PASTORALISM IN CRISIS. THE DASANETCH AND THEIR ETHIOPIAN LANDS

by

Claudia J. Carr
The University of California, Santa Cruz

THE UNIVERSITY OF CHICAGO
DEPARTMENT OF GEOGRAPHY
RESEARCH PAPER NO. 180

1977

Library of Congress Cataloging in Publication Data

Carr, Claudia J. 1942–
  Pastoralism in crisis.

  (Research paper—University of Chicago, Department of Geography;
    no. 180)
  Bibliography: p. 315
  1. Dasanetch (African people) 2. Nomads—Ethiopia. I. Title. II.
Series: Chicago. University. Dept. of Geography. Research paper; no. 180.
H31.C514 no. 180 [DT380.4.D3] 301.31'0963'3
ISBN 0–89065–087-X
77-1252

Research Papers are available from:

The University of Chicago
Department of Geography
5828 S. University Avenue
Chicago, Illinois 60637
Price: $6.00 list; $5.00 series subscription

For my good friend, Lokiriakwanga (Atiko), and all the other Dasanetch who have taught me much about strength and warmth in the face of pain and hardship, and about laughter which can accompany a struggle for survival and self-determination.

PREFACE

The problems confronting pastoral societies indigenous to the dry lands of
East Africa and elsewhere are often forgotten or ignored, largely because of
the onrush of concern for "modernization" and the more profitable development
of lands with higher agricultural potential. This accurately characterizes the
situation now facing the Dasanetch tribe of southwest Ethiopia. These proud
and traditionally strong people are now experiencing the repercussions of powerful external political and economic forces--most notably, the severe reduction
of their tribal lands--which have greatly altered both their environment and
their society. These reprecussions have combined with significant environmentally induced changes to produce a level of economic and environmental deterioration involving much human death and suffering and perhaps threatening the
very survival of the tribe. Nevertheless, the Dasanetch have remained effectively isolated in their struggle to overcome the effects of these forces. Although the Dasanetch themselves are most familiar with the conditions of their
own struggle, they are at present unable to make themselves heard by the
larger community. This monograph is an attempt to create an awareness of
these conditions on the part of individuals and institutions having the capacity to
offer help. It is my conviction that this study may serve as the basis for a rational and effective set of solutions to the present deterioration of Dasanetch
socio-economic relations and their environment, and realistically so within the
present political/economic context of East Africa.

This monograph represents the product of three major objectives. First,
to understand the precise nature of the interaction between the Dasanetch tribe
and their environment, and this in the context of the tribe's increasingly deteri-
orating struggle for survival. Such understanding calls for a grasp of the central processes of Dasanetch society, the lands to which they are presently confined, and the problems and changes of both. Second, to demonstrate how such
an understanding is useful in the framing of alternative courses of action which
address the issue of survival and self-determination for such a people. Third,
to develop a theoretical framework for the study of the above relations which

may be applied to other societal/environmental contexts.

The third objective results from my efforts to comprehend the complex web of societal and environmental interactions--namely, through the use of a system approach. To my knowledge, the type of system analysis developed here* is the first such attempt to view a traditional society in interaction with its environment at such a scale, and as such the ideas presented are necessarily exploratory and tentative. It is my hope that they will serve to help stimulate criticism and further work along similar lines. Insofar as the methodology offers a means for understanding other societal/environmental systems in addition to the one discussed here, I will be gratified.

To a large extent the scope of this study has grown out of my initial innocence as a field worker attempting to understand the complicated set of phenomena pertaining to the relation between plant ecology and land use in the lower Omo Valley. My original work in the Lower Omo Basin with the Omo Expedition was primarily of a general plant ecological nature, beginning with questions concerning the natural scope of vegetation in this type of environment and the major determinants of it (see Carr, 1967a and b). The presence within the area of the Dasanetch and their northern neighbors, the Inyangatom, made it clear that a precise understanding of the environmental impacts of their activities was basic to any full ecological interpretation. I therefore undertook to survey the most basic land use patterns in order to identify and compare regions subjected to fundamentally different types and intensities of utilization. Soon I learned to recognize the relatively undisturbed types of biotic communities as well as those obviously disturbed by human activities. Within this framework, it became possible to surmise basic ecological changes occurring in the past.

My interest in the ecology of riverine and other mesic (relatively wet) environments of the Omo Valley is related to the fact that little is known about the plant communities of such localities. In addition these communities are likely of some importance in the interpretation of paleoenvironments such as those being investigated by the Omo Expedition, of which I was a part. The lower basin offers a unique opportunity for the study of tropical riverine ecosystem development by virtue of the large scale physical changes which have occurred there in the last hundred years. Much of the riverine woody vegetation development is very recent, and it is possible to study the various phases of plant community

_____

*In my brief discussion of system concepts in the following chapters, I have assumed no formal acquaintance with such concepts on the part of the reader.

changes from simple riverine grasslands to riverine ("gallery") forests.

Testimonies by the Dasanetch people revealed much about the changes over the last several decades within the riverine zone, and it became clear that these changes have been intimately bound up with the other past ecological and social dynamics of the area. Consequently, I investigated all of these in a coordinated fashion from place to place. It became increasingly apparent to me, through my conversations with the Dasanetch (and Inyangatom) tribespeople in the initial land-use surveys, that there had been enormous feed-back effects of recent environmental changes into these societies, and certainly there was strong conditioning of the environment and the Dasanetch's means of survival within it by the specific character of Dasanetch society. Consequently, I continually deepened my study of the structure and function of Dasanetch social relations, and the connectedness of environmental and societal processes became a major focus of my work. From nearly the outset of my studies I began intuiting that the conceptual tools I had been socialized into accepting and formally trained to use were inadequate for this task. This intuition became increasingly verified for me as my experience progressed, but I was immediately faced with the absence of a new form of analysis with which to replace the previous, narrower paradigm. I soon became susceptible to the exhilarating if frustrating process of allowing the limits and focus of my investigations to take shape as a result of my experience of the Dasanetch themselves. Specifically, I learned from the Dasanetch that the material conditions of the environment were intimately connected with the nature of their concrete productive activities, their decision-making structure and its immediate social matrix, their symbolic codes, and the many sources of their biases and flexibilities in dealing with their own institutions and their environment amidst radically changing conditions. In this way, the conceptual boundary between society and environment which I had for so many years taken for granted (even with a rhetoric to the contrary) became sufficiently blurred that I began directing my energies to understanding more about the blurring process itself. Thus I began to shape a new conceptual framework which would facilitate my grasp of the deep level interactions between society and environment rather than merely produce a description of the impact of one upon the other.

As a result, the basic concepts presented here, both with regard to the Dasanetch situation in particular and the theoretical framework in general, have evolved slowly and unevenly over a period of several years. In addition to the framework of analysis emerging only gradually, the absence of ecological or ethnographic description prior to my work greatly conditioned the early phases of research. If I were to rewrite the present monograph, I would offer much of the explicit model and many of the principles surrounding it--presently developed in the concluding chapters--at the outset, and the earlier material which is presented here in a general descriptive way could then be fitted into the system (and mode of production) framework as it is introduced. However, the book as written more accurately reflects the way in which the perspective evolved.

There have been so many individuals and groups who have been helpful to me from the beginning of the research to the completion of the present analysis that it is impossible to offer thanks to them all. Nevertheless I wish to express my appreciation to at least some of them here. My deep gratitude to the Dasanetch people is perhaps the most difficult to express. They have greatly affected my life on many levels, and have taught me much through their patience with my unending questions and probing into their lives, all for reasons which remained largely enigmatic to them except for the objective of describing their struggle to survive in the hope that those agencies with the potential to act might do so. Without exception I have been welcomed into Dasanetch villages, and I have learned from countless cooperative and friendly people. I shall not forget their pride and courage in fighting for survival on a daily level as well as their willingness to talk with me regarding their economic and social activities and their plight -- all in the knowledge that I may or may not be able to help effect any change in their behalf. My special thanks go to one Dasanetch friend in particular who will never read this book but who knows much about its content and conclusions--Lokiriakwanga (Atiko), son of Akiro of the Oro tribal segment--as he was my constant companion and friend over many months.

F. Clark Howell (University of California, Berkeley), director of my contingent of the Omo Expedition, has offered his complete support of my work over the years and did much to facilitate my being able to broaden my studies from a purely taxonomic or descriptive plant ecological base. I have developed great respect and friendship through my association with him and it has been a great privilege to learn from and work with him. Karl W. Butzer (University of Chicago) was the individual who first moved to make my work in the Omo possible, and I spent a month of intensive joint field work with him in 1968, during which time his highly perceptive and integrative approach to geomorphology was invaluable to my initial orientation and understanding of the region. This experience was augmented by my experience with him in post-field work interpreta-

tion, classes and many discussions. For several years, I have drawn a great
deal of personal support as well as help in logistic, plant ecological and physical environmental matters from Frank C. Brown (University of Utah), whose
inexhaustively expansive interests in the natural environment served as a constant information and energy source for me. I am greatly indebted to him.
Christopher Matolo of the Wakamba tribe in Kenya was of tremendous help to
me by assisting in all phases of the plant ecological field work, and without him
my work would have been incomparably more difficult. Gerald Eck (University
of California, Berkeley), another member of the expedition, offered help in
many ways, particularly in his capacity as field coordinator.

        I wish also to thank the many Ethiopian officials who were supportive of
the Omo Expedition's research in general, and the study presented here in particular. Jan B. Gillett of the East African Herbarium in Nairobi has offered
much basic support and detailed advice in all stages of my work regarding plant
taxonomy, and his long standing experience in East African botany was of tremendous help. Christine Kubaye, presently Chief Botanist of the East African
Herbarium, and the other members of the herbarium who participated in identifying specimens, were also important in the ecological aspects of this study.
Marion T. Hall (Morton Arboretum, Chicago) offered much advice on field meth-
odologies, extensive criticisms on a manuscript regarding Chapter 3, and
general encouragement in all phases of my work.   William Burger (Field
Museum, Chicago) first oriented me to the botany of Ethiopia, about which he is
an expert. Robert and Norrie Swart of the American Mission at Kalam, Ethiopia, frequently offered me great hospitality as well as information regarding
their activities and knowledge of the lower Omo valley, all of which I greatly
appreciate. Marvin Mikesell (University of Chicago), both as my teacher and
as chairman of the Geography Department, offered his support in numerous
ways and at all phases of my work. Finally, Terence Turner (University of
Chicago) aided me in numerous and important ways in the planning of ethnographic work and also in the subsequent interpretation of important aspects of
Dasanetch social relations.

        Concerning the later phases of analysis and writing I am particularly
grateful to John T. Grinder (University of California, Santa Cruz), with whom I
have spent long and exciting hours discussing the specific results of my research in the context of structural approaches and system theory, and from
whom I have received much support. Both Terence Turner and Dean Boyd (University of California, Santa Cruz) have figured in my development of system

concepts from very different but equally valuable standpoints, both in discussing our mutual research and in offering criticisms for portions of this monograph. Illustrations were prepared by Marion Sirefman, Judy Ogden, and Judy Cohen, whose efforts I very much appreciate. Of those who have been involved in the various phases of draft editing, I especially wish to thank Barbara Crum and James Carr, whose interest and support as well as unique senses of humor did much to bring the monograph to completion.

This research was supported primarily by the National Science Foundation (grants to F. Clark Howell), with secondary support from the Committee on African Studies (University of Chicago), the Committee on Evolutionary Biology (University of Chicago) and the University of California at Santa Cruz Faculty Research Fund.

TABLE OF CONTENTS

Appendices

LIST OF TABLES

LIST OF FIGURES

CHAPTER 1

INTRODUCTION TO THE SYSTEM

Societal/Environmental Relations as a System

I have learned from the Dasanetch themselves that one can only understand their society and their immediate environment through carefully studying
the specific interactions between them. It is with this conviction that I have
attempted to put together a synthesis of both social and environmental processes, although it has been necessary to emphasize those aspects of Dasanetch
society and physical environment which are most relevant to the interactions
between the two. The set of principles which I have developed to achieve my
purpose here--i.e., integrating environmental and social processes in such a
way as to make explicit the forces and nature of stability and directional change
of those processes--is embodied by what is best described as a system analysis.

There are many definitions of a system available in the literature. One
particularly demystified and therefore highly useful one is that given by Boyd
(n.d.) in his forthcoming introduction to systems: "A system is a connection of
many different parts that interact to produce consequences or outcomes." Of
the many other definitions used, that proposed by Weiss is often quoted, so that
I will use it as a basis for discussion here.

> A system . . . [is] defined as a complex unit in space and time so consti-
> tuted that its component subunits, by 'systematic' cooperation, preserve its
> integral configuration of structure and behavior and tend to restore it after
> non-destructive disturbances. (1971: 14)

The phrase "integral configuration of structure and behavior" emphasizes that
the elements of the system are patterned and thus constitute a relatively stable
arrangement, barring destructive inputs. Given a system approach allowing
one to discern structure, the effects of any input of change, or deviation, into
that system may be more readily grasped. The existence of such a patterned
set of relations allows one to generalize across a set of different inputs to the
system. In this way, what might otherwise be regarded as a disassociated series of events is revealed as an interrelated complex of processes which togeth-

er form a recognizable structure. Thus generalizations become possible which allow some predictability regarding the system.

The term "systematic cooperation" indicates that the elements of the system are connected and that at least some deviation introduced into the system will tend to be compensated for by adjustments in a number of interacting elements, rather than being confined to the point of initial contact with the system. This integrated adjustment involves a diffusion among the system's elements from the point of entry.

There is some difficulty with Weiss' notion that a system's components "preserve . . . and tend to restore it." One can imagine three major logical reactions of a system to a deviation generated: (1) maintenance of the system's same basic structure (homeostatic processes), (2) movement toward greater structural order or complexity of the system (morphic processes)[1] or (3) decrease or breakdown in structural order or complexity of the system (entropic processes). Actually, all of these types of processes may occur within a system simultaneously, and it is through studying their interaction that the net effect on the system may be understood. I shall discuss this matter further for the Dasanetch context in Chapter 6.

I have chosen to develop a model for the system of Dasanetch societal/environmental relations as a tool which facilitates studying a very large number of interrelated elements which function together in a non-linear and dynamic fashion. A system approach calls for the analysis of constituent elements in terms of their functions relative to each other, rather than mere description of their internal structures in isolation. Modelling in such an approach also may facilitate differentially weighting the many elements or variables, through the establishing of some hierarchical structure of the system within which the various elements must be placed.

The precise structure of the system model for societal/environmental interactions I wish to discuss is presented in Chapter 6, and only the most basic character of the model is relevant here. Some comment on the subjective content of the model is also reserved for that chapter. I have chosen to consider the societal and environmental elements of the system as comprising two distinct but interrelated subsystems.

In trying to sort out and understand the various interactions between a society and its environment, one cannot hope to undertake an exhaustive study

---

[1]Definition of "morphic processes" is from Whyte (1969).

3

of all societal and environmental aspects and subsequently weigh their differential importance. Consequently, some referential center is needed from which the various elements comprising the system may be given greater or lesser priority for analysis. I propose that the center of this system model (i.e., the baseline of analysis) be defined as the collection of points of interaction between societal and environmental elements. Further, it is obvious that the elements of the system, once identified, bear certain relationships to one another, and the basic relationship of <u>connectedness</u> between any two elements will be represented by a simple line between the elements (or units) involved in that relation. Thus, the relationship of elements to the interaction baseline constitutes the basis for laying out the structure of the system. The elements comprising the two levels contiguous with the baseline are defined as those which <u>either directly affect or are affected by</u> elements of the other subsystem. Those social or environmental features removed from the line of greatest S/E^2 interaction are more peripheral in the system and have relatively less influence in the system's general functioning. Additional levels of the system model are established on the basis of the number of steps removed from the interaction point (the baseline) with the other subsystem. The diagram below is a highly simplified version of the model:

S/E Baseline

Environmental Subsystem ↓   Societal Subsystem

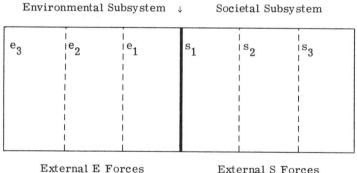

External E Forces   External S Forces

The precise point of input of change or deviation into the system (i.e., its initial impact on a particular element [unit][3] or sub-element [subunit] within a par-

---

[2] S/E is henceforth used as an abbreviation for societal/environmental.

[3] The term "unit" will be used synonymously with "element" in this study.

ticular level of a subsystem) can thus be determined, and the repercussions of that impact within the system may be traced. I suggest that this model, as developed conceptually in the last chapters, is one which may be of use for better understanding the functioning of numerous societal/environmental interaction contexts, in evaluating the relative instability or stability of these relations, and in predicting the effects of present and possible future inputs.

The discussion of environmental and social processes in the next four chapters, although it is not explicitly presented in terms of the system model, nevertheless does take account of the units as laid out in Chapter 6. Furthermore the emphasis given various topics generally conforms to their relative centrality as units within the model.

Introduction to the Dasanetch People
and Their Environment

The lower Omo Basin of southwest Ethiopia. --The environment of the lower Omo Basin of southwest Ethiopia has undergone a series of pronounced physical changes in recent history.[4] It is highly sensitive to human and geomorphic stresses placed upon it, and alterations of it are highly significant for the immediate and long range future of the indigenous tribes.

The lower Omo Basin (Fig. 1-1) is a synclinal depression forming a northern extension of Lake Rudolf (Butzer, 1971), which is part of the East African rift valley. Lake Rudolf is fed principally by the Omo River, the largest river of western Ethiopia, which nearly bisects the lower valley. It is a highly unstable region in terms of precipitation and winds throughout the year, with great fluctuations often erratic in occurrence. Seasonal extremes occur, with precipitation ranging from periods of torrential rains to months totally devoid of rainfall, and winds ranging from periods of relative quiet to storms of gale force. Temperatures are predictably less erratic (see below). Soils and sediments throughout most of the lower basin, excluding the peripheral highlands and the volcanic localities, are depositional in origin.

Both the harsh climatic conditions and the recent large-scale geomorphic changes affecting much of the lower basin combine to produce a rather homogeneous area in terms of the numbers of plant species. Nevertheless, there are zones with widely varying physical conditions which account for striking differ-

---

[4]Butzer (1971) presents a detailed analysis and interpretation of recent geomorphic changes.

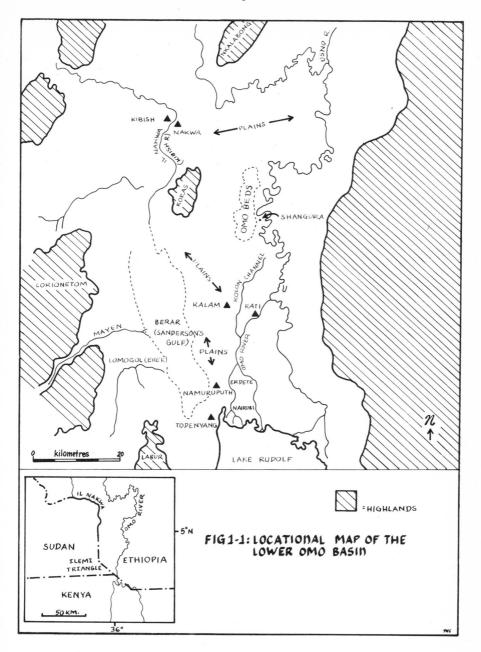

FIG 1-1: LOCATIONAL MAP OF THE LOWER OMO BASIN

ences among plant communities, e.g., plains[5] vs. riverine communities. This variation is augmented by anomalous areas such as the modern delta of the Omo River, the Lake Rudolf shoreline, volcanic highlands, a large expanse of uplifted and eroded series of fossiliferous sediments (the Omo Beds), and a large secondary depression (Sanderson's Gulf).[6] These variations offer the Dasanetch a more diverse natural resource base, but some of them also correspond to conditions such as the presence of disease and aridity, limiting the degree of human exploitation of large areas during much of the year. Of all the types of environments present, the rangelands of the plains are most fully exploited and most directly modified by the Dasanetch.

The Dasanetch tribe.--The Dasanetch are known by several names, and the mixing of these names indicates a long-standing confusion concerning their identity. The most common are the Geleb or Geluba (the name most commonly used in other parts of Ethiopia) and Marille or Merile (the names most commonly used in Kenya and Uganda). They have even been considered to be two different tribes due to the use of these two names (Cerulli, 1956). In addition, Reshiat was the name used by von Höhnel (1894), and Rusia by Cavendish (1898). As their name for themselves is Dasanetch, this will here be considered the correct one.

The Dasanetch live both east and west of the Omo River (see Fig. 1-2); this analysis focuses on the Dasanetch living west of the river (Fig. 1-3). Although there is some economic and social interaction between the peoples east and west of the Omo River, and this interaction fluctuates somewhat with both seasonal and longer term conditions, these two geographically defined groupings are easily distinguishable for the purposes of analysis. The only significant exception is the narrow strip of settlement along the river and the modern delta region.

All population estimates of the Dasanetch are highly conjectural. Estimates by travellers since the late nineteenth century during occupations by foreign forces (Italians, English, and Amharic-speaking Ethiopians) range from a few hundred to 15,000. For example, Smith (1897) reports them as numbering about 500, whereas the Italian estimates are highest. Although an accurate esti-

---

[5]Plains are defined here as the smooth, semi-arid and undulating lands occupying most of the lower Omo valley.

[6]Sanderson's Gulf is referred to as "Berar" by the Dasanetch, and this name will be used frequently throughout this study.

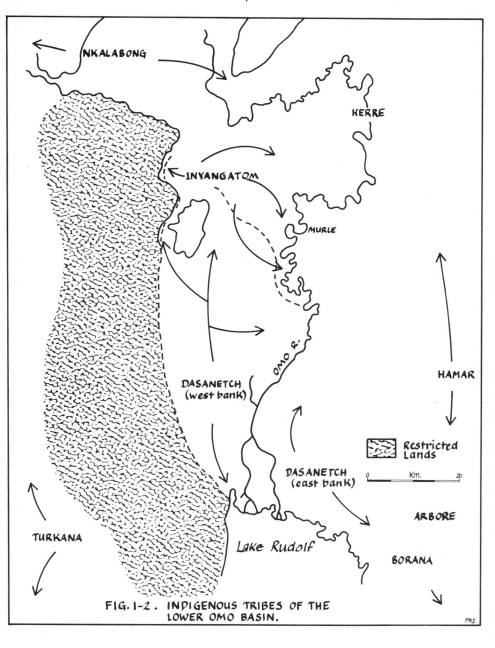

FIG. 1-2. INDIGENOUS TRIBES OF THE
LOWER OMO BASIN.

Fig. 1-3.--Aerial View of Dasanetch Village Complex

mate is still impossible at this point, my own figure is 9440 for Dasanetch inhabiting the lands west of the Omo River alone (see below). This figure is based on a complete count of all huts on the west bank in 1972, made possible by the concentrated settlement during a war between the Dasanetch and the neighboring Inyangatom tribe to the north. The resulting population estimate of 18,000 for the whole tribe is an upward revision of the highly incomplete survey conducted by myself and U. Almagor (of the Hebrew University) in 1969. This 1972 estimate assumes a roughly equal number of Dasanetch on the east bank, whereas there may in fact be an even greater number of east bank tribal members.

The Dasanetch are a people of at least several distinct origins, and there has been a gradual assimilation of groups from various surrounding tribes. The diversity of origins of groups now within the tribe is also reflected by the non-uniformity in physical appearance. Physical build varies from tall and very thin to average height and quite stocky; skin color from very dark (sometimes reddish) brown to light brown tone. Similarly, facial features vary from rather sharp features to rounded or smooth ones (see Fig. 1-3).

No detailed and in-depth studies of Dasanetch society have been made until those by myself and Uri Almagor who began working one year after my studies of 1968. Numerous brief accounts of questionable accuracy have been published, most of them describing either the physical environment exclusively, or certain material economic or settlement distribution aspects of the tribe. These accounts are not of great relevance for the present discussion, but they include: Austin (1902); Brooke (1905); Cavendish (1898); Cerulli, Enrico (1942); Cerulli, Ernesta (1956); Maud (1904); Nalder (1937); Pauli (1950); Ricci (1943); Smith (1896, 1900); Stigand (1910); Vannutelli (1899) and von Höhnel (1894).

The Dasanetch define wealth in terms of their cattle and to a lesser degree, small stock (sheep and goats). This is true even for those who are virtually devoid of stock. Predictably, pathways of stock exchange are usually analogous to pathways of social interactions, and the whole set of Dasanetch political, ideological and symbolic relations both reflect and condition their emphasis on stock. The traditional cultural centrality of cattle and herding is also correlated with the Dasanetch strong preference for mobility, a mobility clearly reflected by the physical and social character of their villages so adapted for rapid locational shifts.

The languages of the tribes of this region are still not all identified and classified, and in fact it is not yet known exactly how many distinct tribes exist in the lower basin. The Dasanetch language is considered Eastern Cushitic in the most recent and reliable work (Ferguson, 1974), and this classification is described in Chapter 4.

The known tribes surrounding the Dasanetch at present include the Turkana (Buma),[7] Inyangatom (Donyiro), Kerre, Murle, Nkalabong (Moruzo), Arbore, Hamar, and the Borana (Fig. 1-2). Of these, the status of the Murle and the Kerre seem most uncertain. Historically, the Dasanetch have also had contact with the Toposa to the west and the Rendille and Samburu (now both south of Lake Rudolf). Relations with the Borana are continuously hostile and they are a constant threat, particularly to the east bank Dasanetch. Those with the Hamar are less consistently hostile[8] and in spite of the periodic fights between them, the Hamar do occasionally come to the Omo River for bartering. Some of the most serious clashes in which the Dasanetch have engaged over the past decades have been with the Turkana (e.g., the 1920's and the late 1950's). The Dasanetch also continuously engage in trading with the Turkana, however, and the two tribes pass years at a time in peace, even sharing some of the same grazing lands[9] and watering holes. Some intermarriage has occurred, and there are currently (as of August, 1970) at least 200-250 Turkana living among the Dasanetch, many of whom have evacuated Turkana lands during famines there and immigrated to do herding or other work for Dasanetch households. The Inyangatom and the west bank Dasanetch have lived closely for many years now, and although they rarely intermarry, much economic and some social interchange occurs; they also sometimes share a couple of settlement areas (e.g., Nakwa; see Fig. 1-1). Although the Inyangatom and Dasanetch have for the most part maintained friendly relations, there have been periodic hostile outbreaks (e.g., about 1948 and again in 1972). The Kerre and Dasanetch do have some trading relations but otherwise have little contact. Relations between the Dasanetch and the Nkalabong (Moruzo), who now live primarily around Mt. Nita in Sudan and more diffusely eastward to the Omo River, have been quite complex. Various modes of interaction between these two tribes have included

---

[7]Underlined names are those used by the Dasanetch which differ from the one listed.

[8]Genealogies I have compiled revealed individuals from the west bank who had been killed by the Hamar in scattered instances for many years, particularly when Dasanetch people have travelled singly along the east bank of the Omo River.

[9]This is now precluded by the tribal separation enforced by the Kenya police, as described below.

heavy fighting, small raids, and peaceful trading (at one time the Nkalabong were apparently an important source of cattle for the Dasanetch); less contact is reported for more recent years.

Recent Political History of Dasanetch Lands[10]

The first record of European contact with the Dasanetch was made by von Höhnel (1894) in an expedition with Teleki in 1888. The Dasanetch were referred to in this work as the Reshiat. Subsequently, a succession of travellers' accounts are available.

From the late 1890's through about 1903, during the reign of Menelik in Ethiopia, a succession of Ethiopian troops invaded Dasanetch lands, causing many deaths, wholesale destruction of huge numbers of stock, and burning of horticultural plots. During this time the surviving Dasanetch were driven far to the south (reportedly as far as Lodwar, Kenya) along the western side of Lake Rudolf. The invasions came in waves, the first of which was most severe in terms of deaths among the Dasanetch. They included troops led by Ethiopian Amharic-speaking people, and during this time the Russian militarist Leontieff figured prominently in the region (Leontieff, 1900). According to Dasanetch oral tradition, one of these waves included the enslavement of many of their tribe who had returned from the Kenyan lands following a previous wave of the Amharic-speaking troops.

The Ethiopians were involved in many battles against the British before their occupation became stabilized at a series of posts in Dasanetch territory, and the Turkana were split between those under Ethiopian and those under British control (Gulliver and Gulliver, 1953). When the Dasanetch returned, peace was made with the Ethiopian foreigners then occupying their lands, and the Dasanetch maintain that they were required to present them with ivory tusks as a peace gesture. The Ethiopians subsequently withdrew from the area, not to return until the 1920's. During the first decade of the 1900's the Dasanetch began obtaining rifles from the Ethiopian highlands, and they apparently became well-armed in a short time. Meanwhile, the British colonialists of Kenya began disarming the Kenyan tribes, including

---

[10]The historical information here results from the oral testimonies of the Dasanetch themselves, several officers at Kibish and Todenyang posts, Mr. Whitehouse (the former District Officer of Turkanaland), and from selected literature. Some of the dates are necessarily only approximate. This account focuses on the west bank Dasanetch lands in particular since they are the subject of study.

the Borana and Turkana. This left the Dasanetch militarily superior to their hostile neighbors to the south. [11] The Dasanetch have a rich oral tradition depicting this era of their successes, and their acquisition of arms is clearly reflected by a whole series of successful campaigns and retaliations against surrounding tribes, particularly the Borana, the Rendille, and the Turkana. Contacts with the Toposa to the west were frequent, especially for the purpose of trading.

Although the east bank lands and the Dasanetch people inhabiting them are not dealt with in any detail in this study, it is pertinent that the eastern Dasanetch were periodically heavily engaged in battles with the Rendille, Borana, and Samburu tribes over the lands east of Lake Rudolf. The Rendille and Samburu now live much further south in Kenya, but Dasanetch oral tradition, as well as available literature on them, strongly suggest that these two peoples have contributed to the Dasanetch tribe within the last century and a half.

In 1914, according to Kenya police records in Nairobi, a portion of extreme southeastern Sudan (the Ilemi Triangle) was placed under Kenyan administration. This was agreed to by Sudan primarily because the area was inaccessible to Sudanese troops due to the natural barriers created by the large swamps to the west. In the years following, there was intense and frequent fighting among the Dasanetch, Turkana, and Inyangatom tribes. No doubt for political and economic reasons (in addition to whatever element of European-style morality existed) the Kenyan, Ugandan, and Sudanese colonialist governments undertook to punish these tribes for their hostile interactions and to bring them under control. The punitive expedition, however, was without success. The 1920's were marked by a large and highly significant war between the Dasanetch and Turkana (referred to by the Dasanetch as Os Kalas) with the Dasanetch apparently having the upper hand. The fighting resulted in a considerable increase in Dasanetch territory. These years of heavy inter-tribal fighting coincided with the Kenyan government's move to establish a post at Lokitaung in the late 1920's. Sudan's relinquishing of still more of the Ilemi area to Kenyan administration soon followed, and the British colonialists of Kenya then created a "no-man's land," or restricted territory, in the western plains of Dasanetch territory. This was ostensibly to serve as a buffer zone between the Dasanetch and Inyangatom tribes on the one hand, and the Turkana on the other. It was a devastat-

---

[11] Shortly after the turn of the century, there were also significant battles between the Dasanetch and the Murle as well as Nkalabong (Moruzo) to the north.

ing and directly hostile act from the standpoint of these tribes, in that these lands were vitally important to the people for grazing of their domestic stock: much of this zone receives higher rainfall than the plains to the east and it therefore supports a relatively luxuriant vegetation.

In the years 1937-38 the Italians moved into the area. They were extremely friendly with the Dasanetch, supplying them with guns and other material aid, and the Dasanetch regard this period as the only one when foreigners have operated as their friends. The Italians apparently tried to negotiate for some extension of Italian territorial control before their armed conflict with the British, and this was seen by the Dasanetch as the Italians supporting Dasanetch claims to their traditional tribal lands. Of course, the Dasanetch were only too happy to receive arms and, in some cases, even to join the Italian forces in the effort to defeat the British, who were responsible for excluding the Dasanetch from their rightful lands. The British were forced far south of Lokitaung (i.e., southwest of Namuruputh, see Fig. 1-1) for a time, but ultimately the Italians retreated altogether from the area and it subsequently was occupied by the British. Most of the west bank Dasanetch were concentrated in the modern delta (Erdete, Nairobi) during the British-Italian war, and when the British reoccupied the area they attempted to disarm the Dasanetch. This attempt was defeated because the delta was heavily ridden with disease, and the British were forced to evacuate. There are Dasanetch reports of bombing by the British in the delta during this period. In the end, the British managed to maintain and even expand the restricted Ilemi lands. Those Dasanetch who had once been able to at least graze their stock in the lands west of Berar (Sanderson's Gulf; Fig. 1-1), including Labur, Lomogol, Liwan, Lokomarinyang, and Kokuro, were now confined to the lands east of Berar, south of the Kibish Ethiopian Police Post (at Nakwa), Il Nakwa (Kibish River), and west of the Omo River (War).[12] Lands east of the Omo River were then, as now, predominantly occupied by different segments of the tribe than those of the west bank (see Chapter 4). New Kenyan police posts were established in 1942 at Kaimothia, Kokuro, Lokomarinyang, and Kibish. A stricter exclusionary policy was enforced by the Kenya police who were instructed to shoot intruders within the lusher restricted zone, or to seize all stock found there.

The Amharic-speaking Ethiopians, who had retreated after their invasion at the end of the last century, returned to the area for a time after the Turkana/

---

[12]Henceforth, Dasanetch location names will not be underlined, unlike other vernacular terms.

Dasanetch fighting in the 1920's and again after the British, in 1943 or 1944. Their troops in the area have always been few, however, and presently they number only about 200 among the Namuruputh, Rati, Kalam, and Kibish posts. From the standpoint of Dasanetch stock raising activities, the Kenya posts at Todenyang and Kibish are most significant since these are the two which are most active in preventing them from using their lands west of Berar (Sanderson's Gulf) and Il Nakwa (Kibish River). The clash between the Dasanetch and the Inyangatom in about 1948 was a decade after both tribes were excluded still more stringently from the plains to the west. Overall, the west bank Dasanetch were free of large-scale wars in the years following the British-Italian war; there were only occasional skirmishes with the Turkana and with the Kenya police. Tensions with the Turkana were mounting by the 1950's however, and in 1957 another large-scale war between these two tribes broke out. [13] The records generally describe this war as initiated by the Dasanetch, but Dasanetch informants and Mr. Whitehouse (see footnote 13) who dealt personally with the Dasanetch, describe it otherwise. According to them, this war was a very strong retaliatory move by the Dasanetch against a whole series of murders perpetrated by the Turkana. At least several hundred Turkana were killed by the Dasanetch, most of them during one major offensive, and there were again clashes between the Dasanetch and the Kenya police. The result of this was once again a determination by the Kenya officials to maintain the restricted zone in Sudan, and this was carried out. Since independence in 1963, Kenya has pursued the same basic policies in the area, which include periodic allowing of grazing of the restricted zone by the Dasanetch, Inyangatom and Turkana. Understandably, there is much bitterness among the Dasanetch and the Inyangatom tribes about their containment by the Ethiopian and Kenyan police.

The actual motives for this containment can only be surmised, but one would assume that governmental control over the tribes in these borderlands would have been desirable from the standpoint of the creation of "order" (in terms of "social stability" and stability of national borders) as defined first by the colonialists and later by the national governments. Another possible motive for containing these tribes might have been to facilitate taxation. Negative repercussions of this territorial restriction are dealt with in detail in the following chapters, and possible solutions are treated at the end of the last chapter.

---

[13] Just previous to the major outbreaks of fighting, according to Mr. Whitehouse, a former commander at Lodwar in the Kenya Turkana District, the Dasanetch had been granted temporary grazing rights in parts of the western plains.

CHAPTER 2

RANGELAND ENVIRONMENTS OF THE DASANETCH

An Introduction to East African Rangelands

Rangeland may be defined as land carrying natural or semi-natural vegetation which provides a habitat suitable for herds of wild or domestic ungulates. High evaporation, low precipitation and high temperatures characterize most of the East African rangelands. More than 400,000 square miles within this part of the continent are available for pasturage (excluding parks and forests), amounting to 90 percent of the land mass of East Africa. This area supports most of the 20 million cattle, 11 million goats, 7 million sheep, and 1-1½ million donkeys and camels (MacGillivary et al., 1967) of that part of the continent. Although these lands vary widely in suitability for grazing, the vast majority of them are of medium or low potential. Although pastoralism is practiced in all rangeland types of East Africa, it is most widespread in the arid zones. In Kenya, the most nomadic pastoralists are the Turkana, Rendille, Orma, Boran and Somali peoples who live in the driest zones (Pratt, 1968). Generally, the less arid zones are characterized by more sedentary forms of pastoralism and with more mixed economics.

The late nineteenth and twentieth centuries brought vast changes to the vegetation cover of East Africa, in particular through altered patterns of grazing and burning which caused the deterioration or severe destruction of grassland communities. For this reason, existing plant life is often a poor indication of the potential or natural vegetation, and this fact must be taken into account in the interpretation of any system of grassland classification. Various methods of classifying grasslands in East Africa have been used, including floristic composition or dominant grass species (Heady, 1960; Rattray, 1960), physiognomic character (Edwards and Bogdan, 1951), and a combination of climatic (precipitation) and physiognomic characters (Pratt et al., 1966). Because of their emphasis upon the form and relative importance of woody plants vs. grass cover, the system adopted by Pratt et al. is most useful for the Lower Omo Basin, although it is modified to take into account differences in grass density

15

which are of utmost importance in any discussion of range potential for domestic animals. Essentially this involves the refinement of physiognomic categories.

There is no specific soil type associated with East African rangelands, and a general quote from Heady is useful in summarizing the situation.

> . . . range soils . . . are either too shallow, too stony, too sandy, contain too much clay or are too wet at certain times of the year to facilitate cultivation. Others may be too alkaline or salty to permit crops. Most important of all is that the rainfall is insufficient for agriculture. . . . Therefore, there is no definite range soil even though the grazing of the natural plant cover is the best use that can be made for many soil types. (1960: 3)

The range soils of East Africa range all the way from very light sands to extremely dense clays, and from rapidly draining soils to heavily impeded ones. This is also an accurate characterization of the Lower Omo Basin rangeland itself.

A whole complex of physical characteristics including precipitation, soil type, topographic relief, drainage and geomorphic processes are responsible for the complex patterns of range vegetation throughout East Africa. This is well illustrated by the studies of Anderson and Talbot (1965), for instance, in the Serengeti Plains. In these they showed the importance of wind erosion, soil depth, soil texture and salt concentration as they affect soil moisture availability and, consequently, plant life within the Serengeti region. It is well known that termites have a profound effect on tropical grassland soils and vegetation, and a brief description of some of the probable influences is given below.

There is little known of the ecology of the termite genus present in the Lower Omo Basin (Macrotermes); only a brief discussion of the overall significance of termites in rangelands is presented here. Literature regarding tropical termites or so-called white ants, is abundant although difficult to generalize from. The best general introduction to the subject is that found in Goodland (1965) and Hesse (1955). Even within a small taxon (there are at least 170 genera and 2100 species) the activities and effects of the termites may vary with the type of vegetation present, soil type, season, and size of the population. These nearly ubiquitous soil animals have a potentially huge effect in modifying soil structure and chemistry. Effects on the soil are apparently confined to the subsoil rather than the topsoil though the literature varies somewhat on this matter. Termite mounds themselves may be important in supporting small islands of woody growth otherwise not present in the surrounding grasslands. This is especially true where burning occurs since termite mounds are very compact and usually have bare sediment around their bases, thus serving as a firebreak and protecting whatever woody growth is able to establish there.

Mounds may also have an increased salt content (an observation disputed by some workers) and they are used as salt licks by many wild and domestic animals.

Aardvarks, the African counterpart of South American anteaters, construct large holes into the lower mounds in order to feed on the termites, and these may be significant in breaking up and scattering some of the mound material. These holes may subsequently be occupied by the bat-eared fox, jackal, hyena, and warthog, all of which are present in the plains of the Lower Omo Basin.

Effects of drought. --Both plants and animals in East African arid rangelands must be adapted to alternating periods of rain and drought, the latter often being severe and prolonged. Even though a relatively rich plant cover may develop during rainy periods, the more mesophytic plant communities typically vanish rapidly with the absence of precipitation, greatly reducing the total vegetation cover and the grazing potential. Lands which are heavily grazed during or immediately following rainy period development are left particularly vulnerable to severe drying out and erosion during subsequent drought months; drought and overgrazing are thus strongly related. According to studies on the pronounced effects of overgrazing on recovery of rangelands following drought, the growth of tops and roots cannot occur unless there is a food reserve which can be used in the growing process. Thus, grasses with weakly or moderately developed root systems are usually the most sensitive to destruction by drought (De Vos, 1969).

Effects of burning. --Fire has certainly been a force in most vegetation types of East Africa in recent times but burning as a controlling influence over vegetation in tropical grasslands is still not understood. The subject is treated extensively by Phillips (1965), West (1965), Batchelder and Hirt (1966) and Daubenmire (1968).

Tropical grasslands are generally considered to require either periodic grazing or burning in order to be useful as rangelands. This is accomplished through the removal of old grass which may otherwise become sufficiently dense to choke out vegetation. This may produce bare patches which are then colonized by annual weeds, leaving the grassland changed in composition and pattern (Rattray, 1960). It is commonly recognized that burning may eliminate or inhibit woody growth while favoring the desired grasses. But burning may also have deleterious effects when it is done too frequently or at unfavorable times. In combination with heavy continuous grazing, its potentially harmful effects are increased. The state of research on the relationships between grazing influences and the effects of burning is still unsatisfactory. Climatic character of the region and the condition of the rangeland before burning are of great importance in assessing the potentially harmful effects of too frequent or too intense burning. When, for instance, the region is highly arid and some deterioration has already occurred, burning may cause very rapid retrogression to a critical point. Wetter climates and a less deteriorated rangeland condition may tolerate a relatively high pressure from burning.

The intensity, frequency, and time of a burn are primary variables determining its effects on the physical and biotic character of the rangeland involved. Infrequent and hot (because of high accumulation of litter) fires are often sufficient to kill shrubs and trees and maintain grasslands without woody growth. By contrast, frequent fires which are not as hot (due to less accumulated litter or combustible plant matter) may not kill woody growth. In fact, Riney (1964) reports an actual increase in shrub invasion and annual grasses with frequent fires in perennial grassland. Actually, the heat produced from the burning of herbaceous vegetation results from factors other than just the amount of fuel; factors such as dryness, the season of the burn, the initial temperature, the direction of spread of fire in relation to wind (Daubenmire, 1968) and fire tolerance by woody vegetation (West, 1965). The temperature effect on soils below the ground surface falls off extremely rapidly so that soil chemical and structural properties are usually not directly altered. At the soil surface, however, microclimatic conditions may change following firing (Daubenmire, 1968). Soil moisture may either be increased or decreased, depending on a number of factors, but in East Africa fire tends to reduce the water-retaining capacity of the soil, leaving the grassland more subject to drought injury. When vegetative material is burned, much of the nitrogen and sulfur is volatilized, but other nutrients are changed to simple salts that are water soluble. In addition, the nitrogen and sulfur released into the soil surface layers are liable to leaching, removal by runoff or wind erosion before they may be absorbed by soil or organisms. However, the ash buildup following burning of grassland, according to Daubenmire (ibid.) is negligible. Data regarding soil pH changes are still inconclusive.

Although burning may actually increase plant productivity in mesic grasslands, it usually has a destructive influence in arid regions of Africa (West,

1965). In perennial grassland, fire may either increase or decrease plant cover; while in annual grassland, it normally reduces cover through destroying the current seed crop. In arid regions, repeated firing lessens the total plant cover, promotes sheet erosion[1] where gradients are slight and encourages the success of annuals over perennials. When grasslands are lightly burned just preceding the new growth, however, both protein and mineral contents of the fresh shoots are usually increased, thus rendering the grass more nutritious (Daubenmire, 1968). In tropical areas where dry periods are analogous to cold ones in their importance for plant growth, grass regrowth may occur very rapidly following a burn, and there are numerous reports of regrowth occurring earlier after burning (Phillips, 1936).

Herbaceous vegetation is generally favored over woody plants by fire, particularly since the perennating buds or seeds of herbs are often located just at or below the soil surface (where temperature is much reduced). It must be noted, however, that adjacent plants may respond in widely divergent ways to burning, depending upon the size of the seed of an organ (Byram, 1948), the positions of seeds and buds, the phenologic condition at the time of burning, the presence or absence of protective tissues, growth stage, and other factors. Woody species which do not have shoot regrowth from their roots are likely to be killed. This is important as a large number of tropical woody species do not have this growth habit. Finally, forbs are very often favored over grasses in both annual and perennial grasslands subjected to fire. Among the detrimental effects on individuals which may result from fire damage (other than death), are a greater susceptibility to disease organisms through fire wounds at the stem base of woody plants (Daubenmire, 1968) and increased susceptibility to drought by herbs which are hastened in their development during the rainy season following a burn (West, 1965).

Effects of grazing and overgrazing. --Grazing plays a vital role in modifying grassland environments throughout the tropics. Grassland ecosystems have probably evolved under the perpetual influence of herbivorous animals, particularly the ungulates. Tropical grasslands are adapted to utilization by wild herds of ungulates without deterioration (barring excessive concentration of herds due to human influences). Different species of wild ungulates utilize different strata of the grassland communities, according to recent research in

---

[1]Denudation is the predominant form of erosion in arid and semi-arid tropical savanna lands where chemical weathering is dominant.

East Africa (Bell, 1971). For example, zebra feed on the top of the herb layer; topi, the higher protein leafy levels below; and gazelles, the high protein fruits from the ground. According to Bell's work, the most important characteristic of the herb layer from the standpoint of the graziers is its length. A rhythm was shown for the Serengeti Plains, whereby a succession of grazing ungulates follows the seasonal changes in structure and composition of the grasslands, and the various types of ungulates involved are intimately related in their effects on each other through modifying the habitat.

Heavy grazing and overgrazing of substantial areas of the tropical grasslands is nearly always the product of domestic ungulate utilization. An important distinction exists between heavy grazing and overgrazing. Heavy grazing does not necessarily imply harm to the ecosystem, and in fact may even be beneficial to the grassland community under certain conditions. Overgrazing, on the other hand, leads to the deterioration of both the structure and composition of the grassland and reduces its future potential. Many of the effects of overgrazing are similar to those caused by drought; overgrazing is also closely related to the frequency of burning in that the reduction of grass cover by grazing generally reduces the incidence of fires. A useful general description of the effects of overgrazing was made early in the development of plant ecology by Weaver and Clements (1938: 79).

> The more palatable species are eaten down, thus rendering the uneaten ones more conspicuous. This quickly throws the advantage in competition to the side of the latter. Because of more water and light, their growth is greatly increased. They are enabled to store more food in their propagative organs as well as to produce more seed. The grazed species are correspondingly handicapped in all these respects by the increase of the less palatable species, and the grasses are further weakened by trampling as stock wanders about in search of food. Soon bare spots appear that are colonized by weeds or weedlike species.

Grasses are differentially susceptible to destruction by grazing as a function of the time of the impact, i.e., the period of the growing season. There are, generally speaking, three critical periods of sensitivity to such damage: (1) beginning of growth, when the first few leaves produced are mainly from food materials stored in the perennial roots the previous year, so that when the young leaves are removed, additional ones must develop from the stored food in the roots, making the second leaves less vigorous (15-25 percent of the plant growth is attained before the photosynthetic activity of the leaves catches up with the plant's needs); (2) seed maturity, when removal of the seed crop lessens chances of reseeding and also the vigor of the plants; (3) foliage maturity, when food materials are being produced and accumulated in the roots so that grazing prevents the food storage process vital to the next year's pasturage (Heady, 1960). Although the grazing of completely dried out grasses apparently has no direct effect on the next growth, it may have an indirect one through the raising of soil temperatures and reduced conditions for water infiltration of the soil.

Heady (1960) refers to the proper utilization of a range as at about 30-40 percent of the current growth on the ground, although this depends on both the time of grazing and the plant composition. Favored bunch grasses, he maintains, cannot be subjected to more than about 50-60 percent removal, whereas grasses with rhizomatous systems can withstand more intensive grazing. The estimated carrying capacity of the Dasanetch lands (under conditions of low human disturbance) is given in Chapter 7.

Some of the major effects of overgrazing on grasslands may be summarized as follows: (a) reduction of ground level plant cover; (b) possible erosion by wind and/or water following exposure of the soil surface; (c) trampling of vegetation and soil compaction; (d) killing of perennial grasses, with replacement of palatable perennials with annuals or less palatable perennials; and (e) invasion of forbs, often unpalatable or toxic ones. These retrogressive changes in grasslands have become predominant in many East African pastoral lands where changes such as constriction of grazing territory, growth of herds through innoculation and other disease prevention, and others have occurred.

Physiography and Climate of the Lower Omo Basin

The Lower Omo Basin is a depression formed by down-warping more than 4 million years ago. It extends northward from Lake Rudolf approximately 375 meters in altitude (Butzer, 1971). It is bordered on the east by the Amar-Kokke Highland, on the west by highlands which dip to the west (Walsh and Dodson, 1966), and on the north by Ethiopian highlands which extend as far south as Mount Nkalabong (Fig. 1-1). Although the Lower Omo Basin is within Ethiopia, its accessibility by land from the highlands of that nation is very limited and the roads are hazardous. Travel from northwestern Kenya is far easier. The region is also virtually inaccessible from the principal cities of Sudan, as mentioned in Chapter 1. This differential accessibility is significant both from the standpoint of inter-tribal relations and also jurisdiction over the area by the Ethiopian, Kenyan, and Sudanese governments. Except for the anomalous volcanic highlands of Koras (synonym Nakwa on some maps, Fig. 1-2), the plains of the lower basin are between 400 and 500 meters in altitude (Butzer, 1971).

They may be subdivided into the geomorphic units described below.

Weather records are scarce for the lower basin, and those available derive mostly from Kenyan police posts and Ethiopian stations slightly peripheral to the basin. Although quite incomplete, other records from the basin exist including some from the Kenya Kibish Police Post (Fig. 1-2), the J. R. Swart family at Kalam, and the Omo Expedition during its field work of 1968, 1969 and 1971 (see Appendix by Carr and Butzer in Butzer, 1971). Altogether, the records are quite inadequate for anything but the rough estimate that conditions are semi-arid to arid (Köppen BShw to BWhw) regimes with at least some years of arid conditions. Climatic patterns of the larger region are well summarized by Butzer (1971).

Local informants from the Dasanetch tribe, and records available suggest great seasonal variation and rainfall; and the Dasanetch themselves also describe large changes in winds and temperature. Two rainy periods are characteristic: a larger one (ir gudoha) between about March and late May, and a smaller one (nyerobe) ranging between late August through October. Both are extremely irregular in occurrence and intensity and sometimes they do not occur at all. Erratic small rains (ir ninika) or occasional deluges may occur during months which are usually without precipitation. These intermittent rains are of crucial importance to the Dasanetch in permitting grazing of areas otherwise prohibitively far from water sources. Records from Todenyang, Lokitaung, and Kibish suggest that the total precipitation of Dasanetch lands is within the range of 340-380 millimeters per year. During the major rainy periods temperatures may drop markedly, especially when the chilling northerly winds are strong. Although the Dasanetch welcome the rains because of much needed new pasturage, they dislike the cold of these periods.

Temperature has been recorded at the Kenyan police posts less consistently than has precipitation. Measurements taken during the period of June-August of 1968 (see Appendix A in Butzer, 1971) indicate a maximum daily range of from 22 through 39 degrees centigrade. However, temperatures below 20 degrees centigrade have been recorded and their chilling effects may be greatly accentuated during rainy periods by winds. Generally speaking, rainfall is the most critical factor in determining the character of vegetation throughout most of the lower basin and its absence creates harsh conditions with which the Dasanetch must contend.

Vegetation and Its Principal Factors

General. --In combination with water, vegetation of the lower basin in the
form of pasturage and browse is the most important natural resource for the
Dasanetch, whose principal subsistence activity is stock raising. Previous to
the present study, no taxonomic or ecological field work was done in the region,
and the only sources of vegetational classification available are for the region
much more generally. The lower basin is included in Naveh's (1966) xerophyl-
lous Acacia savanna belt which extends from Sudan and northern Kenya southward to the central region of Tanzania. Pichi-Sermolli (1957) describes the
general area as undifferentiated savanna and xerophile scrub; Keay (1959)
terms it wooded steppe with abundant Acacia and Commiphora and subdesert
steppe; Good (1964) refers to it as Sudanese park steppe. These authors' classifications, while useful for plant geography, are not adequate for the more detailed understanding attempted here. More precise vegetational description
must consider a whole complex of environmental factors as described in the
next section.

The establishment of eco-climatic zones presented in the Atlas of Kenya
(see Kenya, 1969) is one of the more useful classifications, especially from the
standpoint of comparing the Lower Omo Basin with adjacent dry lands of Kenya.
According to its criteria for zonation, the lower basin may be described as follows:

Climatic Zone: Arid (moisture index -42 to -51).

Vegetation and Land Use: Zone 5.

Land only very locally suited to agriculture, the woody vegetation being dominated by Commiphora, Acacia and allied genera, mostly of shrubby habit.
Perennial grasses such as Cenchrus ciliaris and Chloris roxburghiana can
dominate, but succumb readily to harsh management; more than 4 hectares
is required per stock unit. . . . Burning requires great caution but can be
highly effective in bush-control.

Although conditions imposed by the limited and highly fluctuating rainfall
within the lower basin are severe, there is nevertheless considerable variation
among plant communities. This is especially true when the whole Lower Omo
Basin is considered, rather than the Dasanetch lands alone. There is, in all
probability, a substantial increase in precipitation from the northern shoreline
of Lake Rudolf northward to the latitude of Mt. Nkalabong (Fig. 1-1). Vegetation in the northern sector of the lower basin does in fact show some increase
in mesicity, with slightly greater floristic similarity to the Mt. Nkalabong highlands. Even within the Dasanetch lands alone, however, there is considerable
variation in physical and biotic conditions, ranging from aridic, open plains to

the wet environments near the Omo River and within the modern delta. Vegetation throughout the plains varies among grassland, tree-shrub grassland, grassland steppe, tree/shrub or shrub steppe, and shrub thicket. This variation must be explained both in terms of physical and biotic factors as well as human activities, as discussed earlier. It is possible to accurately predict some basic physical characteristics on the basis of indicator plant species and structural types of vegetation. Within any given locality, a number of factors influence the existing plant and animal life: soils, topography and drainage; floral and faunal character of the more broadly defined region; anomalous physical environmental features; and environmentally related human activities.

Soils, topography and drainage. --Basic geomorphic units which are relevant to the study here are as follows:[2]

(i) Omo River (War) and adjacent levees.

(ii) Delta flats (a term employed by Butzer).[3]

(iii) Modern Omo delta.

(iv) Plains: includes ridges, inter-ridges, and mudflats.

(v) Sanderson's Gulf (Berar): a large mudflat depression (Fig. 1-1) of clay deposits, described below.

Almost no specific information was available regarding soils of the lower basin until the limited sampling done by myself and K. Butzer, both independently and together. Much more extensive study is necessary.

The superficial sediments of the Lower Omo Basin within Dasanetch territory are depositional and basically of fire texture; they include deltaic, littoral, and alluvial beds of Holocene age (Butzer, 1971). Because of the fine texture of sediments and also the predominantly shallow gradients, forces of denudation (surface wash, etc.) predominate over those of dissection. Variations among these types often correspond to only very slight changes in topography and drainage, and these are often clearly reflected by the vegetation. A mere foot in topographic relief may, for instance, produce markedly different moisture conditions and this often corresponds to significant differences in vegetation pattern and species composition.

Intrazonal soils are typical of the plains and sediment variation is primar-

---

[2] Detailed physical descriptions of most of these and other units are given by Butzer (1971).

[3] Butzer (ibid.).

ily the result of facies changes or surface drainage (Butzer, 1970). Several types of soils associated with the particular depositional forms mentioned above are recurrent throughout most of the lower basin, and since they typically correspond to distinctive plant communities they are briefly characterized here.

(a) Ridges, high in sand content, identified by Butzer (1971) as beach ridges. Drainage is rapid and good. Relief varies, but the maximum measured was 11 meters above the surrounding land. Termit mounds are often present and are sometimes very pronounced features of the landscape.

(b) Inter-ridges, high in sand although with higher silt content. Drainage is fair to good, though apparently less favorable than on the ridges. Termite mounds are frequently present.

(c) Clay mudflats with dark and heavy clays which characteristically are waterlogged during rainy periods, and develop cracking patterns during dry months. Cracking may occur to depths of about one meter. These margallitic clays are alternately termed vertisols, or black cotton soils. Termite mounds are absent from the clay (margallitic) mudflats except at their periphery.

Locally within the lower basin, drainage conditions vary from relatively rapid and ideal (e. g., within the porous ridges and high inter-ridges) to greatly impeded (e. g., within the clay mudflats), depending primarily on topography and soil type. In the case of the latter type, the Dasanetch report the existence of standing water on some mudflats for weeks after the large rains (ir gudoha). Drainage within the plains is internal, with the shallow streams and washes essentially unintegrated. The scattered and undeveloped minor streams and washes may become active during rainy periods (usually only for hours or a few days at most), but their waters typically dissipate within a very short distance. There are numerous very small washes west of the Kolon (also pronounced Kolom) channel (Fig. 1-2), for example, but only one or two of them actually reach Kolon itself, and even swales there are widely spread and shallow. Swales between ridges or otherwise higher ground often remain as relatively green patches or bands against the surrounding parched grasses throughout the dry season. The swales and minor drainage channels characteristically receive extra moisture to support a relatively dense growth of trees and shrubs (Fig. 2-1) as well as a more luxuriant growth of grasses and forbs. Small streams are of real significance in draining adjacent higher ground, providing seasonal surface waters, and supporting small, more mesophytic plant communities.

The Omo River (War) is the only perennially flowing river within the low-

26

Fig. 2.1.--Woody Vegetation along Drainage Channel in Plains

er basin. Originating in the western Ethiopian highlands, it bisects the lower basin until it terminates at Lake Rudolf (Fig. 1-2). The relatively lush green vegetation bordering the Omo River stands in sharp contrast to the surrounding landscape during most of the year. Next in order of magnitude are Il Nakwa (Kibish River) and the Usno River (Fig. 1-1); both are ephemeral and highly irregular in flow. Il Nakwa is an important source of water for both the Dasanetch and Inyangatom tribes and their stock, and simple water holes are often dug to depths of over 20 feet during long dry spells. Presently, the waters of Il Nakwa dissipate into low-lying clay mudflats to the west and southwest of Koras (Mt. Nakwa). Older Dasanetch informants describe this river as having once flowed into Berar (Sanderson's Gulf).

Floral and faunal regional affinities. --Floristic affinities of the Lower Omo Basin are predominantly East African, a characteristic related to the region's arid character and its contiguity with similar lands in northern Kenya. Even the species of the riverine forest, geographically linked with the more mesophytic vegetation to the north by an almost continuous band of riverine communities, are most aligned with the East African flora. Both Hedberg (1962) and Gillett (1955) describe the southern Ethiopian highland taxa as more closely related to East African highland vegetation than with that of northern Ethiopia. Taxonomic diversity within the lower basin (see Appendix A) as indicated by my collections[4] is low (with 76 families, 193 genera, 321 species so far recorded). This limited floristic variability is primarily accounted for by the extreme harshness of the environment, the recent large-scale geomorphic changes, and the high disturbance by human activities.

Anomalous localities. --Two localities stand in sharp contrast to the plains more generally: the Omo Beds (Shungura Formation) and Koras (Mt. Nakwa).[5] The Omo Beds (Fig. 1-1), so named by the paleontologist Arambourg in the 1930's, are Pleistocene to recent fossiliferous deposits resulting from major northward extensions of Lake Rudolf and of the delta and floodplain of the Omo River. These beds of silts, sands, clays, and volcanic tuffs form a large exposure in the lower basin due to erosion following stratigraphic uplift. They

---

[4]Plant collections were contributed to the East African Herbarium, Nairobi, Kenya.

[5]Henceforth, the Dasanetch terms for localities will be used in all instances except the Omo River (War) and Lake Rudolf (Bas).

are now partially exposed, especially east of Koras (Fig. 1-2) where they consist of tilted exposed tuffaceous ridges alternating with relatively flat areas of various sediment types. A large percentage of the Omo Bed exposures is bare area, with both tree/shrub steppe and shrub thicket with numerous succulent plants. This large exposure of the Omo Beds offers little potential for utilization by the Dasanetch and Inyangatom tribes, aside from a few species useful for wooden implements, some plants for medicinal purposes, and vegetation for sporadic grazing and browsing by domestic stock. Unexposed and partially exposed sediments of the Shungura Formation extend south and southwest of the large exposures (e. g., north, west and southwest of Kalam) as well as east of Koras. Where partial exposures occur or where the Shungura Formation sediments are very near the surface a distinct patterning of vegetation results. The strong influence exerted by stratigraphy on the vegetation is striking, for example, in a locality just west of the Shungura Formation exposures and east of Koras where alternating bands of shrub steppe and grassland exist, and these bands generally parallel the ridges of the exposures. Structurally controlled vegetation is also pronounced in localities northwest of Kalam. Partial exposure of uplifted Shungura Formation and more recent sediments produces a vegetation which may be considered disturbed, one which is often nearly indistinguishable from plant communities resulting from overgrazing (see below).

Koras (Mt. Nakwa) is a volcanic highland with an unevenly developed lithosol (and scattered termite mounds). Plant cover is highly irregular on these inhospitable slopes, and varies among shrub thicket (dominated by Acacia and Commiphora), tree/shrub steppe with succulents, and grassland steppe. Koras is only lightly used by the local tribes, though it is fairly commonly utilized around its lowermost slopes for small stock. Fires are infrequently on Koras slopes but they do have local significance for plant growth. Koras is an important factor in the availability of water in the region, chiefly due to extensive runoff from its slopes during and following rains (and retained by adjacent mudflats, etc.). Surface pools resulting from this run-off render much grazing land otherwise too far from water seasonally accessible.

Human activities. --Economic activities of the Dasanetch which have some bearing on the present character of the plains will be discussed in detail in Chapter 5. These include intensive grazing and browsing by domestic stock; burning in some localities and cutting, clearing, and planting in riverine and delta zones. At present, the impact of domestic stock constitutes the most profound influence on the vegetation, and the plant life of most of the Dasanetch's present territory is now seriously disturbed. The map in Fig. 2-2 shows the spectrum and distribution of land uses within the Lower Omo Basin, and this distribution is of crucial importance to the existing state of the ecosystems.

Studies of Natural and Deteriorated Plains Communities

General. --Virtually all utilizable lands within the lower basin are exploited by the local tribes for grazing. At least four types of constraints are operative in rendering large tracts of land unutilizable for domestic stock during some or all of the year: (1) presence of disease organisms seasonally or year-round (e.g., tsetse); (2) seasonally prohibitive distances from water; (3) restriction by the Kenyan and/or Ethiopian police (e.g., the Ilemi lands); and (4) hostile relations with neighboring tribes (e.g., the Hamar and Borana). Because of the large scale exploitation by the indigenous tribes, much of the region is significantly altered ecologically and the problem arises as to how to discern natural plant communities from the varying phases of deterioration through overuse by the Dasanetch and Inyangatom in particular. An understanding of these phases is obviously necessary to an assessment of the impact on the environment by the Dasanetch people in the form of estimating the present and probable future quality of their lands.

The objective of determining the sequence of relatively natural and subsequent disturbed phases of plant communities was undertaken through quantitative ecological studies. The studies were basically to examine the plant ecology within the context of both basic depositional/sediment units and land use patterns. Three geographical zones were defined which formed a general gradient of land use pressure:

Zone I --lands essentially unutilized for the past 30-40 years.

Zone II --intermittently grazed, on seasonal basis.

Zone III--intensively grazed, year-round.

These locations are shown in the map of Fig. 2-2 (burning is described separately for each of the zones). Within each zone, line-belt ecological transects were used for two contrasting physical units: (A) sandy and silty sand ridges and inter-ridges, and (B) cracking clay mudflats. The results of the transects were compared among the three sites of each unit separately. Soils were also sampled and collected. [6]

---

[6]Methods of transecting are briefly described in Appendix B.

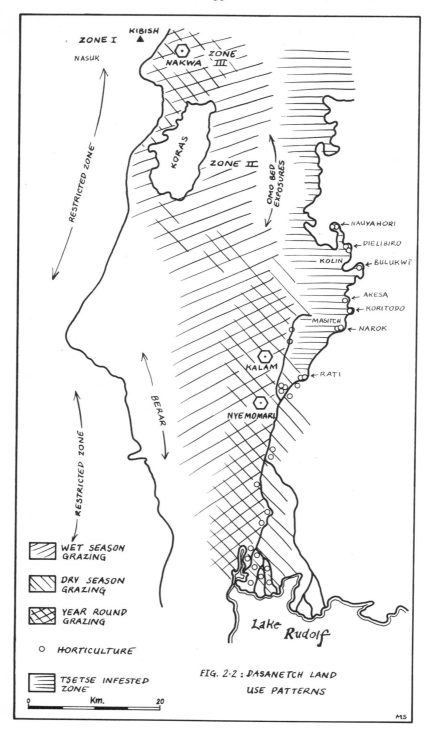

ZONE I

KIBISH ▲

NASUK

NAKWA

ZONE III

KORAS

ZONE II

RESTRICTED ZONE

OMO BED EXPOSURES

←NAUYAHORI

←DIELIBIRO

KOLIN

←BULUKWI

←AKESA

←KORITODO

MASITCH

←NAROK

KALAM

←RATI

BERAR

RESTRICTED ZONE

NYEMOMARI

Lake Rudolf

WET SEASON GRAZING

DRY SEASON GRAZING

YEAR ROUND GRAZING

○ HORTICULTURE

TSETSE INFESTED ZONE

0   Km.   20

FIG. 2-2 : DASANETCH LAND
USE PATTERNS

MS

Ridges and inter-ridges (Fig. 2-3) were combined as a category for study since variations in both vegetation and soils are minor. Although the ridge/inter-ridge and mudflat communities do not account for all of the plains, they are highly significant throughout them, and a good percentage of the remaining communities may be viewed as variations from them. Results from selected sites are presented here in order to demonstrate the most basic types of ecologic and floristic changes accompanying human-induced disturbance.

Unit A: Silty sand and sand ridges and inter-ridges. --Results of line-belt transects are described here for each of the zones. Composite data for Unit A within each of the three zones is shown in Table 2-1. Further details concerning these communities are given in Carr, 1976b.

Zone I: The Ilemi Plains

Land use: The Dasanetch, Inyangatom, and Turkana tribes have been prohibited from using these plains within the Ilemi since the 1930's. The Dasanetch and Inyangatom have been allowed to graze their stock there only during extreme drought, [7] and apparently the lands within a short distance from Il Nakwa is the only area where they are not bothered by the police, providing their situation is absolutely critical. Previous to 1930, grazing was intermittent and relatively light, allegedly because of the distance from water being prohibitive for much of these rangelands during most months of the year. Some temporary Inyangatom villages and cattle camps used to cluster around the edge of the large clay flat Nasuk (Fig. 2-2) when water was present, but these dispersed as the water disappeared. Burning is described by both Dasanetch and Inyangatom informants as being practiced quite frequently several decades ago, but not in recent years. [8] For the purposes of this study, this zone was sufficiently undisturbed by human influences during the past several decades so as to provide an extremely valuable ecological reference point for studies of the effects of human activities.

---

[7]These ecological studies were completed in 1970. In 1971 the Dasanetch and Inyangatom were permitted to graze the area again, which resulted in widespread and serious ecological deterioration which I observed in July of 1972.

[8]The recent prohibition of burning in the Ilemi was confirmed by the Kenya police officer in charge at Kibish.

Fig. 2-3.--Aerial View of Relict Beach Ridges

TABLE 2-1

SELECTED VEGETATION TRANSECT RESULTS FOR UNIT A OF RANGELANDS:
SANDY AND SILTY SAND RIDGES AND INTER-RIDGES

	Zone I			Zone II			Zone III		
Physiognomic Type	Tree/Shrub Grassland	Tree-Shrub Grassland	Shrub Grassland	Tree/Shrub Steppe	Shrub Steppe	Tree/Shrub Grassland	Shrub Thicket & Steppe	Shrub Thicket & Steppe	Shrub Thicket & Steppe
	Site 1	Site 2	Site 3	Site 1	Site 2	Site 3	Site 1	Site 2	Site 3
% of total plant cover	80-85	89-90	80-85	50-55	55-60	65-70	15-20	15-20	10-15
% ground cover (3 ft.)	75	80-85	80	40-45	50-55	60-65	2-3	4-8	1-3
% woody cover	5	2-5	1	5-8	5-8	2-4	15	10-12	8-12
Grass height (average)	18-24"	19-23	17-22	12-15	11-15	12-18	4-7	2-8	3-6

Important Species (excluding termite mound spp.)

Zone I:
Acacia mellifera
Acacia tortilis
Cenchrus setigerus
Cordia sinensis
Dactyloctenium sp. nov.
Grewia tenax
Heliotropium spp.
I. ciferrii
Indigofera volkensii
Maerua crassifolia
Sporobolus marginatus
Ziziphus mucronata

Zone II:
A. reficiens
Acacia nubica
Aerva persica
Barleria acanthoides
Cadaba rotundifolia
Cenchrus ciliaris
Chloris roxburghiana
Cordia sinensis
Dactyloctenium sp. nov.
Grewia tenax
Indigofera spinosa
Maerua crassifolia
Sporobolus marginatus

Zone III:
A. reficiens
Acacia mellifera
Barleria acanthoides
C. glandulosa
Cadaba rotundifolia
Cenchrus ciliaris
Indigofera spinosa
Sporobolus marginatus

Topography and drainage: The ridge/inter-ridge unit within this zone is characterized by relatively porous silts with fair to very good drainage.[9] The highest
ridge studied in this zone has only $8\frac{1}{2}$ meters total relief, while most have considerably less. Topographic change was recorded along each transect made,
and the variation recorded for each site was very slight.

Ridges are numerous in this part of the Ilemi, and together with the inter-
ridges they form a large expanse of nearly uninterrupted silty sands and sands.
Small clayey swales are scattered within this unit (A), and these small localities support plant communities with more woody growth, and less ground cover.
No significant evidence of soil erosion is present in the ridge/inter-ridge unit,
although there is some limited sheet wash where small, compact, bare patches
occur on the steeper sides of the largest ridge studied.

Toward the highlands of Kenya and Sudan Unit A grades into the piedmont
alluvial plains (Butzer, 1970), interrupted only by a few clay mudflats.[10]

Soils: As stated earlier, soil data gathered for the lower basin as a whole is
only preliminary so that soils are only characterized in general terms for each
unit. The complexity of their variation can only be understood following much
more detailed and systematic study. Soils of the ridge/ inter-ridge unit within
this zone (described in a forthcoming paper) are high in sandy content and are
predominantly loose single grain with little aggregation. Generally, the topographically lower inter-ridge soils are apparently higher in silt content. Rooting, as observed in sample pits, is almost entirely fibrous; dense rooting occurs to a depth of ca. 25-30 centimeters, with a few larger roots interspersed.
Organic matter is very low (less than 1 percent); potassium is low, and manga-
nese, nitrogen and phosphorous were highly variable in amount among the samples taken.

Vegetation: Total vegetation cover is relatively high for this unit, with 80-90
percent frequently recorded (Table 2-1). Although tree/shrub grassland and
shrub grassland characterize the whole ridge/inter-ridge unit here, considerable variation exists regarding the importance of woody vs. herbaceous cover.
Trees and shrubs are generally more abundant in the lower inter-ridge portions

---

[9] The term "ridge/inter-ridge unit" will subsequently be used interchange-
ably with "silty sand and sand ridges and inter-ridges" and also with "Unit A."

[10] These piedmont alluvial plains assumedly contribute significantly to the
total amount of moisture received by the adjacent mudflats.

(Fig. 2-4), and the total number of woody species encountered there is higher. Woody growth may also be clustered on termite mounds, even when it is excluded from the surrounding plain (Fig. 2-5). On the highest ridge in the zone (Site 3), small Acacia tortilis shrubs are the only woody plants (see below). Throughout the rest of this ridge/inter-ridge unit, however, woody species are much more diverse (e.g., Maerua crassifolia, Ziziphus mucronata, Acacia mellifera: see Table 2-1). Some floristic differences in grasses exist on the higher ridges, and there are typically more grass species present in the inter-ridge communities. Likewise, forbs show significant contrast between the better-drained ridges and the inter-ridges.

The ratio of grasses to forbs is high throughout most of this unit; in addition, grass heights of 60-90 centimeters are common. Fire-sensitive trees and shrubs are scattered throughout the grasslands, especially in the inter-ridge regions. Woody species commonly browsed in other parts of the lower basin (e.g., Acacia tortilis and Maerua crassifolia) show little evidence of utilization here, and branching frequently is maintained to near ground level. A representative vegetation profile is shown for this Zone I in Fig. 2-6.

Termite mounds: Termite mounds throughout the lower basin are highly variable in construction. For example, towers have been observed up to 9 meters in height, and they may be engineered to have one (most commonly) or multiple towers (Fig. 2-7). Mounds do not occur in the heavy clay flats (nor in the riverine and delta zones), but they are quite common throughout better-drained sandy and silty sand sediments. Their unusual density in the Ilemi area (Zone I), particularly on the highest ridges, is remarkable even to one familiar with the lower basin. An awareness of them is heightened for the land-rover traveler, because of the ever-present possibility of a nearby large aardvark hole, dangerously well camouflaged by high grasses. Samples of mounds indicate some variation from surrounding sediments, but on the basis of the limited data collected, this variation does not form any recognizable pattern. Sediments forming the mounds are always highly compact, almost cement-like, except for fresh deposits near the opening at the top. Active mounds are indicated by this freshly deposited sediment at the top, and the percentage of active mounds in a given locality differs among localities. Mounds frequently support dense clusters of woody plants (mostly fire-sensitive) which may include Cordia sinensis, Cadaba farinosa, C. glandulosa, Maerua crassifolia, M. oblongifolia, M. subcordata, Grewia tenax, and G. villosa. The ground surrounding the base of the mound is

Fig. 2-4.--Undisturbed Tree/Shrub Grassland in Plains

Fig. 2-5.--Undisturbed Grassland on High Plains Ridge

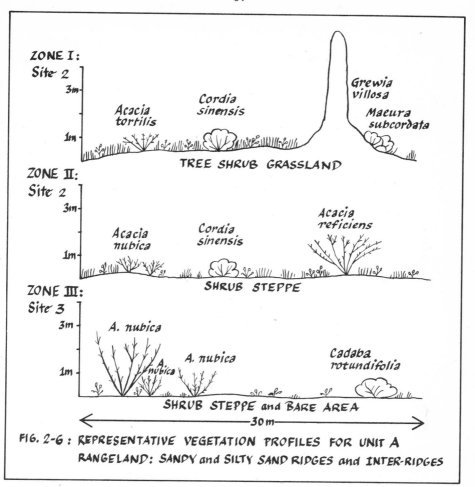

ZONE I:
Site 2

3m

Acacia tortilis
Cordia sinensis
Grewia villosa
Maeura subcordata

1m

TREE SHRUB GRASSLAND

ZONE II:
Site 2

3m

Acacia nubica
Cordia sinensis
Acacia reficiens

1m

SHRUB STEPPE

ZONE III:
Site 3

3m

A. nubica
A. nubica
A. nubica
Cadaba rotundifolia

1m

SHRUB STEPPE and BARE AREA

← 30 m →

FIG. 2-6 : REPRESENTATIVE VEGETATION PROFILES FOR UNIT A
RANGELAND: SANDY and SILTY SAND RIDGES and INTER-RIDGES

Fig. 2-7.--Termite Mound in Plains: Multiple-Tower Form

often devoid of herbaceous growth and the resulting rings of bare ground are
striking from an aerial view.

Fauna: Indigenous large fauna in the Lower Omo Basin are most abundant within the Ilemi region, east of the Omo River (and north of about Rati: Fig. 1-2),
and in the northern sector of the west bank lands. In Zone I, large herds of
Grant's gazelle (with herds containing as many as 80-90 individuals), and smaller ones of oryx and zebra roam the grasslands. Topi are also fairly common
here both in large groups (the largest one observed with over 70 animals), or
more commonly in groups of two or three. Other conspicuous fauna observed
here include cheetah, lion, jackal, antbear, bat-eared fox, warthog, ostrich
and kori bustard.

Discussion: The variation in presence or absence of woody plants and in growth
form among these communities is clearly correlated with drainage properties.
The higher ridges with comparatively rapid drainage apparently discourage
most woody growth, and the fact that the woody growth Acacia tortilis is the
only prominent woody species here is best accounted for by its well-known deep
root system. A. tortilis trees grow to heights of 13-15 meters in small swales
of this sandy region, and thus trees are surrounded by a lush understory of
grasses to heights greater than 1 meter. On the basis of the above, one would
predict a higher density of woody plants and a greater number of woody species
in the lower, siltier, and therefore, less well-drained lands. This is in fact
the case in this unit of Zone I.

The trees and shrubs concentrated on termite mounds may be in response
to alterations in the nutrient content there or for protection from fires due to
the bare area commonly surrounding the base of the mound. A second possibility is protection from fire, but burning is probably not significant within this
zone during recent years. Strong evidence of the exclusion of fire from this
zone (I) for a number of years is provided not only by local informants but also
by some scattered fire-sensitive woody species (e.g., Cordia sinensis, Maerua
subcordata, Acacia mellifera) surrounded by dense grass growth. On the basis
of Dasanetch accounts, it is probable that burning had greater importance in the
past.

Vegetational patchiness, both physiognomic and floristic, is characteristic of some localities within this ridge/inter-ridge unit, especially in association with termite mounds. Small swales within the sandy complex of soils

which support clusters of primarily Acacia tortilis create an irregular appearance to the woody plant distribution, thus increasing the total amount of pattern.
Aardvark holes, sometimes are constructed to depths of 2 meters, collect
large amounts of moisture during rains, and these localities support grasses
growing to heights of 60-100 centimeters which remain green far into the dry
season. Such growth stands in sharp contrast to the surrounding shorter and
dry vegetation. One grass in particular, Dactyloctenium sp. nov., was widely
observed to form pure or mono-specific rings about the mounds (this grass apparently does not compete successfully with the dominant Sporobolus marginatus elsewhere within the unit). The absence of forbs (particularly the widespread Heliotropium) from these rings accentuates the patterned appearance.
Overall, termite activity and the resultant mounds are significant for plant life
through the modification of soil conditions, the concentration of woody growth,
the providing of possible inroads for this growth into communities strongly dominated by grasses and in the creation of considerable patchiness.

Zone II: East of Koras

Land use: This zone (Fig. 2-2) is utilized for grazing by cattle and small stock
on a seasonal basis only. The primary factor limiting its use on a year-round
basis is absence of water. In addition, tsetse is present in the lands slightly to
the north during wet seasons, according to informants.[11] Grazing may be intensive locally during wet periods but it is never prolonged, and temporary stock
camps are generally quite mobile within the area. Grazing here begins in about
March or whenever the large rains (ir gudoha) occur, and stock (especially
small stock) may continue to feed here through late May or into June when the
last of the surface waters disappear. The high irregularity which characterizes the rainy seasons then, insures that this zone undergoes grazing by domestic stock during many but not all years. During wet months a number of villages cluster along the northeast edge of Koras, and the stock associated with
them graze the relatively lush grasslands just east of Koras, where water collects for prolonged periods following the rains. Burning is infrequent and irregular, and when it occurs it is usually just preceding the rains. According to
Dasanetch informants, burning was more widely practiced here in the past,
when the zone was more intensively used by their tribe. Perceptions vary wide-

---

[11]These lands are used primarily by the Inyangatom tribe but Dasanetch villages and temporary stock camps are present in smaller numbers.

ly among the Dasanetch as to whether this zone between Koras and the Omo Beds is disease-ridden during the rainy periods; certainly a number of older men who once relied upon it heavily no longer use it.

Topography and drainage: Ridges within this zone are generally less well defined and lower in elevation than those of the Ilemi (Zone I), and the lower sand and silt environments often form subtle gradations into adjacent clayey and silty clay mudflats. Since local topographic relief is generally less pronounced here compared to much of the Ilemi, extremes of drainage (namely the rapid drainage of the high ridges and the excessive waterlogging of the mudflats), are less characteristic. The maximum relief recorded from a sandy ridge community into an adjacent clay mudflat within this zone was $5\frac{1}{2}$ meters.

Soil: Pits dug in different localities within Unit A of this zone indicated soils to be predominantly loose single grain, with rooting well developed in the first 20-25 centimeters, though less dense than in the same unit of Zone I (an exception to this is the ridge, Site 3, Zone II, which is adjacent to the Shungura Formation sediments and where grass cover is very well developed). Where ground cover is much reduced and where there is sufficient topographic gradient, some surface washing of materials and gullies suggests minor erosional processes.

Vegetation: Two of the transect sites summarized in Table 2-1 are tree/shrub steppe;[12] the third is tree/shrub grassland, though even it has reduced cover compared with sites of the same unit within Zone I. There is a tendency for woody growth to be more restricted to termite mounds, with two exceptions: trees and shrubs are common where some bare area exists; and one species of small tree (Maerua crassifolia) survives well in the grassland even where ground cover is continuous. Maerua is usually browsed to heights about $1\frac{3}{4}$ meters, i.e., the height to which goats are able to reach. Species which are able to establish in small bare areas where grass cover has been removed through grazing (Fig. 2-8) include most notably Acacia nubica, but also A. mellifera, A. reficiens, Cordia sinensis, Cadaba rotundifolia, C. glandulosa and Maerua subcordata. A. tortilis is only occasionally encountered in most of this zone, in contrast with Zone I. Generally, a higher proportion of forbs to grasses constitutes the herbaceous ground cover in this zone than is the case for Zone I.

---

[12]Steppe, by its usage in this discussion, indicates a discontinuous, irregular ground cover.

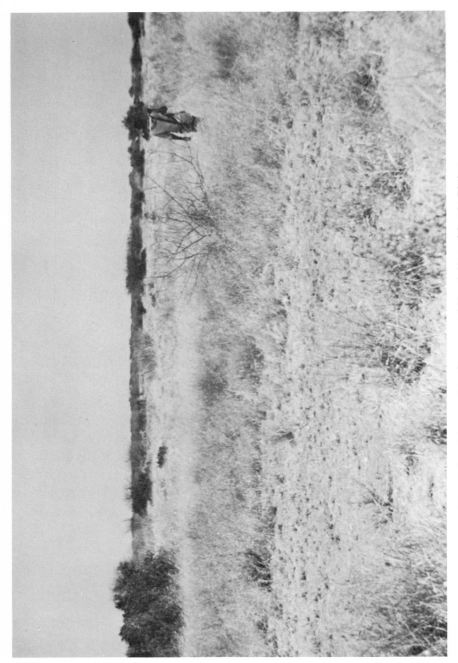

Fig. 2-8. --Intermediate Overgrazed Vegetation of Sandy Plains

Among the forbs most widely and strongly represented are Indigofera spinosa and Aerva persica, both of which are characteristic of disturbed communities. Heliotropium, highly significant in the ridges of Zone I, is of relatively low frequency in most of Zone II (with the exception of Site 3), except after favorable rainy periods. Of the grasses characterizing Zone I, several of the dominant ones are significant within Zone II (Sporobolus marginatus, Dactyloctenium sp. nov. and Cenchrus setigerus). Cenchrus ciliaris on the other hand, while not significant in Zone I, increases greatly in frequency and density throughout most of Zone II, and in some localities it is clearly the dominant grass. This kind of grass is usually associated with a relatively low total ground cover on sandy or silty soils. A representative vegetation profile is presented in Fig. 2-6.

Termite mounds: Mounds are abundant throughout most of the sandy and silty sand environments of this zone, though not nearly as abundant as on the highest ridge of Zone I. Aardvark holes here, as in the Ilemi, may reach the large proportions of 2 by 2 meters, and in Zone II in particular, the grasses of this more mesic microhabitat grow to heights much greater than in the surrounding plains. Vegetation around the mound bases is similar to that of Zone I, with a few species deletions (e. g., Grewia bicolor).

Fauna: Correlated with the deterioration of the rangelands and the increase in domestic animals and human traffic in Zone II, there is a marked change in the large fauna present. Topi and zebra are absent and oryx observed only very occasionally and then only singly or in pairs. Grant's gazelle are common but move in pairs or small groups rather than in the large herds characteristic of the Ilemi. Other fauna observed within this zone include silver-backed jackal, bat-eared fox, warthog, kudu, hyena, aardvark, cheetah, lion, and dikdik. Warthog, hyena, and dikdik in particular are common throughout the shrub steppe communities which comprise a large percentage of this zone, and the latter two especially are not common in the undisturbed rangelands.

Discussion: The high proportion of fire-sensitive woody plants growing on termite mounds where surrounding grass cover is sufficient to support fires is correlated with the protective function the mounds serve, the bare area surrounding the mound base presumably serving as a firebreak. The thick rough bark of Maerua crassifolia renders it fire-resistant (it was observed to survive heavily

burned areas) and it is the only woody species consistently recorded for localities subjected to burning other than fire resistant invader species (Cadaba rotundifolia, C. glandulosa, and Salvadora persica). The most widespread woody
invader following disturbance by overgrazing is Acacia nubica. This species
establishes rapidly in bare sandy and silty sand areas and can grow more than a
meter in one year. It is a reliable disturbance indicator throughout the lower
basin. Although it is usually avoided by domestic animals, cattle will consume
the pods of this weedy acacia when grass or palatable forbs are absent, so that
they may serve as seed dispersal agents. A. nubica does not establish where
grass growth is continuous and it is almost totally absent from the ridge/inter-
ridge complex of Zone I. [13] The unpalatable shrub Cadaba also does not establish where grass cover is continuous. The increasingly ubiquitous member of
this genus, Cadaba rotundifolia, is extremely hardy and fire resistant, and is
now common throughout most of the lower basin in disturbed areas. Once having successfully invaded a disturbed plant community, this shrub maintains a
high competitive ability vis à vis other plant taxa. It has a dual root system,
with both vertical and lateral roots, so that it is well adapted to draw moisture
from both superficial and deeper soil levels. C. rotundifolia was also observed
on many occasions to survive burns, both by resprouting and by the low combus-
tibility of its shoots.

Zone III: Nakwa Vicinity

Land use: Much of Inyangatom settlement is concentrated around Nakwa (Fig.
1-1) and the region to the north. Inyangatom villages along the Omo River form
the major settlement zone. Domestic stock are excluded from the lands adjacent to the river because of tsetse. Consequently, all Inyangatom stock are
kept in the western sector. The combined domestic stock of both tribes at Nakwa creates a year-round and intense grazing pressure on nearby rangelands.
The plains just east of Nakwa (Fig. 2-9) are here designated Zone III. The prohibition of grazing west of Il Nakwa (except for the immediately adjacent land,
where it is not strictly enforced) has created a tremendous intensification of
overgrazing throughout this zone. Of the sandy and silty sand areas present,
those nearest Il Nakwa are grazed and browsed most heavily. Watering holes
are dug in sandy reaches of the dry river bed during drought months, and these

---

[13]One exception to this is a conspicuous A. nubica thicket in Zone I at the
base of the highest sandy ridge, where ground cover is greatly reduced and
where water reportedly collects following heavy rains.

Fig. 2-9.   Severely Overgrazed Vegetation of Sand/Silt Plains

holes constitute the basic water source during that time for both humans and livestock (Fig. 2-10). Burning occurs only in a few localities which are slightly less heavily grazed, primarily in the eastern sector of this zone; elsewhere, grass cover is too low to support fires. Traces of stock camps (foretch) are scattered throughout the zone, and cattle trails are virtually everywhere (Fig. 2-11).

Topography and drainage: Sandy and silty sand environments here typically have fair to good drainage, and generally comparable to those described for Zone II.

Soil: Samples from pits here revealed soils to be mostly loose single grain near the surface but with more subsurface compaction than in Zones I and II. The bare expanses of soil have allowed the development of numerous short unintegrated gullies commonly to one half meter or more in depth, and gullying is present even where there is small local relief. Sorting of soil particles indicates that sheet erosion is also a widely spread phenomenon. Generalizations concerning the precise structural and/or chemical effects of overgrazing on the soil must await further research.

Vegetation: Plant life of this unit is critically destroyed to the point where its capacity for regeneration is clearly questionable within any reasonable time period. Shrub steppe and shrub thicket alternate with large bare areas (Table 2-1) and are the predominant vegetation within this zone. Woody growth (mostly unpalatable) comprises the bulk of total plant cover rather than herbaceous growth (Table 2-1), distinguishing this zone sharply from the other two. Acacia nubica is dominant among the woody species (Fig. 2-12), and this noxious thorn shrub sometimes forms impenetrable thickets. Numerous seedlings of this invader species grow throughout the sands and silty sands near Nakwa, suggesting its successful reproduction. The bright green shrubs of Cadaba rotundifolia (Fig. 2-12), so numerous throughout this zone, are misleading in that they are strictly unpalatable and therefore are of no browse value. Other woody growth, both scattered and on termite mounds, include Maerua crassifolia (heavily browsed), Cadaba glandulosa, Acacia mellifera, A. reficiens, and Grewia tenax (browsed heavily where not protected). Grasses are almost entirely annuals and they generally only grow to a few centimeters before they are grazed off, thus seldom reaching the flowering phase; only where they are protected by

Fig. 2-10.--Il Nakwa (Kibish River) Watering Holes

Fig. 2-11.--Aerial View of Severely Overgrazed Vegetation on Sandy Ridge

48

Fig. 2-12. --Severely Overgrazed Sand Plains with Thorn Scrub

shrubs do they attain greater heights. Among the grasses, Cenchrus ciliaris and Tetrapogon cenchriformis are proportionately much more significant than in Zones I and II. Forbs present are generally unpalatable or of low range value (Zaleya pentandra, Orthosiphon somalensis, Tragus berteronianus). Those species most conspicuous in Zones I and II are occasional or absent here. The representative profile of this zone which is shown in Fig. 2-6 shows the marked contrast between this region and the other two zones.

Termite mounds: Mounds are similar to the ones earlier described in that they are abundant and often support clusters of woody growth, though, the number of woody species occurring on them is fewer.

Discussion: Continuous and severe overgrazing within this zone has resulted in deterioration involving the reduction of total ground cover, increase in annual grasses over perennials, increase in density and frequency of unpalatable and toxic species, and greater vulnerability to erosion. In addition to scattered shallow and incomplete gullies and surface washes through much of this region, dust devils are numerous. Thus both water and wind operate as erosive forces to some degree. Fires are, predictably, excluded by the lack of ground cover. What palatable herbaceous growth does manage to establish during and following the rains is quickly grazed off; little of it actually survives to reproductive stages, and reseeding from surrounding areas is probably of great importance.

Although Zone III is located near Nakwa, there are larger areas of sands and silty sands further south (in strictly Dasanetch lands) which are presently in similar condition. Thus, the sequence of disturbed communities described by this study is applicable on a much larger scale. A diagram summarizing the physiognomic changes with increasing land use intensity is presented in Fig. 2-13. One major question still unanswered is whether or not there is a disturbance threshold, beyond which retrogression or deterioration is so severe as to effectively prevent recovery of the community within the foreseeable future.

Unit B: Clay mudflats.[14]

Zone I

Topography and drainage: The large clay mudflat (Nasuk) of the Ilemi plains

---

[14]In the descriptions of Unit B, sites, land use and fauna are omitted since these aspects are basically the same as described for Unit A. Discussion of these zones follows their brief description.

50

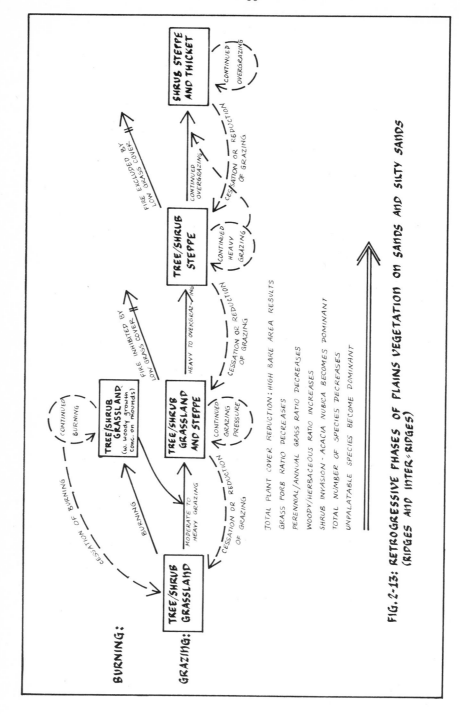

FIG. 2-13: RETROGRESSIVE PHASES OF PLAINS VEGETATION ON SANDS AND SILTY SANDS (RIDGES AND INTER-RIDGES)

(Fig. 2-2) was studied in considerable detail. This mudflat receives considerable drainage from adjacent beach ridges (Fig. 2-14) and also from the highlands to the west. Drainage here is greatly impeded, with surface water remaining in at least the center portion of the flat for some weeks following the large rains (ir gudoha) according to local informants. On several occasions during field work, I have observed standing water even after moderate sporadic rains. A 300-meter transect measuring topographic change from the periphery of the mudflat toward the center of the flats indicated a drop of slightly under 1 meter, and the drop almost surely increases to the actual center.

Soil: The soils comprising the mudflats here (as well as elsewhere within the lower basin) are margallitic clays, usually considered intrazonal. Synonymous terms are vertisols (Smith et al., 1960), grumusols, black cotton soil, black earth and others. Margallitic clays are dense, tropical pedocals (Bunting, 1965) of blackish or dark brown color. This dark color is associated with the humus-montmorillonite clay complex. These clays are well known for their swelling during the wet season and subsequent drying out which produces cracking systems (Fig. 2-15). In numerous localities within the Lower Omo Basin, they are topographically situated so as to retain surface water during and after rains. Even after light rains these soils are characteristically sticky and plastic, making movement very difficult. The alternating wet season swelling and dry season drying out and cracking has a mixing effect which tends to break up roots of woody or perennial plants. Margallitic clays in the interior of the large mudflat in Zone I are very soft on the surface in the period preceding the development of cracking, and during this phase the previous year's cracking patterns or the beginning of the new year's cracking is evidenced by a system of furrows. Concomitant with the development of cracking is the formation of holes, particularly at the intersections of cracks. These holes are often present before cracks are apparent and they sometimes extend to depths of greater than one meter. The periphery of the mudflat (approximately the outer 100 meters) typically develops cracking sooner than the interior, and by the end of the dry season the cracking system near the periphery is far better developed than that of the interior. The data in Table 2-2 show basic contrasts between the peripheral and interior portions of this mudflat. Maximal depth of cracks of slightly greater than one meter was recorded in the outer portion. The width of these cracks achieved the maximal values in Zone I, but variation is enormous (e.g., from 5 to 30 centimeters). Rooting is very dense to about 30 centimeters deep in the outer region but is sparse and shallow in the interior.

Fig. 2-14.--Undisturbed Grassland in Cracking Clay Plains

Fig. 2-15.--Close-up of Cracking Clays

TABLE 2-2

SELECTED VEGETATION TRANSECT RESULTS FOR UNIT B OF RANGELAND: CRACKING CLAY MUDFLATS

	Zone I						Zone II			Zone III		
	Outer Mudflat Zone			Inner Mudflat Zone								
Site No.	1	2	3	4	5	6	1	2	3	1	2	3
Physiognomic Type	Grassland	Grassland	Grassland	Grassland Steppe	Grassland Steppe	Grassland Steppe	Grassland/ Shrub Steppe	Shrub Steppe	Shrub Steppe	Shrub Steppe/ Shrub Thicket	Shrub Thicket- et & Steppe	Shrub Thicket- et & Steppe
% total plant cover	85	95	90	10-15	20-25	12-18	60-65	50-55	45-50	25-35	30-35	25-30
% ground cover	85	95	90	10-15	20-25	12-18	50-55	45-50	25-30	10-15	5-10	< 5
% woody cover	0	0	0	0	0	0	10-15	10-15	15-20	15-20	25-28	15-20
Important Species	Abelmoschus esculentus Abutilon spp. Cyathula orthocantha Digeria muricata Echinochloa sp. Ocimum hadiense Panicum poaoides Portulaca quadrifida Sporobolus helvolus						A. paolii Acacia horrida Aristida mutabilis (Sporobolus helvolus) (Panicum poaoides) C. glandulosa Cadaba rotundifolia Cyathula orthocantha Ocimum hadiense Pontulaca quadrifida Tetrapogon tenellus (A. reficiens)			A. horrida Acacia paolii C. glandulosa Cadaba rotundifolia Cyathula orthocantha Ocimum hadiense (Aristida mutabilis)		

Termite mounds: Termite mounds are absent from the mudflats here and elsewhere within the lower basin, although some do occur along the interface between this unit and Unit A (sands and silty sands). These are very dark in color, high in clays and considerably smaller in height.

Vegetation: (1) Outer region. Vegetation here is grassland without any woody growth except at the thin periphery where the ground is higher and the soil type is somewhat altered. Total plant cover is variable, between about 60 and 75 percent, but mulch is extremely thick so that the living and dead plant cover combined is over 90 percent. The forb/grass ratio is highly variable. Grass height averages 60-90 centimeters, but it may be greater where rooting occurs in more moisture-laden depressions. The vertical facies of cracks are without vegetation, an absence explained by the development of cracks after the wet season annual growth is established. Common species include Sporobolus helvolus, Eriochloa nubica, Panicum poaoides, P. coloratum, Digeria muricata, Corchorus trilocularis, Portulaca quadrifida and Abelmoschus esculentus. Others are mentioned in Table 2-2. There is almost no overlap in grass species between Unit A and Unit B communities. (2) Inner region. Plant life here is sparse relative to the outer region: it is a grassland steppe with large expanses of bare area. Total plant cover ranges from 5 to 20 percent, with little regularity of pattern. It is poor in both plant cover and plant species, and although dead grass culms and shoots of forbs are scattered there is no real mulch development. A marked difference in growth was observed between 1969 and 1970, and again between 1970 and 1972, when species composition shifted strongly--a feature not found in the more stable peripheral part of the flat. The forb/grass ratio here, in contrast to the outer region, is very high and although the grass species are essentially identical in both regions the forbs differ considerably. In particular, Abutilon spp., Ocimum hadiense, Cyathula orthacantha and Ipomoea sinensis are very common. Overall, this inner region is one of high irregularity, both structurally and floristically. Representative profiles of the outer region are shown in Fig. 2-16.

Zone II

Topography and drainage: These seasonally utilized margallitic clay mudflats are smaller in extent and with less topographic relief relative to surrounding environments (with some exceptions, notably the cracking clay grasslands just east of Koras). Consequently, drainage in mudflats of this zone is predictably

55

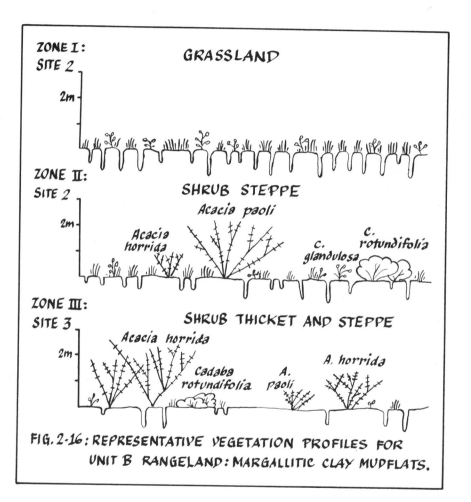

FIG. 2·16: REPRESENTATIVE VEGETATION PROFILES FOR UNIT B RANGELAND: MARGALLITIC CLAY MUDFLATS.

less impeded than in the inner part of the mudflat in Zone I. Nevertheless, seasonal waterlogging does occur, and local informants report that some mudflats of this region retain water for several weeks following substantial rainy periods, thus opening up these lands for grazing by stock.

Soils: Barring sporadic rains, cracking is well developed in most of the mudflats by the end of the dry season. General soil character is comparable with that described for Zone I. A few differences, however, are noteworthy: some shrubs occur where bare area has permitted their establishment (e.g., Acacia reficiens at Site 1) and a ring of non-cracking clay may surround the shrub. This might be explainable in terms of the moisture-drawing power of the shrubs' root systems whereby sufficient moisture is retained to preclude cracking. Wide variation in the time and ultimate degree of cracking development was noted from one dry season to the next. At no time, however, was cracking observed to attain the maximum depths recorded for the Ilemi (1 meter), and holes or depressions were also more shallow.

Vegetation: Physiognomy of the mudflats within this zone varies between grassland and shrub steppe, with limited shrub thicket. These may exist in combination within one mudflat. Bare soil surface occurs mostly in small and irregularly distributed patches. Where shrubs occur they are almost invariably surrounded by steppe or small amounts of bare area rather than by thick herbaceous cover. The forb/grass ratio is again variable, but it generally increases as the total herbaceous cover decreases. Woody species include two shrubs which are largely limited to margallitic clays within the lower basin: Acacia horrida and A. paoli (the former also grows in the Shungura Formation exposures). These two species are invaders (Fig. 2-17) which grow singly or in clusters, and are clearly dominant over other Acacia species here. A. reficiens occurs sparsely in some sites, as is A. mellifera (it is more commonly found in localities with a higher silt content). Also occupying bare patches or extensive bare areas are Cadaba rotundifolia and C. glandulosa, as well as some C. gillettii. Grasses most common include Aristida spp., Dinebra retroflexa, Tetrapogon sp., with much less Sporobolus helvolus and Panicum poaoides than in Zone I. Forbs prominent here include Ocimum hadiense, Cyathula orthacanthan, Abutilon spp., and Solanum incanum. A representative profile is included in Fig. 2-16.

Fig. 2-17. --Intermediate Overgrazed Clay Plains Vegetation

Zone III

Topography and drainage: No essential difference in local relief or drainage exists from those described for Zone II, with the exception that some of the clays near the base of Koras (e.g., between Koras and the Nakwa settlement area) receive considerable runoff.

Soils: Cracking patterns are only well developed in tiny protected areas for the most part (e.g., beneath large thorn shrubs). What cracking develops is usually shallow and incomplete, and cracks tend to become obliterated by trampling in bare areas (Fig. 2-18). Surface soil is loosened by large numbers of stock, thus sometimes making these clays difficult to recognize as margallitic without examining subsurface sediments (except for vegetation indicators). Rooting is very sparse throughout the soil here.

Vegetation: Shrub steppe with patches of shrub thicket are the predominant vegetation forms occurring among large expanses of bare area throughout Unit B of Zone III (Table 2-2). Among the shrubs present, Acacia horrida is less common than A. paolii. Cadaba rotundifolia is a major invading, highly persistent shrub in these disturbed communities, attesting to its wide adaptability to different environmental conditions (note its abundance in Unit A of this zone, described above). Unpalatable forbs clearly predominate over grasses although scattered tufts of a few grass species occur, including Tetrapogon cenchriformis and Aristida spp. Most important among the forbs which served as disturbance indicators are Ocimum, Cyathula, Barleria and Solanum species. Vegetation here is schematized in Fig. 2-16.

Discussion: The diagram in Fig. 2-19 suggests some possible phases of the retrogression of mudflat plant communities. One critical factor affecting the vegetation within this type of environment is the degree of drainage impedance, i.e., the amount and duration of inundation of the mudflat. This characteristic, sometimes in combination with the level of human disturbance, is critical in determining the presence or absence of woody growth and in the maintenance of bare area. Where there is excessive waterlogging, herbaceous cover may be greatly reduced, yet woody plants are also unable to invade and maintain themselves. This is true, for example, in the interior of the large mudflat in Zone I. In this case, the amount of bare area simply increases with continued overgrazing until the area is nearly devoid of vegetation except for unpalatable forbs

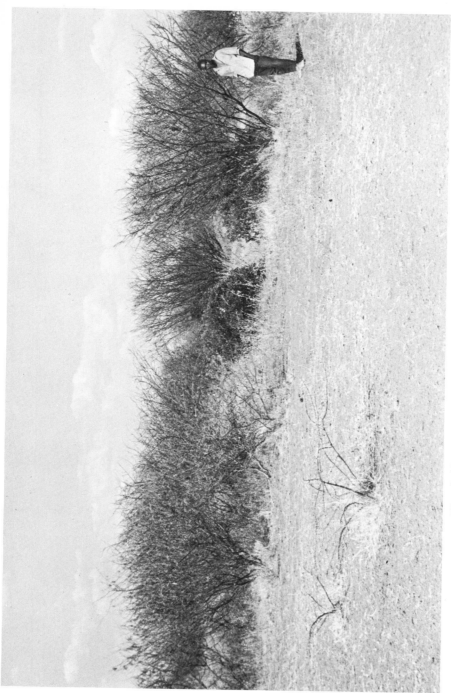

Fig. 2-18. --Severely Overgrazed Vegetation of Clay Plains

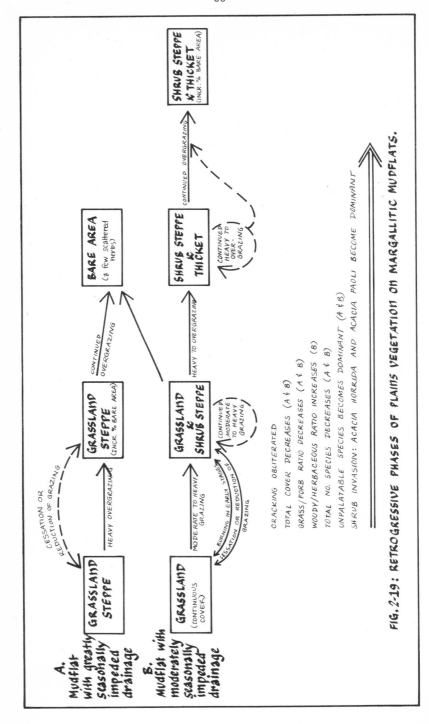

FIG. 2-19: RETROGRESSIVE PHASES OF PLAINS VEGETATION ON MARGALLITIC MUDFLATS.

and a few protected grasses. There is, then, a convergence in the plant life between those localities where the initial phases of overgrazing preceding bush invasion have occurred but where drainage is sufficient to permit woody growth, and those localities where drainage is severely impaired so that woody growth is prohibited and herbaceous cover is sharply limited, even in the absence of domestic grazing. That is to say, certain physical habitat characteristics and disturbance through human activities may favor similar plant communities. Zones II and II contain some clay localities where woody growth is excluded because of excessive and prolonged seasonal waterlogging, but most disturbed clay mudflats in Dasanetch territory do have shrub invasion following the removal of herbaceous cover. With periodic burning, fire-sensitive shrubs predictably succumb. The absence of these fire-sensitive shrubs in smaller clay flats with well-developed grasslands in Zone I, where burning does not occur, suggests that these species (e.g., Acacia horrida, A. paolii and A. reficiens) also do not compete well with the grasses. Severe and prolonged disturbance of mudflats which potentially may support woody growth, I suggest, may ultimately result in substantial amounts of virtually impenetrable shrub thicket. The diagram of Fig. 2-19 represents the major changes in this sort of environment with increasing grazing pressure.

Summary and Existing Range Conditions

The above sections have described in detail the nature and extent of range deterioration which occurs throughout the lands of the Dasanetch. Retrogression sequences were suggested for two recurrent geomorphic soil units; from these it is clear that the structural types of disturbed vegetation for these units are convergent. Major effects of overgrazing are the reduction of total vegetation cover including pasturage, invasion by bush, and an increase in annual grasses over perennial grasses and an increase in forbs (especially unpalatable ones) relative to grass. Even though burning may be practiced in the grasslands which are little disturbed, the seriously deteriorated areas no longer support sufficient grass cover to allow fires. When there is sufficient grass, it is usually only enough to produce a fast, relatively cool fire. Consequently, once bush invasion and the reduction of cover have reached a certain point the fire-susceptible invading bush can no longer be controlled by burning.

The resulting quality of rangeland for virtually all the territory presently accessible to the Dasanetch is very low. Large areas are virtually devoid of pasturage during much of the year, and much of the rest is only sparsely vege-

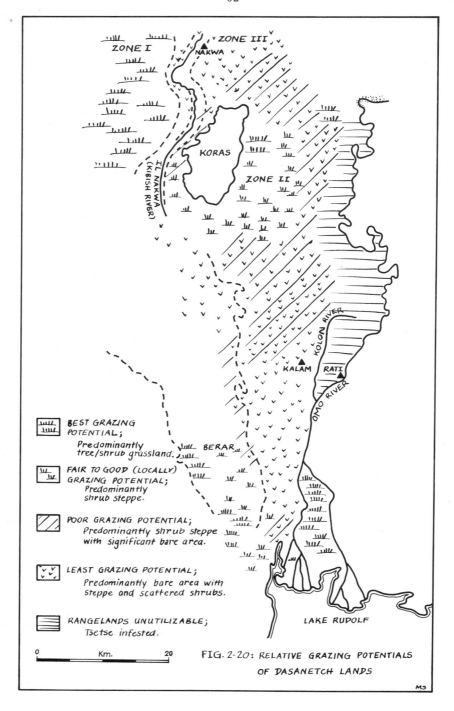

FIG. 2-20: RELATIVE GRAZING POTENTIALS OF DASANETCH LANDS

tated. A very general estimate of range potentials and distribution for Dasanetch territory is given in the map of Fig. 2-20. Since it would be impossible to separate those rangelands undergoing deterioration because of overgrazing alone from those with a disturbed vegetation aspect because of the combination of overgrazing and stratigraphically controlled erosion, the classification of rangeland is made on the basis of grazing potential.

Because the majority of the Dasanetch rangeland is already subject to very serious overgrazing, the prognosis for these lands and the people attempting to subsist from stock living on them is extremely negative. Questions regarding the potential of the retrogressed communities to recover if pressure were to be reduced or removed are only academic, since virtually no means are available to accomplish this at the present time. It must simply be pointed out here that there is not enough known about range deterioration and control to make an informed, accurate judgment about what if any recovery threshold might exist for both types of units (A and B) described, i. e., whether or not there exists a degree of deterioration beyond which recovery is virtually impossible within any reasonable period of time.

Although there are no accurate estimates available of the total stock held by the Dasanetch, the cattle alone certainly number in the thousands for the west bank Dasanetch and small stock number much more. The relationship between the carrying capacity of this type of land and the existing population (estimated from my survey between Lobemkat and Kalam) is discussed in the last chapter.

CHAPTER 3

RIVERINE ENVIRONMENTS OF THE DASANETCH

Introduction

The Omo riverine zone and other important mesic environments of Dasanetch territory, including the modern delta region, Berar (Sanderson's Gulf), Il
Nakwa (Kibish River) and Kolon (Kalaam River) offer both resource opportunities and problems which are radically different from those of the plains. Of
these, the riverine environments will be described in most detail in this chapter. These are here defined as land contiguous with the Omo River (War) and Il
Nakwa (Kibish River). Of these two, the Omo riverine area is much more significant, both because it is a perennial river and because it is centrally located
with respect to Dasanetch settlement. The following sections describe and attempt to explain some of the basic ecological features of the mesic environments. This is useful as a basis for understanding the traditional Dasanetch
exploitation of those lands as well as interpreting recent ecological changes
within the lower basin which have greatly affected the Dasanetch way of life.

The Omo River

Lake Rudolf is in the northern end of the Eastern Rift, and receives the
vast majority of its water from the Omo River. There are a few seasonally
active rivers draining into the lake, such as the Kerio River and the Turkwell
River, but they apparently contribute little to its total volume (Butzer, 1971).
The Omo River travels from an altitude above 2000 meters in the Ethiopian highlands, through cataracts, gorges and an entrenched valley before opening into
the valley which terminates at Lake Rudolf. The altitude of the lake is presently accepted as approximately 375 meters (Butzer, 1971).[1] The climatic data
for the catchment area of this river, and their significance for the general patterns of it, are discussed in detail by Butzer.

---

[1]The plains of the lower basin were described in Chapter 2 as lying between 400 and 500 meters, illustrating the low topographic relief for the region.

Although no precise information exists regarding the fluctuations of the Omo River in Dasanetch land, a general pattern of flow is suggested on the basis of observations during field work and descriptions by local inhabitants. Apparently, the Omo is at its lowest about January; it then rises very irregularly from about May until it reaches maximum flood stage between late August and early October. This pattern shows considerable variation from year to year. The numerous rises and recessions which occur in the weeks preceding and during its maximum flow are difficult or impossible to predict with any precision, and this fact is of critical importance to those Dasanetch engaging in horticulture. During maximum flow, the Omo frequently breaches the relatively low natural levees near the lake, and spills into the southern end of the large mudflat depression of Berar (Sanderson's Gulf). [2]

Butzer (1971) has estimated that Lake Rudolf has fluctuated within a range of 20 meters during the past 80 years, and that since 1896-97 it has dropped about 15 meters to its present level. A precise reconstruction of the northern shoreline of the lake at its highest point is impossible on the basis of existing descriptions, but on the basis of Butzer's synthesis of numerous lines of evidence regarding this dramatic shift, it seems clear that the lands contiguous with the present Omo River on both sides were either submerged or highly inundated as far north as 5° N. With the subsequent lake retreat southward, the natural levees and adjacent lands were exposed and increasingly drained. This progressive improvement in drainage favored the development of woody vegetation, resulting in a southward advance of forest and woodland along the levee. Since there has been a greater time period for development of this woody vegetation at the northern end of this previously submerged and inundated zone, there exists along the levee and backslopes a south to north gradient of vegetational successional development. A synchronic view of this process shows a range of vegetational development extending from aquatic grasslands to riverine forests. Such vegetational change must be correlated with changes in the physical conditions associated with the river as well as with the length of time of development.

The most basic changes in the morphology of the Omo River from its terminus at Lake Rudolf northward through the lower basin are related to its sinuosity. The sinuosity of the meandering system is fairly well developed as far south as Narok although it decreases markedly south of the latitude of Kolin

---

[2]This depression has, according to Butzer, functioned as a northern extension of Lake Rudolf in the past, but for many years has primarily received flood waters from the Omo River.

(Fig. 1-1). In the locations where the river exhibits strong sinuosity, there are numerous cutoff meanders and some backswamps (Fig. 3-1). These are completely absent south of Narok, where the river is only slightly winding. Increasing width (lateral to the river) of riverine-associated mesophytic vegetation is strongly correlated with high sinuosity of the river. Farther south, where the river has less curvature, mesophytic communities survive only along the natural levee itself except where flooding or lateral inundation occurs. In this area the natural levee backslope grades into lands with numerous old distributary channels and non-functional interdistributary basins and mudflats (Butzer, 1971). Finally, in the modern delta[3] and within the flats immediately adjacent to it, the Omo is only slightly winding. Along the lowermost reaches of the river (within the modern delta region) predominantly herbaceous plant communities line the natural levees. These communities gradually phase into semi-aquatic communities where the natural levees extend into the lake in the form of attenuated peninsular ("birdfoot") profiles. Since all riverine environments from grassland to forest are significant in the system of Dasanetch societal/environmental interactions, studies of these environments are summarized in the subsequent sections.

Riverine ecological studies: approaches. --Vegetational development along the natural levees of the Omo River, and some of the most basic physical correlates of such development, were studied along a south to north gradient, with particular emphasis placed on the phases from open woodland to forest.[4] Two environments which are treated in the following sections are defined here: (1) riverine adjacent flats zone refers to the monotonous clayey and silty flats just lateral to the river, between the mesophytic riverine vegetation and the plains, and (2) riverine transitional zone refers to the zone between the natural levee forest and closed woodland, and the riverine adjacent flats.[5] Both the variegated pattern of the transition zone and adjacent flats vegetation and the

---

[3]The term "modern delta," throughout this study, refers to both (a) the lands between the two innermost major branches of the Omo (Dielerhiele and Erdete), including the lands of Nairobi (Fig. 1-1) and (b) the lands adjacent to (a) which are of comparable mesic character.

[4]A more detailed presentation of riverine and other mesic environments is presented in Carr, 1976a.

[5]Henceforth, these environments are abbreviated to "transition zone" and "adjacent flats." Further discussion is presented in Carr, 1976a and b.

Fig. 3-1.--Aerial View of the Omo River and Surrounding Lands

large area selected for study necessitated the limitation of preliminary work in
these two zones primarily to general description and limited transecting. Vegetation of the riverine zone from Rati north to the end of Dasanetch lands was
mapped in detail (Fig. 3-2). Detailed studies of plant community changes leading to riverine forest were made along the south to north developmental gradient for inside bends of the river, since where river sinuosity is present the
inside (convex) bends of the river typically support the better-developed riverine vegetation at any given point along the river. At each riverine forest or
woodland study site selected, general collection and description was done in
addition to quantitative studies of plant community structure and floristics (transecting methods are described in Appendix B). The general developmental
changes in vegetation from south to north, the associated vegetation types lateral to the river and their implications for the Dasanetch are summarized below.

Riverine plant life in southern Dasanetch lands. --Vegetation bordering
the relatively straight Omo channel (i.e., south of Rati) grows on the most recently exposed and/or drained natural levees. Much of this land is subjected to
continual heavy disturbance through burning, watering year-round, grazing and
browsing by domestic animals, and planting by the Dasanetch. Bank overspill
frequently occurs south of the Kolon-Omo River junction, and during August and/
or September flood waters commonly inundate the southern portion of Berar.

Bankside vegetation along the lowermost segment of this portion of the
river is predominantly aquatic and semi-aquatic (Fig. 3-3). Specifically, the
aquatics Ceratophyllum demersum, Pistia stratioides (Nile lettuce) and Nym-
phae lutea (water lily) grow along the river margins; the tall semi-aquatics
Phragmites australis, P. ?karka, Loudetia phragmatoides, Typha (cattail); tall
semi-aquatics and numerous sedges and shorter mesophytic grasses cover the
middle and upper banks (Cyperus spp., Echinochloa haploclada, Eragrostis
namaquensis, Cynodon dactylon) along with some forbs (Cassia italica, Indigofera spp., Tephrosia spp.). The crests and immediate backslopes of the levees often support a tree/shrub grassland or, in a few localities, an open woodland, with the riverine shrub Cordia sinensis most common among the larger
individuals. Scattered fig trees (Ficus sycomorus) along the levee crest grow
to heights of ca. 8-12 meters, with numerous smaller ones common there and
on the immediate backslopes. Some of the large figs are dead or with dying
upper crowns and submerged bases. It is possible that this phenomenon is associated with the lake rise during the early sixties which has caused root damage

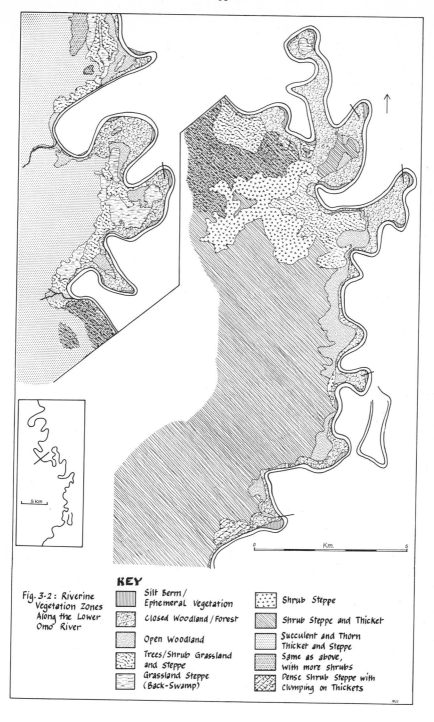

KEY

Fig. 3-2: Riverine Vegetation Zones Along the Lower Omo River

Silt Berm / Ephemeral Vegetation

Closed Woodland / Forest

Open Woodland

Trees/Shrub Grassland and Steppe

Grassland Steppe (Back-Swamp)

Shrub Steppe

Shrub Steppe and Thicket

Succulent and Thorn Thicket and Steppe

Same as above, with more shrubs

Dense Shrub Steppe with Clumping on Thickets

5 km

0   Km.   5

Fig. 3-3. --Riverside Vegetation in the Modern Delta Region

through reduction of aeration and/or increased salinity. Levee backslopes
along this lower section of the river are largely devoid of vegetation or are with
unpalatable species of plants, due to its year-round intensive use by Dasanetch
stock.

The land between the Omo and Kolon channel and north of the Kolon-Omo
(Fig. 1-1) junction is green in appearance relative to the adjacent plains which
are parched and dry during the months without rain. The comparative lushness
here indicates a substantial subsurface water supply between the Omo and the
intermittently filled Kolon distributary channels. Riverine vegetation along this
segment of the Omo River is shrub thicket with some open woodland, the most
conspicuous woody species being Cordia sinensis, Acacia mellifera, Ziziphus
mauritiana, Ficus sycomorus, and a few Ximenia caffra and Grewia fallax. Cordia sinensis grows as a large spreading shrub along the river throughout the
lowermost basin.

Silt berms. --Because of the high level of disturbance on silt berms and
the resultant simple structure of the ephemeral vegetation, only a few general
observations regarding plant life are relevant here. The silt berms are loci of
recent channel deposits and are numerous along inside (convex) banks of the
Omo River (Fig. 3-4). The waterside edges of the berms are often sandy with
scattered ephemerals, both forbs and grasses. It is the silty portions of the
berms which are the locations of almost all horticultural activity along the river. Disturbance of these berms is highly intensive through cutting, burning,
and planting. Since these are annual activities, plant regrowth seldom survives
more than one year. Vegetation consists primarily of annual herbs with some
rapidly growing trees and shrubs. The most common species on the berms
include Cayratia ibuensis, Rhyncosia minima, Indigofera spicata, Tephrosia
uniflora, Eragrostis namaquensis var. diplochnoides, Securinega virosa, Echinochloa haploclada, Sesbania sesban and Racinis communis. Silt berms are
flooded very irregularly. Horticulture, therefore, is unreliable since the
crops require sufficient moisture and nutrients from flood waters in order to
mature.

Riverside plant life of central and northern Dasanetch lands.

Topography and drainage.

The map in Fig. 3-5 shows the selected study sites from which much of
the following information is derived. Riverine woodland and forest owe their

Fig. 3-4. --Aerial View of Silt Berm and Riverine Forest

73

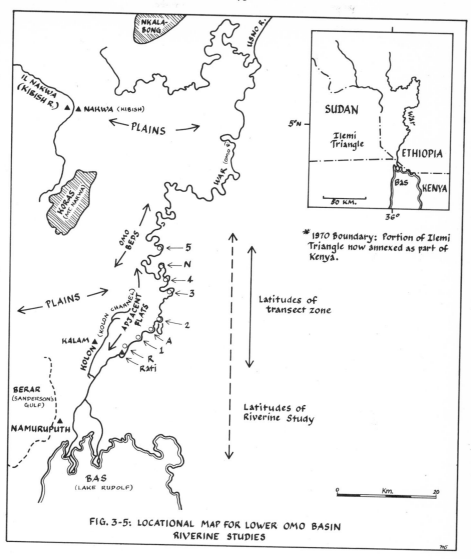

FIG. 3-5: LOCATIONAL MAP FOR LOWER OMO BASIN
RIVERINE STUDIES

existence to ground water from the Omo River, and although this water supply fluctuates greatly in superficial layers with seasonal changes in river volume, deeper levels provide enough year-round moisture to support the semi-deciduous and evergreen riverine species. Given a general decrease in ground water contributed by the river, a decrease which correlates roughly with distance from the river, the sequence of vegetation types lateral to the river, from the mesophytic communities on the natural levee to xerophytic communities in the adjacent flats or plains, becomes comprehensible. Drainage may be assumed to have generally improved within the riverine-associated lands of Dasanetch territory following the recent lake retreat to the south. This situation has no doubt been complicated by topographic and depositional variations, so that the observer of riverine-associated plant communities sometimes does not find an orderly progression of community types lateral to the river. According to observations and informants' accounts, bank overspill does not occur within the zone selected for study, although a few localities permit levee breaching (e.g., site 5, see Fig. 3-5).

Riverine woodland and forest developmental changes.

(a) Structural changes. Vegetation along the outside (concave) river banks generally increases in mesophytic character with increased period of vegetational development (following emergence and/or improved drainage) and increasing river sinuosity. This is true with regard to both the species present and density of riverine vegetation lateral to the Omo. Riverine forest attains a maximum width of only 200-250 meters from bankside along the lower basin Omo River, although riverine woodland may extend considerably farther from the river. Continuous bands of forest and woodland occur on the banks of outer bends just north of the study area (see Fig. 3-5), but along the deepest meanders the xerophytic vegetation of the adjacent flats may extend clear to the river's edge, breaking the continuity of riverine forest. Thus, the south to north trend toward unbroken mesophytic vegetation between inside and outside bends from Site R (Rati) to Site 4 (Dielibiro) apparently continues only to a point in the developing meandering system, beyond which the pattern of plant life is more diversified. The marked contrast between vegetation of inside and outside bends where sinuosity is very high, with xerophytic plant communities on outer bends breaking the continuity of forest and woodland, is probably correlated with widespread burning (e.g., north of Shungura along the west bank, where Inyangatom settlement occurs), increased evaporation from the steep banks of strong outside bends (Butzer, personal communication), lessened infiltration from the river into outside bend bank sediments, and natural levee heights (with reduced moisture in superficial soil layers). These factors may be operative singly or in combination, depending on the specific locality.

Table 3-1 describes some of the more basic structural and floristic changes along the developmental gradient from Site R to Site 5. Total vegetation cover is relatively similar at all six sites, even though considerable differences arise when comparing height classes (Carr, 1976a). On the levee immediately adjacent to the river, ground cover decreases northward to Site 4 and then increases at Site 5. Canopy cover (i.e., plant cover 7 meters or more in height) increases northward to Site 4, again with the trend reversed at Site 5. Overall density of woody plants (2 meters or taller) increases from south to north along the community age gradient, with the exception of Site 5 which again approximates the younger site values. Growth habit changes from predominantly multi-stemmed and spreading shrubs (Fig. 3-6) in the younger woodlands to single-trunked, columnar trees in the forest, with Site 5 intermediate. No distinct stratification is apparent even in the forest.

Predictably for a ground water forest, epiphytes are not present; but lianes are very conspicuous in closed woodland sites and along the edges of the forest. Ground cover is sparse where forests are well developed (Sites 3 and 4), making them easily penetrable even without paths (Fig. 3-7). This is in strong contrast to most woodland communities, which often have extremely dense undergrowth. There is a general increase in maximum tree height with the phases of development from site R through Site 4 (Site 5 is intermediate between Sites 1 and 2), with a maximum height of about 80 feet. On the basis of vegetation transects constructed, it is clear that the structural complexity of woodlands and forests increases along the developmental gradient from south to north (again, intermediate in this respect at Site 5). The detailed results of these and other transects are presented in Carr, 1976a.

Clearings in the forest and woodland vary in size and composition among the sites, but almost all of them support plant species more common to the drier plains or the transition zones. Where the canopy is broken, shafts of sunlight reach the leaf-carpeted forest floor and a dense growth of grasses, forbs and shrubs typically forms. Clearings within the forest may result from cutting by humans, or from the death of large trees due to old age, wind or disease.

TABLE 3-1

RIVERINE WOODLAND/FOREST SUCCESSIONAL DEVELOPMENT

	Site R	Site 1	Site 2	Site 3	Site 4	Site 5
Bell Profile Transects:						
% Cover						
0-30 Meters canopy (≥ 20 ft.)	60	65	70	85	95	85
60-90 Meters canopy (≥ 20 ft.)	5	45	60	90	95	80
Canopy species of highest density						
0-30 Meters (in descending order)	Cordia g. Acacia mellif. A. sieb.	Cordia g. Ficus syc. Acacia sieb.	Cordia g. Maytenus sen. Ficus syc.	Trichilia r. Ficus syc. Maytenus sen.	Trichilia r. Ficus syc. Ziziphus pub.	Trichilia r. Ziziphus pub. Ficus syc.
Point Center Quarter Transects:						
Total number of woody species (≥ 6 ft.)	-	15	11	15	12	14
Number of woody plants per acre (≥ 6 ft.)	-	964.8	1191.1	1770.6	1889.5	1472.1

Fig. 3-6.--Riverine Woodland Interior

Fig. 3-7.--Riverine Forest Interior at Dielibiro

(b) Floristic changes.[6] Even though the number of species comprising the forest canopy alone (Fig. 3-8) increases with succession, there is no accompanying increase in the total number of woody species (Table 3-1). The high seasonal fluctuation in the volume of the Omo might be an important selective force in the limitation of numbers of species present, as might be the small time span of woody vegetation development (about 80 years) from the submerged or heavily inundated state of the levees at the end of the last century. Some woody species clearly increase in importance with age of community (at least northward to Site 4), and these include Ficus sycamorus, Tapura fischeri, Melanodiscus oblongus, Celtis integrifolia, Uvaria sp., Ziziphus pubescens and Trichilia roka. Others decrease along the same gradient to Site 4: Cordia sinensis, Maytenus senegalensis, Ximenia caffra, Securinega virosa, Grewia fallax, Allophylus macrobotrys, Acacia tortilis and A. sieberana. Contagious distribution, or patchiness, of certain species is common within closed woodland/forest communities and this phenomenon is quite pronounced in some localities (Carr, ibid.).

A central problem in interpreting the changes occurring within the south to north developmental gradient of vegetation is the character of the northernmost site (5). Floristically, the vegetation at Site 5 indicates that this community represents a further developmental phase with respect to sites immediately to the south (3 and 4). In other respects, for example, the high percentage of spreading shrubs and the lower tree density, Site 5 more closely resembles the earlier developmental phases of Sites 1 and 2. A large backswamp forms the interior of the Site 5 river bend where water was observed to reach to the boundary of the adjacent woodland and forest during flood stage. The presence of this interior backswamp suggests the possibility of an increased moisture content (i.e., decreased drainage) within the Site 5 adjacent forest at least relative to the forest sites to the south. If increased moisture content or decreased drainage is characteristic of the upper soil layers in the levees nearer the lake where natural levee vegetational development is in its early phases, then this characteristic of the forest at Site 5 may be linked to the retrogression or inhibition of forest development there. This might be predicted to take the form of an increase in the large spreading shrubs of earlier phases. Other highly sinuous meanders northward of Site 5 (in Inyangatom territory) are also characterized by comparatively narrower forests, sharp boundaries between woodland/

[6]Also see Carr, 1976a.

Fig. 3-8.--Riverine Forest Exterior at Bulikwi

forest and the inundated interior (backswamps are common in many of the bends
to the north), and a higher presence of spreading shrubs. If high sinuosity is
found to correlate with lessened drainage, some threshold of river meandering
may exist above which this inhibition of development is operative. These backswamps are of great importance to the Inyangatom, who utilize a number of
them for horticultural purposes whenever possible.

Some features generally considered to characterize succession (e.g., increasing tree height and complexity of height distribution, productivity increase,
and overall greater cover) are indicative of the changes observed from Sites R
through 4. However, other common traits of successional processes are more
problematic in their application to this sequence of phases. As species diversity is closely and directly related to the level of stability, any assumption of
an overall increase in stability for the communities constituting the later
phases of riverine forest succession is premature. In fact, the whole notion of
vegetation stability is of questionable relevance in a riverine environment
where geomorphic changes (e.g., meander development and channel shifting)
and associated physical environmental alterations are continuous and pronounced. To reiterate an earlier statement, any analysis of successional processes in riverine communities must take special account of the changes associated with the evolution of the river system itself.

The major structural changes occurring within the developmental gradient
of riverine woodland and forest are included in Fig. 3-9.

The Dasanetch impact on riverine forest and woodland.

Unlike the situation for silt berms, modification of the riverine forest and
closed woodland communities by the Dasanetch is not great. This fact is in line
with the limited settlement presently within the riverine zone north of Rati, particularly since the invasion of tsetse (see below). The only significant human
disturbance of natural conditions within the woodland/forest is from the sporadic cutting of large trees for dugout canoes. Other minor modifications are
caused by (1) the cutting of scattered woody plants favored for making utensils,
frames for huts, etc.; (2) the gathering of fruits and other wild plant parts for
subsistence; (3) the burning of small patches of ground along paths and around
settlements, done to clear the paths and discourage snakes; and (4) the clearing
of ground for villages (only a few are actually within the woodland/forest, and
even these are relatively permanent).

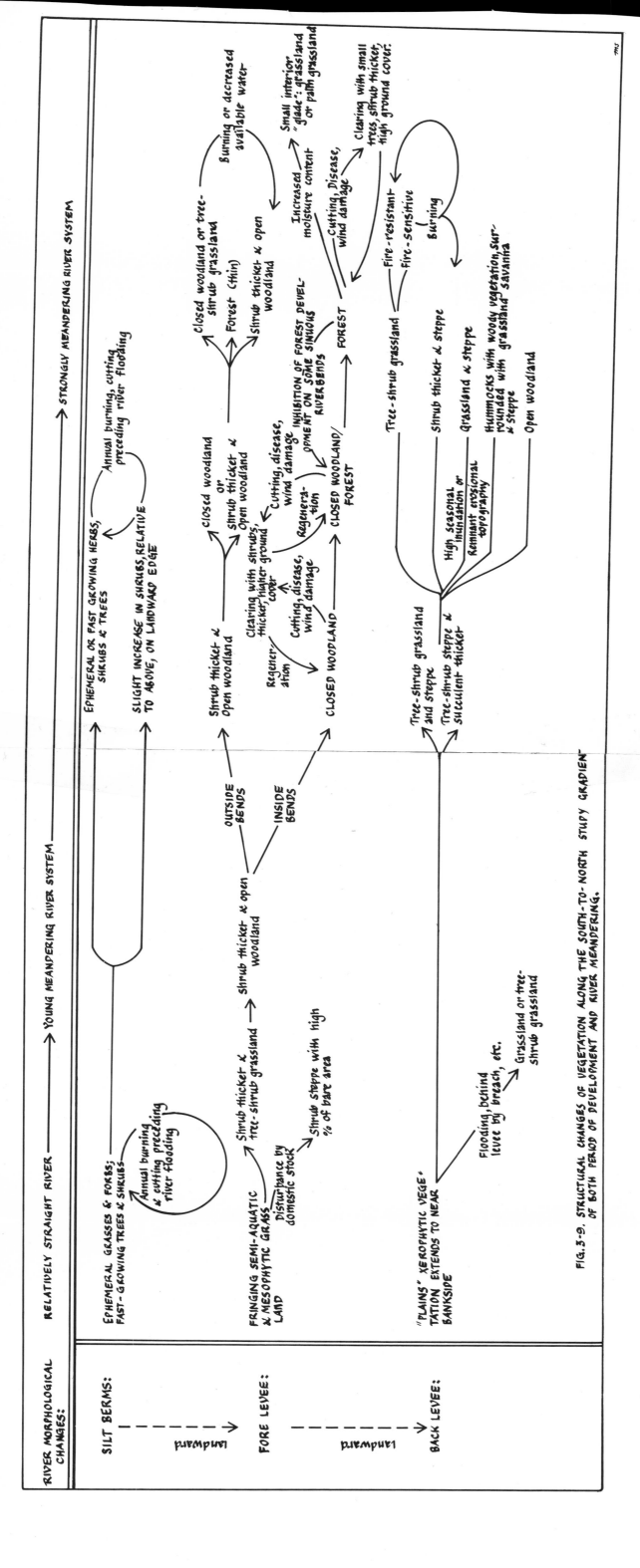

FIG. 3-9. STRUCTURAL CHANGES OF VEGETATION ALONG THE SOUTH-TO-NORTH STUDY GRADIENT OF BOTH PERIOD OF DEVELOPMENT AND RIVER MEANDERING.

The riverine transition zone. --Transitional vegetation was earlier defined as that between riverine closed woodland/forest and the drier vegetation of the adjacent flats. It therefore occurs only where closed woodland or forest occupies the immediate backslope, and not along the southernmost levees and outside bends. On inside bends, transitional vegetation is variable and sometimes forms a complicated mosaic of different physiognomies. Where woodland occurs at the transition, it tends to be with very dense undergrowth and is often impenetrable. Even though woody species composition is similar among most of the localities studied, physiognomic types and the relative importance of species within those types differ considerably. The major determinants of what physiognomic types occur at any given place are topography, drainage, edaphic character, burning, and river morphology and lateral movement of water from the river. Soils of the transition zone are predominantly silty alluvium, except for some clayey backswamp localities.

Transitional plant communities are widely varying and include tree/shrub grassland and steppe (Fig. 3-10), open woodland, open woodland and thicket, shrub thicket and steppe, grassland, and grassland steppe of backswamps (Fig. 3-2). Large, spreading Cordia sinensis shrubs are common throughout the transition zone and their low density in the adjacent flats indicates reduced moisture availability in the flats. Dead riverine shrubs with the growth form of this species occur in much of the transition region from slightly downstream of Site 1, north to Site 5; these are even more numerous in the adjacent flats and their significance is noted below.

Woody species diversity within the transition zone is generally higher than that of the adjacent flats, riverine forest, or riverine woodland, and this is attributable to the transition's combination of habitat conditions from the zones to either side, facilitating the presence of species from both environments. The higher total number of species present in the transition is correlated with mosaics of different structural types of vegetation, especially where small scale topographic and/or edaphic variations occur. Abundant examples of both structural and floristic patchiness occur throughout the transition (Carr, 1976a).

Although some cutting is done within the transition zone, the major ecological impact on the land is through burning by the Dasanetch and Inyangatom people. Burning has been even more extensively practiced in the riverine areas in the early decades of this century, when settlement and grazing were widespread there (see Chapter 7). It is more common during the dry months and in the

Fig. 3-10. --Shrub Steppe and Open Woodland: Transition Zone

weeks just preceding the smaller rains (nyerobe), nights present a spectacular visual array of fires scattered throughout the region surrounding the highlands, in the delta, in some plains areas and in the transition zone. Fires range in extent from those which sweep over extensive grassland areas of the plains or the delta to those only a few meters in diameter, as in some transition locales with low ground cover. Burning is done for various reasons, such as to prepare silt berms, seasonally flooded levees, and the delta for planting; to arrest bush encroachment; to eliminate existing bush around trails and settled areas; to reduce cover which shields predators and snakes; to eliminate shrub cover associated with tsetse; and for pleasure, particularly by children.

The use of fire is often associated with sharp boundaries between vegetation types within the transition zone in particular. Burning on outside bends along the transition may sometimes extend to the river bank, particularly in the region inhabited by the Inyangatom (Site 5 and northward), where sinuosity is high. Where riverine closed woodland or forest does occur, however, fires do not penetrate these communities so that numerous fire-sensitive species survive there. Riverine forest or closed woodland may form a razor-sharp boundary with burned grassland and steppe communities of the transition, or there may be fire-resistant thickets intermediate between the riverine and transition communities including Cadaba rotundifolia, Salvadora persica and Cissus quadrangularis. Grasses associated with grasslands and steppe show varying degrees of tolerance of fire, and some grasses and forbs actually spread in regularly burned areas. One possible mechanism to help explain the distribution and effects of burning in the lower basin transition zone is as follows. The available water for plant growth generally lessens with increasing distance from the river (exceptions occur where backswamps or complex topographic or sediment patterns exist). In order for woody growth to achieve sufficient density to produce a canopy cover that can effectively shade out most combustible grasses and forbs, a critical level of soil moisture content is required. Below this critical point of soil moisture or, equivalently, at a certain distance laterally from the river, the combustible plant understory is dense enough to permit fire to penetrate the community and thus select for fire-resistant species. Such fire can reach toward the river only to the point where soil moisture is sufficient to support dense woody growth. In absence of burning, fire-sensitive woody species apparently decrease only gradually in frequency with increasing distance laterally from the river, and they produce a wider zone of scattered trees and shrubs in grassland. Burning, on the other hand, may greatly nar-

row (or condense) the transition zone, locating it roughly at the critical moisture threshold mentioned above. Other factors such as the incidence and season of burning and the fire resistance of the plant species involved must also be
considered for individual localities. This schema is shown in Fig. 3-11.

Succulent thickets (of shrubs and herbs) constitute a very common transitional vegetation type, and serve as an effective fire barrier. When soil moisture is insufficient to support a solid mass of thicket, or when other conditions
so dictate, succulent thicket may form clumps, with fires able to penetrate between them, producing an irregular thicket and steppe community (common in
parts of the transition zone). A somewhat similar physiognomic type of vegetation results where low-lying, seasonally waterlogged grassland is dotted with
better-drained hummocks of earth which support woody growth and often resist
fires (e. g., the transition zone between the Omo Beds and the Omo River, north
of Site 5).

Riverine associated adjacent flats. --This monotonous zone is problematic
from the standpoint of developing an ecological explanation of its essential character. It was traditionally of real significance for grazing of stock and settlement.

Drainage is internal and there are numerous incomplete distributary channels throughout these flats. The largest such channels are bordered by a
sparsely growing large Acacia tortilis and some A. sieberana trees and they
may also support a relatively luxuriant growth of the same plant species common to the flats more generally. Topographic relief of the adjacent flats is
very slight compared to that of the plains, and the flats seem highly uniform to
the new observer. Sediments and soils of this zone are predominantly silts and
clays (both cracking and non-cracking). The micro-topographic features which
characterize most of the flats have real significance in creating small-scale patterns among the different structural types of vegetation. Even a small topographic feature as pits, for instance, may result in significant variation in
moisture conditions which is reflected by the vegetation. Cracking patterns,
where developed, are reminiscent of the cracking clay flats of the plains. Many
of these features offer micro-habitats of increased mesic conditions during at
least part of the year, judging by the species and luxuriance of plants growing
within them. Although water does remain in some of them following heavy
rains, the only standing water in the flats during dry months is in several localities along the periphery (e. g., in Kolon channel) where drainage from the

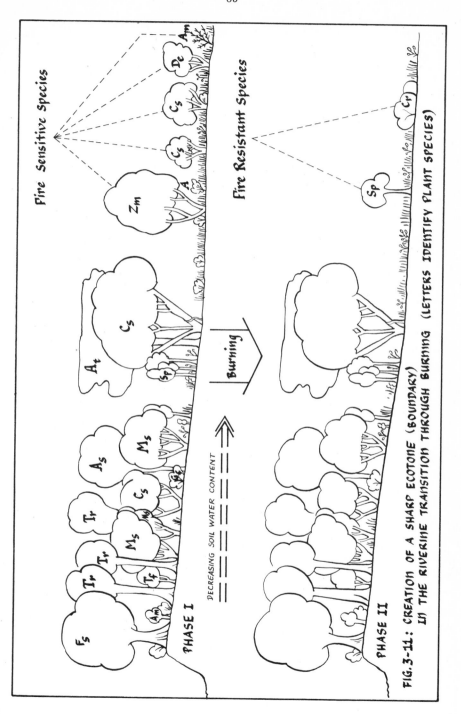

Fire Sensitive Species

Fire Resistant Species

PHASE I

DECREASING SOIL WATER CONTENT

Burning

PHASE II

FIG. 3-11: CREATION OF A SHARP ECOTONE (BOUNDARY) IN THE RIVERINE TRANSITION THROUGH BURNING (LETTERS IDENTIFY PLANT SPECIES)

plains to the west is apparently sufficient to produce relatively permanent pools with aquatic vegetation.

Some of the northern adjacent flats (in Dasanetch territory) are comparatively lush in the plant life they support, with higher vegetative cover values and greater overlap of species with the transition zone than is characteristic of the southern flats. This is especially true in the latitudes of the highly sinuous Omo where a variegated pattern of plant communities is produced. Physiognomic types of vegetation alternating within the flats include shrub steppe and thicket (see Fig. 3-12), shrub steppe with scattered trees, tree/shrub grassland, grassland and steppe, and succulent thicket and steppe (Fig. 3-2). These have in common a highly irregular and sparse plant cover. The large amount of bare ground surface is a striking feature throughout much of the flats and gives the appearance of a disturbed area.

Large dead riverine shrubs were earlier described as scattered within the transition and adjacent flats, and there is a notable absence of their living counterparts, i. e., the riverine form of Cordia sinensis with its tall, spreading growth form. (These dead shrubs are sometimes more numerous within the topographically lower, clay-filled old channel cutoffs). Evidence of cutting or fire scars are not present on these shrubs, suggesting some other cause for their death. Whereas shallow-rooted plants of the flats (e. g., many grasses and forbs) are dependent on the moisture content of upper soil layers, some more deeply rooted woody plants are at least partially sustained by the ground water supply. The large dead riverine type spreading shrubs are very possibly indicators of a time of greater moisture. The availability of water was likely greatly lessened due to the water table drop accompanying the lake retreat or, alternatively, the shrubs may have been casualties of the rising lake waters with their high salinity. There is some support for the former possibility, that of death caused by water table drop, for two reasons. First, these dead shrubs are taller and more numerous in the flats than in the transition zone; the flats would predictably have suffered a greater moisture loss with lake retreat than the transition zone which still receives considerable ground moisture from the river. Second, Cordia sinensis, the likely species of these shrubs, now grows (in its riverine form) exclusively under wetter conditions than the flats now offer, with living individuals of this species virtually excluded now, clearly suggesting a change in conditions. Further, large deeply rooted Acacia tortilis trees are the only woody plants greater than about 7 meters surviving in the flats (except for a few A. sieberana near the transition zone and along internal

Fig. 3-12. --Shrub Steppe in the Riverine-Associated Adjacent Flats

drainage features). These trees can utilize a very deep ground water supply. The precise time of death of these shrubs cannot be determined, but Dasanetch descriptions suggest that it may have been only several decades ago. It seems likely that the drop in water table suggested here would correspond to both the southward advance of the woodland and forest along the levee and the invasion of tsetse fly.

It is doubtful that the disturbed appearance of the flats is attributable to human activities, since settlement and land use are extremely limited in the flats north of the Rati latitude and east of Kolon (the dearth of settlement is primarily due to the invasion of tsetse). More likely causal factors of the low cover or disturbed aspect of the flats include soil salinity and/or internal drainage patterns with high seasonal fluctuation in soil moisture. These fluctuations between extreme drought with high evaporation from upper soil levels on the one hand, and waterlogging of the soil with reduced aeration on the other, may greatly inhibit shallow-rooted plant growth and thus reduce the total cover.

Tsetse in the riverine zone. --The occurrence of animal trypanosomiasis is related to the distribution of tsetse fly (Glossina spp.) which is found only south 14° N latitude in Africa. All domestic animals are susceptible to one or more species of the animal trypanosomes. Zebu cattle,[7] although hardy and well adapted generally to an arid environment of the lower basin, are in fact more susceptible to animal trypanosomiasis than other African breeds.

G. palpalis fuscipes is reported for the north end of Lake Rudolf. Tsetse has apparently migrated along the Omo River concomitantly with the woodland forest advance in that direction, and it has been observed numerous times by the writer as far south as Rati. Although indigenous animals are either little or not at all afflicted by the tsetse-transmitted trypanosomiasis, domestic stock are not resistant. Large numbers of cattle and small stock deaths in the lower basin from bash keething (literally, "fly disease"; Swahili equivalent is nagana), have forced the Dasanetch to evacuate their herds from the riverine woodland zone to the plains. The accompanying changes in settlement pattern and grazing movements have certainly reduced the human-induced disturbance of the riverine environments during the past decades but the overall environmental and economic repercussions of this evacuation have been severe (see Chapter 7). Some stock are watered along the Omo during about January, when

---

[7]Zebu is the cattle type raised by the Dasanetch.

the river is reportedly lowest and tsetse populations are greatly reduced or nearly absent. During rainy periods, standing water collects in mudflats of the plains and tsetse extends its normal riverine distribution via shrub thicket which is contiguous with riverine vegetation. The exact distribution of tsetse in the plains during the rainy periods is not known. Its presence in the lands between the Omo Beds and Koras during ir gudoha (the large rains) is insisted upon by some informants, though there is not uniform agreement on this. The avoidance of this area by some stock owners partially explains the diminished utilization of these lands for grazing compared to previous decades; a change described numerous times by older informants. A large portion of the northern lands of the Inyangatom (Fig. 1-2) is covered with shrub thicket and shrub steppe. In addition to infestation of the adjacent flats by tsetse, it also enters the Kolon channel region north of the Kalam area, but only during rainy periods. Local distributional patterns and seasonal population variation of tsetse are somewhat predictable on the basis of its breeding requirements: shade for the puparium, some protection from excessive isolation for the adult, and trees for perching by the adults. Tsetse penetration of grasslands, for instance, is usually greatest during cooler damp seasons (Glasgow and Duffy, 1961), and then it is normally dependent on the presence of woody growth.

Conspicuous wild fauna. --Larger mammals within the transition zone and adjacent flats include Grant's gazelle, kudu, warthog, hyena, baboon, lion, garinook, buffalo and dik-dik. Leopard is present in the forest but it has reportedly become scarce in recent years. Monitor lizards measuring up to several feet in length are common along the levee edges and may be seen climbing among the low branches of the huge sycomore fig trees overhanging the river. Crocodiles frequent the point bars, emergent logs and other accessible places along the river banks; in recent years, the crocodile population has unfortunately become a target for European hunters.

Primates identified in the forest so far are Colobus monkey, baboon and vervet monkey. Baboons live along the riverine zone to as far south as Rati (note that Rati is the approximate southern extent of woodland along the natural levee). Baboons (noroitch) were observed moving and feeding through most of the riverine forest/woodland, transition zone and adjacent flats studied, and they were also observed in the relatively uninhabited fringes of the plains near the river. On numerous occasions, they were encountered moving from the flats and transition areas into the riverine woodland in the early morning, and in only a few instances were they seen in the adjacent flats during midday. The baboons apparently utilize the woodlands more heavily than the high forest (e.g., those at Sites 3 and 4), although they are not at all unusual in the forest and certainly pass through it to reach the river for watering. Troops from the Site 5 forest were observed to water at the backswamp in the interior of the river bend, however, rather than at the Omo. Baboons were also noted in the Omo Beds on numerous occasions (in the A.M.). Movement of troops along the river within the forest and woodland was noted only casually. Several troops of 30-50 each were observed to simultaneously move within one river bend along the west bank closed woodland, suggesting the possibility of some territorial overlap between them, or else considerable mobility along the river. Baboons eat several kinds of fruits very commonly (Ficus, Cordia, Ximenia, Grewia, A. tortilis and A. sieberana), in addition to their habit of stealing the Dasanetch's crops as they mature--a practice which makes them very unpopular with the riverine villagers. Baboon skins are frequently worn for decoration during the large Dasanetch ritual, dimi (see Chapter 4).

Colobus monkeys (lol) were seen only in the riverine forest and closed woodland (also to a latitude just north of Rati), and then usually in the highest canopy available. Groups of Colobus were never seen to exceed 5 or 6 individuals, and most were 2 to 4. Some habitat divergence exists between Colobus, which typically occupy the higher forest and tallest portions of woodland shrubs, and baboons, the latter typically more common among the shrubs of closed and open woodland, the transition zone and the adjacent flats. The Dasanetch kill Colobus on occasion, using their skins for decoration at dimi.

The Modern Delta

For the purposes of this study the modern delta is defined as (a) the lands between the lowermost two major branches of the Omo River (Butzer's Dielerhiele and Erdete branches), including the lands of Erdete and Nairobi (see Fig. 5-12); and (b) the lands adjacent to (a) which are of comparable mesic character. The modern delta is presently a critically important region to the lives of many west bank Dasanetch. Utilization of the delta[8] has, however, drastically oscillated during the past three or four decades. Grazing by cattle is very intense here during months without rain, though stock are evacuated during rainy seasons, due to both flooding and disease. Horticultural plots of a very large num-

[8]Henceforth, "delta" is used synonymously with "modern delta."

ber of west bank Dasanetch have been in Nairobi and Erdete for years, though Nairobi is now mostly submerged. Inevitably associated with planting is cutting and burning, both of which are done extensively throughout the delta (Fig. 3-13), usually before the flooding of the Omo. Fishing, though an important subsistence means for many in the delta (see Chapter 5), has little or no environmental impact.

The modern delta is a complex of slightly sinuous Omo distributaries, interdistributary flood basins, mudflats, prodeltaic deposits, natural levees, and interdistributary bays, bars and spits (Butzer, 1971). Sediments are diverse and form patterns which include silty (mostly alluvial) deposits, cracking and non-cracking clays, and combinations of silts and clays. Giant cracking patterns are clearly visible from the air in portions of the mudflats.

Vegetation bordering the northern end of Lake Rudolf is typically a narrow zone of aquatic and semi-aquatic vegetation, except in the modern delta where it is much more extensive. The northwest shoreline supports a loosely zoned fringe of salt-tolerant grasses and sedges. Along this northwest shore, small sandy ridges alternate with submerged swales, the ridges being unvegetated except for their inner margins which support mesophytic grasses and some sedges. Swales are dominated by Typha (cattail) and Cyperus (sedge). There is a steep gradient of vegetation change from this semi-aquatic community into tree/shrub grassland and grassland of the adjacent plains, and this gradient has been steepened by the recent lake rise. The northeast shoreline of the lake reflects the low wave action there compared with the northwest shoreline. Plant life here forms a notably wider zone of semi-aquatics with long strips of sedges, and large stands of cattail alternate with open shallow water. Here too an abrupt transition to the dry plains vegetation occurs, further emphasized by the intense overgrazing by domestic stock and the recent lake level change.

Along the lowermost reaches of both branches of the Omo River (in and very near the "birdfoot" portions), the plant life reflects year-round poor drainage, with communities dominated by semi-aquatic grasses and sedges along the banks and highly mesophytic species of grasses and forbs more laterally removed from the river. Near its terminus War Erdete, the western branch of the Omo River, is bordered with narrow bands of cattails and sedges, and scattered small pools of water support aquatic life. An aerial view here reveals its complicated mosaic pattern of vegetation types (Fig. 3-13). Slightly upstream are the grasses (to ca. 3 meters in height) Phragmites australis, P. ?karka

Fig. 3-13. --Aerial View of Delta Vegetation and Burning

and Loudetia phragmatoides which line the banks there. Along the water's edge are aquatic plants including floating masses of the water lettuce, Pistia stratioides and the submergent Ceratophyllum demersum. The eastern branch of the Omo River, War Salalitch (Dielerhiele Branch in Butzer, 1971) is similar in many respects, but differs in that it has a good deal more woody growth; Cordia sinensis and Ficus sycomorus are most numerous among them.

The vegetation of the delta environs outside of Erdete and Nairobi, and east of the river, consists of a complex mosaic of physiognomic types. It is basically controlled by topographic and edaphic variation which in turn corresponds to changes in moisture content. Mesophytic vegetation extends farther north on the east side of the Omo compared to the west side, suggesting the former to be topographically lower or to otherwise receive more moisture. Vegetation types comprising this mosaic include: (a) dry mudflats with tree-shrub steppe and bush thicket, (b) seasonally or slightly inundated flats with ephemeral herbaceous vegetation, similar to that of the silt berms along the Omo, and (c) aquatic pools, sometimes formed at intersections of cracking patterns, with submergent and floating-leaved species. Type (a) probably results from seasonally intense grazing by domestic stock. Although the lusher wetlands grasses are also presumably under heavy pressure by domestic stock, they tend to maintain rather solid plant cover.

Kolon Channel and Il Nakwa (Kibish River)

Kolon channel. --This channel is a catchment which possibly also serves as a gathering stream, and vegetation associated with it is often strikingly lush during much of the year relative to the surrounding sparse and highly xerophytic plant growth (Fig. 3-16). It borders the littoral deposits to the west and the adjacent mudflats (clays and silts) to the east. Kolon is a critical link in the survival of many Dasanetch households, since it is used for watering vast numbers of stock, grazing and browsing, some limited horticulture and gathering. Surface water is retained year-round in several of Kolon localities (Fig. 3-14), even during the driest months, and stock are brought here from many miles away. During the large rains (and possibly some of the small rain periods), however, tsetse invades the channel, north of Kalam at least (as it does the adjacent flats). During these times west bank Dasanetch stock utilize standing pools of water in the plains. There are no villages along the Kolon, although many are found nearby on higher ground. A small amount of horticulture is practiced where flooding occurs on the clays of Kolon after the large rains in

Fig. 3-14. -- Fishing in Standing Pool of Kolon Channel

June,[9] but it has been sporadic at best and extremely unproductive during recent years. Oral tradition consistently describes a time (at least several decades ago) when there was much horticulture here (Chapter 7).

Kolon apparently collects seepage from the higher ground to the west, but numerous small gullies leading into it indicate that it also receives some runoff or sheet wash from these lands. Throughout most of its length it is comprised of one major channel, although a complicated braiding of short channels develops in several places (e. g. , near the Kolon/Omo River junction and at its northern terminus). The best-defined channel of Kolon terminates in the north in the riverine adjacent flats. The following description treats this channel almost exclusively since it is of the greatest significance for the Dasanetch.

Local relief along Kolon is highly variable, due to the alternating deposits of sands, silts, and clays, and the localized alternation of banks from trampling. Sandy portions were on several occasions noted (in topographic transects) to be slightly higher than those of clay and silt, and after small rains standing water remains in some clayey localities (see Fig. 5-6). Directional flow in the Kolon channel is, at least in recent years, only a highly localized phenomenon, although much of it may be with superficial water during and after the large rains. Back-up into Kolon from the Omo during flood stage usually occurs, probably accentuated by the recent lake rise. This causes flooding of lands adjacent to the Kolon/Omo junction, and many horticultural plots are activated at such times in this region. According to older Dasanetch informants who have long lived in this part of Les Dasanetch (translated as "land of the Dasanetch"), the Omo River used to flood into Kolon at two places: at the present junction mentioned above, and also in one locality much further north.

The lands along Kolon have suffered severe overgrazing, and their deteriorated appearance obtains almost throughout. Acacia tortilis trees are common along the Kolon banks, as are the mesophytic (riverine) form of Cordia sinensis, some A. sieberana trees, and Ziziphus mucronata. Much of the bordering woody vegetation is more xerophytic (and unpalatable or avoided by stock), however, such as Cadaba rotundifolia and Salvadora persica. A walk along the channel itself reveals vegetation ranging from aquatic and semi-aquatic plants where pools are maintained, to scattered xerophytic herbs and shrubs on other stretches. Vegetation along Kolon has both riverine and upland species and this is explainable in terms of its wide spectrum of habitats.

[9]This is the same planting rhythm as is maintained by the Inyangatom at Nakwa.

Il Nakwa (Kibish River).--This intermittently active river is the largest
of the ephemeral channels in Dasanetch territory (Fig. 3-15). The lower Il
Nakwa (Nyongolol to the Inyangatom) flows southward to where it dissipates into
a large clay plain west/southwest of Koras (Fig. 1-1). Its greatest flow is in
or near May (Butzer, 1971), at which time it usually floods the large west bank
horticultural flats of the Inyangatom tribe. As in Kolon channel, during the driest months water is retained above ground surface only where clays occur, and
the channel surface deposits vary among sands, silts and clays. Some year-
round watering localities exist where these clays occur, but water holes are
dug elsewhere in the porous sands (see Fig. 2-10). These have been observed
to extend over 7 meters in depth, are crudely prepared by rotating a large, ver-
tically held branch in huge circles and are used to supply both stock and humans.
Only clays and silts are used for horticulture. The combination of the sandy
nature of much of the lands adjacent to the river, limited flooding by the river,
and the restriction by the police of the Inyangatom and the Dasanetch to the west
bank of Il Nakwa, effectively limits the total amount of horticulture carried out
in this area.

Plant communities along Il Nakwa are generally mesophytic relative to
the surrounding plains, ranging from closed woodland dominated by Acacia tortilis and A. sieberana, to open woodland and shrub thicket. Undergrowth is
greatly disturbed by domestic stock grazing and browsing, so that grasses and
forbs are greatly reduced, and large areas are without ground cover altogether.
The disturbance indicator shrubs of Cadaba rotundifolia, C. glandulosa, and
Salvadora persica are scattered throughout the woodlands. There are also numerous (though very irregularly distributed) shrubs of Combretum aculeatum and
Terminalia brevipes. Immediately west of Il Nakwa are the restricted Ilemi
lands, once freely used by both the Dasanetch and the Inyangatom tribes.

Implications of Riverine Environment
Changes for the Dasanetch

Recent large-scale changes in the level of Lake Rudolf and subsequent
changes in the Omo River have resulted in a south to north gradient of both river sinuosity and vegetation development along the Omo. This gradient is described in detail in the preceding sections. As the following remarks suggest,
the patterns resulting from the above changes have had profound effects on the
Dasanetch's way of life.

The lower reaches of the river, south of about Rati (see Fig. 3-5), are

Fig. 3-15. --Aerial View of Il Nakwa and Adjacent Closed Woodland

relatively straight, with mesophytic grasses, forbs and scattered shrubs form-ing a thin border along the bank. This vegetation is predominantly open in char-acter, and this in combination with the relatively low levee along much of the river here makes the river easily accessible to human and domestic stock. This section of the river is utilized intensively year-round by the Dasanetch for domestic stock grazing and browsing, watering and horticulture.

Vegetational development of riverine lands, from open woodland to forest, was described earlier for the zone north of Rati. Although the riverine vegeta-tion within this zone is luxuriant relative to the surrounding semi-desert and therefore desirable for grazing purposes, the continuous bush cover proximal to the water has led to tsetse infestation over the past decades. This invasion along the river in the transition zone and in the flats has caused large-scale evacuation of villages and domestic stock. Consequently, grazing pressure on the drier plains has increased greatly. This northern riverine sector now sup-ports only limited human settlement by the poorest Dasanetch households, with horticulture the predominate activity (see Chapters 5, 6 and 7). The relation-ship of these physically generated pressures on the Dasanetch to politically gen-erated pressures will be dealt with in detail in the last chapter.

As described in Chapters 5 and 7, Kolon channel remains of great impor-tance to the Dasanetch for watering purposes although it has become drier in recent decades to the point where it is presently of little value as a horticul-tural location.

The above described physical changes constitute the major environmental shifts in the lake and riverine zones which have had far reaching implications for the Dasanetch people. These have been greatly intensified by their conver-gence with the politically generated (i. e., territorial restriction) deterioration of the range quality of the plains environments described in Chapter 2. The interaction of these two sets of changes and their combined effects on the tribe will be analyzed in the last chapter.

CHAPTER 4

AN INTRODUCTION TO DASANETCH SOCIAL RELATIONS

For the reasons stated in Chapter 1, the basic features of Dasanetch society will be described primarily synchronically in the present chapter. Aspects
of ideological change and social processes will be considered in Chapters 6 and
7. A full ethnographic account of Dasanetch society is not attempted here. Instead, the focus is upon those features of Dasanetch society most relevant to
the objectives of this study, i.e., the system of societal/environmental interactions and the states of tension and change in the system resulting from these
interactions as well as from external forces.

The Roles of Cattle

Cattle occupy a central position in Dasanetch society, and their roles
form a wide spectrum of variation, from what is conventionally referred to as
economic, through many other aspects of concrete social relations, to symbolic.
As with the Pakot of East Africa, as described by Schneider (1957), the subsistence role of cattle is much greater for the Dasanetch than is indicated by the
"cattle complex" as developed by Herskovitz (1926). The economic importance
of cattle to the Dasanetch centers on their role as a source of milk and related
products, meat, blood, skins and numerous implements. Further, it centers
on their role in the bridewealth system and in other ways as a medium of exchange. Although the economic role of small stock (goats and sheep) is also
highly significant, making the concept of "stock complex" as suggested by Gulliver (1951) for the Turkana appealing in a superficial sense for examining the
Dasanetch system, when the ideological and other functional roles of cattle are
considered there is a clear qualitative difference in the importance of cattle vis-
à-vis small stock, such that this conceptualization is also unsatisfactory.

The traditional centrality of cattle among the Dasanetch is clearly indicated by their complex terminology for cattle, their close identification with cattle as reflected by naming systems (e.g., names adopted by social groups, the
institution of an individual male adopting the name of a favorite ox, i.e., einbe-

siyet, involving both a strong emotional attachment as well as serving a direct social function) and the recurrent cattle themes in song, dance, myth and ritual (Fig. 4-1). Cattle are the essential medium (direct and indirect) of social relations, and indeed social relations are largely defined by rights and obligations concerning cattle or their equivalence in small stock. Economic wealth is defined primarily in terms of cattle, though there are other sources of social prestige, as described below.

Cattle are therefore central in the organization and functioning of Dasanetch society, both through their high use value, i.e., their subjective value associated with human wants (Eaton, 1963), and their exchange value, i.e., their quantitative value in exchange transactions. This interpretation strongly contrasts with those which emphasize either the prestige value of cattle (Herskovitz, 1952) or their exchange and transfer values (Gulliver, 1955).

Tribal Segments

Names, components and relative sizes. --Dasanetch society is organized into eight tribal segments. These units are only quasi-territorial, each with its own traditional tales of origin. Although marriage within the segment is predominant, marriage between members of different segments is common. A segment (en) functions as an autonomous fighting unit during warfare, although the segments typically coordinate their actions. Each en is divided in turn into clans (tur), sub-clans (bil), age sets (hari) and sub-age sets (modo). These segments, listed below, vary widely in size and importance for the society as a whole.

Sheer	{Inkabela	Koro
	{Inkoria	Oro
	{Naritch	Randel
	Eleli	Rieli

Another segment, Ever, was described by some informants as having once existed but either dying off or migrating out of the area. Informants who reported it at all agreed that it had been a very small segment. Of the existing segments, Inkabela is easily the largest, with at least 6,000 or more members. Among the segments present on the west bank, Eleli and Oro are next in order of magnitude, with Randel, Rieli and Koro following. Rieli and Koro are both very small segments, each with no more than several hundred members.

Inkabela is clearly the dominant segment. It serves as a reference structure for the other segments (en), and it occupies numerous leadership roles within the tribe. Inkabela, Naritch and Inkoria are bracketed in the above list

Fig. 4-1.--Cattle Slaughter at Dimi Ritual

because the latter two are regarded as derivatives of Inkabela, and the three function as one segment (Sheer) in several basic respects (see below). An Inkabela will often respond with Sheer to the inquiry as to the name of his or her segment.

Origins and territoriality. --Oral traditions prevalent among the different segments clearly indicate that the present tribe was constituted from at least several groups of widely divergent origins. This tradition is supported by the high degree of physical variability (in stature, facial features, skin tone, etc.). The points in time when individual segments originated or became absorbed by the tribe as a whole varies widely, with Inkabela and Oro being the oldest. Randel and Koro are said to be the most recent segments, and Rieli is also considered by many to be of relatively recent origin. Inkabela's position within the tribe as the dominant segment is unquestioned and is consistent with Dasanetch oral tradition which fixes this segment as the core and first element of the tribe. Long before the formation of Naritch and Inkoria, Inkabela is described as Sheer in oral tradition, and the earliest name reported was Nyeupe. Dasanetch informants describe the Nyeupe as having come from Ger, a land south or southwest of Lodwar, Kenya. One version of the oral tradition regarding the early history and migration of the Nyeupe into the present area is translated in Appendix C.

The Oro segment is considered to be traditionally very closely associated with the Inkabela and its ancestor group, the Nyeupe. This view is congruent with the fact that the segments Inkabela and Oro are today bound by very strong economic, political, and social ties as well as the fact that the majority of Oro segment members live within traditional Inkabela lands on the west bank.

Eleli is a segment which apparently came from the west (see Appendix C). Oral tradition describes this segment as either having been separated from the other segments until entering the Lower Omo Basin, or having been associated with the Sheer and the Oro before passing a period of relatively independent existence, after which it reunited with them in the Omo region.

Rieli, Randel and Koro, according to informants from those segments, were basically absorbed from other tribes which were hostile: the Rieli possibly from the Borana, the Randel from the Rendelli, and the Koro from the Samburu. There are numerous records of Dasanetch fighting with these tribes. The social structures of Randel and Koro are significantly deviant from that of the Inkabela, as noted below. Altogether, the tribal origins claimed for these segments in the oral traditions which I have collected vary considerably. Different versions identify the Donyiro (Inyangatom), Moruzo (Nkalabong), Borana, Arbore, and Rendelli tribes as sources for segments or portions of segments of the Dasanetch tribe. Whatever the validity of these accounts, their reliability is high and there is certainly a strong consciousness of the different origins and a complicated history of absorption of diverse social units into the tribe.

At the present time, there is much variation in the degree of territoriality for tribal segments. There is considerably less correspondence between segments and clearly defined territories today than in the past (see Chapter 7). Segment distributions are here defined only according to where the men of the segment in question are settled (as described below, women generally settle after marriage in their husbands' villages). Those segments which are best defined geographically are Naritch and Inkoria, the two segments which comprise the majority of the Dasanetch population on the east bank. To a lesser degree but still relatively well defined is the Rieli segment, largely concentrated around Dielirieli (see Fig. 5-12) but with scattered individuals among the Oro, Eleli and especially the Inkabela of the west bank. The Eleli are settled both on the east bank near the Omo River, especially near Turangoli, and on the west bank from the Kalam vicinity northward, particularly in the eastern half of Dasanetch lands. They are also settled along the river north of Rati. The Inkabela are extremely widespread with the largest portion of them settled from Kalam southward on the west bank, in the modern delta and proximal regions of the east bank. There are, however, Inkabela settlements as far north as Nakwa (see Fig. 1-1) and scattered elsewhere. Most Oro are settled on the west bank among the Inkabela, although a few live in predominantly Eleli regions (e.g., Rati, Koritodo along the Omo River) or in Randel villages. Randel and Koro are strongly co-resident, as are the Inkabela and Oro. Randel villages are most numerous in the western plains between Kalam and Nakwa where their villages greatly overlap geographically with the Eleli, but they mix freely with the Inkabela so that some Randel villages are also encountered from Kalam southward to Lake Rudolf (e.g., at Lobemkat). Randel are not settled along the Omo River nor on the east bank of the Omo.

Some regions within Les Dasanetch have considerable segment mixing during at least parts of the year, such as the modern delta (Erdete and Nairobi), the Kalam vicinity and Nakwa. The large west bank settlement complexes are clearly dominated by certain segments: Lobemkat and Nyemomari (see Fig. 5-12) are predominantly Inkabela; Kalam (south) is mostly Inkabela and Oro;

Kalam (north) is virtually all Eleli; and riverine villages north of Rati (Masitch, Akesa, Bulukwï, Koritodo, and Kolin) are almost entirely Eleli (see Figs. 1-1 and 5-12). There is no major settlement area with a high concentration of Randel or Koro, as these segments are traditionally very mobile, and the Randel in particular are spread over a wide area between Kalam and Nakwa.

Language of the Dasanetch

The language spoken by the Dasanetch (rendered orthographically as Dasanech in the most recent linguistic surveys of the area: Ferguson, 1975) is included in the large Afroasiatic language family. This family includes Cushitic-Omotic whose first order daughters are shown in the figure below.

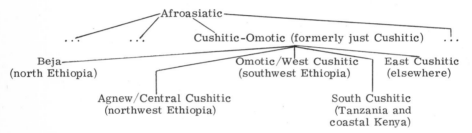

This classificatory schema is based almost exclusively on lexical evidence and must, therefore, be regarded as tentative. More specifically, the more refined classification below shows the position of Dasanetch (Dasenech) within the hypothesized proto-East Cushitic group.

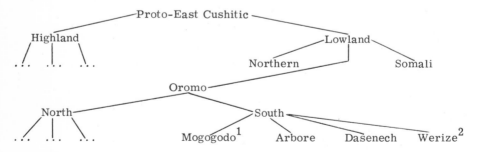

Consistent with the family tree structure, "Dasenech" shows the most marked lexical overlap with Mogogodo and Arbore.

---

[1]A language of Tanzania.

[2]Pronounced Wariza by some Dasanetch informants.

Relations of Moiety, Clan and Age Set

The following discussion of social categories is derived primarily from my work with the Inkabela, Eleli and Oro segments with whom I had the greatest contact. Major differences between these segments and the remaining ones are noted. Unless otherwise stated, the social structural and functional characteristics described are for the reference Inkabela segment (which is alike in almost all details for Oro and Eleli).

Moieties. --The presence of a moiety system is one of the more unusual features of Dasanetch society. Its significance within the structure as a whole is discussed at the end of this chapter. Each moiety (dolo) is based on a system of alternating generations. That is, the moieties Dolgerga and Dolbariyet alternate with successive generations within each patrilineal descent line. Thus male and female siblings are of the same moiety, and their moiety is identical with that of their grandfather and opposite to that of their father. There is no correlation between moiety and wealth, status or residence pattern.

Two tribal segments, Randel and Koro, lack the moiety system. A possible significance of this structural difference is suggested below, along with other structural differences between these two segments and the rest of the tribe.

Marriage and sexual relations with members of the opposite moiety (dolo) are strictly prohibited (i. e., the moieties are endogamous) within each tribal segment having a moiety system. An individual may, however, marry into either moiety of another segment (en). An exception to this rule is the Sheer group composed of Inkabela, Naritch and Inkoria segments, none of whom allow marriage between members of the opposite moiety of any of the three segments (i. e., where endogamy exists for moieties). This marriage rule, indicating an especially close connection among these three segments, is consistent with the common origin of Naritch and Inkoria from Inkabela which is described by the Dasanetch. For all tribal segments in which moieties are present, the endogamous moiety rule is the most extended constraint on possible marriages.

Moieties form the primary organizing principle for dimi, which is the most important ceremony in the life of a Dasanetch man. This ceremony (Figs. 4-1, 4-2) is passed by a man when his first daughter is of the age just preceding breast development, and after he has fulfilled certain other prerequisites such as having undergone circumcision and having completed small stock bridewealth. It is of the utmost significance to him because it marks his passage to the prestigious status of big man (ma gudoha). Dimi is held separately though

Fig. 4-2.--Dasanetch Male Passing Dimi Ritual

consecutively for each moiety of an individual tribal segment. It is often held simultaneously for some segments (e. g., Inkabela, Oro and Rieli all held dimi in the region of Rap, near Nyemomari, in August-September of 1969), and it is not held every year, even by the larger segments. An important role in dimi is played by the judges of the segment, the ara (bulls), who are chosen according to moiety such that, normatively, half the total number of ara for a segment are from each moiety. Dimi is not held by the two segments without a moiety system, i. e., Randel and Koro.

Clans. --Each tribal segment is divided into a system of patrilineal clans (tur), which are in turn subdivided into bil. Most informants from the west bank clans claim a common ancestor for their clan, although many do not know the name of this individual. Younger informants often are not familiar with traditional tales of clan origin, save perhaps a very well-known one, such as Galbur of Inkabela (described in Appendix C). There is, normatively speaking, a ma gudoha (big man) for each clan, and this individual is also an ara (judge), except in the Randel and Koro segments where no ara system exists. Gal gudoha (big men) are often very important in the settlement of disputes both internal to the clan and between a clan member(s) and a member(s) of some other clan. A big man of a clan is also often the preferred member to perform certain clan functions (see below).

Clans of a tribal segment are regarded as differentially related to each other in terms of origin, although descriptions of their precise ordering varies from one informant to the next for some segments. Although male informants claim a genealogical relationship with all members of their clan, only those in the smallest clans can trace their specific ties to all other members. Clans with the same name occur among some of the tribal segments, but there is no consciousness of a common origin between them, and no marriage prohibition (exogamy) exists (although in fact I found very few cases of such marriages). Exogamy reportedly also exists in a few instances between segments where two clans of different name are considered to be linked in origin.

Significant functions and activities of the clan include: (1) holding and transfer of property, in particular, stock; (2) bridewealth transactions; (3) co-residence (often); (4) collective functioning at certain ceremonies (e. g., circumcision or bilte); (5) performing of everyday, ceremonial or special duties designated for that clan; (6) inheritance of wealth and taking of levirate wives.

Table 4-1 lists the clans for most segments of the west bank Dasanetch.

TABLE 4-1

CLANS OF SEGMENTS PREDOMINANTLY ON WEST BANK[a]

INKABELA	ORO	ELELI
Turnyerim	Turnyeim	Turnyeim
Fargaro	Fargaro	Fargaro
Turat	Turbur (Turat)	Urubur (Turat)
Ili	Ili	Turthitch
Galbur		Mekgoti
Etha		Deritch (Ili)
Murle		
Tiemle		

KORO	RANDEL
Agala	Agala
Muhsi	Nagan
Lorokuchu	Sanli (Turat)
Lukumoi	Wageli
	Myleti
	Baldor
	Guium
	Dobalvien
	Galora (Syn. Bule)
	Bulier
	Bilse

[a]Names in parentheses are those sometimes given when informants from those clans are responding to someone from a different segment, or to a person from outside the tribe, presumably because the alternate name is considered analogous and the "foreigner" is more apt to be familiar with the Inkabela term.

Those segments with clan names most divergent from the rest of the tribe are clearly Randel and Koro. The reasons for the relatively large number of Randel clans, which includes some extremely small ones, cannot be treated here. But it is interesting to note that there are various combinations of exogamy which occur among the clans of this segment.

Clans are further characterized by cattle brands (gui) and by ear notches (hethe), the former by far the more important. Whereas some clans have only one brand, others are considerably differentiated, e.g., six for one important clan. There are numerous tales of fissions within or between patrilines which have resulted in new brands; I have recorded numerous instances of arguments between brothers or between brothers and father's brothers which resulted in cattle brand fissions. Some fissions have, according to Dasanetch descriptions, occurred because of too many cattle for one brand. Some overlap in type of brand exists between different clans of different segments.

Most clans have certain duties and/or rights which are of importance in Dasanetch life, and these may include everyday, ritual (e. g., dimi) or special (e. g., times of war or epidemics) activities. These duties are very widely known throughout the segment, although they are sometimes confused when described by a member of another segment. A closer examination of some selected characteristics of these clans shows both the mixing of clan functions between tribal segments and the pervasiveness of some environmental concerns in social processes. These are given for Inkabela, Oro and Eleli, by example, in Table 4-2. While some clans have similar duties for different segments (e. g., Turnyerim of Eleli and Inkabela), others of the same name strongly contrast in duties between segments (e. g., Turnyerim of Inkabela and Oro). Further, a clan in one segment may have a duty or privilege analogous to that of another segment.

Age sets.

Social significance and organization of age sets.

The age set (hari) system is a central organizing principle of Dasanetch society, and its structural/functional relation to clans is suggested in the last section of this chapter. The age set system is critical in an individual male's increasing ability to form a broad spectrum of social and economic ties, his overall socialization, and the political functioning of both individual segments and the tribe as a whole. An age set system with political authority based on seniority is a common feature of many East African societies (Beattie, 1964), including the Dasanetch. The Dasanetch system is unusual, however, in that its age sets are paired, with the age sets comprising each pair alternating with generations within patrilines. Thus, within an individual patriline, all the sons of a particular father belong to one age set. This age set is identical with that of their grandfather, [3] aand alternates with that of their father. A patriline, then, has the following sequence for the age set pair A/A': Generation$_1$ (G$_1$)--A; G$_2$--A'; G$_3$--A; G$_4$--A'. In this respect, age sets are similar in pattern to moieties. Unlike other East African age set systems which have a small span of years comprising any given age set such as the Masai as described by Jacobs (1968) or the Karamojong as described by Dyson-Hudson (1966), the recruitment prin-

---

[3] This identity of age sets between alternate generations of a patriline may be obscured where age set name changes have occurred.

TABLE 4-2

CLAN DUTIES AND POWERS FOR THREE WEST BANK TRIBAL SEGMENTS

Clan Name	Duties/Powers
Inkabela	
Turnyerim	Converse with God to get help in war; dimi: prepare white and black paint; prepare fire.
Fargaro	Bring rain; sacrifice small stock to bring millet growth; cure headaches; can build fire if no Turnyerim.
Turat	Treat burns; dimi: cut ritual tree (Miede).
Ili	Cure scorpion bites.
Galbur	Perform ritual to protect stock from crocodiles during river crossing.
Etha	Treat eye sickness; dimi: call the wind to prevent spiders, scorpions, etc.
Murli	No work.
Tiemle	No work.
Oro	
Turnyerim	Give blessing before war; dimi: prepare white paint.
Fargaro	Beg God for rain if no Turnyerim near; treat spider, scorpion bites.
Turbur (Turat)	Treat burns.
Ili (Deritch)	Cure headaches; dimi: cut ritual shrub.
Eleli	
Turnyerim	Help stock crossing of Omo River; beg God for water; dimi: prepare fire with ritual shrub.
Fargaro	Can beg for rain if no Turnyerim near.
Urubur (Turat)	No work.
Turthitch	Aid stock in drinking and crossing Omo River.
Mekgoti	Heal sores from ticks; heal knife wounds; bring wind to get rid of mosquitoes.
Deritch (Ili)	No work.

ciple for the Dasanetch age set (hari) results in a broad age spectrum. There are sub-age sets (modo) within each age set, and it is a male's modo with which he is most intimately associated. A male child knows his future hari from the beginning of his social awareness, and he begins playing and associating with his future age mates at that time. Only in his young manhood, however, is he formally incorporated into that age set.

A female, on the other hand, deviates from the alternating generational age set pattern of fathers and sons in that she initially follows her father's age set. The prefix -ini (meaning daughter) followed by the father's hari name constitutes the age set name for a female child. A female maintains membership in her father's age set until after marriage and, more specifically, until after the completion of bridewealth payment by her husband when she is formally incorporated into her husband's age set. Thus a female is considered a member of the age set of one of the two dominant males during her life cycle. This is one important reflection of the structural bias against females in Dasanetch society.

Names and origins of age sets.

Age set pairs are similar for most of the tribal segments except Randel and Koro (these two segments recently have only one age set pair each). A comparison of number and names of age sets is shown in Table 4-3. There is a wealth of oral tradition regarding name changes of age sets, although some series of changes are reported with much variation from one informant to the next. Fission of age sets has been of primary importance in the social structure of the Dasanetch. For instance, the origin of the tribal segment Inkoria allegedly occurred following a quarrel between younger and older members of one age set within the Inkabela segment.

Some explanation or ordering principle is necessary to integrate the following three dimensions of age sets: (1) there are pairs of age sets which, for males, alternate with generations within patrilines; (2) there is some differential average age among age sets, which is both suggested to the foreign observer as well as part of the Dasanetch consciousness; (3) there is a rotating sequence of age sets from which the ara (judges) are selected, i.e., a rotation of senior age sets. There are several major logical possibilities for integrating these apparently incongruent features of age sets: (a) no real differential in age exists, although oral tradition has perpetuated the notion of an age/seniority sequence; (b) the ara phenomena is explained by the ara simply being chosen from the oldest sub-age sets (modo) of each age set within the rotating sequence; (c) there is a real age differential, resulting from the relatively recent formation (through fission) of some age sets.

On the basis of Dasanetch testimonies based on oral tradition regarding family, segment and tribal history, (c) is the correct explanation. At least several generations removed, age set A' (Nyongolomongin) split into two age sets,

TABLE 4-3

AGE SET PAIRS OF WEST BANK DASANETCH TRIBAL SEGMENTS

Inkabela:
      Numor (A) . . . . Nyongolomongen (A')
      Nilimeto (B) . . . . . . Nikorio (B')
      Nilimkorio (C) . . . . . Nigabite (C')

Oro:
      Numor (A) . . . . Nyongolomongen (A')
      Nilimkorio (C) . . . . . Nikorio (C')

Elele:
      Numor (A) . . . . Nyongolomongen (A')
      Nilimeto (B) . . . . . . Nikorio (B')
      Ngyrisii (C)* . . . . . . Nigabite (C')
      (Nilimkorio)

Randel:
      Ngynyangakabor . . . . Ngymerimong

Koro:
      Ngymerikobir . . . . . Ngytira

---

*Ngyrisii is considered analogous to Nilimkorio.

A' and C (Nilimkorio), along age lines such that the older sub-age set(s) remained as A' while the younger sub-age set(s) formed C (see Fig. 4-3 and Table 4-3). From that point of fission, A' continued to alternate with A (Numor) with successive generations, whereas the creation of age set C resulted in a new alternating sequence with C' (Nigabite). Thus, two age set pairs existed where only one had existed prior to the fission. Since C was constituted by the younger sub-age set(s) involved in the split, their sons (in C') would have been younger, on the average, than the sons of A', i.e., the members of A. Since A' was reportedly the older hari (between A' and A) at the time of the fission, i.e., the age set of the ara (judges) at the time, the sequence of descending average age resulting from the split would have been: A' > C > A > C'.

    Subsequent to the above fission, age set A split, not along age lines but rather, between patrilines (a few informants maintain that it was within patrilines and between half-brothers, but in either case the effect is the same). Thus A split into A and B (Nilimeto), with the sons of the latter forming the new age set B' (Nukorio). With this fission, the average ages of A and B were similar, as were those of age sets A' and B'.

    The two fissions may be summarized as follows.

Fission (1)

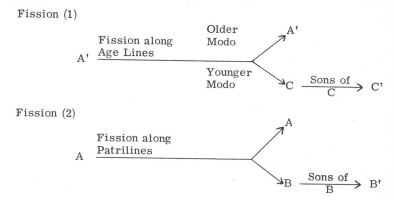

Fig. 4-3.--Two Primary Fissions among Dasanetch Age Sets

The nature of these fissions and their significance will be the subject of a forthcoming paper, but a few aspects of Dasanetch society may be briefly described which substantiate the above theory of recent age set formation. First, there is exogamy (marriage prohibition) within each given age set (e.g., A', A), both within and between tribal segments, and these exogamy patterns are in agreement with the suggested mode of age set formation. For example, consistent with fission (2) is the fact that A is exogamous with B, and A' is exogamous with B'. Similarly, A' and C have been exogamous until a ritual breakage of the exogamy was performed (see below), as have been A and C'. There is no exogamy rule between age set members of a given pair (i.e., A and A'; B and B'; C and C') and in fact marriages between opposite age sets of a pair are extremely common. Second, members of A' and C, since originally of the same hari, addressed each other as "my brother" (nyar chu) previous to the exogamy breakage ritual (bershō), but as "my father-in-law/my son-in-law" (soz chu) after the ritual. These linguistic forms reflect precisely the age set membership rule: namely that brothers are of the same hari and father-in-law/son-in-law must be of different age sets, since age sets are exogamous and daughters belong to the same age set as their fathers. Third, the ara (judge) age set rotation occurs in the following sequence: C (presently the senior age set)-----→ A/B (combined)-----→ C'-----→ A'/B' (combined)-----→ C. This sequence is in agreement with the age order established by the above theory of age set formation. Fourth, a member of age set A and a member of age set B reciprocally refer to each other as of "my age set" (hari chu), and a similar situation obtains for members of A' and B'.

Activities of age sets.

Functions and activities of individual age sets are great in number and importance, and include the following: (1) passing of certain ceremonies together, e.g., circumcision (bilte), and the hairdress ceremony (when young men of an age set begin wearing the traditional elaborate hairdress: Fig. 4-4); (2) fighting together in warfare against other tribes (each tribal segment is divided into fighting units according to age set); (3) eating of meat, drinking and singing together at special occasions (e.g., the ritual dimi); (4) slaughtering of a name ox, einbesiyet, or other stock belonging to an age mate (upon numerous occasions); (5) herding together as boys and young men, especially when on extended treks with stock (foretch); (6) celebrating bridewealth completion by one of the hari members, at the gol ceremony (see Fig. 4-5); (7) settlement of numerous disputes involving one or more of the hari members; (8) gathering periodically at the village of the age set pair chief (Makansitch eka), his assistant (megaseli) or another member's village to discuss matters related to the age set, etc.; (9) participating in a member's marriage ceremony; (10) sharing labor power at the disposal of age mates (e.g., the herding labor of sons); (11) participating in collective dances with song (adum) when young (and unmarried). A number of the above activities are defined by individual sub-age sets (modo) rather than the broader age set (hari) as a whole. Throughout an individual male's life a large share of his close friendships and strong ties are within his age set, and particularly within his sub-age set of his own segment (Figs. 4-6, 4-7). Members of the same age set from different segments may also be closely associated (e.g., in residence, at certain ceremonies, as bond friends).

Within each age set pair, a distinction is made between the senior and junior age set. This designation changes with the passage of generations, as indicated in the above discussion regarding age set origins. There is a considerable political power difference between the senior and junior age set of each pair (i.e., A versus A', etc.) in favor of the senior one. Within each age set, relations between junior and senior sub-age sets are extremely important. Arguments and disputes between different sub-age sets, sometimes resulting in beatings, are common and these occur for various reasons: younger modo members refusing to prepare a place for the older modo members to cut meat; older member's disapproval of younger member's herding practices; younger modo member's active interest in or attempt to seduce the same young woman an older modo member is interested in, etc.

Fig. 4-5.--Dasanetch Male with Face Painting for Bridewealth Completion Celebration.

Fig. 4-4.--Dasanetch Adult Male with Hairdress and Earrings.

Fig. 4-6.--Age Mates in Conversation at Dimi

Fig. 4-7. --Age Mates Relaxing in Woodland near Horticultural Plots

Bond friendships.

Types of bonds.

Bond friendships are of great importance in a Dasanetch male's life, especially from the standpoint of increasing his array of social and economic relations. These relations are centrally bound up with his immediate family's economic well-being and his own developing social status. There are four basic
types of bonds, and these vary considerably in strength obligations, and period
of life cycle when they are formed.

The basic types of bond friends are as follows: (1) Name-giving bond
friend. This bond is a very strong, virtually unbreakable one, established
when a friend of the newborn child's father (often from his own age set or clan)
takes part in the naming ceremony for the infant. Reciprocal kin terms are
often used between the male child and his name-giving bond friend. Co-residence between these two partners or friends does occur but is not common.
(2) Gift exchange friend. This bond is highly variable in strength, ranging from
a relatively light-hearted tie between young men to a much more serious one,
and this bond may progressively deepen with the aging of the individuals involved. Such a bond is often used in a rather exploratory fashion in order to
expand a socio-economic base. The value of the gifts exchanged strongly indicates the seriousness of the bond. (3) Smearing friend. This bond is a strong
one between two males of the same age set, where one is chosen by the other to
smear him with domestic stock entrails at the smearing ritual, which occurs
near puberty for males. (4) Holding friend. This friendship bond is between a
man who is circumcised and the man he selects to hold him during the cutting.
Like smearing and name-giving, a holding bond is considered a very strong one,
and a holding friendship bond is considered strongest by most informants.

Social and economic aspects of bond friendships.

Exogamy is associated with bond friendships, especially name-giving,
smearing and holding bonds, but Dasanetch informants describe these marriage
prohibitions as basically flexible for all but holding. Many bonds are formed
between members of exogamous units anyway (e. g., between clan or age set
members). At any rate, the degree of exogamy resulting from bond friendships
is certainly minor by comparison to the moiety endogamous restriction within
each segment (en), and the age set and the clan exogamies.

Bond friendship formation and development are important and dynamic

aspects of a male's life, and he may choose to strengthen or perpetuate some
ties while weakening or even breaking others, depending on his socio-economic
interests. Both the formation and proliferation of a male's bonds are often intimately related to his family's pre-existing bond patterns and to his changing
needs. A large number of bond friendships are formed with individuals already
bonded to close kin, age mates or otherwise previously connected to the initia-
tor of the bond. It follows then that a male typically deepens or expands his
base in a pre-existing social network more than he creates wholly new inroads
into social and economic reciprocity relations.

Socio-economic advantages initiated or intensified by bond friendships
may include: sharing of herding labor (especially if the friends are co-resident);
receiving or allocating of horticultural plots; sharing during times of hunger,
sickness or other hardships; stock gifts, including goats, sheep and oxen; stock
loan or gift for the dimi ritual (usually from a man's holding bond friend); receiving right to bridewealth from marriage of a bond friend's daughter (after
the presentation of an ox to the woman's father); support in disputes; and, the
utilization of a bond friend to establish further economic or social relationships.

Marriage and Bridewealth

Marriage rules and patterns. --Primary marriage rules among the Dasanetch include: (a) moiety endogamy within tribal segments, and across segments within Sheer (Inkabela, Inkoria and Naritch); (b) clan exogamy within the
tribal segments (and again across the three segments of the Sheer group), between certain clans of different names across segments (e.g., Sanli and Randel
and Turat of Inkabela), and between certain clans within one segment (Randel);
(c) exogamy within age sets;[4] and (d) exogamy with certain affines, siblings'
affines, and bond partners' close kin.

Intermarriage between tribal segments occurs throughout Dasanetch society, although the frequency and type of intermarriage varies greatly. On the
basis of data gathered primarily within the Eleli, Oro, and Inkabela segments,
the percentage of segment intermarriage within any one genealogy recorded
varied from less than 5 percent to more than 75 percent. Traditions and prefer-

[4]Randel and Koro are unusual in that they differ in some important organ
izational principles. For example, according to both Randel and Koro informants, there is exogamy between the Ngynyangakabor age set of Randel and the
Ngymerikobir age set of Koro, as well as Ngymerimong of Randel and Ngytira
of Koro (see Table 4-3). I have not had the opportunity to explore this further.

ences of marriage with certain other segments do exist for individual segments, and this will be described in a later section. The major factors regulating the amount of inter-segment mixing by marriage include physical proximity and wealth status, type of economic activity and traditional segment and family associations.

Inter-tribal marriages will not be dealt with in detail here, as only the general tendencies are relevant to the subject at hand. Genealogical information and informants' testimonies indicate intermarriages with nearby tribes include the Nkalabong (Moruzo), Arbore, Borana, Turkana (Buma), and Inyangatom (Donyiro) in the past. Of these, intermarriages with the Inyangatom and especially the Turkana were most frequent. Presently, the Turkana is the only tribe which intermarries with the west bank Dasanetch, and it almost invariably contributes women to the marriage rather than men. There are a few cases described by the Dasanetch where Turkana men have come to Les Dasanetch during times of famine in Turkanaland and subsequently settled, been incorporated into the Dasanetch social structure, and even married Dasanetch women.

The Dasanetch are polygamous, with the number of wives ranging from one to five. The majority of men interviewed had one to three wives. There is a strict order in which the sons in a family may marry. The oldest unmarried son must marry first, and I have recorded several occasions where a younger brother who married out of turn was chased away from the father's or older brother's village (en), at least for a time.

Marriage occurs in several ways among the Dasanetch: (1) Elopements. This type of marriage is extremely common, especially for young men and their prospective brides. It usually involves the man bringing the young woman secretly to his village, with the woman's immediate male kin (e.g., her brothers) following within a few days. If the discussion between the appropriate kin of the woman and the man (or his father) is settled in favor of marriage, the two families arrange the bridewealth terms. (2) Arranged marriages. These are of two basic types. Usually, a series of negotiation sessions are held between the father of the woman (although the father's brothers, or abayam, are often the primary decision-making force regarding the woman's marriage)[5] and the prospective groom and/or his father just prior to the marriage. The sec-

---

[5]The prospective bride's brothers are not directly instrumental in the marriage agreement, and this is consistent with the very strong dominance by the ascending generation in all the patriline's affairs.

ond type of arranged marriage described by informants is that contracted by the two families (that of the bride and groom) years before the marriage, but I encountered no instances of this during the course of my field work. (3) Stealing the bride.[6] Done either by a man alone or with his sub-age set mates, the capture of a young woman comes as little or no surprise to the close kin of both parties involved. If, after the woman has been stolen and negotiations between the two families end by approving the marriage, they typically arrange the bridewealth terms immediately. Arguments both about whether the marriage will be allowed and the terms of the bridewealth are not infrequent. Some shifts have apparently occurred in recent decades regarding the relative frequency of the different types of marriage as noted in the last chapter.

It is important to point out that although a young woman may theoretically marry anyone whom she is chosen by (respecting, of course, the marriage rules described earlier), in actual fact her marriage is largely conditioned by her agnates' social and economic relations. Her brothers in particular are usually very important in the active encouragement or discouragement of suitors, even though they defer to her father's brothers in the actual marriage arrangements. Concentration of brothers marrying into the same family is structurally avoided by the prohibition of marriage to a sibling's spouse's sister. Thus, the composite affinal ties of any given set of brothers usually forms a broad net of social relations.

A husband's social ties with his affines may include a wide range of economic and social associations. These social ties are reflected concretely in a number of ways. The husband may live in his wife's father's village or his wife's brother's village, but I found no cases of uxorilocal residence except where either the husband was less wealthy in stock than the wife's patriline or where he was engaged in labor sharing with them. Since brothers cannot marry into the same household, uxorilocal residence effectively disperses a given set of brothers. The husband may gain access to the control over the labor power of his younger affinal relations, especially for herding he may also offer the labor power of his younger brother to his affines if his father is dead or if he agrees; later in life he may offer the labor power of his son. A husband may also obtain a horticultural plot from his affines; this allocation is most frequently from his wife's father. Sharing with affinal relations may also be important in times of hunger or illness. Finally, affinal ties may be used to obtain stock

---

[6]This type of marriage is, according to Randel informants, rare within their segment, whereas (2) is greatly predominant.

for slaughter at select ritual occasions. Since both the husband and his affines have long-range reciprocal interests, they may nurture their good relations with small gifts (e. g., coffee or tobacco from the debtor to his immediate affines) and acts of hospitality (e. g., slaughter and eating of a sheep or goat). Thus, a male's basic motives in establishing a particular marriage tie focus on the extension of existing socio-economic ties, possible social prestige and labor needs.

Bridewealth. --Bridewealth is a central institution in Dasanetch society. It is primarily through this system that an individual male attempts to build and maintain a strong socio-economic position. Bridewealth payments both reflect and condition the social relations of the debtor (the husband) and recipients (his affines). Through his skill in maneuvering within the bridewealth system, a male may initiate, terminate, intensify or attenuate existing relations as he deems necessary or desirable.

Bridewealth is paid by the groom in the form of both cattle (guo) and small stock (ayi, including sheep and goats), and these types of payment are termed guo foitch and shebedam, respectively. Both shebedam and guo foitch are paid either immediately or in installments over an extended period of time, and much variation occurs in the timing of payment. The Dasanetch describe an overall change in the proportion of stock paid in immediate versus extended bridewealth payments in favor of the latter. When payments are extended, they may be deferred up to twenty or thirty years, and many males die without having completed bridewealth for more than one wife.

The termination of shebedam, or small stock payments, usually occurs prior to the completion of cattle payments, but it sometimes occurs simultaneously. Completion of shebedam marks the attainment of legal status of the marriage. After this time, separation or divorces are much more unusual, and the wife's agnates can no longer break the marriage by returning her to her father's village if they are not satisfied with the progress of bridewealth payments. Along with the completion of the circumcision ceremony (bilte), completion of shebedam is a prerequisite for passage of the dimi ceremony.

Completion of guo foitch, or cattle bridewealth payments, is marked by two celebrative events, it galan and gol. Gol, the more significant of the two, is attended by many of the bridewealth debtor's age mates (from his own and other tribal segments), [7] and it formally completes the marriage. It is a time

---

[7] Males of the opposite age set, i. e., the other age set of the pair, do not

for dancing, drinking and feasting with much meat, provided by small stock slaughter, and age set mates attend with faces elaborately painted (Fig. 4-5). An older brother must complete the gol ceremony before his younger brothers. This situation thus parallels the strict birth order requirement in contracting a marriage among a set of brothers stated above.

The dominance of the ascending generation is a broad principle applicable throughout Dasanetch society, and this is clearly illustrated by the bridewealth system. The range and terms of bridewealth payment are decided primarily by the bride's father's brothers, her abayam, although they typically consult with other members of the patriline. The abayam are also powerful in forcing payment when it is delinquent, and the younger generation recipients (e.g., the bride's brothers, nyarum le yabka) usually defer to them when there is a question or problem regarding payment.

The full range of possible cattle bridewealth recipients is theoretically large, but the most common guo foitch recipients presently include (stated in relation to the bride): father's brothers, brothers (half and full), father's sister, father's bond friend (usually his holding partner, ma kernoka), and mother's brother. The range of recipients is described by Dasanetch informants as having been greater in the past, and this is congruent with the reduced herds in recent decades, as described later. Note that the father of the bride does not himself receive bridewealth payments. An individual recipient usually does not receive all the cattle due him/her at one time, so that the actual distribution of cattle at any point in time prior to completion appears irregular.

Women cannot own property, neither horticultural plots nor cattle, even though they may acquire milking rights to cows. Instead they serve mainly as transfer agents for males; for instance, a father's sister transfers the head of cattle she receives in bridewealth to her husband.

One rather uncomplicated bridewealth payment record is summarized below by example. The debtor is Ekorisep, an Inkabela of the Etha clan and Nilimkorio age set who is a judge (ara). The bridewealth promised and paid is shown only for his first wife, also an Inkabela woman, whom he married in the early 1930's.

---

participate in gol (e.g., A does not participate in an A' gol ceremony although age set B' may).

Shebedam (small stock):

>Paid to 13 individuals--all immediately
>Recipients were (named according to relation to the new wife):
>>10 father's brothers--of these 10, 5 actually received the
>>>2 head of small stock which is the nor-
>>>mative payment, and the other 5 re-
>>>ceived equivalent payment in coffee
>>2 father's sisters --2 small stock each
>>1 mother's brother--2 small stock
>
>>13 total

Guo foitch (cattle);

>Promised 45 total
>Paid immediately:

oldest father's brother	5 head
2nd oldest father's brother	3 "
3rd " " "	2 "
4th " " "	1 "
(i.e., youngest)	

>Paid 1 month later:

2nd oldest father's brother	1 "
3rd " " "	1 "
4th " " "	1 "
oldest full brother	5 "
2nd oldest full brother	4 "
3rd " " "	3 "

Paid 2 months later:

oldest half-brother	5 "
2nd oldest half-brother	4 "
3rd " " "	3 "
4th " " "	2 "
mother's brother	2 "
older father's sister	1 "
younger " "	1 "
father's holding bond friend	1 "
	45 total

Although the total number of cattle to be paid is agreed to by both debtor and recipients, the timing and actual sequence of individual payments involves much discretion on the part of the debtor. There are, however, certain priorities conventionally followed by the debtor, as well as several traditional channels of pressuring the groom by the recipients (see below). One basic principle which is usually maintained is the priority of payment to the ascending generation close kin, i.e., the wife's father's brother (pl., abayam). I have recorded numerous instances of a father's brother (sing. abaya) forcing payment by the husband and successfully exerting pressure on the wife's brothers (nyarum yabka) to defer payment until his is completed. The wife's brothers themselves receive strong priority for payment relative to recipients other than the aba-yam, but the payments may be extended over a much greater period of time. Other recipients, such as mother's brother, father's sister, bond friends and more removed patrilineal members are, in recent years, less likely to receive payment. Exceptions occur where some economic or social interest is served by changing the order of payments, thus promoting the particular individual into a higher position in the normal sequence of payment. A major characteristic of the functioning of the bridewealth system is the constant negotiating regarding the order and rate of payments.

A relatively young debtor is concerned in particular with his relations with his wife's brothers, who tend to be near his own age (and possibly even within his own age set). He therefore wishes to develop lasting ties with them which will be exploitable economically, socially and politically. The wife's brothers' right to receive bridewealth from the marriages of any daughter their sister has (if the bridewealth for their sister is not completed) augments this situation. The father's brothers, however, are predictably very anxious for rapid payment. They wish to make the acquisition within their own lifetimes, and since their socio-economic ties are already established and more or less consolidated they have little reason to tolerate, let alone favor, highly extended payments. Exceptions to this principle are common where they have strong and long-standing ties with the debtor's patriline.

It is not unusual for no cattle to be transferred at all until after the birth of the first child, and it is generally easier to delay payment to a recipient group which is already bound in some way to the debtor or his patriline. Those only distantly connected previous to the marriage, on the other hand, often demand more regular and frequent payments. [8] I have encountered cases where virtually no cattle have been paid for years after the first and even the second child was born, even when the debtor had a fair-sized herd. Bridewealth may also be almost insignificant in amount when the debtor and/or the recipients are very poor. One very poor Oro man, for instance, paid only coffee and small gifts for his wife, and promised (but did not pay) only a few small stock. He was able to maneuver this because his bride's mother was a widow and there were no close agnates still living. This very limited bridewealth is very com-

---

[8] Randel informants have, on several occasions, stated the pressure for rapid payment which is applied by other segments as a clear reason that intra-segment marriages are predominant among the Randel.

mon among the poor Dasanetch living along the river and in the modern delta region.

A husband's skill in dealing with the range of bridewealth recipients is an important index of his ability to manage his whole economic and social base throughout his married life. This ability is largely dependent on his family's social and economic position as well as his own personal qualities. A young husband's decisions regarding payments are delicate ones, as he must create a balance between the crucial building of his own stock numbers on the one hand and the cultivating of economic and social bonds on the other. He withdraws stock from his father's herd (or his older brother's, if his father is dead) upon his first marriage, but must for the most part handle his own payments subsequently. A grown son often is called upon to help his father with contributions toward the latter's bridewealth payments, and this may be the cause of unspoken resentment. Finally, a man's sons incur his outstanding bridewealth debts upon his death. Implications of these facts for father/son relations are suggested below.

A husband may respond to strong pressures exerted on him by the recipients by threatening to send his wife away or actually doing so, especially in the early period of his marriage. Pressures on the debtor for payment of small stock or cattle may precipitate arguments or disputes which are settled in generally prescribed ways. These may result from a delay in cattle payments by the debtor, or because certain individuals feel slighted, or for other reasons. In any case, individuals (particularly a wife's brother or her father's brother) may come to the village of the debtor and discuss the matter, and they are either promised payment or put off in some way. Strong means of pressuring the debtor may also arise, such as the return of a wife by her father's brother(s) or her brothers (before shebedam is completed). The extreme form of protest by the recipient patriline is blocking the debtor's stock from leaving the kraal (nu) for the day's grazing. The latter action is very severe and may even result in stick fights. Even when arguments become heated and disputes become widespread among members of the debtor and recipient families, however, it is in the interests of both groups that the argument be settled, and the judges (ara) may become involved.

Divorce and death of spouse. --A wife who has been sent away (divorced) may remarry after a short time. If the divorce of a wife occurs before she has given birth to her first child, bridewealth is normatively refunded (except for one head of cattle). In the case of a wife's death prior to the birth of her first child, bridewealth is typically refunded. If the debtor wishes to maintain social/ economic ties already formed with his affines, however, he may marry a sister of the deceased woman, or he may not demand the return of the portion of the bridewealth already paid.

When a husband dies, the wife may be taken in levirate, especially when members of the dead husband's patrilineage wish to perpetuate or strengthen their ties with the wife's family. Any further children the woman has with a clansman of her husband taking her in levirate (usually the dead man's brother) are considered those of her dead husband, and the brother still retains the position of father's brother with respect to the children. If the wife is beyond child-bearing age, she may remain in co-residence with her husband's brother(s) or with a son or daughter. Some villages described (e. g., Kolin, described in Table 4-4 below) have a significant number of older widows as members of the village.

Inheritance. --When a male dies, any stock in his possession (i. e., those not already under the control of one of his sons or already spoken for by individuals he is indebted to) are divided among his sons; his brothers, by contrast, receive none. Widows receive no stock as owners, but they do retain milking rights. As mentioned above, a woman really serves more as an agent of transfer of wealth, in this case from her husband to her sons. The eldest son may retain the stock for his younger brothers until they reach marriageable age. It is not uncommon for this practice to result in the younger men receiving fewer than their anticipated share of the original number, due to stock deaths, bridewealth payments of the eldest brother, etc. Both cases where there was an equal division of a father's stock among his sons and those where the division asymmetrically favored the eldest son were encountered. Irregularities and disputes related to inheritance do occur, and one example of such is described briefly here:

Morita (Oro, Numor) described very poor relations with his father's brother's sons (his paternal cousins) which have involved bitter arguments and occasional stealing of his stock by his cousins. This resulted from Morita's father having taken his dead brother's wife in levirate, and instead of giving his dead brother's cattle all to the man's sons, he gave some to his favorite son, Morita, who was not really entitled to stock under Dasanetch custom. This precipitated much trouble over a number of years between the younger generation men long after the death of Morita's father. . . . It was particularly aggravated by Morita's stock number greatly depleting, through bridewealth payments and stock deaths by disease, so that restitution is not possible (if indeed desired by Morita).

128

TABLE 4-4

SELECTED VILLAGES: SOCIAL COMPOSITION

	Individual	Segment	Relation
Village I Location: Mort Kaliku	1 (Morita)	Oro	
	2	Oro	Age Mate of 1
	3	Oro	Age Mate of 1
	4	Inkabela	Husband of Daughter of 1
	5	Inkabela	Brother of 4
	6	Eleli	Age Mate of 1, 2, 3
Village II Location: Siri Gabite	1 (Lorokwacor)	Eleli	
	2	Eleli	Son of Father's Sister of 1
	3	Eleli	Sister's Husband of 1
	4	Eleli	Age Mate of 1
	5	Eleli	Youngest Brother of 1
	6	Eleli	Sister's Husband of 1
Village III Location: Siri Nakure	1 (Maen)	Inkabela	
	2	Inkabela	Son of 1
	3	Inkabela	Daughter of 1 (Widow)
	4	Inkabela	Daughter of 1 (Widow)
Village IV Location: Siri Barakonetch	1 (Lokwita Alun)	Eleli	
	2	Eleli	Younger Brother of 1
	3	Eleli	Younger Brother of 1
	4	Eleli	Younger Brother of 1
	5	Eleli	Age Mate of 1
	6	Eleli	Age Mate of 1
	7	Eleli	Wife's Sister of 1 (Widow)
Village V Location: Kolin (Poor Riverine Village)	1 (Karamit)	Eleli	
	2	Eleli	Age Mate of 1
	3	Eleli	Father's Brother's Son of 1
	4	Eleli	Sister's Husband of 1
	5	Eleli	Widow of 2 (Elderly)
	6	Eleli	Brother's Widow of 2 (Levirate)
	7	Turkana	Father's Wife of 1
	8	Randel	Widow of Brother of 1
	9	Rieli	Sister's Husband of 5
	10	Eleli	Son of 7
Village VI Location: Siri Morti	1 (Kinetch)	Inkabela	
	2	Inkabela	Brother's Son of 1
	3	Inkabela	Age Mate of 1
	4	Inkabela	Brother of 3
	5	Inkabela	Brother of 3, 4
	6	Inkabela	Brother of 3, 4, 5
	7	Inkabela	Brother of 3, 4, 5, 6
	8	Inkabela	Brother of 3, 4, 5, 6

TABLE 4-4--Continued

	Individual	Segment	Relation
Village VII Location:	1 (Ngytamoi)	Inkabela	
Siri Kalam	2	Inkabela	Age Mate of 1
	3	Inkabela	Mother's Brother of 1
	4	Inkabela	Wife's Brother of 1
	5	Inkabela	Wife's Father of 1
Village VIII Location:	1 (Siri)	Koro	
Siri Kalam	2	Randel	Sister's Husband of 1
	3	Koro	Wife's Sister's Husband of 1
	4	Koro	Mother's Brother's Son of 3
	5	Koro	Eldest Son of 3
Village IX Location:	1 (Narengamoi)	Randel	
Siri Barakonetch	2	Randel	Younger Brother of 1
	3	Randel	Younger Brother of 1, 2
	4	Randel (Note: Father Is Dead)	Younger Brother of 1, 2, 3

Cases of favoritism among brothers by a father are common and these may precipitate poor relations between the brothers involved in addition to worsening
the already existing, though usually unspoken tensions between the unfavored
brothers and their father.

Village Social Organization

Village size, in terms of the number of beehive huts, fluctuates among
the Dasanetch, and my field surveys indicate a range of from two to twenty huts.
A given village may itself oscillate in size within a year's time due, for example, to differences in herding location decisions by different stock owners within the village or insufficient pasturage in the immediate vicinity of the village
for all to remain together, attendance of an extended ritual by some of its members (e.g., dimi), etc. Although not exhaustive, the following factors are important in determining the size and social composition of villages: (1) location
of the village; (2) season and available resources (e.g., water, pasturage, and
horticultural land); (3) economic relations of individual males associated with
the village; (4) horticultural plots of males or heads of households (e.g., the
need for a plot); (5) potential mobility of households within villages under consid-

eration; (6) other close social relations of members (e.g., affinal and consan-
guinal); and (7) the traditions of a segment, patriline, etc., including relative
mobility.

Both males and females may change village associations a number of
times during a lifetime. A female, for instance, might experience the following shifts or readjustments, among others, in her primary village associations:
father's village, husband's village with his patriline, husband's village with his
age mates, and married children's or husband's brother's village subsequent to
her husband's death. For a male, residence shifts may be based on a broad
spectrum of possible associations, including his father, father's brother(s), sister's husband, wife's father, age mate(s), and brother(s). These shifts for
males and females reflect quite different magnitudes of change in the actual
functioning of the individual. Specifically, even though a woman's social ties
are structurally disrupted during her lifetime and she may change villages a
number of times, her concrete activities and functions in the village closely correspond from one to the other. By contrast, a man's movements from one village to another very often immediately reflect his changing responsibilities and
actual labor inputs, etc.

Tribal segments of males are often mixed within villages, but with widely
differing tendencies toward affiliation among specific combinations of segments.
These are considered here with regard to the segment affiliation of men, since
women are less often the pivotal figures in determining co-residence of households. The most common residence principle for all segments is one where
males from a single tribal segment form the social core of the village. There
is at present considerable mixing among the west bank segments, the most frequent combinations being:

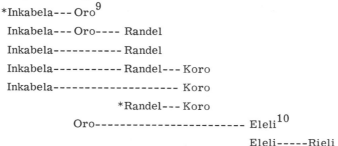

*Inkabela--- Oro[9]

Inkabela--- Oro---- Randel

Inkabela---------- Randel

Inkabela---------- Randel--- Koro

Inkabela------------------ Koro

*Randel--- Koro

Oro---------------------- Eleli[10]

Eleli-----Rieli

---

[9]Combinations marked with an asterisk are particularly common.

[10]Oro/Eleli and Eleli/Rieli combinations were largely limited to the impov-
erished riverine zone.

Other combinations do exist but are less common (e.g., Eleli/Inkabela; Randel/ Oro). These emphases within the full range of possible combinations strongly reflect the differential friendships and traditional relations among segments. Randel, and to a lesser degree the Eleli, villages are often without males from other segments. Some shift toward greater mixing of segments within villages has apparently occurred within recent decades (see Chapter 7).

There is marked heterogeneity of social relations actually functioning as the organizing principle for co-residence, and these are difficult to hierarchize in terms of importance. Those which were most frequently encountered are listed here according to two categories based on higher or lower frequency of occurrence. These are expressed in terms of relations to males and include only married males.

Relatively Common	Relatively Less Common
father/son(s)	sister's husband
brother(s)	father's brother's son
age mate(s)	wife's father
	bond friend (other than age mates and fellow clansmen)
	wife's brother

Whereas there are a fair number of villages organized basically along descent lines (e.g., ego's brothers, ego's sons and/or brother's sons), many sharply contrast in their basic organizing principle. In particular, many are organized on the basis of age set (and often sub-age set) membership, usually with members from within one segment, but sometimes cross-cutting tribal segments. It is often difficult to distinguish the actual initial principle operative in the formation of a village, for example, when age mates are co-resident and also have strong economic bonds such as having all received a horticultural plot from one of the members. There is a high frequency of combined organizational principles for a given village, where clan, age set and other relations are all operative in shaping the social composition of that village. Randel villages are apparently less frequently organized along age set lines relative to a patrilineal organization, as compared with the Inkabela, Oro and Eleli segments. Some examples of village social compositions are presented in Table 4-4.

Juridico-Political Patterns

Although political or authority patterns cannot be presented in full here, some of the more important features are described because they are clearly relevant to even the most basic understanding of Dasanetch society, and specifically to later sections of this monograph. These patterns are described for men, since women do not figure into the basic authority relations of the tribe. Within a household, there is a clear hierarchy of authority among women which is based primarily on marriage order, from the first-married through the most recently married wife. (This hierarchical order is reflected in everyday activities such as water treks, which are commonly done by the younger wives.)

Elders and judges. --Members of the senior age set (presently hari C, Nilimkorio) enjoy great social prestige, and younger persons defer to their demands and authority in most situations. Most elders have many fewer stock compared to the number that they had in previous mature years, because they have provided stock for each of their sons upon his marriage and they have been constantly subjected to wealth-redistributive pressures (particularly if they have passed dimi or are otherwise considered "big men"; exceptions to this occur where an elderly man continues to live with his sons and the collective herd is acknowledged to be his). Much of the economic prestige which an elder once had as a stock owner is, therefore, often gradually transformed into social prestige. It is important not to overstate the case, however. Elderly men are strongly influential with respect to their many younger agnates and affines, so that they are not without economic power, although this power is less direct. An elderly father, for instance, may frequently ask for (and nearly always receive) stock and many other items from his sons for his own consumption, or in order to make his own bridewealth payments. A mature man may, over a period of years, give his father a considerable number of stock for such purposes, and this is a reversal of his obtaining his initial herd from his father upon his marriage. An elderly man (e.g., as an abaya, or father's brother) also holds considerable power to both determine the size of and to demand payment of bridewealth from his brothers' sons-in-law.

Judges (ara) are chosen within each tribal segment from the senior age set. The word ara is translated as "bull," and this name is consistent with the economic and social centrality of cattle for the Dasanetch. Judges are selected from the senior age set of an age set pair designated according to a rotating pattern, as mentioned in an earlier section. In the Inkabela or normative segment, this rotational pattern is as follows:

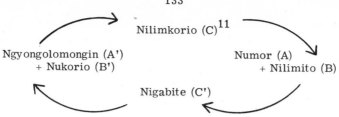

Fig. 4-8. --Rotational Pattern among Age Sets of Ara Membership.

The change from one age set of judges to another in all segments with a moiety system is signaled by the change in the Inkabela judges, and occurs when their numbers are substantially diminished. One exception to this occurs in the Rieli segment, where the judges have already rotated to Numor (A), apparently because the Nilimkorio individuals had mostly died. [12]

Two types of judges exist, a junior category and a senior one, or gal ethika and gal gunite, respectively. The death of a senior judge is followed by a replacement from the junior group, and a new junior judge is then recruited by the existing judges. In addition to being drawn from the senior age set, judges are selected according to moiety (dolo). The ara system of Inkabela provides for twenty judges, though this number did not exist at any time during my field work. No orderly distribution of judges by clan is operative in their selection, and in 1972 the number of Inkabela ara per clan varied from zero to five. One ara of each clan (tur) is considered the big man (ma gudoha) of that clan, and much of the business concerning individuals in his clan is dealt with through him although he meets with the other ara in the settlement of many disputes.

Some of the more important specific powers, duties and rights of judges may be mentioned here. (1) A major event for the judges is dimi, where they occupy an exclusive circle (nap) in the center of the ring of huts which are arranged in two semi-circles, according to moiety. At dimi the judges are given very special treatment and play a central role in the lengthy ritual event. It is at dimi that new judges are incorporated into the ranks following the deaths of previous ones. Although dimi is held separately (and consecutively) for each

---

[11] Nilimkorio (hari C) is the present age set of judges (as of 1972).

[12] Only those members of sub-age sets within the judges' age set who have passed a certain ritual (held infrequently) may actually become judges, so that the youngest modo of Nilimkorio who have not passed it are ineligible. The Inkabela ara, by example, are drawn from only the oldest three sub-age sets, excluding the fourth or youngest one.

moiety (<u>dolo</u>) of a given segment, the judges of one moiety may visit the judges of the other, and they frequently do. Thus, the separateness but also the complementarity of the moieties is evident. (2) Homicide is handled by the judges of the segment, who describe their responsibility as one of killing the guilty person (or seizing all the stock if that person flees). I found very few instances of homicide among the Dasanetch, however, and these were mostly accidental or where the individual killed was allegedly mistaken for a Turkana during a war. (3) Judges may intervene when an ox (<u>yer</u>) is stolen to be eaten, whether by an individual, sub-age set, etc. They do not become involved, however, unless the matter cannot be settled otherwise. (4) If a male obtains an ox from another male for slaughtering because of hunger in the former's household, but later refuses to repay the lender, the man demanding repayment may go to the <u>ara</u> (i. e., to his own clan's <u>ma gudoha</u>) for help. Several Inkabela <u>ara</u> indicated this type of dispute has increased in occurrence in recent years, but this is exceedingly difficult to verify. (5) When an unmarried young woman (<u>marti</u>) becomes pregnant, the immediate kinsmen of the woman typically go to the village of the man assumed to be the father, and demand the compensation (<u>nyaki-chul</u>) of eight cattle. If a marriage agreement is made, instead, bridewealth arrangements are made and some immediate payment is usually forthcoming. Again, although judges may be drawn into the conflict, they typically are not unless the parties involved are unable to resolve the situation. An important exception to this pattern of the Inkabela occurs, however, within the Randel segment. If an unmarried Randel woman becomes pregnant, the matter is much more severe in that she is chased away from her father's village and, in fact, from the tribal segment altogether. The woman is never allowed to return to the segment, and she usually takes refuge in and joins another segment (in the instances I encountered, the woman joined the Inkabela segment). The young man involved is usually severely beaten. (6) When adultery occurs and becomes known, the husband of the woman involved is the lawful recipient of six cattle. The judges retain one of the cattle transferred (which they slaughter and eat together) and transfer the other five to the husband. Again, exception to this type of settlement occurs among the Randel, where only small payments of coffee, tobacco and other items are made in the place of cattle. [13] (7) Bridewealth disputes are frequently brought before the <u>ara</u>. The blockage of a male's kraal (described in the section on bridewealth) in order to prevent his

---

[13] I found no instances of this offense among the Randel in the course of my field work.

stock from grazing is a highly serious form of dispute between a debtor and recipients of bridewealth, [14] and this conflict often necessitates the intervention of the ara. Individual ara are active in helping settle disputes within their respective clans, even when their counterparts from other clans may not be involved. They also have roles in certain rituals for their own clan members.

A few brief descriptions of some disputes which have involved the Inkabela ara during 1972 are illustrative of the judges' roles in Dasanetch society.

(1) One young, married male of the Etha clan of Inkabela took a young calf from the herd of another man of the same clan (but distantly related), while the herd was on trek and looked after by the young son of the owner. The owner was angry and went to the village of the ara of the Etha clan who was an od ethika (senior judge). This ara then sent for another judge of the clan, an od gunite (junior judge). The junior judge then went to the man who had stolen the calf and told him to return the animal, which he did. The owner was pleased and called all of the Inkabela ara to come to his village for coffee and feasting on the meat of an ayi (sheep or goat). Only ten of the ara came, as many were far away.

(2) An Inkabela man of the Etha clan and a Turnyerim (also Inkabela) man argued bitterly over the fact that the cattle of the Turnyerim man ate the regrowth in the millet plot of the Etha man, whereupon the Etha man chased the cattle away. The argument erupted into a stick fight, and the Etha man his his opponent over the head with his alcho (a type of stick) so hard that the Turnyerim man was killed. The ara of Inkabela heard about it and immediately gathered. The gal ethika, or senior ara, wanted to kill the man but many others (mostly gal gunite) believed it wasn't the Etha man's fault and that he shouldn't be killed for an accident. The gal gunite finally refused to kill him, and the man was left alone.

(3) A young Randel man was involved in an Eleli marti's (unmarried woman) pregnancy, and the woman's close agnates wanted to take all of the Randel man's father's cattle (the man himself was still unmarried). The Randel offender went to the Inkabela ara, asking for help. The Inkabela ara told the Eleli men to wait for them to settle the matter, and they then instructed the Randel father to pay eight cattle (as nyakichul) to the Eleli patriline. The ara themselves kept none of the cattle.

(4) A Koro man (makabana) "stole" an Oro marti, and a marriage settlement was then made between the Oro and Koro patrilines. The woman had no children and so before shebedam (small stock bridewealth) was finished, the Koro man sent her back to her father and demanded the return of the cattle bridewealth (i. e., guo foitch) which he had paid. The Oro father refused, and after an argument the Koro man went to the Inkabela ara for help. He first went to a junior judge, who in turn called the other judges. The Inkabela ara then consulted with the Oro ara, who in turn instructed the family to return most of the bridewealth cattle to the Koro man.

Judges are often close friends within any given tribal segment, since they have been associated as age mates for many years and have developed an ongo-

---

[14] This type of dispute erupted twice within the Inkabela segment in the first half of 1972, and at least three times in the previous year.

ing daily solidarity as well as experienced rituals, wars, feasts and countless other events together. They gather frequently for coffee and general visiting and often slaughter a head of stock for feasting. Relations between ara of different tribal segments vary, and they basically conform to the general patterns of friendship which obtain for the segments.

The Randel and Koro segments have neither ara nor moieties (dolo), but the elders (especially the big man, or ma gudoha, of each clan) fulfill some of the functions carried out by the ara of other segments. There is one most prominent political authority figure for the Randel segment, with the title of ma gudo eka, who is considered basically analogous in function to the ara of other segments. [15] Finally, as indicated by the dispute described above, the Inkabela ara are frequently active in settling disputes between Randel or Koro and other tribal segments.

Age set leaders. --This political office is one of leadership for an age set pair (e.g., A and A', B and B', C and C'). The office is usually patrilineally passed to the eldest son, although this principle is not always followed (e.g., as in the case of the recent Inkabela Nigabite successor who was even of a different clan from that of his Nilimkorio predecessor). [16] Succession to the office of the son often occurs before the father's death, as when the father is too old to continue with it or when he becomes an ara, providing his age set becomes the senior one. Although the individual man holding this position of age set leader (makansitch eka) usually has high authority and esteem, several galkansitch eka of the age set Numor (A) planned to give the office up in order to become ara just as soon as the judgeship rotation from C to A/B age sets occurs. The ma-

---

[15] The ma gudo eka of the Randel, for instance, can enter the exclusive circle (nap) of the ara at dimi. This office is passed along one patriline and passage of the office from one individual to the next occurs at a large ceremony. It is presently held by Acheriameri of the Agala clan, who has also the position of doing the actual cutting at circumcision (bilte) for all segments (until recently when an ara of Inkabela took over the function for that segment). The office was previously held by Acheriameri's older brother, Dabo, a man of great repute far beyond the Dasanetch tribe and widely revered within it.

[16] The hereditary principle for the makansitch eka office within the Randel segment is reportedly at variance with the normative pattern. According to Randel informants, including the present makansitch himself, it may pass from an eldest brother to his younger brother(s), and then to the eldest son of the eldest brother. This variation awaits verification, however. It is interesting to note that the present makansitch eka for the Randel described numerous duties he has performed which overlap considerably with those of the ara in other segments.

kansitch eka office in the Inkabela, Oro, and Eleli segments is occupied by an individual of the Nigabite (C') age set, whereas the Nilimkorio age set (C) is that of the ara, so that there is no overlap in the holding of these two offices within the same age set. Age set pair leaders are not necessarily of different clans within one segment; one segment, for instance, has two of the three age set leaders from the same clan. Their basic functions relate primarily to dispute settling and role modeling within their respective age set pairs, and each leader is powerful in both the junior and senior age sets of his pair (though this is not true for the makansitch eka from the age set which is junior to that of the ara). The political influence of a makansitch eka may also extend beyond his own age set pair and even beyond his tribal segment, depending upon his personal qualities, existing inter-segment relations and other factors. Age set leaders almost always have an assistant (called megaseli) of their own choosing, and in all cases studied the assistant was of the same age set, though frequently of a different sub-age set. This individual male assistant (megaseli) often shoulders many of the routine duties of the leader, especially if the latter is very old. By the time the son of the makansitch eka, who is of the alternate age set within the pair, is an adult he is often the major force in dealing with his own age set rather than his father, although final authority is his father's.

The responsibilities and powers of a makansitch eka sometimes overlap with those of the ara, but he is primarily associated with matters pertaining to his own age set pair. His functions and duties include the following: (1) Trouble arising between junior and senior age set members may be dealt with by him (or his assistant), and also that which may occur between younger and older sub-age set members if it reaches large enough proportions (cf. earlier section on age sets). (2) The age set leader may participate in the settlement of some disputes with which the judges are involved if his aid is needed, especially those involving a member(s) of his own age set pair. The following example describes such a situation.

> One Oro man (of the Turnyerim clan and Numor age set) stole an ox from another man (also Oro and Numor, but of the Ili clan), in order to buy a rifle. When the owner found out, he demanded the replacement of his ox, and the guilty man gave him one young cow (made). But the cow died within a month of disease, and the owner angrily sent the skin to the Turnyerim man, demanding replacement again. This time the Turnyerim man refused, so the Ili man went to the judges for help. The judges were unable to settle the matter as to whether the debt had in fact been paid, so they sent for the Numor makansitch eka, who decided that the Ili man should receive no further payment.

(3) An individual may go to the village of the makansitch eka or the megaseli for

138

refuge, and the latter is obliged to protect him until some settlement is reached. One case will illustrate how far an age set leader may be obliged to go in order to prevent severe trouble.

> Bilili, a megaseli for the Eleli, reported a Randel man sought refuge in his village because he feared physical harm by the Eleli man (of Bilili's own age set) whose ox (yer) he had stolen and slaughtered out of hunger. The Randel man had no stock at all, so Bilili scolded him severely and warned him never to do such a thing again, and sent him away. He then sent for the Eleli man whose ox had been stolen. Bilili gave his age mate one of his (Bilili's) own oxen, and warned him that if he harmed the Randel man he would have to return the ox and that he might also be beaten by his own age mates.

(4) The age set leader instructs the members of his age set pair in acceptable behavior patterns, as well as reprimands them for any wrongdoing, and members may come in groups or all together to his village for coffee and visiting.
(5) He settles trouble arising from incidents such as when an age mate (or group of age mates) goes to a stock camp and alters the horns of an owner's ox, slaughters or steals one of another man's stock, or becomes involved in a dispute of another kind with an age set mate or age set pair member.

Since the age set leader (and his eldest son, who is next in line for the office) frequently welcomes his megaseli and/or members of his age set pair by giving them coffee and slaughtering a head of small stock for meat, some demands are continually placed on his economic resources. These demands are usually not great, however, and they are probably offset by certain advantages he may gain through his office, such as favors and friendships with other big men (gal gudoha), which may include easy terms of bridewealth for his own wives. The prestige of the makansitch eka varies considerably from segment to segment, and is not only dependent upon the qualities of the individual himself, but also on the relative prominence of the ara of his segment. In the Oro, Eleli and Randel segments the office is presently a very strong one. Since age sets are a major institution in the lives of Dasanetch males, the office of the makansitch eka is a structurally significant one.

Government leaders. --The political office of government leader (makansitch ushomba) is not a traditional one, but instead was established subsequent to the Ethiopian occupation of the area. The number of individuals holding this office varies from one segment to the next: Inkabela--3, Oro--1, Eleli--1, Randel--1, Rieli--0,[17] Koro--0.[18] For Inkabela, there is one government

---

[17]Koro and Rieli are dealt with through the Inkabela makansitch ushomba.

[18]This distribution of government leaders was recorded in 1970.

leader for each age set pair. Like the age set pair leadership, this office is
normatively patrilineally passed. The social prestige of the makansitch ushomba is limited relative to that of the makansitch eka, though some government
leaders are members of patrilines which are traditionally very powerful ones.
In the latter case, such individuals may hold more influence.[19] Basically,
these individuals are liaisons to the Ethiopian government, their primary function being to serve as tax collectors. In return, the government pays them
small monthly salaries, which, along with the salaries for the Dasanetch who
join the Ethiopian police force, constitute most of the inflow of currency to the
Dasanetch (outside of the sale of Dasanetch stock or other items to foreigners).

Relations among Tribal Segments

Tribal segments were earlier described as quasi-territorial, with some
of them more clearly delineated geographically than others. The fact that most
of the segments were even more territorial in the past strengthens the predic-
tion that there would be considerable differentiation in the relations among them.
There is, in fact, strong variation in the degree and nature of economic and
social interactions among individual pairs of them. This is true with regard to:
(a) sharing of grazing and settlement lands; (b) co-residence in villages; (c) intermarriage; and (d) other socio-economic ties (through bond friendships, horticultural plot sharing, etc.).

Differentiation among inter-segment relations is clearly indicated not
only by synchronically viewed patterns of interaction, but also by numerous
oral traditions concerning segment origins, past disputes and modes of social
structural change. The structural change from endogamous to freely intermar-
rying moieties between segments, which is described in Dasanetch oral tradition, for example, indicates a widespread consciousness of traditionally strong
friendship between the Inkabela and Oro and a corresponding relative lack of
friendship of both with the Eleli. There is also an oral tradition of a dispute
involving physical violence between the Inkabela and Eleli. The selected oral
traditions of segment origins which are given in Appendix C show a recognition
of close ties between the Inkabela and Oro segments of a scale not shared by
any other combination of west bank segments. According to Inkabela and Oro
informants, the Eleli are considered relatively unfriendly and troublesome, and
the former two are more friendly with the Randel and Koro. Intermarriage, co-

---

[19]Such was certainly the case for Dabo of the Randel segment.

residence, and to some degree traditional grazing lands also show this differential alignment of Inkabela and Oro to the exclusion of Eleli. There are some Eleli men and their households who are members of predominantly Inkabela and Oro villages, but the presence of a man from one of the latter two segments living in an Eleli village is an unusual occurrence. One notable exception is the co-residence of some very poor Oro men with the Eleli of the riverine villages north of Rati.

Although of acknowledged different origins, the Eleli and Rieli segments overlap considerably in settlement (especially at Dielirieli and Turangole, see Fig. 5-12), and they have considerable intermarriage and other economic ties, [20] and generally carry on very friendly relations. It is significant that the average wealth status of these two segments overlaps greatly, and is below the average for the Oro and Inkabela segments. The west bank Eleli, as described earlier, are heavily concentrated in the region just north of Kalam, between Kalam and Koras and along the Omo River north of Rati. This Eleli settlement is rather stable and apparently long-standing. There is considerable overlap between Eleli and Randel settlement and grazing in the plains north of Kalam (see Chapter 5), and intermarriage is fairly common between Eleli women and Randel men. Incidences of Randel men living in predominantly Eleli villages are not common, however, and this is correlated with the general differential in economic wealth between the two segments (in favor of the Randel). The Randel express a very strong dislike for horticulture, and consistent with the general tribal value placed on stock raising (which the Randel exemplify), they tend to look down upon the Eleli who engage heavily in horticulture. This is illustrative of the general pattern whereby men of economically more favored or more prestigious segments (in terms of the emphasis they place on stock raising) tend to avoid co-residence with those engaged in less prestigious activities.

Randel and Koro segments have lived in co-residence for many years, according to older informants. Intermarriage is common between them, although some exogamy occurs. They are further bound by their mutual strong emphasis on herding and by their marked social structural differences from the other segments. Both segments intermarry and share numerous ties with the Inkabela in particular.

Segment interaction is also exercised along other lines, such as sharing

---

[20] Both segments have a strong subsistence emphasis on horticulture, for instance, and they share many planting locales.

at ritual times and during periods of hostility with surrounding tribes, and in
the performance of certain clan functions between segments. [21]

Discussion and General Conclusions

Changing social relations during male and female life cycles. --The above
sections have concerned themselves with a description of the essential social
institutions which determine the web of social relationships into which an individual Dasanetch is integrated. This may be viewed as the normal socialization
process within the tribe. These institutions were described as relatively autonomous entities for the purposes of presentation. From the viewpoint of the Dasanetch themselves, however, the elements of the social organization which
have been discussed separately are fully integrated. In order to develop an
appreciation of the Dasanetch's experience as well as to gain some insight into
the way in which these organizational principles interact to serve as binding
forces within the tribe, we may consider the relative importance of the various
social units and their appropriate social functions at different points within an
individual life cycle. It should be clear from the previous discussion that no
single characterization of a life cycle, even in an idealized form, can accurately represent both females and males for this system. Consequently they will be
treated separately.

Dasanetch males.

The schema presented in Fig. 4-9 is an idealized life cycle for a Dasanetch male, including both the major events in his life as well as the changes in
different social relations in changing phases in his life. [22]

The strength and nature of a male's relationship to his patriline, though
always maintaining a functional significance, undergoes considerable change
during his life cycle. In his earliest years (childhood and early boyhood) his
position within the patriline is one of dependence, in which the most closely
related members of the patriline exercise the greatest amount of control.

---

[21] For instance, a member of the Galbur clan of Inkabela may be called by
members of another segment (if no person of their segment with an analogous
clan power or duty is available) to help protect cattle from crocodiles during a
crossing of the river. The Galbur, it is believed, can perform a ritual which
causes the crocodiles to sleep, thus enabling the animals to cross safely.

[22] For the purposes of this schema, the pattern is shown for a man with one
wife only.

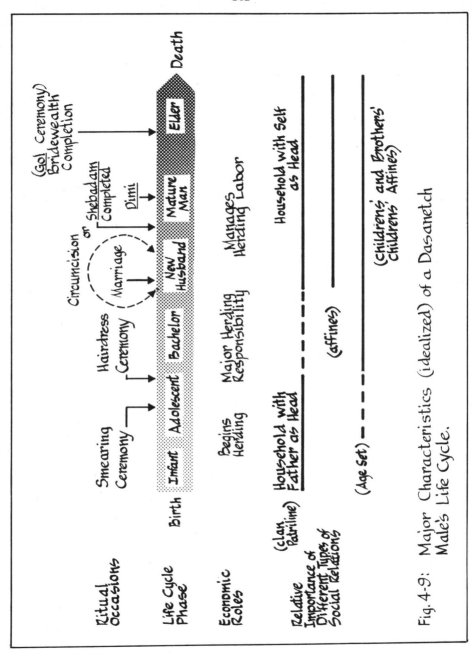

Fig. 4-9: Major Characteristics (idealized) of a Dasanetch Male's Life Cycle.

There is a gradual lessening of the control exercised by patriline members over his daily activity as he approaches adolescence and bachelorhood. This period is marked by a corresponding increase in the amount of time spent with and the amount of influence exerted by age set mates (and especially sub-age set mates). But even in the years immediately preceding a man's first marriage, when his ties with his age set mates are very strong, he must maintain his relations with his father, from whose herd he will withdraw the stock necessary for beginning his new role as household head (upon his marriage). At the time of marriage the choice of residence location presents itself. Not surprisingly, those sons who continue to live in the same village as their father and/or brothers maintain stronger patrilineal ties, while those who begin uxorilocal residence or co-residence with age mates undergo a somewhat greater attenuation of functional lineage ties. After his marriage, a man usually continues strong ties with his patriline, all the while gaining in authority and prestige within it. His position within the patriline shifts dramatically with the establishment of his own household as he now becomes relatively autonomous, as a manager of his own herd and a manager even of others' labor power (e.g., his wife's and later his children's). Establishment of his own household has another significance: it represents the successive regeneration of the basic unit of the patrilineage. In the latter years of a man's life, it is clearly to his advantage to maintain strong ties within the patriline, particularly with his brothers. Even after the transfer of wealth (cattle and small stock) to his sons, he carries considerable authority in many situations and typically participates in decisions central to the maintenance of the lineage interests (e.g., bridewealth arrangements). He of course continues receiving bridewealth from his brothers' daughters' marriages, and this is a primary means of obtaining stock. Increasingly, though, his strongest bonds are with his age mates (and a few bond friends).

From the time a young boy is able to walk and talk, it is very likely that he will be playing and developing skills with other children (especially boys) of the same age. As he becomes old enough to herd small goats and sheep (see next chapter) and to do other small chores, he begins developing ties with future age set mates, especially of his own sub-age set group (modo). Particularly by the time he is in charge of a herd and spends much time at foretch (stock camp, often some distance from the village), he is profoundly influenced by his age mates, and this period can be characterized as one in which he is extending his social ties laterally within the social hierarchy. The above schema indicates that these age set bonds are maintained throughout the remainder of the life cycle. There is a structural complementarity between the social units of the patrilineage and the age set, and this is crucial to the resolution of systemic tension.

Dasanetch females.

The major distinction between the female and male life cycle patterns for members of the Dasanetch tribe with respect to social units lies in the fact that within her life cycle a female shifts her functional membership in both clan and age set, whereas the lifelong membership of a male in these units is determined and fixed at birth by reference to those of this father. This shift for the female is a major discontinuity in her life experience.

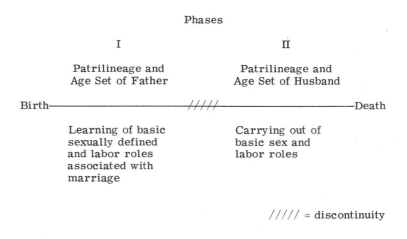

Phases

I	II
Patrilineage and Age Set of Father	Patrilineage and Age Set of Husband

Birth——————————/////——————————Death

| Learning of basic sexually defined and labor roles associated with marriage | Carrying out of basic sex and labor roles |

///// = discontinuity

Fig. 4-10.--Discontinuity in the Dasanetch Female's Life Cycle

As described earlier in this chapter, the age set recruitment principle for females is that a daughter's age set is of the same name as her father's (with the prefix ini-, meaning "daughter") making other age set membership opposite to that of her brothers; women are officially adopted into the age set (and clan) of their husband upon completion of the payment of the cattle promised in the bride-wealth agreement. Note that while the time between the change in residence (living with her husband) and the full recognition of the woman as part of the social units to which her husband belongs is usually considerable, the actual contact and development of ties between a woman and members of her husband's primary social units are immediate upon her marriage. This is reflected by the more detailed schema of the female's life cycle shown in Fig. 4-11. A Dasanetch female, then, is at each point in her life functionally a member of the same primary social units as the dominant male to whom she is attached. There can exist for females, therefore, no structurally determined experience of solidarity with other females comparable to the solidarity available to males in the age set and patrilineage. A male undergoes no comparable major disruption and instead only broadens and deepens ties within the same age set and patrilineage as well as widens his social relations beyond them. This structural block to social unit continuity for women is consistent with their exclusion from any property holding (whether stock or horticultural land). Consequently, women are effectively prevented from attaining any economic independence or social solidarity.

Relationships among structural units. --The discussion earlier in this chapter has identified the three major structural constituents of the Dasanetch social system as the clan (and more particularly, the patriline), the age set and the moiety. This section focuses on the relationships which hold among these constituents, with the purpose of identifying those aspects of the relationships which induce either stability (a binding effect upon individuals within the social matrix) or tension (a splintering effect upon individuals within this matrix). In other words, the question addressed here is what adaptive value these organizational principles have.

With this purpose in mind, let us first consider the lineage system. The effects of this structure, especially the tensions generated, will form the basis for the consideration of the other two principles. This is because the patriline, as the basic property holding group and the organizational focus of the main economic functions, is the chief source of structural tension in the Dasanetch society. In examining the age set organization, for example, we shall focus on how it helps to deal with the tension generated in the lineage structure. Since the Dasanetch economic and social order is centered upon the Dasanetch male, following remarks necessarily assume as their subject the Dasanetch male. A commentary on the applicability of these principles for the Dasanetch female is held until after this section.

Binding and splintering tendencies within the patriline. --The most powerful economic and social binding forces within the Dasanetch social system are located within the descent line. The minimal patrilineage of two generations

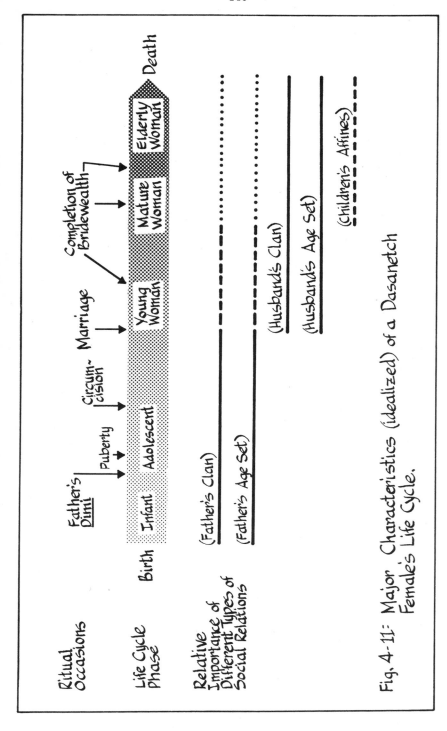

Fig. 4-11: Major Characteristics (idealized) of a Dasanetch Female's Life Cycle.

manifests these economic and social ties in their strongest forms. In general, as the size of the lineage unit under consideration increases, the strength of the bonds between any two randomly chosen individuals in that lineage decreases.

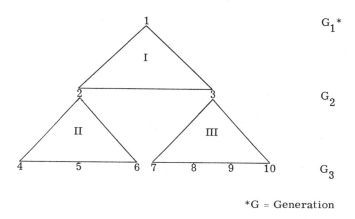

*G = Generation

Fig. 4-12. --Schema for Minimal (Two-Generational) Patrilineages

In the schema above, showing three such minimal (two generational) patrilineages[23] (I, II, III), several types of binding forces may be identified. For example, brothers 4, 5, and 6 depend upon their father 2 for food (before establishing their own households), initial stock to establish their own herds upon marriage, and inheritance. The father 2 is, in turn, dependent upon his sons 4, 5, and 6 for labor power in order to maintain and augment his own material and social capital (see Chapter 5). The relationships between the father 2, and his sons 4, 5, and 6 are mirrored exactly at the next higher step of the patrilineage by the relationships between the grandfather 1, and the fathers 2 and 3, respectively.

A given generation within a minimal patrilineage unit (e.g., brothers 4, 5, and 6) is bound by the practice of levirate wife-taking, their common interest, in their sister's marriage and bridewealth arrangements (and later, in their daughters' marriages and bridewealth arrangements), and mutual aid in certain disputes and sharing in times of need. In addition to bonds deriving from their position with respect to individual number 1, the bonds between 2 and 3 created

---

[23]Henceforth, "minimal patrilineage" is to be understood as denoting the two-generational or two-step patrilineal segment formed by a father and his offspring, with attached wife or wives.

by their mutual interests as the ascending generation relative to their respective sons (individuals 4 through 10) clearly coincide with their interests as members of the same minimal, two-generational, patrilineage unit. These ascending generational interests are typically effectively asserted. The interests of the younger generation (individuals 4 through 10) coincide structurally (with respect to the lineage system) to a lesser degree as they are not all members of the same minimal patrilineage unit. This, in combination with the strength of the principle of age seniority, insures that their generational interests are not as strongly asserted as in the case of individuals 2 and 3. This is an example of the general tendency for relationships between individuals of larger lineages to be less intense than those between individuals within smaller lineages.

An individual Dasanetch male within a patrilineage experiences continuity in his relationships with close agnates as he passes during his lifetime from a position of complete dependence and subjugation to one of independence and authority (e. g., from junior generational status within a household to senior generational status as head of a household). The dependent position of children with regard to their physical survival as well as their critical early socialization leads to the establishment of intense personal bonds within their own lineage. Other binding relations within the patrilineage include food-sharing during times of hardship, unity through ritual occasions and everyday functions, and the consciousness of a common origin.

Thus, the descent group is the locus of strong binding forces within the Dasanetch social system. But this same organizational principle also contains structural relations which generate the strongest internally induced social tensions found in that system. If one considers the minimal two-generational patrilineage it can be clearly seen that the major tensions arise between generations, that is father/son, as opposed to intra-generational conflicts, although this is not to suggest that the latter are absent. Among those situations which generate father/son tensions are the following:

(1) Father's control over the son's labor power. This includes not only the power to decide where and how the son will spend his labor power in activities directly supporting the household's economic position, but also the power to place the son's labor power under the control of other males (e. g., the father's age mate or bond friend, his brother, or his affines) for herding or horticultural activity.

(2) Father's control over the son's marriage. This control takes the form of the father's authority to decide when to release the stock necessary for

a son's initial bridewealth payment and for the establishment of the son's own herd.

(3) The incurring of debts by the father which are inherited by the son(s). An example of incurred debts by sons is bridewealth debt not completed by the father.

(4) Father's demands on his sons even after their marriages and establishment of their own households. It is clear both from normative reports from informants and from cases which I encountered in the field that even after the son's marriage the father continues to exercise some control (albeit more indirectly) over the stock wealth and the labor power of his sons. This implicit although real control over the son's herd, for example, is easily seen in the affirmative response by sons to the request of their fathers for stock to be used in ritual, for the latter's bridewealth debts, for slaughter to welcome guests, or for consumption during times of hardship. The amount of control exercised by the father and recognized by a grown son varies widely as a function, for example, of whether they reside together as well as of the individual personalities involved.

(5) Father's association and solidarity with his brothers in relation to their common father, as head of their minimal two-generational patrilineage. As previously stated, the father and his brothers have structurally convergent economic and social interests with respect to their father. These interests tend to be maintained with respect to the next generation, the sons of these men. One particular situation in which these convergent interests are clearly revealed is the bridewealth negotiations and payments: this may take the form, for example, of the father's brothers receiving preference in bridewealth payment resulting from the marriages of the father's daughters.

(6) Father/son competition for young women. A structural tension resulting from the polygamous system of the Dasanetch is that women are the focus for competition among men, including fathers and sons. This last situation is somewhat restricted because of the endogamous marriage rule with regard to moiety within a given segment, so that such competition between father and son is confined to women from other segments.

While it might at first glance appear that the binding and splintering tendencies within the patriline are fairly well balanced, this is somewhat misleading. If we review the two sets of structural situations, a certain asymmetry emerges. The set of binding forces associated with the patrilineage generally have their strongest effect in the earlier years of a Dasanetch male's life and

tend to wane as he approaches marriage. Conversely, the splintering tendencies tend to increase in intensity as the male reaches the point in life where he
will establish a new household. The way in which these increasing tensions are
dealt with structurally forms the basis for the subsequent discussion of the age
set pair and moiety systems.

The patrilineage discussion has thus far concentrated on horizontal or generational situations. Within the patrilineage, one may also identify and discuss
the binding and splintering effects found in collateral relationships. Relations
among brothers, for instance, which tend to induce solidarity include: (1) their
convergent economic and social interests with respect to the patriline's ascending generation in general, (2) their common interests with respect to their father in particular, (3) their shared experience in performing labor tasks (especially in herding) and in their early socialization, (4) their convergent interests
in the selection and acceptance of husbands for their sisters, and (5) levirate
wife-taking. By contrast, the features of their relations which tend to induce
tension include: (1) competition for the same stock; (2) competition for the
same material goods in terms of inheritance; (3) competition for the same wom-
en; (4) tensions among brothers resulting from birth order differences (e.g.,
relating to marriage order, membership in different sub-age sets, the hierarchy of authority with regard to herding). In addition to these filial tensions,
problems sometimes result when a father dies and his eldest married son assumes control of the stock of any unmarried sons until their respective marriages.

In the structural situation which obtains between patrilineal cousins, certain of the binding and splintering forces listed above continue in importance
(e.g., shared experience within the segment as a binding or consolidating influence, and competition for the same women as a tension-producing situation).
An additional splintering tendency results from the fact that males who are patrilineal cousins are members of distinct economic and social units, that is,
their wealth accumulation and holding and transfer units are different. Given
an infinite amount of natural resources, this situation would be uninteresting.
In the actual case under consideration, however, the natural resources available to the tribe as a whole are severely limited. Thus, some structural competition among the wealth accumulating, holding, and transferring patrilineage
units for these natural resources follows under the conditions presently prevailing in Dasanetch land.

In summary, then, it appears that the balance of forces induced by the organizational principle of the patriline favors the splintering or disintegrative tendencies along the following two dimensions: (1) between generations (a generalization of the basic father/son tension), which results in a horizontal fragmentation within the Dasanetch social system; and (2) between minimal or n-step patrilineages, which is a conflict rooted primarily in distinct socio-economic interests and results in a vertical fragmentation. It is clear from the above discussion that the tensions generated within and between patrilines do not cause critical vertical and horizontal ruptures in the social fabric. This calls for some explanation. The first portion of the explanation derives from a consideration of the way in which the age set system functions.

The age set system as a stabilizing force. --The age set (hari) system, I suggest, displaces the focus of inter-generational tension from the patrilineage(s) onto a structurally distinct institution, thereby countering the patrilineal tensions. Consider the recruitment principle for the age set pair: this principle insures that a man's father and sons are identified as members of the age set in opposition to himself. This shared membership in the same age set for grandfathers and sons unites alternate generations in a way which tends to structurally offset the tension between adjacent generations (e. g., father and son), the main locus of patrilineal tension. Thus, cohesion of the patriline is promoted and the tendency for fragmentation along generational lines is alleviated (Fig. 4-13). The age set principle also addresses the problem of vertical fragmentation or splits between minimal patrilineages. Age set membership within a segment crosscuts the individual minimal patrilineages as members of different minimal patrilineages identify with each other as members of the same hari. This is true both within one generation and between alternate generations of different patrilineages.

The partial displacement of the conflict between adjacent generations, then, is accomplished by removing that conflict from within the individual patrilineage and projecting it onto the generalized relationship between the two sets of an age set pair. The adjacent generational conflict is generalized across the society and institutionalized by channeling it into a framework of prescriptive deference and respect (the normative pattern of behavior of the junior age set toward the senior age set), which in turn allows it to be contained. Now the makansitch eka, i. e., the authority figure of the age set pair, may be recognized as a significant unifying force. The makansitch eka functions to lessen certain generational tensions as well as other hari problems which were de-

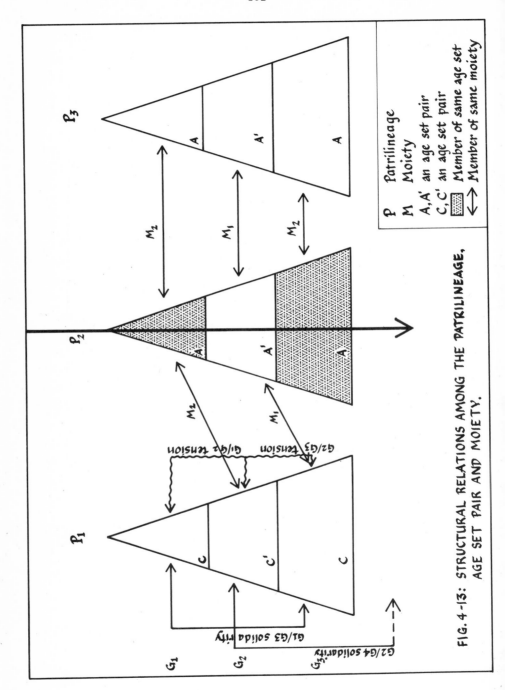

FIG. 4-13: STRUCTURAL RELATIONS AMONG THE PATRILINEAGE, AGE SET PAIR AND MOIETY.

scribed earlier. He accomplishes this both by direct intervention and by the power implicit in his position as acknowledged leader of the age set pair. In sum, the age set pair principle of organization integrates individuals along both the vertical and horizontal planes of structural cleavage, in both cases bringing together into solidarity groups individuals who are otherwise set in structural opposition to each other within the lineage system.

The moiety system as a stabilizing force. --The second social organizational principle which addresses the tensions generated within and between patrilines is the moiety (dolo) system. The functional significance of the moiety system is best revealed by considering the two major occasions for which it serves overtly as an organizing principle, marriage and dimi.

Marriage is a time of considerable structural tension for Dasanetch males. There are two cases to consider: (1) Assume the position of the prospective groom's patriline. From this point of view the father/son structural tensions are significant in that marriage is a time when the son makes an immediate demand on the herd, both for his initial bridewealth payments and for the animals which he will use to start his own herd. The father and son are united with respect to the bride's patriline, however, on the issue of bridewealth negotiation. (2) Assume the position of the bride's patriline. Her father (ya) and father's brothers (abayam) are the key figures in the bridewealth arrangements (although the father is not a direct recipient himself), and they are responsible for securing the most advantageous terms for the patriline. From the point of view of the bride's patrilineage, her labor power is being lost, and this loss must be offset by securing some degree of economic and social compensation in return. In the context of this structural opposition of the two lineages, sensitivity and skill is required of both negotiating parties. At the same time issues such as the portion of stock to be given in immediate versus delayed payments and the order of distribution of payments may create generational tension (structural and sometimes quite evident) within the bride's patrilineage once the negotiation is made. Thus, within both of the lineage groups both generational and inter-lineage tensions are associated with marriage.

It is with this perspective that the stabilizing effect of the moiety system may be understood. The moiety principle cross-cuts the patrilineages involved in a way reminiscent of the age set pair principle. The moiety endogamous marriage rule guarantees that the father of the bride and the father of the groom (if of the same tribal segment, or en) are of the same moiety. Further, within the same segment the brothers of the bride and the groom will always be of the same moiety. [24] The moiety system imposes upon the basic pattern of inter- and intra-lineage relations, a larger structure: a set of endogamous groups, the relations between which are defined by the impossibility of marriage, and which contain no adjacent generational (e.g., father/son) relations to become foci of intra-group tension (since the adjacent generations within any given patriline belong to opposite moieties). Although father/son tensions still exist within the patrilineages, one of the forms of competition between father and son with regard to marriage between segments is eliminated within the segment through the moiety endogamy rule, by insuring that they may not compete for the same women. [25]

Dimi is the other major occasion besides marriage for which moieties form the organizing principle. This lengthy ritual (lasting several weeks) is held successively for the two moieties within each tribal segment in which it occurs (all but Randel and Koro). The passing of dimi is one of the most important single events in a Dasanetch male's life, and at this point he enters the status of "big man." [26] This status in turn corresponds to high demands on him for bridewealth payments and various gifts and sharing gestures, so that dimi also marks the growing tendency for this individual to transform his economic wealth into social wealth. The many days of dimi include the (concentrated) large scale slaughter of cattle and small stock. This slaughter of animals may be considered a sort of bridewealth-in-reverse, whereby the father of the future bride (a man passes dimi when his daughter is near puberty) sacrifices stock before his patriline is to receive stock as bridewealth payment for her when she marries. Perhaps the most revealing aspect of the dimi ritual is the presence and activities of the ara. The ara are the recognized bearers of political power in terms of the moiety system, and by their position of power over members of both moieties, then, serve as a unifying force. They have the ability to serve as a redress mechanism for disputes arising both within and be-

---

[24] Note that there is no necessary relationship between membership in the same age set and membership in the same moiety, and the moiety principle may function to bring together Dasanetch males who are in a structurally antagonistic position with respect to the age set as well as the patrilineage principle.

[25] It should be recalled that the Koro and Randel segments have no moieties.

[26] As indicated earlier, the term "big man" (ma gudoha) is used in other ways among the Dasanetch, including for those males holding political office, those having relatively great stock wealth, etc.

tween moieties. Even though the judges are drawn from the moieties (as well as from the senior age set), their roles as agents of political appeal and unification are, as explained earlier, much broader than those institutions which are moiety determined.

Summary.--The principles of age set and moiety have been presented to show the way in which they interact with tensions generated within and between the patrilineages. These two principles, as well as the political figures associated with them, have a high adaptive value for a system where considerable generational (intra-lineage) and inter-lineage structural tensions exist, i.e., they act as mechanisms or agents to bring together individuals set in opposition to each other by the patrilineal principle. More specifically, inter-generational tensions occurring within the patrilineage are displaced onto and generalized by the age set system, thus institutionalizing these tensions. In combination with the unity derived from alternate generations of a patrilineage having identical age set membership, this tends to preserve the integrity of individual patrilineages, thus addressing the problem of horizontal fragmentation. Cross-patrilineage age set identification (within and between segments) serves to reduce possible tensions between patrilineages, i.e., vertical fragmentation. Further, the moiety system counters horizontal fragmentation through elimination of competition between fathers and sons for women and through the unity derived from alternate generations of a patrilineage having identical moiety membership. It too may provide identification which crosscuts patrilineages and thus reduces the tendency for vertical fragmentation.

Given the economic position of women in the Dasanetch tribe, it should not be surprising that there is no requirement for similar interaction patterns regarding their position in their patrilineages, age sets, and moieties. For instance, one adaptive value of these interactions in the case of males is grounded in the fact that the age set system institutionalizes the conflict generated within the patrilineage, arising primarily although not exclusively from economic tensions. Since women are structurally barred from holding property in the Dasanetch system, there are no such inter-generational tensions. Therefore, there is absolutely no adaptive value from the standpoint of social stability in providing a system of solidary female groupings. In other words, without this root economic conflict, the existence of a female solidarity unit (such as the age set for Dasanetch males) might prove to be the basis for disruption of the pattern of economic exploitation of women, rather than being of high positive adaptive value in promoting stability. The structural transformation of a woman's membership from her father's age set to her husband's serves as an indicator of the recognition that property has been transferred between the two patrilineages.

It may be predicted, on the basis of the preceding discussion of structural relationships and displacement mechanisms operative within Dasanetch society, that the overall structural and functional stability of the system is relatively high. This is true, not only because of the complementary functions of the age set and moiety systems with respect to patrilineally generated tensions, but also because there is considerable overlap among pathways of redressing disputes. That is, a number of types of disputes may be settled alternatively by the parties involved (exclusively), their respective patrilineages, the makan-sitch eka (or his megaseli) of one or more of the age sets of the parties involved, the ma gudoha of the involved parties' clan(s), or the judges (ara). Multiple ways of settling a given dispute is a situation particularly adaptive in a society which is basically mobile and which is fluid in its organizational patterns of settlement, seasonal movements, etc. After a basic examination of the material production system of the Dasanetch in Chapter 5, the present significance of this relative stability of social relations will be considered within the context of the large scale environmentally and governmentally induced changes.

CHAPTER 5

DASANETCH PATTERNS OF PRODUCTION

AND UTILIZATION OF PRODUCT

Introduction

The previous chapter has discussed the most basic social processes of
the Dasanetch system. One of its conclusions was that the combination of structural principles of lineage, age set and moiety result in a high level of societal
stability. The present chapter examines the Dasanetch system of material production, [1] after which the interrelations of material production and the societal
and environmental complexes as a whole will be discussed within the conceptual
frameworks of a S/E system model and that of mode of production (in Chapters
6 and 7). Although this chapter treats the Dasanetch branches of production separately for the most part, it should be clear that the branches cannot be fully
understood apart from the broader set of productive relations, and for that matter its social and environmental framework. This is expressed well by Polanyi
(1957) where he says: "The human economy, then, is embedded in institutions,
economic and noneconomic. The inclusion of the noneconomic is vital. For
religion and government may be as important for the structure and functioning
of the economy as monetary institutions or the availability of tools and machines
themselves . . ." (p. 250).

The Dasanetch system of production may be described as "primitive" only
with some careful definition of this term. The meaning I intend closely corresponds to the description given by Firth:

> The term primitive is a relative one . . . it implies a system of simple non-
> mechanical technology, with little or no innovation, directed to maintenance
> rather than increase of capital assets, and with relatively low differentiation
> of economic roles of people in production, entrepreneurial and management
> functions. Usually it is without overt market institutions or generally accept-
> able media of exchange for rapid conversion of one type of resource into
> another. (1965: 17)

---

[1] "Production is employed here in its more narrow sense, the totality of
the operations aimed at procuring for a society its material means of existence"
(Godelier, 1972).

A number of more refined characteristics of primitive[2] economies are offered
by Sahlins (1972) in the context of his discussion of primitive exchange systems.
But although more precise, these characteristics are still in part impressionis-
tic. Those which are applicable to the Dasanetch system of production are:
(a) food holds a commanding position in the economy; (b) day-to-day output does
not depend on a massive technological complex nor a complex division of labor;
(c) a domestic mode of production, whereby there are household-producing
units, division of labor by sex and age dominant, and production that looks to
familial requirements; (d) direct access by domestic groups (or producing units)
to strategic resources; (e) rights to control returns go along with rights to use
resources of production; (f) there is limited traffic in titles or income privi-
leges in resources; (g) societal ordering is primarily by kinship.

Meillassoux (1964: 90), in his economic anthropological study of the Guoro of the Ivory Coast, emphasizes the quality of self-subsistence as primary in
defining an economy as traditional or primitive:

> Self-subsistence is the major characteristic of so-called traditional or primi-
> tive societies organized according to a system of kinship. To be sure, few
> societies are totally self-subsisting but the conditions of subsistence remain
> the same as long as exchange with the outside world have not introduced spe-
> cialized labor into the groups, that is, so long as they do not reach a critical
> threshold beyond which the group is incapable of doing without the imports
> without disrupting its fundamental structure.

Meillassoux defines only one mode of production for the Guoro (see discussion
in Chapter 6), and his description of lineage-based and segmentary societies as
based on "the exploitation of the soil,[3] self-subsistence, the utilization of short
term techniques and the use of human energy as the principal energy source"
(p. 89), is largely applicable to the Dasanetch system of production. Some criticisms of several aspects of Meillassoux's work are discussed briefly in Chapter 6.

---

[2]The term primitive is explained by Sahlins in this manner: ". . . the
indicative condition of primitive society is the absence of a public and sovereign
power: persons and (especially) groups confront each other not merely as distinct interests but with the possible inclination and certain right to physically
prosecute those interests. Force is decentralized, legitimately held in sever-
alty, the social compact has yet to be drawn, the state nonexistent" (p. 140).

[3]Exploitation of the soil may include, when considering the Dasanetch system, stock grazing and browsing, horticulture and gathering. Hunting and fishing are exceptions.

Branches of Production: Range of Variation

Although the Dasanetch are primarily a pastoral society, and were described in Chapter 4 as part of the "cattle complex" of East Africa, production does not focus only on stock, particularly in recent years. Instead it includes different combinations of stock raising, horticulture, fishing, gathering and hunting. Although detailed information from individual households reveals strong variability in emphasis among these branches, an idealized representation of combinations along the continuums of variation is shown below.

Stock raising only ---> Mostly stock raising, ---> Nearly equal
with limited horticulture dependence on stock
raising & horticulture

No stock, with entire <--- Heavy emphasis on horticulture,
subsistence from horticulture, with few stock. Limited or
fishing, gathering, hunting sporadic reliance on gathering
(especially crocodile) and/or fishing or hunting

The continuum from reliance on domestic stock raising alone to diversification of productive activities correlates with decreasing wealth status, as wealth is defined by the Dasanetch.

The trend toward means of subsistence alternatives to stock raising which connote a lower wealth status, and the whole ideology supporting the centrality of cattle (and stock generally), dictates that a given individual prefers to occupy a position as close to stock raising alone, or stock raising with limited horticulture as possible. As described earlier (Chapter 4) the main social institutions, including social structural features, bridewealth, important ritual occasions and so forth, are intimately connected with relationships to cattle. Although horticulture is not the favored activity, a vast number of households have relied on it in recent years, and it carries no real stigma when supplemental to stock raising.[4] There is, however, a strong cultural bias against fishing, even though many have no recourse but to engage in it. Consequently, those at the lower end of the wealth spectrum are at a strong disadvantage in numerous social respects as well as in subsistence terms. These include the range of potential marriages open to them, their ability to enter exchange relationships which are often crucial in times of stress, and their ability to obtain sufficient stock in order to pass certain rituals which are of extreme importance in Dasanetch life (such as gol, dimi, and so forth). Disruption of the so-

---

[4]Stock raising will henceforth refer to the production of both cattle and small stock.

cial fabric of an individual's life which is characterized by economic depriva-
tion is well expressed by Firth: "In primitive communities, the individual as
an economic factor is personalized, not anonymous. He tends to hold his economic position in virtue of his social position. Hence to displace him economically means a social disturbance" (1951: 137).

The above range of production branches or activities is applicable to Dasanetch society as a whole and partially coincides with major geographic settlement areas in that those households which are poorest (i. e., without stock) are
settled along the Omo River or in the modern delta area rather than in the
plains. Those households which are wealthy in stock, on the other hand, are
almost invariably residents of the plains. Some individual settlement areas do
include households representing nearly the whole wealth spectrum (e. g., Nyemomari), so that geographic location of villages is often not a reliable indicator
of economic status. Furthermore, the types of economic activities and their
relative emphasis may fluctuate from the standpoint of the tribe as a whole over
a period of many decades, from the standpoint of a given individual's lifetime,
and even from season to season.

A few generalizations may be made here regarding the various tribal segments' (en) subsistence emphases, especially between stock raising and horticulture. The Randel and Koro rely almost entirely on stock raising and members of both segments express a very strong dislike of horticulture, though
some poor households must resort to gathering and sometimes fishing (they
rarely undertake horticulture). Almost all members of the Eleli segment, by
contrast, do regularly engage in horticulture, and although most express a
strong preference for raising stock a large amount of attention is given to planting relative to some of the other segments. A fair number of Eleli are extremely poor and rely entirely on horticulture and other alternative subsistence means. The Oro and Inkabela segments are both highly mixed with regard to production activities, representatives of the whole spectrum of productive activity shown in the above spectrum. Members of these segments uniformly state a strong preference for stock raising, and available wealth is usually
transformed into stock when possible. Finally, the tiny Rieli segment is predominantly poor in stock and engaged in horticulture along with the other activities alternative to stock raising. Few Rieli households have more than a small
number of stock. The Naritch segment, resident on the east bank of the Omo
River and not dealt with in the present study, has a strong emphasis on horticulture and is periodically an important source of grain for the west bank Dasa-

netch. The Inkoria segment, also resident only east of the Omo River, is similar to the Inkabela in their mixed productive activities and their strong ideological focus on stock.

The Forces of Production

Land, capital and labor[5] are elements of the forces of production, and
will be discussed in the next chapter as one of the two components of the economic base (as that term is employed in the concept of mode of production).
Some important aspects of land as a productive force are reviewed here, and
major characteristics of capital and labor are discussed. Applications of these
three elements in the contexts of specific production branches are made in the
following sections.

Land. --Land as a production force is primary to Dasanetch survival
from the standpoint of its exploitation for grazing and browsing by stock, for
gathering of plant foods and for horticulture. It may be considered from the
standpoint of several questions: how much land is theoretically available; how
much is actually utilizable; of what quality is that which is available; and what
patterns of land allocation exist? Land as a production force is described here
primarily with reference to the dominant production branch of stock raising.
Horticultural lands are dealt with below in the section treating that branch of
production.

The total land theoretically available to the Dasanetch is approximately
1375 km^2, though only a portion of this amount is actually utilizable for domestic stock. The great reduction from theoretically useful land to that actually
exploitable is due primarily to factors as (a) the presence of disease organisms
over large areas (e.g., tsetse along the river); (b) the seasonal absence of water over large areas during at least the majority of the year; (c) hostile relations with surrounding tribes;[6] and (d) police restrictions.

---

[5]Much information concerning land (or, more accurately, natural resources) was given in Chapters 2 and 3, and various aspects of social relations
affecting labor arrangements (e.g., those between father and son, among adult
males) were discussed in Chapter 4.

[6]The lands just east of the Omo which are threatened by the Hamar tribe
inhibit the utilization of a large area on the east bank. The 1972 war between
the Dasanetch and their neighboring tribe to the north, the Inyangatom (Donyiro),
provides a useful example of the importance of this factor in the short term at
least. For months following the outbreak of hostilities between the Dasanetch

As to the quality of land actually available to the Dasanetch, Chapter 2 describes the generally very poor quality of much of the available grazing lands[7] (e. g., with very low total cover and most of what vegetation exists over large areas is unpalatable to domestic stock), and Chapter 3 describes the uncertainty of planting in much of the horticultural lands[8] utilized by the Dasanetch.

The degree of rights to lands contrasts sharply for grazing and horticultural lands. Some such rights do exist on the macro social level, i. e., the en (tribal segment) level, for grazing lands, although there is much overlap among the segments (see Chapter 4), and none of the west bank segments graze lands considered to be exclusively theirs.[9] Rights to grazing lands are not significant on social levels below that of tribal segment (except for grazing of horticultural lands). Lands for planting, on the other hand, are characterized by recognizable ownership and allocation patterns, and ownership may be described at both the macro (segment) and micro (patriline and households) levels. These patterns are briefly treated in a later section of the present chapter.

Capital. --Because the use of the term "capital" is often ambiguous and when defined is done so in very different ways from one writer to the next, it is useful to briefly review several perspectives before applying a definition to the present system.

Heilbronner (1972: 9) defines national capital as "the portion of . . . productive wealth that is man-made [sic] and therefore reproducible." According to this definition, capital is said to include a nation or society's structures, producers' equipment, consumer durables, all inventories, money, etc. Capital includes all that the "nation" (or tribe) has produced up to the present time, and that it has not used up or destroyed. Firth has stressed that capital is a stock

---

and the Inyangatom, the Dasanetch were unable to graze their stock in lands they had traditionally depended heavily upon because of their proximity to Inyangatom territory. They were therefore forced to concentrate their herds in the lands to the south and to some extent on the east bank and in the modern delta. Consequently, already severely overgrazed lands underwent an even further acceleration or deterioration, with increased hardship for humans and stock.

[7]The stock-carrying capacity of the Dasanetch rangelands is estimated in Chapter 7.

[8]The loss of much horticultural land in recent decades, as well as the social and environmental impacts of this loss, is discussed in Chapter 7.

[9]Tribal segments were, at least in part, very probably more territorial in the past, before the tribe's confinement to the lands it now occupies.

of goods and services which is used in the productive process by being "immobilized" (i.e., not used by the entrepreneur for immediate consumption) and which is used to meet any changes in the productive situation. Elsewhere, First restricts the idea of capital to certain types of goods which facilitate production and stresses that capital is not commonly invested with the notion of obtaining a return from it. Salisbury, in From Stone to Steel (1962: 141), offers a definition of capital which is close to that of Firth: "In real terms, then, capital will be defined as a stock of goods, present before a productive act is performed, used in production, and 'immobilized' from direct consumption while the act is in progress." Both the Firth and Salisbury expressions of capital are, then, consistent with that offered by Heilbronner.

Godelier (1972), on the other hand, asserts a definition of capital contrasting considerably with the above when he sets out two conditions for judging a thing used to be called capital. These two conditions are: (1) the thing must be bought and sold (i.e., it must be a commodity for its owner), and (2) the thing must bring its owner something more than its initial value (i.e., a profit). Assuming that capital possesses the property of growth, capital exists in any agricultural or pastoral society since these utilize plants and/or animals. He further emphasizes the social character of capital when he says, "In its essence, capital is not a thing but a relation between men realized by means of the exchange of things. It is a social fact" (ibid.: 286).

There are many other definitions of capital which could be surveyed here, but these are sufficient to suggest a range of parameters from which I suggest that the usage of capital most appropriate to this study is as goods used in the production process but not consumed in that process. This meaning of the term is in relatively close agreement with the definitions of Heilbronner, Firth and Salisbury. It is important to stress that capital is a sub-set or type of wealth, i.e., there are forms of wealth which are not considered capital by the above definition. Land, for instance, is a form of wealth which is not considered capital, for it is not human-made nor is it reproducible. Further, control over labor power and other forms of social wealth such as prestige, etc., are not considered capital by the above definition, although they may be employed to produce capital.

The forms of wealth which are considered capital by Heilbronner (see above) may be applied to the Dasanetch system to specify the types of capital for this particular society. Dasanetch capital identifiable from the categories of structures, producers' equipment, consumer durables, inventories and money include: huts, granaries, spears, horticultural implements, herding sticks, knives, cooking pots, frames used for transporting and storing goods (on wild ass and in huts), skins, rifles, stock, and grain. An individual adult male, as the owner of capital, is considered of high economic status primarily if he possesses a large number of stock, especially cattle. Cattle (guo) are easily the most important kind of capital, not only in terms of social prestige and as a means of payment (and other forms of social interaction), but also for milk, meat, blood, skins, and numerous implements and other products. Cattle are not only the preferred store of value, but also the most primary standard of value. Small stock (ayi) too are productive capital for the Dasanetch, as are camels (galte) and wild ass (olo). Small stock are particularly important economically in exchange relations since (a) they are a smaller denomination and (b) the system of values of both the Dasanetch and surrounding tribes permits them to freely utilize small stock in barter for numerous other goods (e. g., grain, cattle when possible). Pertinent to the latter point is the upward transformation of wealth by most Dasanetch whenever possible in the form of transformation of grain into small stock (and into cattle when possible).

Finally, it is important to distinguish between ownership and control of capital, since in Dasanetch society, as in many other political economies, control without ownership of capital is highly significant in socio-economic power relations. For instance, an elderly Dasanetch man who does not live with his married sons nevertheless frequently makes demands on the latter's stock (and capital more generally).

Labor: types, division and control. --Considered as a whole, human labor power in the production process is utilized primarily toward the production of consumption products in traditional economies, though this does not always mean short-term consumption, as in the pastoralists' raising and maintaining of cattle which are only slaughtered after some years or which are used for reproductive purposes. Labor processes include the controlling of the production process by the indirect producers or managers (see below), the direct producing (e. g., the actual growing of livestock or crops), and the managing of space in which the production processes take place (e. g., burning of grazing lands, managing horticultural plots). In any account of the Dasanetch political economy, it is also important to include productive activity as contrasted with production. Whereas the latter may be defined as the process of actually producing a good or service, productive activity is labor directed toward produc-

tion of a good or service but not necessarily with success. Raising of
stock which later die from disease, planting with subsequent loss of the
crop due to drought or an unpredicted flooding, and hunting, gathering or
fishing without success are all examples of productive activity but not production per se. In the Dasanetch system, the ratio of productive activity
to effective production is usually very high.

There are a number of patterns of labor power control which occur
within the different Dasanetch branches of production, but some notion of
the basic division of labor is necessary for understanding those patterns.
The economic activity in which a particular individual will be engaged at
any given time is largely predictable from a small number of variables:
sex, age, marital status, wealth status of the individual's patrilineage, settlement location and season. I will briefly characterize labor as it is differentiated along sex and age lines and within the context of the traditional
production unit, the household.

Female labor.

Relatively little differentiation by age occurs with females compared
to males. Although marriage represents a significant increase in the economic responsibility accorded a young woman, it does not represent a radical change in the type or amount of labor she performs. That is to say,
from the time she is about five or six years old, a Dasanetch girl begins
imitating and learning the skills of her older sisters and mother, gradually
increasing her responsibilities as she becomes an adult woman. The most
basic productive activities a woman typically participates in are: (1) milking and kraal care (Fig. 5-1), including preparation of fires in kraals,
building and repairing of thorn fences for the kraal, and care of the baby
goats and sheep which remain at the village; (2) herding when there is a
shortage of male labor; (3) other domestic work including child care, water
carrying (Fig. 5-2), food preparation, hut building and repair (Fig. 5-3),
and gathering of building materials; (4) horticulture (women and girls do
most of the labor associated with horticulture, except for heavy cutting);[10]
and (5) food gathering of wild fruits, roots and stems, etc. Unmarried

---

[10]The degree of male labor power employed in horticulture is quite variable from household to household (see later section).

Fig. 5-2. --Pregnant Dasanetch
Woman Carrying Water from Omo River.

Fig. 5-1. --Preparation
of Dung Fire in Village Kraal.

Fig. 5-3.--Cooperative Hut Building by Dasanetch Women

168

females, and sometimes married ones, may perform a combination of
some of the above tasks on foretch (temporary stock camps), and they
frequently transport milk and other products between foretch and the village.[11]

Labor of women and girls is highly variable in intensity and duration,
according to the economic status of the individual households to which they are
attached, the season of the year, and their age and position among the wives of
their husband. Working is usually highly cooperative among the women of a particular household (i.e., among wives of one male). This is also frequently the
case on the more inclusive level of village and sometimes between villages.
Within a household, some wives commonly concentrate more on horticultural
work and others on stock care, though all are involved in most of the basic
domestic chores listed above. The dominant role of the first wife (min gudoha)
is usually pronounced, and this is an important aspect of the organization of
labor among a group of three or four wives and their daughters. Division of
labor among women and girls of a family or village may necessitate their living
in different areas for short (or sometimes extended) periods of time. For instance, one or more women may move to a horticultural locality during periods
of intensive activity there, to a temporary cattle camp or to the location of a
lengthy ritual occasion (e.g., dimi). Women and girls often move in groups on
their treks to the river or to the lake for water and from their villages to horticultural lands; they generally converse freely during their daily chores within
the village. These social groups often include a full age span, from young children through old women.

Male labor.

In contrast to the work performed by females, that of males is strongly
differentiated according to age. Major shifts in a male's labor coincide with
other primary changes in his life, such as puberty and the onset of adolescence
and marriage. The primary economic activities of males are as follows.
(1) Herding. Young boys being handling stock from the time they can move
around independently (Fig. 5-4), and their responsibilities for herding of cattle
and (later) small stock increase until just prior to marriage. They are allowed
to accompany the stock on foretch (temporary stock camp) when still very young

---

[11]Unmarried females (marti) are generally only allowed to go on foretch if
they are accompanied by their brother(s) or another close male relative.

Fig. 5-4.--Young Dasanetch Cattle Herder and Infant Boy

and by the time they are in their mid-to-late teens they may be in charge of foretch. Small stock herding and foretch are usually run by relatively older bachelor males since sheep and goats are much more active in their movements and therefore more difficult to manage (Fig. 5-5). Although a young bachelor spends much time with members of his age set (hari) and more specifically with members of his sub-age set (modo), he still participates in herding and is active in overseeing the herding done by his younger brothers. This is particularly true when a male remains in residence in his father's village until his marriage. Although married men may still accompany or direct foretch, most send their herds with others (e.g., younger brothers, affinal unmarried males) after this time. Mature men normally do not herd themselves, but instead manage the herding labor power of young men and boys under their control (often a source of tension between fathers and sons). They are usually present at milking time in the village (Fig. 5-6) to oversee the herd and generally supervise stock care, even though they do not themselves participate in the chores. Mature males do herd, however, when it is necessary, e.g., in wartime or when they must send their stock into the less grazed, government restricted lands to the west where there is the danger of stock seizure by the Kenya police. (2) Horticulture. Male labor is important both for the clearing of horticultural plots and the harvesting of crops. Younger boys also sometimes chase birds from the horticultural plots, a form of work generally disliked.[12] During most of the horticultural period, however, the men who won plots are apt to be seen sitting and conversing in small groups while the females perform most of the labor. (3) Fishing and hunting. These activities are done only by males, and those who have neither stock nor get a substantial horticultural yield. They are undertaken only during hunger periods such as severe drought or disease, if at all. As mentioned earlier, the poorest Dasanetch rely heavily on fishing and hunting in combination with gathering and horticulture. Many individuals who practice fishing and/or hunting deny doing so, as there is a strong stigma attached to them, especially fishing. Younger males, however, may fish in groups openly in months of hunger (Fig. 3-14). Fishing is the more common of the two activities, however, and among the west bank Dasanetch it is done primarily from the shores of Lake Rudolf, in the modern delta, in an ox-bow lake

---

[12]Turkana male refugees (from hunger in their lands in northern Kenya) are frequently utilized for horticultural work, another indication of the low esteem given this kind of labor. Some of these Turkana males remain for some years but ultimately return to their own lands, some die from disease, and only a few settle permanently among the Dasanetch.

171

Fig. 5-5.--Bachelor Herding Small Stock near Temporary Camp

Fig. 5-6.--Milking Time at Mid-Day in Village

near Koritodo, elsewhere along the Omo and in Kolon channel. Among those who practice them at all, fishing and hunting are done only sporadically, and the primitive technology of the Dasanetch greatly limits productivity in these branches. (4) Exchange. Bartering and selling of goods are done mainly by men, though not exclusively. Much exchange of goods occurs among the Dasanetch themselves as well as with the Ethiopian and Kenyan police and with neighboring tribes, especially the Turkana and Inyangatom.

Division of labor specified by household labor roles may be generalized to the larger social and economic context. The household unit is the structural principle which allows the basic patterns of labor roles to be comparable, in spite of variables such as geographical location and wealth status. Labor roles maintain in a distinct parallelism across these parameters of variation. For example, while the poorest men of the riverine/delta zone often hunt crocodile, the poorer men of the plains hunt gazelle and topi when necessary. There is also a parallelism of women's labor roles in the plains and in the riverine/delta regions. Thus while the specific activity which these individuals are involved in are superficially quite distinct, it is the structural homologue of the activity of the other zone. Further, the labor performed by individuals of the same sex and age is parallel, whether the patrilineage with which they are associated is of high or low economic status.

Dasanetch Traditional Unit of Production

The unit of production and the patrilineage. --It is with control over labor power that real economic strength in the sphere of labor as a force of production resides. It is therefore useful to consider the production unit, which is here considered to be determined by the unit of control over labor power (Eaton, 1963: 69). Some alternative subsistence activities (e.g., fishing, hunting) involve variations in production unit organization, and where not identified specifically, the term "production unit" refers to the dominant and traditional unit associated with stock raising. Much of the following description of the traditional, or stock raising, production unit obtains for the other production branches. Exceptions to this are noted in the discussion of the other branches below.

Individuals are not free agents in the allocation of their labor power, but are constrained by authority patterns within the household, and more generally by the set of relations within the patrilineage. This system of organization is

responsible for a general pattern of realization of abstract labor[13] in production processes which is basically uniform for the entire tribe. A married man
or head of household has basic control over the labor power of his unmarried sons,
his wives and his daughters. This individual household head, as already
pointed out, may in turn be controlled to some degree by his own father (or fa-.
ther's brothers). This is especially true when he and his household reside within his father's village. Thus the basic unit of control over labor power is the
one-generational minimal patrilineage unit, with the husband being the controller of that unit. The unit of production is closely related to the units of both
wealth holding and inheritance. These are jointly embedded within the patrilineal system, and their functioning can only be understood in that context. A patrilineage may be characterized as a series of production units linked by inheritance.

Women are critical to the existence of each production unit from the standpoint of their roles in the reproduction, maintenance and socialization of the
labor force. A woman normatively changes her functional membership in a production unit abruptly when she marries, shifting from one patriline (and clan) to
another. A man, by contrast, shifts his production unit only along the continuum of one patrilineage. The generational continuum and the contrasting positions of women and men relative to patrilineages may be represented schemati-
cally (Fig. 5-7). Patrilineages provide the basic structure for wealth concentration and wealth transfer, and when a young woman marries the economic
loss to her patrilineage is normatively compensated by bridewealth from the
husband's patrilineage (see Chapter 4). Although bridewealth may be paid to
individuals outside the bride's patrilineage (for example, her father's bond
friend), such rights exist only by virtue of those individual's connections to her
patrilineage. There is, then, a cyclic dispersion and loss of members of the
productive units on the one hand, and addition of them on the other, whereby the
basic structure is successively reproduced while the social composition is continually changing (not only from the births and deaths occurring, but also the
inflow and outflow of women through marriage; see Fig. 5-7).

Labor cooperation among production units. --Labor cooperation among
units is common, and it is initiated both by production unit heads and the laborers themselves. This is consistent with the strong lineage and age-set princi-

---

[13]Abstract labor is without reference to particular characteristics or purpose (Eaton, 1963: 32).

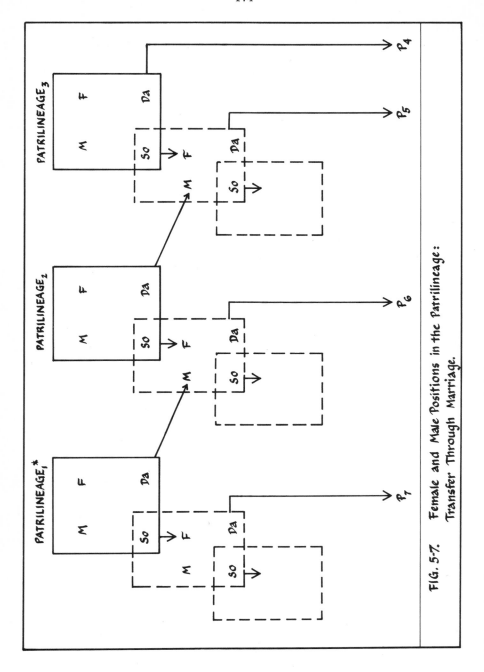

FIG. 5-7. Female and Male Positions in the Patrilineage: Transfer Through Marriage.

ples of the Dasanetch, the high value the Dasanetch place on reciprocal sharing, and the pressures on "big men" (gal gudoha). Most cooperative labor is done on a highly restricted and simple basis, involving only several persons. Ongoing or everyday forms of highly simple and restricted cooperation arranged by production unit heads themselves focus on herding arrangements, but also extend to the sharing of labor power (particularly of young males) for horticultural labor, such as during harvesting. Herding and horticultural cooperative labor is especially common among close kin (e.g., within the same patriline), but also occurs frequently among age mates, especially sub-age set (modo) mates, bond friends and affines.[14] Inter-production unit cooperative labor instigated by the producers themselves include: herding together by young men and boys who are friends (often sub-age set mates),[15] cooperative treks and subsequent labor by women for water-getting, cutting of branches (for kraals, etc.), food gathering, and in many forms of village and horticultural work when co-residence exists.

Periodic forms of labor cooperation are common among Dasanetch production units, and these are similar to the "simple cooperation" of Balibar (1970: 237),[16] whereby the actual numbers of cooperating laborers are still relatively few in numbers and their cooperation is, with some exceptions, of some duration. Omo River crossings with stock, for instance, are occasions when such cooperation is important. Production unit heads of low economic status often cooperate in the hunting of topi or crocodile, etc., and in fishing. Finally, the continuation of production (particularly stock raising) during wartime or in other conditions of stress often requires cooperation. This type of cooperation may generate from social levels higher than individual production unit heads, such as when younger groups of sub-age set mates patrol endangered lands during wartime. It is often essential for small herds to be combined into huge ones at such times, and this has serious negative consequences from the standpoint of ecological destruction through overgrazing and its feedback adverse eco-

---

[14]The latter types of cooperation are particularly common where co-residence exists.

[15]This sometimes causes difficulties or tension when a group of young men desire to herd together and disregard their fathers' wishes concerning locationing of the herds.

[16]Defined by Balibar as cooperation in which "numerous laborers work together side by side, whether in one and the same process, or in different but connected processes."

nomic effects. Generally speaking, cooperation in productive processes is often increased in times of stress.

Stock Raising: The Dominant Production Branch

Stock as a means of subsistence.--The importance of stock within the levels of ideology, ritual, symbolic aspects of social structure, and as a medium of exchange and store of value is intimately tied to their importance for the Dasanetch in subsistence terms. Their subsistence value rests primarily on their utilization for milk, blood, meat, skins and many implements, as well as their exchange value for other products, e.g., small stock for millet grain.

Milk is traditionally the staple of Dasanetch diet, although numerous other foods are important, according to a household's economic status, settlement location, the season of the year and other factors. Milk yields vary greatly from one season to the next. A good yield from a milk cow is considered to be about one wooded vessel or kurum (an average size kurum is about two quarts) or more, whereas a cow often yields only one-quarter or less of a kurum when grazing conditions are very poor (e.g., in drought season and when overgrazing is intense). During most of my own field work, which was carried out primarily during drought periods, milk yields per individual milk cow were frequently below the above estimate for poor conditions. Small stock are also used for milking and even though their milk yields are relatively small they are sometimes the sole source of milk for a village. Goats are generally considered better for milking, although sheep are preferred for oil and skins. Wild ass are occasionally also milked, and the few remaining households with camels use them for milking.[17]

Blood constitutes part of the diet of some Dasanetch, particularly in times of drought and hunger. It is taken from an ox by tying a rope or cord around the neck of the animal, puncturing a large blood vessel anterior to the stricture with a tiny bow and arrow, and draining the blood into a kurum or gourd. Up to a quart or so of blood may be taken at one time. Blood is either drunk alone or mixed with milk. Attitudes toward blood consumption vary considerably from person to person, although males generally drink it more often than females.

---

[17]There were, according to Dasanetch informants, many more camels owned by the tribe when they lived in the plains to the west. Reportedly, most have died from disease since the Dasanetch became confined to the lands closer to Lake Rudolf and the Omo River.

Slaughter of cattle and small stock occurs on numerous occasions, includ-
ing at ritual times (especially <u>dimi</u> and <u>gol</u>; see Chapter 4), as a welcoming gesture (e.g., when an affine or other respected individuals visit), when re-
quested by one's own age or sub-age set mates, and in times of drought and hunger. Although small stock are usually slaughtered first in times of stress,
oxen may also be sacrificed. Stock killed or dying from many diseases are
also eaten, though some types of diseases preclude consumption of the animals.
It is difficult at best to sort out the ritual and social functions of stock slaughter
and sacrifice from slaughter as an adaptation in the form of providing protein;
certainly these functions overlap on most occasions. In fact, slaughter of animals has almost certainly become necessary for the survival of many stock
raising patrilineages in recent years, but this need for slaughtering in times of
extreme hunger places many production unit heads in something of a double bind:
the marked decrease in the average individual's number of stock in recent
years dictates consumption of some stock for survival at times just when there
is an even greater need to maintain and reproduce the existing herd. This constitutes an important link from a production unit's state of almost total reliance
on stock raising to its diversification to exploit alternative subsistence means.

    <u>Stock composition, herd sizes and stock diseases</u>. --Consistent with the
Dasanetch emphasis on herding, there is a complex terminology for the major
stock animals (cattle, goats and sheep). The full terminology is not relevant to
the present discussion, but the most general names for stock animals are: cat-
tle--<u>guo</u>, sheep--<u>wala</u>, goats--<u>erde</u> (sheep and goats collectively--<u>ayi</u>), wild
ass--<u>olo</u>, and camels-<u>galte</u>. An individual male expends much energy trying to
maximize his number of stock. Although this is true for cattle in particular,
small stock are also extremely important as media of social and economic relations. Consequently, a stock owner has both types of animals, and in fact he is
likely to have many fewer cattle relative to sheep and goats. Sizes of herds
vary widely, as does the composition of herds. Cattle herds range from only
one or two head to several hundred head under one man's control (the latter is
an exceedingly rare occurrence in recent years). Many stock owners whose
households are able to subsist with only sporadic horticulture commonly have
40 to 50 head of cattle, though there are certainly exceptions. Even allowing
for individual differences regarding attitude toward planting, there is a clear
tendency for the frequency of horticultural activity to correspond inversely with
herd size for the Dasanetch segments studied. It is often very difficult to ascer-

tain the precise number of a man's cattle, since the Dasanetch are reticent to reveal this type of information--until such time as a level of trust is established--and firsthand observations of the number of them based in the village at night may not take account of those on foretch. Another problem in verifying the number reported is being able to separate out the cattle belonging to different men which are herded and/or kraaled together and which may have the same brand and ear notches (gui and hethe, respectively). Estimates of Dasanetch stock numbers were based on a combination of direct estimates given by the owner, testimony from informants familiar with the owner, and indirect measures based on cross-checks with information given on such matters as lifelong changes in stock numbers, disease, bridewealth payments and the number of bulls.

The size of a man's herd is important not only in his household's subsistence and in the establishment of his economic and social status, but also in the herding arrangements he makes and therefore the social ties he develops or exploits with other individuals. Very small cattle herds, for instance, are typically herded in combination with those of other individuals, whereas large ones may be divided for effective management. Combined vs. divided herds are also a function of the labor supply available to a stock owner, the particular season involved, and the general ecological conditions. There is a general and strong tendency toward an increase in the number of small stock vs. cattle since small stock (ayi) are relatively well adapted to the poor range conditions common to much of the west bank plains. Most men now own a much larger number of them than cattle (guo).

Camels (galte), which are considered valuable for their high milk yield, presently number no more than 30 or 40 for the tribe as a whole. The remaining camels are concentrated in the lowermost portion of Dasanetch lands (south of Kalam), and they are reportedly highly susceptible to diseases. Wild ass (olo) are essential to the transporting of a village from one locality to another. They may sometimes be used for carrying water when the village is a considerable distance from the nearest water source, and may even be utilized for milk when hunger is severe.

No detailed information is available for this region concerning the types and incidence of livestock diseases. Consequently, remarks and descriptions presented here are based on accounts by the Dasanetch, personal observations and brief personal conversations with Getachen Bekele, an Ethiopian veterinarian who has spent a short time in the Omo region. All major stock diseases are well known among the Dasanetch who have any stock at all, and such knowledge is basic to the daily decision-making by stock owners concerning grazing locations to be utilized, the recognition and isolation of diseased animals and trading relations. Dasanetch stock are not isolated from those of the Inyangatom and the Turkana, since the shortage of good land promotes overlapping of grazing areas and since these tribes constantly engage in bartering involving stock. This fact is significant when one is speculating on the spread of stock diseases among the three tribes and the effectiveness of disease control programs carried out by only one government (Kenya or Ethiopia) or for only one tribe in the area. The following are the vernacular names for the major stock diseases found in Dasanetch territory:[18] cattle--ortheno (pleuropneumonia),[19] agonywa, gamoritch, and keething (trypanosomiasis); small stock--isthire (lice), uli, bira, kwunche, gamoritch fasca, ortheno (pleuropneumonia), and gor. According to Bekele, rinderpest, Anthrax and blackquarter bacterial diseases and bovine pleuropneumonia are the most prevalent diseases among Dasanetch stock. Susceptibility to these diseases is increased by the poor health of the animals due to the lack of adequate grass and browse, and communicability of disease is high due to the tremendous population concentrated in the small area to which the tribe is now confined. All of the diseases listed above are described by informants as having occurred in les Dasanetch for a long time although their frequency, seasonal occurrence, duration and severity have changed over time. Pleuropneumonia (ortheno) in particular is almost continually severe in recent years whereas in the past it was of low incidence except for periodic epidemics. Rinderpest reportedly has undergone a similar increase in persistence over time. Although slaughter of diseased animals is extremely common during the dry season, animals dying from certain diseases are not eaten. The dry months (guium marietka) are particularly precarious for the Dasanetch since some stock diseases are very severe then and hunger is at its peak. My surveys of plains villages clearly reveal that very large numbers of stock die annually from disease, particularly agonywa, gamoritch and ortheno, and that these have been decimating the herds of many stock owners. Further, a shift toward small stock increasing as a proportion of an individual owner's total stock is clearly in evidence from my interviews with older stock owners. It is necessary to consider all major stock diseases integrally in or-

---

[18]The term bash means disease and often prefixes these names.

[19]Also called by its Turkana name, loke.

der to accurately predict shifting emphases among cattle and small stock, and
sufficient information to do this is lacking.

There have been no large-scale or extended endeavors by the Ethiopian
government to deal with the problem of disease in this area, although a few vet-
erinarians and small teams of foreigners have visited the region for observations and for small-scale, short-term programs.[20] In any case, there are
severe problems involved with offering any one-dimensional form of aid to the
Dasanetch, e.g., stock inoculation, and these are discussed in the last chapter.

Herding practices. --Among males, the increasing involvement or responsibility for herding which generally accompanies age is clearly reflected by the
hierarchy of authority among brothers. By the time a boy reaches his mid- or
late teens, he may make major herding decisions, and sometimes even acts
against his father's wishes with regard to the grazing localities utilized or other matters, e.g., in order to herd with his age mates. Some fathers openly
complain about their sons' behavior on this issue, as for instance during my
field work when young men would disregard their fathers' instructions by taking
their herds into the prohibited zone monitored by the Kenya police.

Herding associations can be partially predicted by the social composition
of a village. Stock owners of the same village may send their herds out individually to the same or different localities or they may undertake cooperative herding. There may be several herding subgroups even within a single village. Several influences on herding association formation have already been suggested,
such as herd size, labor supply, existing social and economic ties among stock
owners, season and the range conditions of the particular region concerned.
Existing socio-economic ties are clearly a major factor in the formation of cooperative herding arrangements, and an individual male commonly uses his
sons' (or other males') labor power to further develop and consolidate social
ties. An individual stock owner may obtain herding labor by arrangement with
a variety of relations, in addition to controlling that of his own sons (and also
his younger unmarried brothers if their father is dead, etc.). These relations
include brothers and other close male agnates, sister's husband, father-in-law,
father's sister's husband, mother's brother, age mate and bond friend.

---

[20]The Dasanetch are extremely reluctant to bring their stock for inoculation or dipping, and the presence of medical persons or teams for short periods and with a manner quite alien to the Dasanetch has inhibited the development of trust on the part of the stock owners.

The frequent correlation between co-residence of non-agnates and sharing of available labor power (and horticultural plots) was mentioned earlier in this monograph.

Turkana men (sometimes with their wives and children) or boys who have left their tribal lands during times of famine and have entered Dasanetch lands as refugees also may serve as another source of herding labor in return for shelter and food. In 1970 there were at least 250 Turkana among the Dasanetch, but their numbers fluctuate greatly, primarily according to conditions in their own territory and the relations between the two tribes.

Herding involves both daily treks from the village, including watering every day or every other day, and extended periods away from the village with temporary stock camps (foretch). Stock owners utilize foretch to widely varying degrees, from not at all to almost exclusively, with all gradations between these extremes. Foretch may last for only several days or for periods of months and by the end of the dry season a large proportion of the plains villages have some of their members gone on foretch with much of the stock. Although foretch exists for both cattle and small stock, small stock are more frequently kept near the village when range conditions are at their worst during the dry season since they can better utilize the little pasturage and browse remaining near the village. Milk cows and small stock may be kept at the village during the dry season when the other animals are away on foretch, but in the most severe times all stock may be sent to the camps. When milk cows are on foretch, young women may be present for varying lengths of time (accompanied by close male kin).

Cattle and small stock are herded separately, and this is attributable to (1) the must faster movement of small stock, and (2) the difference in adaptability of cattle vs. small stock for water conditions (e.g., small stock are often watered only every other day during the dry seasons, whereas cattle should be watered every day),[21] and (3) the fact that small stock (especially sheep) are better adapted to graze very near the ground so that they can utilize rangelands heavily grazed by cattle, and (4) the ability of sheep and goats to utilize many plants unpalatable to cattle. Cattle are often, though not always, given preference to the best grazing lands, but they too must survive on deteriorated ranges over large areas of Dasanetch lands (see Chapter 2). Interviews with stock own-

---

[21] There are exceptions made to the daily watering of cattle, too, notably during the dry season when pasturage is very far from water so that the animals only trek to water on alternate days.

ers throughout my field work revealed deep bitterness over their confinement to these deteriorated lands, but also a certain sense of resignation to this accentuated and prolonged set of hardships they have endured in the past. Many individuals are aware that their circumstances are with little or no prospect of improvement, unlike the situation in the past.

Grazing units vary widely in size, but generally speaking, units are typically smaller during the dry season than during the wet season. Herds do combine more in the dry months under certain circumstances (e.g., when an unseasonable rain has resulted in a fresh grass growth in one particular locality, or for safety in a particularly dangerous zone). My observations during the dry season alone showed a variation in cattle herd size from less than ten animals to large herds of more than 100, and in small stock herd size from about 20 to a few hundred. Factors of importance in determining herd size include availability of labor, [22] location and quality of pasturage, disease conditions, and season.

A boy or young man responsible for a herd is usually attentive of the herd throughout the day and any negligence may be cause for a dispute or reprimanding, for survival dictates that he guide them to the best pasturage locally available, keep watch for any predators nearby (especially in bush country) and see that they are watered regularly. Otherwise lonely days are broken by conversation with other males and by songs composed by herders. Predictably, these songs are most often about cattle. A favorite ox (inbesiyet) or bull (ar) in particular are the frequent subjects of these songs, and some lyrics and melodies become widely familiar. One such lyric is translated here, and it clearly illustrates the reverence and responsibility felt by a Dasanetch male for his bull as well as how his relation to the bull is closely bound up with his social relations.

> My spotted bull, I call you.
> When I send you for grass, I like you.
> When it is drought time, I am ahead of you
>   to look for good grass for you.
> I have given you the bell of the son
>   of my mother's father.
> People of my age, get ready to decorate yourselves
>   for a dance of my bull.
> Young girls, you said my bull will not grow as big
>   as an elephant--now get ready for a
>   dance of my bull.
> A girl--she jumped, crying "Let us dance today.

---

[22]The availability of labor is in turn often closely related to the degree of economic diversification, as discussed in a later section.

> I have seen his bull--he is good,
>   he is big."
> My bull is liked by everyone.
> When they see him at the well, they like him
>   more because he is handsome and big.
> Bull--why do you say I don't take you to
>   much grass?
> You--eat now, because I like you as I like
>   land of good grass.

A typical stock raising village of the plains. --The size of any individual plains village (eh) is dependent on numerous environmental factors, as well as social and economic ones. Whatever its size, there is rather uniform physical appearance sharply contrasting with that of the riverine villages. Huts are arranged in a semicircular or circular order (Fig. 5-8) and each hut (bil) is beehive in shape. The hut itself is constructed by women as a shell of dried animal skins (usually sheep and goat) fastened with leather or grass cord to a framework of supple branches (see Fig. 5-3). When skins are not available tightly woven grass mats are used, and very often a combination of skins and mats results. A small hole is left in the center top, and another about two and one-half feet high forms an entrance (Fig. 5-9). A bil is easily dismantled and transported by wild ass to a new village site where it is reconstructed in a matter of hours. A whole village or even a village complex may disappear virtually overnight, and this is a necessary adaptation to a land where opportunities for pasturage and water may shift dramatically in one day's time.

Day huts are constructed in many villages for protection from the sun during hot afternoons (usually for women, children, and small animals), for welcoming of and conversations with guests, and for overnight sleeping by a visitor. These shelters are constructed very loosely as half-shells of branches and leaves. Kraals are used more often in regions where danger of predators (or raiders) exists and they are common features of Dasanetch villages. Separate kraals are usually maintained for mature cattle, calves and heifers, and small stock (Fig. 5-8). They are constructed, whenever possible, with acacia or other thorny branches in order to better contain the stock and protect them from animal predators. Granaries are sometimes located in the plains villages for storage of grains harvested in horticultural plots but they may also be constructed near the plots themselves, where they are left unguarded.

A radically different arrangement of the plains village plan is that which is organized around defense against a neighboring tribe. This type of village is constructed of concentric thorn fences with the huts closely grouped in the cen-

184

Fig. 5-8.--Aerial View of Dasanetch Plains Village

Fig. 5-9.--Goat Kids Frolicking on Hut near Dawn

ter, where the women and children sleep. Stock are kept between the thorn rings, and the older boys and men sleep in holes or trenches nearer the periphery (see photo on p. 134 in Butzer, 1971). This type of village is also described in oral tradition for Dasanetch life of many years ago when inter-tribal raiding was a frequent occurrence.

The following is a description of the economic activities of a typical day in a plains village complex during the dry season. This brief account is not meant to be exhaustive but rather to simply convey a general sense of Dasanetch economic life exclusive of the wide array of other social activities which may take place.

Morning: Just before dawn, one is awakened by the rhythmic shaking of milk in a wooden vessel by women who are separating it in order to get the much valued oil. There is an increasing commotion among the cattle and small stock, accentuated by the loud braying of wild ass. The young goats are usually excited by the cool morning air and may be seen chasing each other through the village and climbing on the beehive huts (Fig. 5-9). It is the season when preparation of the horticultural plots is underway, and some women and girls of the village depart for the river or delta before day; these groups can be heard laughing and talking each morning as they pass nearby. Soon the milking begins (Fig. 5-10) and conversation in the village becomes more lively. The children of the village are given milk whenever possible. Before the small stock are sent off for the day's feeding, they are checked over for embedded thorns and other problems. The men spend time looking over the animals before the day's grazing begins, or perhaps they may instead be drinking coffee and chatting around the tiny fires in or next to their huts. The women may then settle down to drinking coffee (when available) or begin other chores, and the herders set off with the stock for the day's trek to feeding and watering locales. The men may remain for a while and then depart for a favorite shady spot with their age mates or other friends; the very old men, however, remain in the village. The village is far from water, so that some of the women and girls have already set off for water at the Omo River or at Kolon. Others tend to basic chores in their huts and in the kraals.

Midday and Afternoon: Men generally spend much of the day away from the village on business or with their age mates, other friends, etc. Women, on the other hand, usually remain in the village unless they have chores elsewhere, such as gathering wood or food or water-fetching. They pass parts of the day straightening their huts, preparing food, shaping or repairing various utensils, doing each other's hair, caring for the children, etc., chatting with each other all the while. The hottest part of the day is a time for sleeping or at least retreating into huts to avoid the sun. Tiny goats and sheep lie sheltered in the thin shade along the bottoms of the outside of the huts. By late afternoon some women set off for water, others begin preparing the kraals by gathering the dried dung into piles for the night fires. The men, meanwhile, spend the day talking of their economic and social matters, shaping ornaments and tools, doing each other's headdresses or earrings, or playing games. Some men go to briefly check on their herds, others engage in bartering at Kalam. By comparison to the women, their days are incomparably freer and more mobile.

Fig. 5-10. --Early Morning Activity in a Plains Village

Evening: In this open plain near Kalam which is relatively devoid of tall shrubs the cattle and small stock which return to the village in early evening are a stirring sight as the lines of slow homeward-bound animals are accompanied by a trail of dust before the sunset. This is a time of high activity in the villages, for the stock are always attended to before a household relaxes. Almost all members of the village are returned. The cattle cluster about the dung fires when they arrive, and once again the milking is begun, along with general grooming and tending to the animals. It is only when this is done that the little bit of porridge and milk available is eaten. The night is relatively cool after the scorching hot afternoon, and the landscape is dotted with innumerable tiny fires from the dung heaps and beside the huts. Families cluster outside around the entrances to their huts, and tiny children are already asleep. Laughter and talking flow, and singing and dancing may begin which involve wives and their young children, and particularly young unmarried women and young bachelors (this is a time of courtship). Dancing is more unusual in the more isolated villages of the plains; hunger is also a strong factor in whether or not dancing and singing are frequent such that riverine and other poor villages are often very quiet at night. (Many Dasanetch go to sleep with virtually no food except a very weak variety of locally grown coffee and some fathered fruits or tubers, etc.) During the night, there is always an occasional shuffling of people within and among huts, the crying of babies, as well as periodic stirring of the stock or the braying of the wild ass on the village periphery, and the laugh of a nearby hyena. Not uncommonly, a disturbance is caused by a snake entering a hut or crawling up on one of them, when many people of the village rush to kill it with sticks. This night, a man stays up during much of the night, walking about and singing to his favorite ox or bull while the animal grazes the sparse grass nearby. To the outsider, it seems a very short time between the final quiet of the village and the beginning of the next morning's pre-dawn activity.

Subsistence Alternatives to Stock Raising

The range of alternatives. --The alternative subsistence activities of horticulture and to some degree fishing and gathering are, unlike herding, highly seasonal in occurrence since they are, to varying degrees, dependent on environmental conditions which are present during only part of the year. Because seasons are extremely unstable from year to year, these economic activities (along with hunting) do not provide a stable base for subsistence.[23] Even though some Dasanetch (especially many of those settled in the delta and the riverine zones) have engaged in these alternatives for many years, each carries a certain stigma so that reliance on them is usually an index of poverty. These people usually refer to themselves as poor and maintain that they would move to the plains if they were able to obtain enough stock to subsist there. Some Eleli and Oro male informants from the poorest villages along the Omo River maintained that they kept some stock in the plains when they clearly had none at all:

---

[23]This is especially true when the primitive technology of the Dasanetch is taken into account.

such testimony was made in an effort to avoid admitting their own poverty. The Dasanetch riverine forest villages studied (Koritodo, Narok, Masitch, Akesa, Bulukwī and Kolin [Fig. 5-21]) rarely receive any milk from stock in the plains and their diets consisted mostly of a little grain (usually gone within a short time if any at all was harvested), gathered fruits and other plant parts, fish and occasionally crocodile meat.

A typical riverine village. --Riverine villages are usually at or near the silt berms where horticulture is practiced (e.g., Narok, Akesa, Koritodo, Bulukwī), or nearby in the adjacent flats (e.g., Masitch, Kolin). Riverine settlement in the early decades of this century was considerably different, as is briefly described in the next chapter.

These villages (Fig. 5-11) strongly contrast with those of the plains in several respects. They are virtually immobile, since the huts are of solid grass. When a move occurs, the huts are simply abandoned. Occasionally, a riverine village hut is of the plains type (i.e., with skins and/or grass mats tied over a wooden framework), but those are invariably--except along the lowermost Omo--only temporarily established for horticultural work.

Since the few riverine households which have any stock cannot keep them in the riverine zone (because of tsetse), there are no kraals. Numerous small granaries, of the same type as those in the plains, are present. Wooden frames or loosely constructed platforms are used for drying crocodile meat, fish and other animal carcasses. Chickens are raised by several of the riverine villagers (e.g., Koritodo, Akesa), primarily for sale to the Ethiopian police. Tiny conical grass huts are used to protect the chickens at night from snakes and other predators. The riverine villages north of Rati in particular are economically extremely deprived relative to those of the plains, and most of the riverine people from Rati northward have a rather limited amount of social and economic interchange with other Dasanetch, except during periods of intensive horticultural work. Given the high incidence of disease and the low economic status generally, an outsider is impressed with the quietude and the low energy of these villages relative to the plains village.

Horticulture

Roles in Dasanetch economy. --Horticulture is the most widespread and also the most important subsistence alternative to herding. It is significant in several ways. To begin with, planting is done by productive units from a

Fig. 5-11. --Riverine Village in Riverine-Associated Flats at Kolin

wide spectrum of economic status, from the poorest units to those with considerable stock wealth. Horticulture is not usually practiced by the wealthiest patrilineages, however. A clear tendency exists for those with herds large enough to provide bare subsistence to plant only irregularly if at all or else for bartering purposes, whereas poorer Dasanetch have little option but to plant during every season possible. In the second place, planting is widespread for households over a wide geographic distribution, not merely those near the river or delta. In fact, virtually all Dasanetch (see section below on settlement nodes) land regions have at least some households which plant, even though there are real differences from one region to the next. Third, all eight tribal segments engage in at least some horticulture, although there are certain clear tendencies (e.g., Randel avoid planting when possible),[24] whereas Eleli and Rieli typically plant as often as possible. Oro and especially Inkabela demonstrate the full gamut of variation, from those who are very poor and rely heavily on it to those who have never engaged in it.

The Dasanetch plant maize (nakapona), millet (ruba), tobacco (dumbo), two major types of beans (am) and several types of gourds. Of these, millet (ruba) is clearly the dominant crop, primarily because it can grow in drier conditions than can maize, and planting conditions are highly unstable in Dasanetch lands. Beans, tobacco, gourds, etc., are usually planted at the periphery of plots and in other places unsuitable for maize or millet.

Horticulture serves several types of economic functions for a given productive unit. It may form the basic means of subsistence, with almost all that is produced being consumed; this situation applies year after year to some production units. It may periodically serve a stopgap function, enabling a household or much of the tribe, for that matter,[25] to survive drought, stock epidemic or famine periods when animal products or the herds themselves are severely limited. Finally, horticulture may be supplemental and the grain produced may be used primarily for barter or for consumption at ceremonial times. Bartering with grain focuses particularly on items such as tobacco, coffee, small

---

[24]In the course of my field work, I found only a few Randel horticultural plots (at Narok and in the delta on the west bank) though I did not exhaustively survey all the west bank planting lands.

[25]Horticulture has played a critical role in the past, according to the Dasanetch, when a severe epidemic, drought or warfare has decimated herds, and the Dasanetch's opportunity for planting (provided by the Omo River and its delta, etc.) has periodically given them a decisive advantage over their neighbors, the Borana and the Turkana.

stock, and cooking vessels, but there are many others. West bank Dasanetch obtain grain from other Dasanetch as well as from the Inyangatom. Lands near the delta on the east side of the Omo River are apparently lower and therefore with better moisture conditions for horticulture, so that crop yields there are often correspondingly higher when efforts fail nearly completely on the west bank. Consequently, the Naritch segment, settled east of the river, is often a source of grain for the west bank Dasanetch, through barter for small stock.

<u>Location and environmental character of horticultural lands</u>. --The map in Fig. 2-2 shows the localities of most common horticultural activity along the west bank and in the modern delta region. Crop growth is dependent on flooding, either by the lake or river waters (or a combination of them) except for a few localities which permit small crops where water from rainfall is sufficient. Predictably from the recent environmental changes (e. g., the lake rise of the 1960's and the irregularity of flooding by the Omo) many productive units utilize plots in different localities from year to year and even during one year in some instances. There is apparently more shifting of plots from year to year by individuals planting in the modern delta and in other localities relatively removed from the river as compared with the silt berms along the river. In spite of this shifting within the delta, yields there are considered good by comparison to other localities (although in the delta too, the crops fail in years of little or no flooding). River flooding was earlier described (Chapter 3) as highly irregular from year to year, and yields on the silt berms north of the delta region are often very poor (see below). Fallowing is <u>de facto</u> practiced in some locales where a plot is abandoned for a time, but there is no systematic effort toward that end.

Along the Omo River all available silt berms within Dasanetch territory are planted except for the east bank berms upriver from Rati due to the Dasanetch's fear of raids by the Hamar tribe from the highlands to the east. Correspondingly, there is almost a complete absence of villages on the east bank north of about the Rati latitude. Most of the horticultural localities along the Omo River have villages nearby, either in the woodland or forest itself or in the adjacent transition zone. These villages contain a segment of the households engaging in horticulture there, whereas others come from the plains. Nauyahori (Figs. 3-5 and 5-12) is an exception to this pattern since it can only be reached by dugout canoe (Fig. 5-13) due to the excessive growth of spreading shrubs and thick undergrowth throughout the interior of that very long river

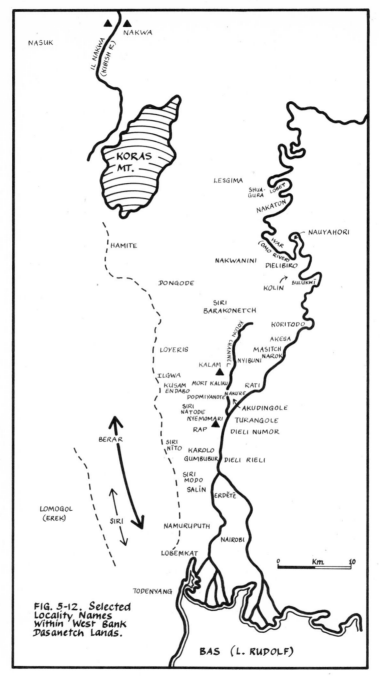

FIG. 5-12. Selected
Locality Names
Within West Bank
Dasanetch Lands.

Fig. 5-12. --Selected Dasanetch Locality Names

Fig. 5-13.--Dasanetch Woman Preparing Dug-Out Canoe

meander. Although the riverine villages are mostly comprised of Eleli, the plots allocated on the silt berms north of Rati include some Oro and a few Koro and Randel.

South of Rati, west bank horticulture is practiced in many localities more removed from the river, especially within the zone bordered by the Omo on the east and Kolon channel on the west. North of the Omo River/Kolon confluence, the land is relatively wet (mesic) compared to that equally removed from the river farther north. Within this zone, Kolon forms a braided system and parts of it support very green and lush plant life well into the dry season. Omo River flood waters back up behind the natural levee from the Omo River/Kolon confluence. Farther south, levee breaching occurs in some localities and horticulture is irregularly practiced where the soil is clay or clayey silt and with sufficient moisture.

Kolon itself is also planted sporadically in a few localities, primarily where it derives moisture from rains, as well as seepage and/or runoff from the plains to the west. The confinement of crops to silts and clays, in combination with the highly irregular presence of sufficient moisture, greatly limits the number of localities where it is possible to plant with a reasonable probability of a good yield. Out of 12 plot localities which I studied along Kolon in 1969, for instance, only two of them had millet which matured at all.

Ownership and subdivision of plots. --Individual males may make numerous shifts in planting location within a short time span, and the system of acquisition, division and exchange of horticultural plots is complex. Some have planted a different locality every year for four or five years: others have used the same plots for decades (rarely without subdivision, however).

In a household which plants, each wife is usually allocated a plot for which she is responsible, although wives of one man usually cooperate in their labor. The real owner of a wife's plot is her husband, however, since women do not have ownership rights. A man does not become a plot owner until his first marriage, and there are several typical ways to receive a plot. The most common traditional appropriation of land is from his father. A man's land is in reality often not equally divided among his sons, and it may also be distributed among other kin and non-kin. An individual male might receive a plot or at least temporary planting rights from other close patrilineal kin (e.g., brother or father's brother), his mother's brother, mother's sister's husband, wife's father, wife's brother, sister's husband, age mate or bond friend. Like most economic transactions, plot receiving will sooner or later involve reciprocity in some form. Aside from close agnates, donors of plots most frequently encountered during my field research were wife's father and age mate. Many elderly men have already allocated most of their horticultural land, and there is heavy pressure on "big men" to do so.

In some parts of Dasanetch lands still another means of obtaining a locality for planting is possible. Land which has lain fallow for some time (variously defined) may be planted by an individual male and his household, although if the original owner reclaims it, the new user must usually go elsewhere. The acquisition of horticultural land, then, does not follow any precise hierarchy of social relations, and pressure for allocation is mostly confined to the relations described above. It was pointed out earlier that whole villages of non-agnates may be organized along a principle of horticultural land division. This situation is usually, however, the result of socio-economic ties already existing rather than the formation of them, and in this respect can be misleading. It is significant that the patterns for allocation and redistribution of cattle are clearly defined in almost all respects whereas those for horticultural land are extremely variable. This is consistent with the relatively low status accorded horticulture as an alternative livelihood and the deeply established patterns of stock exchange which identify prescribed types of social relations.

Subdivision of existing plots occurs frequently among the Dasanetch and the economic implications of the resulting smaller yields for individual households are surely great. The continual division of lands and the instability of yield for most plots are critical considerations in any assessment of the possibilities of horticulture for alleviating the other economic stresses which the Dasanetch face, such as those resulting from the constriction of their territory and the subsequent destruction of rangelands.

Horticultural labor, seasonality and yield. --Environmental conditions vary significantly in their impact on horticultural activity, and yields from one zone to another vary greatly as well as those in one locality from one year to the next. In particular, the delta and upstream riverine zones (in the northern sector of Dasanetch territory) are associated with somewhat different environmental conditions which produce different rhythms of horticultural labor. The most significant difference is that the riverine harvest (simago) is earlier than the delta harvest (hol dim), with a lag time of as great as two months. [26]

---

[26]My studies of horticultural plots were done primarily along the Omo Riv-

Flooding of the silt berms (see Chapter 3) by the Omo River occurs from late August to as late as October, depending on the year. Those Dasanetch households which plant begin burning and cutting the year's weedy growth before this time. Planting occurs after the flood waters subside (if they are considered sufficient), usually in about October, whereas planting is delayed in much of the delta by the backup of the Omo River waters from their terminus at the lake. In December or January harvest occurs on the silt berms, but cutting is usually done in January/February in the delta. Second and even third growths of millet are common in the delta region in particular, and this regrowth in the delta is significant since it may be grazed by stock.[27] Kolon plots follow approximately the rhythm of the Inyangatom horticulture at Nakwa: planting is usually done in about June and harvest (which is not often possible along Kolon channel in recent years) is sometime in August.

According to the Dasanetch, maximum flood level of the Omo may fluctuate many meters laterally on the silt berms from year to year (as well as in the delta). Flooding is essential to the planting of crops in several respects: for the acquisition of new sediment, for nutrients deposited and for sufficient moisture. Thus, the length of submergence of a plot by the flood waters is an important determinant of crop success. Careful judgments must be made regarding the behavior of the river, since errors may cost those concerned their entire crop. Reflooding of the plot by the river after planting may, for example, result in the destruction of the entire crop, and this can occur quite suddenly. Another factor is the possibility of early flooding of the plot before the clearing and cutting of the weedy growth since the last harvest.

The yield from a given unit of horticultural land fluctuates greatly. This is true from one geomorphic unit to another (e.g., silt berms vs. modern delta flats), within similar sediments from one locality to another, and at one locality from one harvest to the next. The wide variation in yield illustrates the precariousness of a production unit's reliance upon horticulture for its subsistence. Riverine silt berm plots are reported by almost all to be less productive than those in the modern delba, but the recent rise in the level of Lake Rudolf has flooded out much of the good horticultural land in the delta. The amount of mil-

---

er from Rati northward, and only secondarily along the west bank in the delta, in Kolon channel and at Nakwa (now planted only by the Inyangatom).

[27] It may be recalled that the presence of tsetse in the riverine zone north of Rati precludes the presence of domestic stock there, except for the short time when the river is at its lowest and tsetse is much less abundant. Even then, most stock owners do not attempt to take stock there.

let actually produced, for instance, vacillates greatly according to factors such as soil type, crop diseases, [28] degree and duration of river flooding, and variations in available labor. Table 5-1 shows some selected millet yields from the plots at Rati, on the basis of a number of square meters of land which yielded a large bag[29] of millet. These are given for a good and bad yield over three to five years planting for individual plots.

TABLE 5-1

FLUCTUATIONS IN SILT BERM
HORTICULTURAL YIELDS

Plot*	Poor Yield** (sq. meters/bag)	Good Yield
1	598	870
2	83	130
3	80	388
4	711	1600
5	350	520
6	558	951
7	498	1666
8	307	470
9	222	280
10	731	970
Total	4138	7535
Average	413.8	753.5

* = Location of plots: Narok.

** = Based on yields for the last ± 5 years.

The sequence of horticultural activities is virtually the same for all localities, whatever the rhythm of these activities for a particular locality, and they are described here with respect to the silt berms. When the river rises (late July or August), cutting, clearing, and burning (Fig. 3-13) of the previous year's growth begins and during this time smoke from the burning of plots all through the delta and along the river is visible all through the lower Omo valley. Planting is done after flooding and inundation, when it is judged that the waters

---

[28] Whole crops have been lost to disease in recent years, on both the Omo River and Il Nakwa (Kibish River) at Nakwa.

[29] One large bag of millet is about four <u>debe</u> (Ethiopian).

have reached their highest point and will not return. Maturation of the crops usually takes one and a half to two and a half months and during this period the plots must be protected from invading birds, small animals and baboons. As described in the earlier section on labor, harvest time is a period of intensive labor when many boys and young men as well as mature men participate, and sharing of labor power by heads of different production units is common.

Fishing

While only a minority of Dasanetch profess a strong avoidance for food derived from maize and millet, all but the poorest Dasanetch (and sometimes even they) express a strong dislike for fish. Fishing is universally associated with the poorest economic status (Fig. 5-14). Even those who must frequently resort to fishing as a means of subsistence will often initially deny it. The Dasanetch term for "fisherman" (fishing is almost invariably done by males) is in fact the same as that for "poor man." It is very difficult to verify the existence of fishing as an economic activity by plains Dasanetch, since they very often do it covertly at night. My field work experience suggested a fair number of plains households or economically mixed production units (especially of the Eleli and Rieli segments, and many Oro and Inkabela near the delta and the Omo River) eat fish at least occasionally.

Most fishing occurs in shallow waters, including in one large cut-off meander along the river's edge, from dugout canoes, from wooden fishing platforms built over the water (in the lower delta), and in Kolon channel. Fishing is neither easy nor particularly productive for the Dasanetch because of their very limited technology. Crude hooks are usually used with grass cord of low strength or a rope is sometimes secured through barter. Spears are used for catching Nile perch (in Lake Rudolf and the lowermost Omo) and for other large fish. Netting is practiced but not commonly. Adult males as well as young boys engage in fishing. Varying degrees of labor organization of this activity occur, from simply a couple or small group of males fishing together (as individuals or more cooperatively such as in spearing Nile perch), to a rather large group of young males such as those who have been observed to collectively beat the water in Kolon in order to trap and spear fish. The product is allocated in various ways rather than in any prescribed manner.

Fig. 5-14.--Riverine Village Man with Fishing Equipment

Gathering

Except for the wealthiest of households, at least some sporadic gathering is done by the Dasanetch, especially in adverse seasons or over longer periods, even if it entails nothing more than the occasional collection of berries by herd-boys on foretch or by others on trek. The vast majority of gathering, however, is done by the poorer Dasanetch and it is considered to be a very low status subsistence means. It has, however, been resorted to by at least some Dasanetch for many years (cf. Smith, 1896, and Austin, 1902). Gathering for the household is done by girls and women and is initiated by them (at least superficially). Most foods gathered are from plants in the wetter localities. Women from the relatively poorer plains villages may bring back certain fruits (especially nchira, a small cucumber fruit, which is usually dried and ground up), roots (lokote; Cayratia imbuensis) when they go to the river for water. Altogether, very few species are commonly utilized for food by them. Riverine and delta families in particular rely quite heavily on fruits during at least part of the year, especially the two mentioned above. Nchira is gathered almost continuously by the riverine Eleli villagers when it is available (e.g., July-September). Other fruits commonly eaten by the poorer Dasanetch of the riverine zone include: kinetch (Ficus sycomorus), morshorte (Ximenia caffra), and miede (Cordia sinensis).

Hunting

Hunting plays only a minor part in Dasanetch economics, and like fishing and gathering, it is generally looked upon with disfavor. Crocodile (anitch) is the only large animal which is eaten rather often by some riverine people. As is true in fishing, the effectiveness of the Dasanetch in this activity is greatly limited by their level of technology as well as the prevailing attitude toward it. The poorest men (hunting is done exclusively by males) do not always have spears, and those Dasanetch who have rifles do not want to use the few bullets they may possess.

Crocodile hunting is done both along the shore and from dugouts, by groups of men using spears, hand axes, etc. This is both difficult and dangerous, as crocodiles are extremely fast in their movements. I was able to observe one crocodile kill by villagers from Kolin during the course of my fieldwork, at Dielibiro (Fig. 5-12). This was accompanied by much excitement which was sustained a good while as many from the village helped cut up the animal and transport it piece by piece back through the forest to their village (Fig.

5-15), a few stopping to roast small portions of it along the way. In addition to
the meat and fat being fully utilized, the bone, skin and nearly every other part
is taken advantage of (i.e., much the way slaughtered cattle are utilized fully
in the plains). Almost all Dasanetch, except the poorest, draw back in disgust
when questioned as to whether they eat crocodile meat, thus indicating the force
of the stigma attached to this form of hunting.

Other animals hunted are Grant's gazelle, topi, and occasionally zebra
(northeast of Dasanetch settlement, and east of the Omo River). Ostrich, Colobus monkey, leopard and several others have traditionally been sought: Colobus and leopard for their skins (used for dimi) and ostrich for its feathers used
in men's hair pieces. Hunting of topi, gazelle and other animals by the plains
people usually occurs during severe drought seasons or other times of hardship.
Small bands of males may sometimes hunt in bush country (e.g., in the transition zone between the riverine forest and the adjacent flats). I have also observed hunting by a large number (20-30) of males in the mud flats of Berar
(Sanderson's Gulf) where, for example, the men chase a group of topi into the
center of the flats where water has collected and where it is extremely muddy
and sticky. As the animals enter the mud and are slowed down, the men encir-
cle them, making it possible for a few men to close in and spear them, killing
four or five or more animals at a time. Some of the meat may be immediately
roasted and eaten by the hunters and the remainder returned to their respective
villages or households for distribution. During the dry season it is not unusual
to visit villages with gazelle (most commonly), topi or zebra skins staked out in
the sun to dry, indicating a recent kill.

Seasonal Movements and Settlement

Environmental and social factors of seasonal movements. --The movements of Dasanetch peoples and their stock are complex and clearly reflect the
interaction of numerous environmental and social forces. The complexity of
decision making regarding movements is not surprising in view of the wide variation in environmental character within the tribal territory, coupled with the
harshness of their conditions during much of the year, the existing combinations of economic activities and wealth, and the wide range of a given individual's social and economic relations. Any movements of individual households,
of the stock on foretch, or of entire villages must take into account a whole
range of variables which may differ relative to place and time.

Dasanetch expressions for season primarily relate to grazing conditions

202

Fig. 5-15.--A Crocodile Kill by Riverine Villagers at Bulikwī

as shaped by the moisture and quality of grass. Some of the more significant terms are: (1) ish ekgelep (green grass within and immediately following the big rains--ir gudoha); (2) ish heri (the green, fresh grass following the large rains); (3) morgotch (the condition of green, fresh grass existing in a mixture with already dried, yellow grass--such as after ish heri and also resulting from a small local rain--ir ninika); (4) ish eshantea or shante (dried out, yellow grass generally, corresponding to guim marietka or "months of hunger"). There are many additional terms describing various combinations of grazing and moisture conditions, and different ones apply to the varying parts of les Dasanetch at one time.

Wet and dry seasons correspond with wide variations in pasturage and browse, available water, and certain disease organisms. Some of the dynamics and basic conditions of the plains (to which most stock are confined) were discussed in Chapter 2; the delta and riverine zones in Chapter 3. An individual stock owner weighs the options available to him by taking into account the three most basic environmental considerations given above, as well as those described below. Decision making with respect to these environmental factors may occur on the level of individual stock owners, or larger groups which herd together (e.g., whole villages or sub-groups of one village). Adjacent villages may and in fact often do follow very different grazing patterns.

For the tribe as a whole there is more foretch (stock camps) during the driest months whereas in the wet months there is usually fresh growth to be utilized near the settlements. When water is available in the plains (e.g., as large and small pools), villages are more able to move with their stock. The relative range potentials of different regions within the Dasanetch territory were contrasted in Chapter 2. Much of the better land theoretically or traditionally available to the Dasanetch is presently inaccessible to them for at least one of these four reasons: (1) it is restricted from use by the local tribes, according to Kenyan-Ethiopian governmental agreement; (2) it is infested with tsetse fly (the riverine zone north of Rati, and parts of the adjacent plains) or other disease organisms during part or all of the year; (3) it is considered dangerous from the standpoint of traditionally hostile tribes (e.g., the lands northeast of the Dasanetch and east of the Omo River); (4) it is nearly inaccessible to the Dasanetch stock during the dry season even though it is relatively less disturbed than most of their territory because of its great distance from water sources (e.g., just east of Koras; see Fig. 1-1). Consequently, the lands which must bear the greatest pressure by Dasanetch cattle and small stock are primarily those which are already severely degraded.

The importance of small, unseasonable rains as well as the small and large rainy seasons (nyerobe and ir gudoha, respectively) can be easily appreciated when one considers both the opening up of grazing lands otherwise inaccessible because of lack of water, and the fresh growth of grass and browse more generally. Even a small rain during the dry season may produce fresh grass and some standing water in a locality (e.g., central and northern reaches of Berar), and a very large cluster of villages and camps may therefore arrive there almost overnight.

A few generalizations about available water for stock (and humans) are important to an understanding of the seasonal movements described below. Water during the rainy months is fairly widely distributed. Watering places for the dry seasons are listed here according to the most general grazing regions (arbitrarily defined):

(1) Lobemkat and regions just north (see Fig. 5-12): water from Lake Rudolf, the lowermost Omo River, and lower Berar: Sirte, near Namuruputh during rainy or river flooding months.

(2) East edge of Berar to the Omo River (and north to latitude of Nyemomari): water from standing pools in Berar or from the Omo River, according to distance and presence or absence of water in former; plains pools during rains.

(3) Nyemomari to Kalam: water from the Omo River, the southern end of Kolon and the vicinity near its terminus during Omo River overflow, scattered plains pools during rains.

(4) Kalam to Koras Mountain: water mostly from Kolon channel during dry months (several watering places); Kalam stock sometimes go to the Omo during December and January (when there is no tsetse because of low river); scattered plains pools during rainy months.

(5) Nakwa and vicinity: water from Il Nakwa (Kibish River) during rains and from water holes there during the dry months; plains pools during rainy months, including large water expanses at the foot of Koras from slope runoff.

Water for humans is obtained at all the above places, in addition to several small water holes (not used for stock) between Kalam and Koras.

The primary social forces influencing seasonal movements need only be mentioned here, as they have been dealt with in previous sections of this chapter and in Chapter 4. Basically they include the following, although this is by

no means an exhaustive list: (a) wealth status; (b) ownership or access to horticultural land; (c) available labor supply; (d) traditional lands of individual tribal
segments;[30] (e) police regulations, and (f) relations with neighboring tribes;
(g) important ceremonial periods (e. g., dimi); and (h) socio-economic ties
along lineage, age-set, and affinal lines. A sample of any large number of individuals reveals significant variation in the hierarchy of controlling factors of
seasonal movements, and, of course, the relative importance of these factors
changes for any individual over time.

Settlement: general distribution. --The overall pattern of settlement and
tribal segment distribution for the Dasanetch has been described in brief form.
However, a more detailed description of the areas of concentration of settlement on the west bank is pertinent to the following sections.

The highest concentrations of villages on the west bank are Lobemkat,
Nyemomari, and Kalam (Fig. 5-12). All three are very stable village complexes, although the individual villages comprising them fluctuate considerably.
The important riverine village areas have been mentioned as Dielirieli, Turangoli and Dielinumor on the east bank of the Omo River, and Rati, Akesa, Koritodo, Bulukwī, Kolin, Narok, and Masitch on the west bank.[31] Although relatively stable in their existence, these riverine villages do not account for a
large proportion of the Dasanetch population (in my 1972 census, only 113 huts
were counted, or roughly 565 people at the highest estimate). A less stable concentration of villages occurs at Nakwa, although this is predominantely Inyangatom.

Remaining villages on the west bank are distributed very widely in the
plains, although fair concentrations of them do form seasonally in some localities (e. g., the sandy ridges west of Karolo, Gumbubur, and Rap; see Fig. 5-12).
Although these areas change considerably in concentration of villages from one
season to the next, this variation may be quite rhythmic in nature (e. g., Salin,
Rap). Overall, settlement is densest between Berar and the Omo River be-

---

[30] As mentioned earlier, there are no strict grazing sections and although
certain general patterns of settlement and utilization may be discerned for segments, there is a great deal of mixing (see Chapter 4 and below).

[31] On the west bank south of Rati are numerous villages near the river (e. g.,
many villages in the Salin region are along the river during the dry season, and
Nyemomari is very nearby). However, since the plains environment extends
nearly to the river's edge from Nyemomari southward, these villages are considered together with the rest of the plains.

tween the latitudes of about Kalam and Lobemkat. Villages (largely of the Randel and Eleli segments) are scattered more widely throughout the lands between
Kalam and Nakwa, with all different degrees of mobility. However, there are
no permanent or semi-permanent Dasanetch villages east of Koras. It is important to point out that the mobility of a village is not necessarily predictable on
the basis of whether it is located in one of the densely populated settlement
areas or one of the thinly settled regions mentioned above. All settlement
areas, for instance, include some villages which remain for only a short time
and there are a number of rather isolated villages which have moved only very
short distances for many seasons or even years. Generally, plains villages
which are relatively stable in location send their stock on extended and/or frequent foretch.

Nodes of settlement and seasonal movements. --One way seasonal movement patterns may be described in detail for the west bank Dasanetch is by identifying geographical settlement areas and comparing the movements generated
from within them. These settlement areas of reference henceforth are referred to as nodes (Fig. 5-16). There are recognizable patterns of village and
herd movements associated with these nodes, even though there is considerable
overlap among them. A village may leave one node for a period of time or may
enter another node and change its base of operations without altering the character of the nodes themselves. The node concept used here is not derived from
density of settlement or from particular patterns of individual villages but rather is defined by its existence as an area of convergence of pathways of movement. Both dry and wet season movements are described for the nodes proposed below, and may be either village movements or stock camp (foretch)
movements. Foretch camps may extend for only a few days before they return
to the village, or they may continue for months on end, moving from one region
to another without returning to the village. The stock movements shown for the
nodes refer to both foretch camps and daily movements outside the node as designated. I have chosen to describe the nodes in some detail in order to demonstrate the potential complexity of movements of a pastoral people. Specific
locations given in the schema of Figure 5-16 are mapped in Figure 5-12.

Node 1: Lobemkat. Lobemkat is the large, southernmost area of Dasanetch settlement, and it is only two to three miles north of Todenyang Kenya
Police Post. This node is here defined as extending northward to and including
the Namuruputh. During my dry season surveys there were 528 huts in the

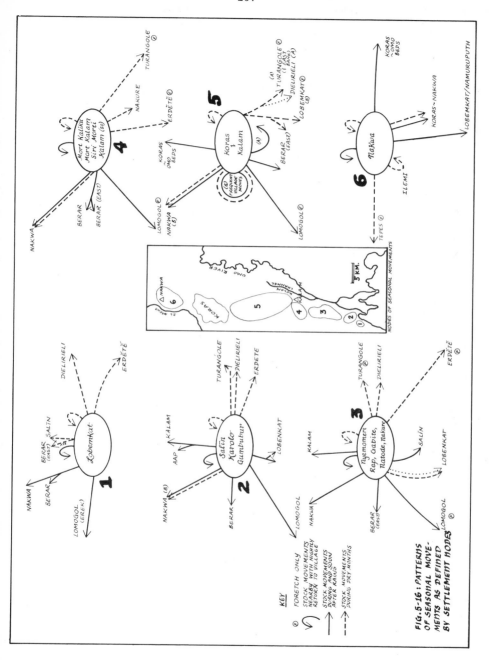

FIG. 5-16 : PATTERNS OF SEASONAL MOVE-
MENTS AS DEFINED BY SETTLEMENT NODES

area in 1970 and 586 in 1972.[32] This complex is often much larger in population during the rainy months. Lobemkat has shifted in the location of its greatest concentration of villages in recent years, primarily in response to lake level changes, the presence or absence of mosquitos, and disease conditions. This area is widely considered by the Dasanetch to offer some of the best grazing land within the area now accessible to the tribe. In actual fact, the area has been nearly denuded of grass cover during the dry seasons in recent years, except for the grass in the southernmost tip of Berar and along the lake's edge. The spectrum of village mobility within this complex ranges from those which are virtually permanent and send stock on foretch for many months of the year to those villages which spend only a few months at a time in the area complex. Village moves to and from Lobemkat most often involve the region just to the north (Salin, Gumbubur, Karolo), the localities along the eastern edge of Berar, and Nakwa. Inkabela is easily the predominant tribal segment in numbers in Lobemkat, although there are also Oro, some Randel, and Koro (I did not encounter any Eleli males here and only a few Eleli females who were married to males of other segments). More Turkana refugee laborers are found here than in any other single area of settlement.

Lomogol (Erek) is an important region for people of this and other nodes, even though it is, according to the Kenyan government, technically off limits to both the Turkana and the Dasanetch. Here the grass is considered better than that of the presently defined Dasanetch lands, and many stock owners risk seizure of their stock or being shot themselves by the Kenya police in order to utilize the resources in this traditional tribal land. Because of the danger involved, however, very few villages move there and instead foretch is usually sent. During both large and small rainy seasons the stock are commonly grazed either near Lobemkat itself (including southern Berar) or near Lomogol. During dry seasons, on the other hand, most cattle are either based in the village in Lobemkat and grazed in Berar (more precisely at Sirte, the southern grassy portion of Berar), or on foretch near Berar or in Erdete. During the dry season following nyerobe (the small rains), from about December or January into March, many cattle are sent on foretch to lands just east of the Omo River, including the delta; this pattern is more true for nodes 1-3 than for other west bank settlement areas. Most small stock, however, remain on the west bank

---

[32]Using the estimate of five persons per hut, which is intended to take account of those persons on foretch, the latter hut count indicates a population of 2,920.

with grazing from the village at Lobemkat, further north along the sandy ridges (and watering at the Omo River) or along Berar's eastern border. Even though the modern delta is one of the best places for cattle during the driest seasons, it must be evacuated during the rains because of the high water (and disease). Foretch from settlements in other nodes is also sent to Lobemkat. A few families based in Lobemkat traditionally send their cattle (and sometimes small stock) to Nakwa during some months, and entire villages also may make this move. As was pointed out in an earlier section, milk cows are frequently retained at the village, even when the rest of the cattle are sent on foretch.

Horticultural plots of Lobemkat households are very commonly located along the lowermost Omo, in the modern delta (Erdete, Nairobi), and in the Dielirieli vicinity. Many plots in these areas have been flooded out in recent years, so that a high frequency of plot location shifting has become characteristic.

Node 2: Salin, Karolo, Gumbubur. Although some village complexes within this node are of significant size during some seasons, most of the individual villages here are fairly mobile. The most common pattern of village movement within the zone is from the relatively higher ridges slightly to the west (just east of Berar), where they remain during the rainy season when large shallow pools and muddy expanses form on the lower sections, to the lower ground east of the ridges and nearer the Omo River during dry season months. A large number of villages have moved into this node when they evacuated the modern delta in the early and mid-1960's as a consequence of Lake Rudolf's rising. This node is a severely overgrazed zone (see Fig. 2-20) during most of the year, but it is very open land, is accessible to water and is considered a desirable place to live by most Dasanetch. Social composition here is very mixed among the west bank tribal sections, but again with a conspicuous absence of Eleli and with only a few Randel. There is much similarity between the patterns of stock movements of node 1 and node 2, but the Salin node (2) is strongly associated with the use of the long ridge between these settlements and Berar. Cattle are often sent on foretch for much or all of the dry period. This may be elsewhere on the west bank, or in the delta or on the nearby east bank. Small stock, on the other hand, usually remain on the west bank either spending nights at the village and grazing fairly nearby, or moving on foretch to the west edge of the above-mentioned ridge. Some complementarity in grazing between cattle and sheep in particular enables both to take maximum advantage of Berar and the adjacent ridge to the east of it. Small stock typically utilize the short and sparse bunch grasses (either stunted from lack of moisture and the sediments poor in nutrients, or already grazed over) and tiny browse on and near the ridges, while the taller grasses in the mudflats of Sirte are grazed by cattle.

There is wide variation from village to village in the degree of dependence on horticulture, and a large percentage of the plots owned by men here are in the delta or on the lower east bank.

Node 3: Nyemomari, Rap, Natode, Nakura, Gabita, Dodmiya Khote. Nyemomari is a huge and long established settlement complex, its actual size and social composition varying with the seasons. Its population reaches its maximum during the rainy months. Even during the dry season I counted 230 huts here in 1970.[33] Villages which have evacuated the modern delta region in recent years have swollen its size considerably. Nyemomari is traditionally a vital political center in les Dasanetch. Although it has a highly mixed social composition, it is predominantly Inkabela with Oro and a few Randel and Koro; again, Eleli males are usually not resident.

A high percentage of the villages here send stock on foretch during much of the year. The other locales included in this node are of much smaller density as well as less stable in settlement than Nyemomari. Much village movement occurs within this area as well as between nodes 2 and 3. This node is in a pivotal geographic position, and the numerous grazing locality options produce a very heterogeneous overall pattern of stock movements. Lomogol is used for foretch somewhat less by stock owners in this node relative to the two nodes to the south and most of the foretch from here is either within or near the modern delta or on the east bank. During and just after the rains, a large number of the stock return to the villages here to graze the new growth of grass.

Horticultural plots of those who do plant are also widely scattered, a fact which correlates with the high degree of social mixing and the heterogeneous geographic locations of the villages previous to their arrival here. Broadly speaking, plots owned by males here are in the modern delta, along the levees very near the lake, or at Turangole or Dielirieli. Some others are between Kolon and the Omo River (e.g., in Akudingole and Nakura).

Node 4: Mort Kaliku, Mort Kalam, Siri Morti, South Kalam. This locality (see Fig. 5-16) is apparently one of relative stability in terms of the number of households that consider it their traditional land of settlement. Social compo-

---

[33] In 1972 I counted 520 huts, but this number was swollen due to fighting with the Inyangatom which caused much condensation of settlement from Nyemomari northward.

sition is very mixed in this node, with Inkabela the most numerous segment, and Eleli, Oro, and Randel also present. This node forms the major interface between the Eleli and Inkabela segments, i. e., it is the northernmost extension of high density Inkabela settlement and the southernmost extension of high density Eleli. Like the lands of nodes 2 and 3, those of this node are severely overgrazed during the whole year (see Fig. 2-20). This area is, however, a favored area for foretch from other settlement areas during ir gudoha (the large rains) through ish heri (fresh, green grass), especially on the well-drained sandy ridges. There is a tendency for stock owners here to retain small stock at the village continually, or at least for some weeks after the cattle are on foretch.

Households within this node represent a wide spectrum of economic wealth; some households are without stock and are essentially immobilized (including some who have no wild ass, which are used for transport), while others are relatively rich in stock and are very mobile. Horticulture is widely practiced among the villages here, with many having plots in Nyibuni (Fig. 5-12) and along Kolon (although most of these areas have dried out in recent years), the Akudingole region and Dielirieli. Cattle foretch during dry months in particular is most often to the modern delta. A few stock owners have sent foretch to the northwest as far as Mt. Tepes in Sudan (far into the zone prohibited by the police), though this region is predominantly utilized by the Inyangatom tribe. Compared to stock movements from node 4, Lomogol is used even less for foretch by villages of this node, and there is a corresponding increased usage of Nakwa and the eastern edge of Berar. The overall high level of differentiation of seasonal patterns here may be accounted for by the geographic centrality of this settlement node and the mixed social composition. In this respect, it is similar to node 4.

Node 5: North Kalam to Koras (Mt. Nakwa). There is no single geographical reference point for this node. Instead, there are two distinguishable subzones which have very similar stock movement patterns during much of the year: north Kalam and the areas of more dispersed settlement between Kalam and Koras (A and B are used in the diagram to indicate movements characteristic of the north Kalam subzone and that between Kalam and Koras, respectively).

The settlement of north Kalam is year-round, relatively stable and is comprised almost entirely of the Eleli segment. Unlike the households of previously described nodes, most here are engaged regularly in horticulture, with most plots located along the Omo River from Rati northward or on the east bank near Turangoli, and a few others along Kolon channel. Many Eleli here have only a few stock, and most of their villages have relatively little, if any, mobility. These Dasanetch usually water their stock at Kolon during the dry months (and less often at Rati), and in the plains where surface water collects in the wet months. A number of herders do water their stock at the Omo River near Rati in the few months when the river is at its lowest.

Settlement between Kalam and Koras is dispersed and consists largely of the Randel and Eleli segments, with the Eleli tending to live more in the eastern sector and Randel in the west. There are no settlement complexes or dense settlements between Kalam and Nakwa. Randel are generally very mobile by preference, and in this way the Randel contrast sharply with the Eleli, at least in recent years. Much of the Randel stock and village movement is within this node itself and in the Nakwa area, although many do utilize the predominantly Inkabela-occupied lands south of Kalam. During the dry months stock between Kalam and Koras mountain must be watered at the few places along Kolon which retain water year-round, so that stock during this period must be within trekking distance of Kolon. They can therefore only utilize the westernmost portion of these rangelands when water becomes available again as standing pools throughout the plains.

Settlement node 5 represents a significant shift with respect to previously described nodes in seasonal patterns of stock movement. Differentiation of the patterns is considerably less than nodes 3 and 4, for instance, and this is probably due to both a less centrally located settlement and a markedly increased social homogeneity. The seasonal patterns of the Randel in particular have changed radically in the past decades, particularly since they were among the Dasanetch who most heavily relied on the Ilemi plains of Sudan and Kenya which are now prohibited.

As mentioned earlier, only a few Randel plant at all (these do so at Narok and along the Omo River near the lake), and all Randel informants clearly indicated a strong distaste for horticultural activity. Randel villagers apparently do not engage in fishing, but many of them (especially women) do resort to gathering in times of hunger. Alternative economic activities for the Eleli between Kalam and Koras are essentially the same as those described for north Kalam.

Node 6: Nakwa and west of Koras. The Nakwa region, although strongly dominated by the Inyangatom tribe, nevertheless usually contains some Dasanetch villages throughout the year and is utilized by numerous Dasanetch for foretch.[34] Since the Inyangatom villages along the Omo River (Shungura and northward) cannot keep stock there because of tsetse infestation, the vast majority of Inyangatom stock must be based at Nakwa or westward on Tepes Mountain. Nakwa is the major center for interaction between the Inyangatom and the Dasanetch.

Those tribal segments which most frequently use the Nakwa village and the lands between Koras and Il Nakwa are Inkabela, Oro, and Randel. Dasanetch village settlement sites in this node vary greatly in degree of permanence, from only a few weeks to four or five years at a time. Although the Inyangatom have extensive horticultural land along Il Nakwa, the Dasanetch no longer have access to planting lands there. In fact, the distance between Nakwa and the Dasanetch horticultural localities along the Omo and elsewhere is prohibitive for many who rely on planting for subsistence. Those households which have sufficient labor power to permit a split of that labor force can manage to continue planting even while their village is based at Nakwa.

The diagram of stock movements from villages of this node shows a pattern similar in form to that of Lobemkat (node 1) in the extreme south of Dasanetch land. In both instances, the stock movements are skewed horizontally (east-west) from the settlement area in contrast to the radial patterns representing nodes 3 and 4. For the most part, the plains east of Koras can be utilized only during the rainy months when pools of water form there (e.g., in clay localities along the eastern base of Koras, where runoff from the mountain is high). During the rest of the year, watering must be done at Il Nakwa, and during the dry season wells as deep as 22 feet are dug (see Fig. 2-10) in the river channel. Lands on the east bank of Il Nakwa near the main settlement area are severely overgrazed (see Fig. 2-20), and frequent trespassing occurs on the Kenya Ilemi lands west of Il Nakwa during the driest months when the situation is desperate for many Dasanetch and Inyangatom at Nakwa. On several occasions this exclusionary policy has been temporarily rescinded by the Kenya authorities so that stock could utilize these rich grasslands during severe droughts.[35] It is clear that this exclusionary policy has had profound effects

---

[34]This pattern was sharply broken in July of 1972, however, when fighting broke out between the Dasanetch and Inyangatom; it is not clear if and when Dasanetch will move back into the area. However, since it has been a much used area for a number of Dasanetch and may continue as such, it is included in this account.

[35]A section of it was, for instance, opened to the Dasanetch, Inyangatom

on both the Dasanetch and the Inyangatom, and the nature of these effects will be considered in detail in Chapter 7.

Dispersal and contraction patterns. --The strong separation between the east and west bank Dasanetch is clearly reflected by the movements of the west bank Dasanetch in the nodes described above. Social and economic interaction between Dasanetch of both banks occurs primarily in the modern delta and in the narrow strip of land along the east bank of the Omo River which is utilized by west bank Dasanetch households for foretch and for horticulture. Thus, the localities of such mixing are: Erdete, Nairobi,[36] Dielirieli, Turangoli and Nyemomari to name the most important. There is a tendency for the relatively immobile riverine Dasanetch to remain within the riverine area, thus reducing the probability of contact with the plains Dasanetch. Many of the riverine Eleli of the west bank, for instance, have more contact with east bank riverine residents than they do with plains Dasanetch on their own bank.

Dasanetch seasonal movements are only partially predictable on the basis of settlement within a given geographic area, as the above discussion demonstrates. This is in line with the Dasanetch perception of most land (excepting horticultural land) in terms of available resources rather than in terms of strict territoriality. Dispersion (centrifugal) and contraction (centripetal) settlement and stock movements vary greatly from place to place, rather than having an overall pattern such as that described by Evans-Pritchard (1960) for the Nuer, whereby there is village contraction in wet seasons and village dispersal to camps in dry seasons. For the Dasanetch tribe as a whole, the total area utilized by the tribe is greatest during the rainy periods because of: (1) the broad dispersion of east bank Dasanetch (Inkoria and Naritch segments) to lands farther north and northeast of their settlements near the lake and the Omo River;[37] (2) the movement of many villages and foretch to Nakwa and the lands nearby; and (3) the exploitation of Lomogol (Erek) and other areas west of Berar during the rains, primarily for foretch.

From the standpoint of individual settlement nodes, there are a number of

---

and Turkana for grazing between my 1970 and 1972 field work periods, and upon my return I found it very badly overgrazed where healthy grassland had existed.

[36]Now mostly flooded by the recent rise of Lake Rudolf.

[37]These movements are greatly affected by relations with neighboring tribes, especially the Hamar.

additional examples of movement patterns which make the situation far more
complex. It is useful to bear in mind the distinction between village movements
and foretch movements, since a group of villages may contract geographically
during a time when the total grazing area is simultaneously expanded through
foretch. Settlement density does increase significantly in some major settlement areas (such as Lobemkat and Gumbubur) during the large rainy season (ir
gudoha), for instance, whereas some of the villages send at least one type of
foretch (small stock or cattle) even farther away at this time.

The strip of land bordering Berar on the east is one example of a region
which undergoes radical fluctuation in settlement from season to season, and it
may receive a large influx of villages and camps a number of times during a
year. During the dry months when water is absent from the extensive mudflats
of Berar, little use is made of this zone (except near Namuruputh), and what
domestic stock are there are almost entirely goats and sheep, since they can
withstand two days without water and therefore make a trek to the Omo on alternate days. After even a small local rain, however, many villages and foretch
camps may appear overnight from different settlement nodes only to disperse
again when the pools evaporate. Generally, although the zone between Kalam
and Koras (node 5) is always with grazing and scattered settlement, there is an
influx of more villages and foretch during the rains due to scattered surface
pools forming in the plains there. This influx is no doubt partially offset by the
expansion northwards to utilize lands east of Koras.

The important factors of settlement contraction and dispersal must be
considered integrally when interpreting the village movement pattern for any
area. Those environmental features which promote dispersal include: accessibility of new rangelands following the rains; stock diseases which are considered highly contagious, causing many stock owners to keep their herds from
concentrating too much with others; and highly limited pasturage, forcing villages to split into smaller units. These are augmented by certain periodic and
relatively unchanging social forces, including the generational tensions associated with the patriline and the highly decentralized juridico-political organization. Those environmental and social forces promoting settlement contraction,
by contrast, include: large-scale flooding or inundation of lands in some areas,
causing villages to move to higher ground where they concentrate; horticultural
activity which requires intensive labor; ritual times, such as during the large
rains (ir gudoha), made possible by the increased amount of food available from
the harvests of January and higher milk yield because of fresh grass growth,

and during dimi; and hostile relations with neighboring tribes, causing small scattered villages to band together for defense purposes.

The complex patterns of movement described in this section provide for a high degree of social mixing at all levels, including individuals of widely varying economic status. It is in light of this fact that the juridico-political mechanisms for dispute settlement and general maintenance of social stability discussed in Chapter 4 take on a new dimension of importance. The highly flexible means of dispute settlement (with a few notable exceptions), the ideology maintaining the strict age principle and specifically the authority of the elders, and the ideology promoting solidarity and the avoidance of intra-tribal violence are thus highly adaptable and important features in this mobile society.

Goals of Production, Wealth and Surplus

Production goals. --In order to understand Dasanetch behavior relative to the various products resulting from economic activity, I find the following classification of production goals useful:[38] (1) direct subsistence--e.g., stock for food and other products, stock for herd building and future consumption, grain for consumption; (2) direct luxury--e.g., production of beer for ritual occasions, slaughtering of stock as a hospitality gesture or non-essential occasion,[39] fashioning of ornaments; and (3) exchange--e.g., millet grown to obtain small stock through barter, production of implements or ornaments for exchange by an individual with an especially well-developed skill or access to an uncommon resource, or stock for bridewealth exchange. The production goal of exchange subsequently undergoes transformation to one of the other two production goals (i.e., direct luxury or direct subsistence) in the context of the other production unit involved in the exchange. It is important to note that the emphases among these production goals vary widely among households or traditional (stock-raising) production units as well as on the level of tribal segment.[40] Labor power,

---

[38]There are a number of alternative classificatory systems which I have chosen not to adopt on the basis of the strong overlap among their categories, such as that of subsistence, luxury and ceremonial use and gift-giving as suggested by Salisbury (1962).

[39]The slaughter or sacrificing of stock for certain occasions may, by one line of thought, be considered essential to Dasanetch life such that what is a subsistence need may be defined quite differently when cultural, as contrasted with physiological, needs are taken into account. This is one of several qualifications which are necessary before the distinction between luxury and subsistence production can be explicated.

[40]Furthermore, non-subsistence (luxury and some exchange) production for

production branches, resultant products and production goals are shown in combination in Fig. 5-17. The outcome of the three major production goals, the material products, comprise much but not all of what may be termed wealth for a given production unit.

Wealth defined and wealth transformations. --The range of Dasanetch material wealth which either results directly from the production branches described earlier, or from any equivalents acquired through exchange, includes: land (e.g., for horticulture), domestic stock, implements or tools for labor (digging sticks, knives, herding sticks, herding spears, canoes, cooking pots), clothing, weapons (fighting spears, rifles), housing materials and luxury items (ornaments, etc.). But wealth in a broader sense may be taken to include not only the material objects held but also the capacity to appropriate or otherwise benefit from the wealth held by others or the wealth-producing capacity of others. This broader meaning includes social wealth such as control over labor power and gift-acquiring capacity through socio-economic position. Much of social wealth, then, may be thought of as one step removed from material wealth in that much social wealth may be traded for material wealth. Consequently there is no clear distinction between the two forms of wealth and even a given level of wealth may undergo a highly complex set of transformations between the two types over a short period of time. An elderly Dasanetch male who no longer directly controls the herds of his adult sons and who has in fact distributed much of his own stock (and his horticultural land) may be considered rich in terms of social wealth, and he has indirect access to considerable material wealth through his power and right to make economic demands of his sons and many other individuals.

The exchange of material wealth is intimately bound up with social relations, both in a generative and a conditioning sense, and exchange must therefore be understood in its social as well as material context. This is evident, for instance, in the exchange of cattle, which involves cattle as of central ideological importance, as a measure of material and social wealth, as a medium for the development and maintenance of social relations, and as a form of wealth storage[41] (i.e., for future expression of social relations through con-

---

a given household certainly does not necessarily indicate an adequate food supply for its members.

[41]Cattle, even though the preferred form of wealth, are unsuitable as a form of wealth storage from the standpoint of their (1) lack of durability (due to

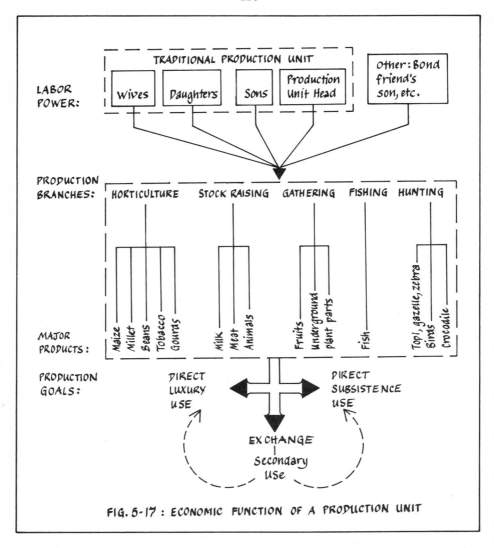

FIG. 5-17 : ECONOMIC FUNCTION OF A PRODUCTION UNIT

sumption or exchange).

The patterns of exchange of material and social wealth are conditioned by a whole complex of environmental and social factors, notably including the use values[42] of particular forms of wealth. Where one form of wealth has a higher use value relative to the others, patterns of wealth flow are correspondingly biased. The types of exchanges made over time by an average Dasanetch male or production unit head reflect the hierarchy of values placed on individual types of goods. The tendency among the Dasanetch to convert grain to small stock to cattle is a case in point.

On the basis of durability (thus, capacity for storage of assets), use value and exchange value [43] the strongly preferred form of material assets is stock, especially cattle.[44] Consequently there is a strong tendency to convert grain (millet or maize) into stock, i. e., in an upward direction of wealth transformation as wealth is culturally defined.

The combination of the use value and the exchange value of a product is the basic determinant of its position in the network of possible transformations. In the case of grain and small stock, use value favors small stock, but grain may be desired by production units with stock as a stop-gap or supplementary food source, for consumption during ceremonies, or for bartering for tobacco, coffee or other items. The higher use value of small stock explains the fact that a production unit head trades grain for a goat or sheep (three to four bags of grain equal one head of small stock) even when the remaining supply of grain is not adequate for the members of his unit.

The exchange values of small stock and cattle are roughly 10 small stock for one head of cattle, but among the Dasanetch themselves the exchange of small stock for cattle is in fact blocked by the cultural bias (use value) favoring cattle. Since the Dasanetch are presently confined to lands far more suitable for small stock than cattle, this strong differential use value favoring cattle

---

their susceptibility to disease), and (2) lack of transportability. These are both related to the utility of cattle as money. They are not a universal equivalent as described by Mandel (1969).

[42] Use value is the subjective value attributed to a product as a function of desirability.

[43] Exchange value is value of a product as a direct function of the labor time required to produce it.

[44] Cattle are, however, with limited durability in recent years, due to the deteriorated environmental conditions and high susceptibility to disease.

over small stock interferes with at least their short-term economic "rationality"
(see below). Transactions in which one major product is exchanged for another
are limited to two products:

$$\text{grain} \longleftrightarrow \text{small stock} \longleftrightarrow \text{cattle}$$

These two forms of exchange do not occur equally within the Dasanetch tribe
and intertribally, however. Dasanetch, for example, most often obtain cattle
from other tribes by bartering with small stock, and they barter for small
stock (usually with the Turkana) with grain.

Theoretically, economic rationality for a Dasanetch production unit head
might involve retaining or investing enough subsistence products and other material assets to provide adequate nourishment and care for his unit, using the
remaining products for exchange or luxury purposes. When rationality is defined by a complex of social and economic presuppositions, however,
a situation quite divergent from this form of strictly economic rationality results. Bartering of grain for small stock would seem at first highly irrational
to an outsider from the standpoint of increased stock pressure on the already
deteriorated lands and the high mortality of stock. But at least two other dimensions are important to consider in evaluating the matter. First, according
to Godelier (1972: 12), an act is only "irrational" if it is a means which is inconsistent with the end pursued or if, on a higher level, the ends pursued are
not mutually coherent. The ideological tenets of Dasanetch society which place
the acquisition and maintenance of stock as of paramount importance, and the
social processes immediately bound up with and dependent on the maintenance
of herds, clearly support the transformation of wealth from grain to small
stock. Second, within a relatively short-time perspective the transformation
of wealth from grain to small stock may also be considered rational from the
standpoint of the acquisition of a form of capital, namely stock, which is
reproducible capital, as opposed to grain which is primarily destined for consumption. [45] Only insofar as the maintenance of herds over a prolonged period
of time takes precedence over short-term increase in stock wealth would such
considerations as destruction of the lands for supporting future stock become
significant. Regarding this latter point, pastoral people in general and certainly the Dasanetch in particular have not, in the face of frequent disease epidem-

---

[45]Grain is used for reproduction of capital (more grain) through replanting,
but the regularity with which planting is attempted--i.e., when the grain is not
all consumed and other factors permit or encourage it and with which successful harvesting actually occurs, is not high for most Dasanetch households.

ics, droughts and wars, had the luxury of planning very far into the future. It should also be borne in mind that the Dasanetch ideological system has evolved over a very long period when the Dasanetch were not confined to a small tract of land (see Chapter 7), so that what is "irrational" to the economist or ecologist viewing the present situation is likely the product of a rational system which developed in a radically different context.

Hopefully, it has become clear by the preceding discussion that a full understanding of the emphasis among production goals (subsistence, luxury and exchange) and of the transformations of wealth by a given production unit requires an integrated consideration of social relations directly and indirectly associated with production, and the ideological system, etc., as well as direct productive economic forces. The above issues have focused on the production unit level, and it remains to consider subsistence and non-subsistence production on a societal level. For this purpose, the Marxist notion of surplus is valuable and is subsequently discussed as it might apply to the Dasanetch context.

The concept of surplus and Dasanetch economy. --Succinctly stated, surplus, or surplus product, is output above the producers' requirements (Sahlins, 1972). It is useful to briefly elaborate the concept, however, before considering it relative to Dasanetch production.

On the traditional (stock-raising) production unit level, all the productive activity done by members of that unit may be divided into that portion of labor required to produce subsistence for the unit, and other productive labor. The latter portion of productive labor is equivalent to surplus labor, and the products resulting from such labor are identified as surplus product. Extrapolating to the societal level, it is possible to calculate what portion of the labor of the members of society over a given period of time is concerned with production deemed necessary for the maintenance of that society (i.e., socially necessary labor resulting in socially necessary product) and that in excess of the above (i.e., resulting in surplus product). Stated in another way, surplus at the societal level is the difference between what the entire society produces and what it requires for its continued existence.

Baran (1957: 23) defines actual surplus[46] as the difference between soci-

---

[46]As contrasted with potential surplus, defined by Baran as "the difference between the output that could be produced in a given natural and technological environment with the help of employable productive resources, and what might be regarded as essential consumption."

ety's actual current output and its actual current consumption, such that actual
surplus is "identical with current saving or accumulation, and finds its embodi-
ment in assets of various kinds added to society's wealth during the period in
question." There are some difficulties with Baran's concept as applied to traditional societies. Specifically, when considering a traditional society such as
the Dasanetch, the existence of a product which is not consumed does not necessarily imply that the subsistence needs of the society are met. There are numerous socio-economic and environmental forces which influence the emphasis
among alternative production goals (direct subsistence, direct luxury, exchange)
for a given household, and it is necessary to consider a whole complex of them
in order to understand the existence or lack of surplus product for society as a
whole.

That it is sometimes necessary to separate conceptually the question of
the existence of surplus product for a society from behavior which is convergent with that accompanying the existence of surplus is clear in the context of
Dasanetch society. A comparison of the number of stock necessary for subsistence of the Dasanetch human population and the number of stock supportable by
the lands now available to them (see Chapter 7) shows that the former far exceeds the latter. When this is considered in conjunction with the fact that there
is a limited amount of alternative production (horticulture, fishing, etc.) it can
be concluded that there is no surplus product for the Dasanetch on a societal
level. In fact, it is clear that Dasanetch production is considerably below subsistence level, and the societal average is a real distortion of the starvation
conditions facing a very large number of Dasanetch households when the unequal
distribution of wealth is taken into account.[47] In spite of a production level considerably below subsistence, however, much Dasanetch behavior is similar to
that accompanying the existence of surplus: two clear examples of this are the
bartering and selling of food staples in order to obtain luxury items, and non-
reciprocated gift-giving (e.g., to bond friends, affines) involving subsistence
goods. Rather than simply considering these forms of behavior "irrational" on
the part of the Dasanetch, it is instructive for the outsider to consider the
broad and complex set of considerations Dasanetch decision makers necessarily
take into account which are therefore "rational" from the standpoint of the integrated levels of short- and long-term economic survival (see discussion

---

[47]This distortion may be considered analogous to that inherent in GNP
(gross national product), which does not take into account the distribution of
product.

above), development of social relations and maintenance of cultural integrity.

The issue of why no surplus product results from the Dasanetch system in the context of behavior consistent with the existence of surplus is primary to an understanding of the present state of the Dasanetch societal/environmental system of relations as set out in the next chapter. It is also essential to any serious suggestion for a solution to existing instability and deterioration. Of the possible explanations for the lack of existing surplus, two major ones are considered here. These are, first, the absence of a drive to generate surplus on the part of societal members, or second, socio-cultural and/or environmental processes inhibiting surplus generation which run counter to an existing drive to accumulate surplus.

With regard to the first possibility, Dasanetch ideology surrounding domestic stock involves a strong drive to accumulate large numbers of stock such that production objectives are, for all practical purposes, limitless. This is not to say that redistributive pressures do not mount as wealth in stock increases, as they in fact do, but rather that stock wealth is desired as a means of attaining prestige which may be expressed socially (e.g., through redistribution as a "big man") as well as economically through material wealth. Thus, rather than being "geared to the production of livelihood, . . . endowed with the tendency to come to a halt at that point" (ibid.: 86), Dasanetch society is instead geared for maximization of stock wealth. Thus the first of the two possible explanations for the absence of surplus in the Dasanetch economy, is certainly inadequate and we may turn to the second.

The inhibition of surplus generation, more generally the limitation of total production, occurs through the interaction of a number of forces: (1) full utilization of labor power does not exist; (2) environmental conditions are limiting, such as the loss of horticultural land in the delta, along the Omo River and in other localities and the deteriorated rangelands; (3) strong cultural biases exist against production activities alternative to stock raising; and (4) external (Ethiopian and Kenyan) controls are placed on Dasanetch territory and activities. Any of these four inhibitory factors may be sufficient to block the production of surplus, and in combination they impose strong counter forces to maximal production, or possible surplus formation. All of these inhibitory forces are discussed in other portions of this monograph except labor power, so I give brief attention to it here.

As Godelier points out, labor is not a scarce resource in most "primitive" societies. Within the Dasanetch system there is considerable unutilized labor power, primarily in the form of (but not limited to) adult male labor power. Even in the event that this additional labor power were utilized, however, the desired form of wealth--namely stock--would not be significantly increased. Its utilization would instead have the greatest impact on production if it were in the direction of economic diversification. It is at this point that the interaction between the limiting factor of unused labor power and the other three forces mentioned becomes relevant, however. Even if the adult male labor power were utilized and the cultural biases against diversification removed, the environmental and external political-economic controls would still be operative in keeping production increases down, thus preventing subsistence needs from being met and surplus from being created.

The Dasanetch economy, then, is characterized by underproduction, even relative to its existing potential. I do not suggest, however, that its existing potential would suffice for "socially necessary production" without at least some shifts in cultural and social patterns. One conclusion which results from even a superficial examination of the reasons for the lack of realization of full productive potential is that societal aspects such as kinship, ritual and juridico-political organization are of real significance to the structure and function of Dasanetch economic relations. For this reason the system of production is one which includes the interplay of components commonly termed economic and social, and these may be considered to comprise a mode of production (see Chapter 6). One dimension of relations which clearly illustrates the interaction of social and economic processes is that of exchange, and this forms the basis for the discussion to follow.

Socio-Economic Interaction in Exchange Relations

Forms of reciprocity. --The dual social and economic aspects to the flow of material wealth are examined in the following discussion of exchange relations. Further, their implications for social and economic stability are discussed briefly. Many of my thoughts are extensions of the discussion to be found in Marshall Sahlins' essay on primitive exchange (1972), and any misunderstandings I might have made are hopefully creative ones.

Polanyi (1957) describes three mechanisms of distribution which are forms of integration for societies. These are reciprocity, redistribution and exchange. In turn these three modes of distribution are associated with the supporting institutions of: symmetrically organized structures (for example, a symmetrical system of kinship groups), centricity (an allocative center), and a market system. Sahlins' (1972) conceptual categories, however, are considerably more refined and more useful. He offers a subset of categories of "reciprocity" and distinguishes it from "pooling" (i. e., Polanyi's "redistribution"). Pooling, or the "collection of products from members of a group, often under one hand, and redivision within this group," is really "an organization of reciprocities, a system of reciprocities." Pooling and reciprocity may be usefully separated, however, in that pooling is "socially a within relation, the collective action of a group," whereas reciprocity is "a between relation, the action and reaction of two parties" (ibid.). In general, pooling is a process which promotes group solidarity. In Dasanetch society, pooling usually occurs in the context of food distribution, and it occurs primarily on the level of the patrilineage, especially within the production unit. It may also occur among a father and his co-resident married sons, among co-resident age mates, or among individuals involved in collective hunting (e. g., of crocodile or topi). Reciprocity is discussed here on the level of its occurrence between patrilineages, or production units of different patrilineages.

The three types of reciprocity defined by Sahlins (ibid.) are: (1) generalized reciprocity (the solidary extreme); (2) balanced reciprocity (the midpoint); and (3) negative reciprocity (the unsociable extreme). These are symbolically represented by Sahlins as: generalized reciprocity, A $\overset{\longrightarrow}{\longleftarrow\text{--}}$ B; balanced reciprocity, A $\rightleftarrows$ B; negative reciprocity, A $\overset{\text{--}\rightarrow}{\longleftarrow\text{--}}$ B.[48] I will discuss these individually for the Dasanetch system.

(1) Generalized reciprocity occurs when a gift is made from a position of strength to another party who may or may not make a return gift (or at least an equivalent one), and where failure to reciprocate does not cause the giver of "stuff" to stop giving: the goods move one way, in favor of the have-not, for a very long period of time (ibid.). A major adaptive feature of this type of reciprocity is clearly stated by Sahlins:

> Primitive peoples have invented many ways to elevate a man above his fellows. But the producers' hold on their own economic means rules out the most compelling history has known: exclusive control of such means by some few, rendering dependent the many others. The political game has to be played on levels above production, with tokens such as food and other finished goods; then, usually the best move, as well as the most coveted right of property, is to give the stuff away (p. 93).

For the Dasanetch system, generalized reciprocity includes: food sharing

---

[48]A dotted line represents a reduced (or zero) amount of goods flow.

among kin and other close relations; gifts of stock, ornaments, etc., to bond friends or age mates; donation of stock by an adult male to young males on patrol during time of war, [49] and gifts by a "big man" (ma gudoha) to others. Generalized reciprocity is particularly common where social distance is small, so that the strength of the social relation outweighs the fact of an asymmetrical material wealth flow.

Although Sahlins maintains that the material advantage actually rests with the subordinate's side in such an arrangement, this is not always clear in the Dasanetch situation. For a big man (whether so-called because of his wealth status, political position, etc.), although he may make an unreciprocated donation and therefore take a material loss in an isolated instance, he may gain sufficiently in rank or prestige through such generosity. In fact, in the long run he may make an equal or even greater economic gain elsewhere, such as in the form of a favorable bridewealth arrangement or a gift from another big man.

(2) Balanced reciprocity, or direct exchange wherein "the reciprocation is the customary equivalent of the thing received and is without delay" (ibid.: 147), implies a greater social distance between the two individuals or groups than does generalized reciprocity. Here the material aspect of the exchange is often at least as important as the social aspect, so that failure to reciprocate may result in social tension or rupture between the parties concerned. Two variables may be considered for this type of reciprocity: economic equivalence and time. For the Dasanetch, immediate reciprocation does not have the importance that equivalent reciprocation does, so that the latter forms a better criterion for identifying this type of reciprocity. For example, bridewealth payments are frequently made over a large number of years, especially in recent years, and often are not completed at all. Thus balanced exchange may actually be expressed superficially (or in the short term) as generalized reciprocity. Among the Dasanetch, balanced reciprocity occurs in many forms: relatively equal gift exchange between bond friends; the loaning of an ox or other stock by one male to another, which is to be repaid; restitution of peaceful relations by payment of a penalty for an offense by an individual (e.g., cattle payment for adultery or for the pregnancy of an unmarried woman, as described in Chap-

---

[49] This is most often in the form of a visit by a group of age mates to an older man of the complementary age set (e.g., age set C' young males visiting a mature man of age set C) to beg the latter for an ox for slaughter. The usual justification given is that the meat is needed by the young men for strength to patrol the tribal lands. I observed this begging and feasting daily during the Dasanetch-Donyiro (Inyangatom) war of 1972.

ter 4); strict bartering of goods intra- and inter-tribally; looser forms of goods and services exchange (e.g., labor power exchange); and contracts of bride-wealth compensation to a patriline for loss of a woman upon marriage.[50]

I include a few comments here concerning barter of goods, since the other types of balanced reciprocity mentioned above are discussed elsewhere in this book. The total diversity of bartering, in terms of types of material wealth exchanged, is limited for the whole lower Omo Valley group of tribes. Two important reasons for this are the relatively homogeneous environmental conditions, resulting in a very small variety of goods produced, and the homogeneity of cultural values such that little variation in use values for the various products exists from segment to segment and among neighboring tribes. Bartering is done for various motives: obtaining subsistence goods for consumption, the building up of longer range capital assets, and the utilization of a change surplus (e.g., a good millet crop) to obtain non-subsistence or luxury goods. Within the tribe barter results from the different emphases among products rather than actual differences in production branches themselves (with few exceptions), at least on the tribal segment level. Contrasting product ratios are in part attributable to tribal segment territoriality in combination with environmental differences.[51]

Although Dasanetch balanced reciprocity relations are based on established exchange equivalents, some fluctuations do occur which are related to supply and demand. For example, the number of bags of millet grain exchanged for a head of small stock varies slightly, depending on such factors as drought and range conditions in the plains, degree of flooding of horticultural land, stock disease conditions, ritual needs, and so forth. Supply and demand modification of exchange values occurs both within and between tribes, and insofar as supply/demand influences signify a transition toward market economies,[52]

---

[50]Sahlins adds a qualification to this last type of balanced reciprocity, i.e., bridewealth, by pointing out that the exchange is of incomparables and therefore possibly does not represent an equal or balanced exchange. It is important to point out, however, that although the consideration of women in terms of cattle is a form of objectification of women, it does in fact represent Dasanetch consciousness.

[51]For instance, the Naritch tribal segment, inhabiting lands east of the Omo River which are better suited to horticulture, often produces a substantially larger millet crop than do residents of the west bank. Consequently, the Naritch frequently exchange millet for stock from the west bank.

[52]See the discussion of marketless, peripheral market and market-dominated economies by Bohannan and Dalton, 1965.

the Dasanetch system illustrates the lack of a clear boundary between market
and non-market systems. A couple of other characteristics of Dasanetch economic behavior also associated with market economies (as defined by Bohannan
and Dalton) and which also serve to blur the boundary between types of economies are production for sale[53] (as opposed to subsistence) and money payment.[54]

Balanced reciprocity among the Dasanetch may serve to initiate and solid-
ify or maintain certain social bonds or relations which otherwise might not be
developed because of social distance or other reasons. Looked at from a different position, balanced reciprocity may serve to avoid adverse social effects of
ruptures or negative interactions in social relations, both within the tribe and
between the Dasanetch and their periodically hostile neighbors. It does not,
however, serve as a redistributive mechanism, and in this respect it contrasts
sharply with generalized reciprocity.

(3) Negative reciprocity is described by Sahlins as "the attempt to get
something for nothing with impunity, the several forms of appropriation, transactions opened and conducted toward net utilitarian advantage" (1972: 148). It
often, though by no means always, occurs between Dasanetch individuals or
groups of relatively great social distance. A few clear examples of negative
reciprocity from Dasanetch society are: theft of stock (whether for herd building or consumption purposes), grain or other goods; adultery; sexual inter-
course between a male and an unmarried woman;[55] and bartering within the
tribe which involves trickery or cheating.

Although the above definition characterizes this form of reciprocity as
occurring when an individual or group has intentions which are counter to the
normative social values, the issue of intentions is often difficult at best when
attempting to apply it to daily social relations. This is true for the reasons
that the precise nature of the intention behind a given act is quite often not clear,
and the fact that an individual act frequently involves multiple objectives or mo-

---

[53]For example, some Dasanetch production of millet is done with the intention of using it for barter with the Turkana tribe to obtain small stock.

[54]This is increasingly common among the Dasanetch as well as between
them and the Kenya police, Ethiopian police, at the Kalam mission, at the
small stores in northwest Kenya at Lokitaung, etc. Money is usually obtained
through sale of cattle, small stock, grain, or chickens (raised only by poor riverine villagers).

[55]"Stealing" a young woman whom a man wants to marry (see Chapter 4) is
here considered not to be an instance of negative reciprocity, since the young
man does not really expect to avoid paying bridewealth.

tivations (e.g., in the case of a stock loan made by a Dasanetch male which is not repaid according to agreement, it is not clear what his intentions were at the time of the agreement). The issue of intentions counter to the normative social values is closely related to an important dimension not taken into account by Sahlins' schema--that of economic exploitation of others' labor power, etc., by individuals who are themselves non-producers or low producers. I use economic exploitation here in the sense of the product itself being "turned against" the producers and increasing their subjection to the controller of their labor power. This usage stands in strong contrast to that of Godelier and Meillassoux in particular, but it is similar to that of Dupré and Rey (1973). Dupré and Rey, however, consider only the use of surplus product as allowing for exploitation, whereas the Dasanetch situation has been described as one having no surplus product. Yet in Dasanetch society there is full appropriation of the labor power of women, girls and unmarried males by relative non-producers or "controllers" (adult males as heads of production units). I submit that the existence of surplus product is not a necessary condition to the existence of exploitation in the sense described above, and that exploitation of labor power along the lines of sex and age is within the realm of normative social processes.

I propose the following as a refinement of Sahlins' conceptualization of negative reciprocity. This refinement is based on the premise that there is a significant difference between exploitation or "transactions opened and conducted toward net utilitarian advantage" which are clearly counter to the normative ideology and/or the juridico-political system of a society on the one hand, and exploitation or such transactions which are normatively congruent with the social system of relations on the other. Thus, one former type may be identified as non-institutional negative reciprocity (e.g., theft, cheating, adultery) and the latter type as institutional negative reciprocity (e.g., exploitation of the labor power of one individual or group by another). A few comments regarding both types of negative reciprocity make this distinction clearer.

Most forms of non-institutional negative reciprocity do have corresponding penalties or compensations within the juridico-political system, and it may even be considered that these forms of deviance, given their relative low frequency and the redress mechanisms evolved for them, may even serve to reinforce and provide for adaptation of the juridico-political organization. Thus this type of negative reciprocity is closely bound up with balanced reciprocity if the actual transactions rather than the supposed intentions behind them are con-

sidered.[56] This adaptive value which exists one level removed from the surface level non-institutional character of the act is an example of the overlapping
nature of the reciprocity types as defined here. With regard to institutional negative reciprocity (e.g., exploitation by an adult male of his wives' and his
young children's labor power, economic exploitation by an elderly man of his
married sons, raids on a neighboring tribe which result in seizure of stock),[57]
this form of exploitation and action which is directed toward net utilitarian advantage is not only advantageous to Dasanetch society but indeed is necessary
to the maintenance of the traditional system of social relations.

The above examples hopefully make it clear, first, that it is important to
take into account both the level of social structure being considered (e.g., intra-
tribal vs. inter-tribal, tribal vs. tribal segment) and the time period[58] involved when applying the conceptual categories of reciprocity to real transactions, and second, that the distinction between institutional and non-institutional
negative reciprocity is significant in the whole system of exchange.

Reciprocity relations: an overview.--Coincident with pooling, balanced
and generalized reciprocity being of high importance in Dasanetch society is the
fact that Dasanetch social relations are rather remarkably stable (see conclusion of Chapter 4). Generalized and balanced reciprocity contribute to this stability in social relations in several respects. First, the creation of a bond involving an asymmetrical transfer of goods and services (generalized reciprocity) provides for a social bond, and collectively in society these result in strong
cohesive forces. Second, generalized reciprocity, as a strong redistributive
mechanism within Dasanetch society, operates in structural opposition to economic inequalities and therefore social tensions associated with them (intensified during times of stress) are at least somewhat lowered. This is not to as-
sert that large inequalities in wealth do not exist, for they clearly do, but that
such inequalities would be considerably greater without significant modes of

---

[56]A bridewealth obligation, considered above to be a form of balanced reciprocity, may never be fulfilled by the debtor, whether or not he actually intended to complete payment. In this context such a transaction could be considered a form of non-institutional reciprocity.

[57]Note that inter-tribal raiding may often be considered normative social
behavior.

[58]In any concrete applications of the notion of the types of reciprocity, these
categories may be found to involve transformations among one another over
time.

redistribution. Those structural tensions which do exist have associated institutionalized or non-institutionalized counterbalancing mechanisms which, at least
in the short run, effectively neutralize them. For example, the lineage-based
generational tensions (see Chapter 4) are largely offset by the age-set and moiety principles, and there exist political redress mechanisms for deviations
from the normative prescription for social behavior, i.e., as non-institutional
negative reciprocities.

Extreme stress conditions have been created within the Dasanetch socio-
economic and environmental system over the past few decades, including the
depletion of stock numbers, scarcity of food much of the time, and stock and
human disease in critical proportions. A question which is pertinent to the Dasanetch situation in the future could be phrased: is there a limit to the increased balanced and generalized reciprocity mechanisms which alleviate the
effects of such stress; or, in the context of the Dasanetch situation, is there a
limit to the extension of generalized reciprocity especially, beyond which the
range of social relations (in terms of social distance) involved may, under conditions of severe economic stress, even constrict from that traditionally established? Is there a threshold of stress beyond which the patterns of reciprocity
which have traditionally been important factors of social stability themselves
break down? If so, then economic stress, coupled with progressive environmental deterioration, may be predicted to be accompanied by a serious rupture
in the social fabric more generally, given sufficient time.

It is now possible to develop the concepts of a societal/environmental
(S/E) system and that of mode of production as they relate to the above processes, and a more formal introduction to these concepts constitutes the bulk of
the next chapter. I will then analyze the major recent changes occurring in the
Dasanetch system and discuss possible solutions to the problems of the Dasanetch and their natural resources.

CHAPTER 6

SYSTEM PROCESSES AND THE MODE

OF PRODUCTION CONCEPT

Having now discussed many of the basic socioeconomic and environmental patterns relevant to the Dasanetch way of life, I turn now to presenting a more formal theoretical framework for examining these patterns. My objectives in developing this framework include offering a means of viewing the full range of processes as a whole, thus enabling a systematic understanding of the phenomena leading to the desperate condition of the Dasanetch people. This involves explicating the scope and nature of changes which have occurred as a result of the political policy markedly restricting Dasanetch territory (see Chapter 7) and, secondarily, those changes associated with the lake level and river shifts which have occurred in recent decades (see Chapter 3). Such understanding in turn constitutes a basis for shaping policy with the aim of reversing the human and environmental destruction now in progress. I will conclude the next chapter with a basic outline of one possible solution which is based on the following objectives: physical survival of the Dasanetch people, reduction of environmental destruction with selective ecosystem management, fundamental socioeconomic changes necessitated by the realities of social and environmental resources available locally and nationally, and maximal participation by the Dasanetch themselves in shaping their own future.

In the course of developing this analysis, I have become increasingly aware of some common weaknesses of system analyses. Some of these I have consciously attempted to avoid by considering Marx's development of a historical materialist analysis of a social "totality" or whole, and within this the concept of mode of production. Because the utility of a system framework for accomplishing the objectives I have set out above is likely more apparent to the reader than the utility of the mode of production concept, I will preface my explication of the societal/environmental system's internal structure with some introductory remarks concerning the mode concept, to which we will return later.

System analyses are often strongly limited in their representation of the world by their emphasis on equilibrium (or "deviance" from equilibrium), as well as by their tendency to represent processes over time (i. e., "diachronically"), if at all, as a series of "synchronic slices." A Marxist historical materialist analysis of productive and reproductive processes, by contrast, strongly challenges these equilibrium and synchronic biases, as well as the frequent omission of individual and social consciousness as a critical agent in system change (misrepresentations of Marx notwithstanding). Such analysis, I submit, provides for a more dynamic understanding of a complex societal/environmental system. A mode of production schema is based on establishing and analyzing those relations which have specified orientations to a society's changing system of material and social productive processes (see below) and offers a set of useful ordering principles for the constituents of a societal/environmental system. The development of this Marxist concept in the present study represents only a beginning in the investigation of its usefulness in understanding traditional or "precapitalist" societal and environmental change.

General Characteristics of the System

The structure of the societal/environmental (S/E) system developed for this study is presented in basic outline in Fig. 6-1. The baseline of analysis was defined in Chapter 1 as the collection of points of interaction between social and environmental units. The relationship between the baseline and the units of the system was also explained. Although the general structural character of the system is hierarchical in the sense of central and peripheral components with reference to the focus of the study (i. e., societal/environmental interaction), this is without connotation of an order of determination.

The basic constituent of the system as presented here is the unit. Each unit of the system is itself internally structured in that it is decomposable into a number of smaller components or processes. A unit is therefore based on its components having qualities which are persistent, tend to covary, and have some intuitive coherence. As in all systems, such classifications are validated primarily by their utility in the analytic framework in which they appear. Examples of units which I have deemed useful for this study include Riverine Environments (Unit$_8$) and Domestic Stock (Unit$_{11}$), for instance. Examples of components (or sub-units) for Domestic Stock are Herd Composition, Stock Diseases and Stock Utilization.

Fig. 6-1 shows the connectedness of units within the S/E system, but without reference to causal relationships between individual pairs of units. While the model presented here makes clear many pathways of change which are possible, it does so in the form of statements of correlation. This is so because the direction of movement of change between two units may vary according to context, including such influences as the points of origin of change within (or from without) the system, the specific nature of the change occurring, and historical conditions. Now with the identification of the baseline and units, it is possible to order the relationships within both subsystems (i. e., environmental and societal) by defining the strata. Societal and environmental units are grouped into strata which are defined by their proximity to the points of interaction between the societal and environmental subsystems (i. e., the baseline). In slightly more formal language, the two strata immediately adjacent to the baseline, s_1 and e_1 (see Fig. 6-1), contain all those units which are <u>either directly affected by or directly affect</u> a unit(s) in the opposite subsystem. Thus <u>Domestic Stock</u> (Unit$_{11}$) is a unit which directly affects (and, as it happens, is directly affected by) environmental units, including <u>Plains Environments</u> (U_7). Once these two strata adjacent to the baseline are defined, those strata one step removed may be defined. For example, stratum e_2 is the set of units directly connected with units of e_1. Units of the strata e_2 and s_2 do not directly affect, nor are they directly affected by, units of the opposite subsystem, but instead interact with the latter through "intermediary" relations of other units. A brief elaboration: the unit <u>Patterns of Exchange and Social Mixing</u> (U_{15}) does not interact directly with any environmental units, but interacts with them through the units of stratum s_1; it is therefore placed in stratum s_2, one level removed from the baseline. The same criterion for membership may be applied to the next two strata toward the periphery of the system, e_3 and s_3. In the actual model developed in this study, there are three strata to the right of the baseline and three to the left. One important constraint on the possible relationships which may hold between any two units of the system model as defined here is that only units of the same or adjacent strata may be connected.

In creating any model of a system, choices must be made along at least three lines: (1) the selection of boundaries for the model, (2) the definition of units within those boundaries, and (3) the organization (hierarchization, connectedness, etc.) of the units within the system once those units are defined. These choices are made by the model-builder, who operates implicitly or explicitly with certain assumptions and objectives. A few examples from the Dasanetch S/E system may serve to illustrate the pervasiveness of such choices.

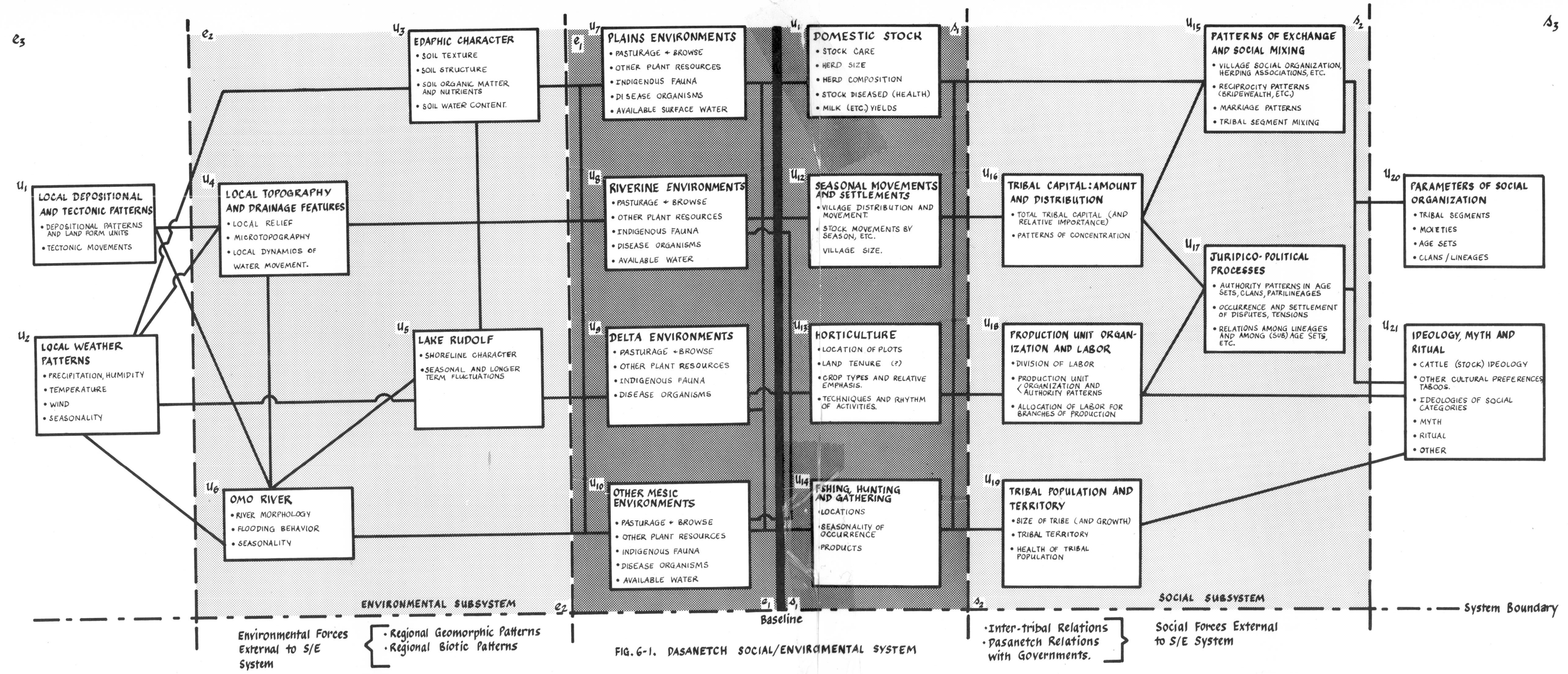

PARAMETERS OF SOCIAL ORGANIZATION
- Tribal segments
- Moieties
- Age sets
- Clans / lineages

u_{20}

IDEOLOGY, MYTH AND RITUAL
- Cattle (stock) ideology
- Other cultural preferences, taboos.
- Ideologies of social categories
- Myth
- Ritual
- Other

u_{21}

System Boundary

b_2

PATTERNS OF EXCHANGE AND SOCIAL MIXING
- Village social organization, herding associations, etc.
- Reciprocity patterns (bridewealth, etc.)
- Marriage patterns
- Tribal segment mixing

u_{15}

JURIDICO-POLITICAL PROCESSES
- Authority patterns in age sets, clans, patrilineages
- Occurrence and settlement of disputes, tensions
- Relations among lineages and among (sub) age sets, etc.

u_{17}

TRIBAL CAPITAL: AMOUNT AND DISTRIBUTION
- Total tribal capital (and relative importance)
- Patterns of concentration

u_{16}

PRODUCTION UNIT ORGANIZATION AND LABOR
- Division of labor
- Production unit organization and authority patterns
- Allocation of labor for branches of production

u_{18}

TRIBAL POPULATION AND TERRITORY
- Size of tribe (and growth)
- Tribal territory
- Health of tribal population

u_{19}

SOCIAL SUBSYSTEM

Social Forces External to S/E System

Inter-tribal Relations
- Dasanetch Relations with Governments.

b_2

A_1

DOMESTIC STOCK
- Stock care
- Herd size
- Herd composition
- Stock diseased (health)
- Milk (etc.) yields

u_1

SEASONAL MOVEMENTS AND SETTLEMENTS
- Village distribution and movement
- Stock movements by season, etc.
- Village size.

u_{12}

HORTICULTURE
- Location of plots
- Land tenure (?)
- Crop types and relative emphasis.
- Techniques and rhythm of activities.

u_{13}

FISHING, HUNTING AND GATHERING
- Locations
- Seasonality of occurrence
- Products

u_{14}

Baseline

e_1 s_1

PLAINS ENVIRONMENTS
- Pasturage + browse
- Other plant resources
- Indigenous fauna
- Disease organisms
- Available surface water

u_7

RIVERINE ENVIRONMENTS
- Pasturage + browse
- Other plant resources
- Indigenous fauna
- Disease organisms
- Available water

u_8

DELTA ENVIRONMENTS
- Pasturage + browse
- Other plant resources
- Indigenous fauna
- Disease organisms

u_9

OTHER MESIC ENVIRONMENTS
- Pasturage + browse
- Other plant resources
- Indigenous fauna
- Disease organisms
- Available water

u_{10}

e_1

e_2

EDAPHIC CHARACTER
- Soil texture
- Soil structure
- Soil organic matter and nutrients
- Soil water content.

u_3

LAKE RUDOLF
- Shoreline character
- Seasonal and longer term fluctuations

u_5

LOCAL TOPOGRAPHY AND DRAINAGE FEATURES
- Local relief
- Microtopography
- Local dynamics of water movement.

u_4

OMO RIVER
- River morphology
- Flooding behavior
- Seasonality

u_6

LOCAL DEPOSITIONAL AND TECTONIC PATTERNS
- Depositional patterns and land form units
- Tectonic movements

u_1

LOCAL WEATHER PATTERNS
- Precipitation, humidity
- Temperature
- Wind
- Seasonality

u_2

e_2

e_3

ENVIRONMENTAL SUBSYSTEM

Environmental Forces External to S/E System

Regional Geomorphic Patterns
- Regional Biotic Patterns

FIG. 6-1. DASANETCH SOCIAL/ENVIRONMENTAL SYSTEM

Socioeconomic features of neighboring tribes, the political character of the Ethiopian and Kenyan governments, or larger scale regional environmental character might have been included within the system, but these were instead considered external on the basis of the central objective of understanding societal/environmental relations within the Dasanetch context. Even though these features are important to the set of relations being analyzed, they may be considered external units which both contribute to and are shaped by the Dasanetch S/E relations themselves. Nevertheless, their formal exclusion from the system is significant.

Varying objectives of the analysis may also lead to different formulations of the system as well as the types of conclusions resulting. If, for instance, the major objective of the analysis were to understand the relations between economic and ritual aspects of Dasanetch society, these two dimensions would likely be centrally located within the system as well as more differentiated conceptually. Similarly, if the major objective were to understand societal/environmental interaction as defined by the Dasanetch themselves, e.g., through their "natural" vs. "social" categories, [1] a strongly contrastive organization of the system would obtain. Finally, the objective of economic survival for the Dasanetch, environmental integrity and maximal self-determination by the tribe likely leads to a radically different system of gathering and interpreting information from the objective of social control or containment of the Dasanetch. The setting of boundaries, defining of units and internal organization, etc., of units of the S/E system presented in this study are justifiable only insofar as they contribute to the objectives I have laid out.

The S/E System through Time

The synchronic model of the S/E system, which is given in Fig. 6-1, although useful in defining and describing the social and environmental relations to be considered, is seriously inadequate for understanding those relations. In the most general sense this is true because any structure, including the S/E system presented here, is only a "stage in process" (Ollman, 1971: 18). More specifically, a synchronic model is inadequate for identifying the components of the system as in an improbable state or typical in character, and such a model

---

[1] A highly interesting analysis of the concepts of "natural" and "social" (as defined by the Northern Kayapo people of Central Brazil) has been developed by Terence Turner in an endeavor to relate these categories and their use to existing social and ecological processes (manuscript, 1973).

may therefore significantly distort the real relations involved. Nor does a synchronic view provide an adequate understanding of the differential importance (or dominance) of some components within the system vis à vis others, even though some ranking of units according to dominance may be of real interest to the model builder. A third and more inclusive point is that a synchronic system provides insufficient information about the forces for change or resistance to change within the system. This information is necessary in order to take any clear account of the overall intactness of the system and its possible future states, including both adaptations and breakdown within and of the system.

One way a diachronic system model may be developed is as a series of synchronic slices, as noted earlier. Ideally these slices are able to be fully stated and conditions for the transitions between them can be specified. In most systems, however, and certainly in the Dasanetch S/E system in particular, this ideal cannot be fully met, both because information concerning many past (and for that matter, present) aspects of both the Dasanetch's society and their environment is not available and because the general characteristic of models is as only partial expressions of the realities which they are created to represent. Nevertheless, the diachronic content of an analysis may be maximized through several procedures, given the acceptance of a system framework. These include, among others: (1) selecting processes important to the major goals of the analysis and examining these historically, with the selection made on the basis of synchronic information, goals of analysis, etc.; (2) extrapolating from the relations within the system as presently functioning, to infer previous states of the system or parts of it (being careful, however, to specify the assumptions regarding constraints to future change, e.g., significant political change); and (3) utilizing whatever means are possible to obtain direct evidence of change over time (e.g., oral tradition, written records, etc.). All three procedures have been utilized in the present study.

A System Overlay: The Concept of Mode of Production

In the following sections I will first discuss the meaning of the concept of mode of production along with its general utility for the objectives laid out above, and then briefly deal with the issue of number of modes of production in a given society as well as suggest some parameters for separating branches of production into distinct modes and note the significance of the number of modes established for a given system. Finally I will suggest the relevance of the mode of production schema for examining system change and resistance to change.

The concept defined. --Because this study is primarily concerned with Dasanetch societal/environmental interaction over time, it strongly focuses on the productive system (broadly conceived, to include distribution and consumption). The social aspects of any production system, as explicated by Marx (1967), are embedded within that society as a whole, i.e., within a "totality" of social relations, or a "social formation." Just as, for instance the Dasanetch system of exchange was discussed in Chapters 4 and 5 as intimately bound up with the social fabric as a whole, so too is the very production of those goods and services which are exchanged bound up with the rest of society, e.g., with its system of authority, social structure and system of values. The Marxist conception of a social totality or social formation, viewed as the set of relations among humans and between humans and their environment, forms a strong critique of the fragmentary and limited nature of most "system" models of economic production, I submit, and strongly supports the breadth of system framework used in the present study. A useful refinement or expansion of the concept of social formation may be made from the perspective of a focus on human/environmental relations. That is, the environmental aspects of any productive system, in parallel form with its social aspects, embedded within the environment as a whole, such that one might think of an "environmental formation." The S/E system developed here and the analysis supporting it provides ample basis for considering this refinement.

The concept of reproduction is essential to the treatment of a social (or, I suggest, a societal/environmental) totality, in that a society not only reproduces its own labor, capital and some natural resources if it is to survive over time but it must also reproduce the conditions for its survival. This includes the reproduction of its conditions for change and adaptation as internally and externally generated pressures unfold. Those natural resources which are transformed in the society's productive processes must also be reproduced, along with the conditions for their reproduction. Much of Chapter 2 was devoted to the system constraints on this natural resource reproductive process in the Dasanetch situation. Consequently, the schema offered here is again broader than one "traditionally" defined by the Marxist concept of social formation although it is certainly congruent with it.

A mode of production may be preliminarily defined as a recognizable set of relations (among producers and the means of production) of economic production and distribution of goods and services. The concept will be developed here as it may be applied to traditional societal production systems in general and the Dasanetch system in particular. There is very little literature which attempts to apply the concept to traditional societies, and in this respect Claude Meillassoux's (1964) analysis of Guoro society is among a few pioneering works, as is Terray's (1972) critique of Meillassoux's work. These have been very important, along with several others acknowledged below, in the development of the thoughts presented below. However, my work has led me to some fundamental disagreements with their ideas, and it is my hope that I have not distorted their own formulations in my discussion of these disagreements.

The literature which does deal with the concept of mode of production is often highly ambiguous with regard to the precise meaning of the concept. A major question arising from the brief definition of mode of production offered above is: just what is included in "a recognizable set of relations . . ."? How much of the realm of social (and environmental) processes, for example, is to be included in a mode of production? One of the most inclusive interpretations is made by Althusser (1970: 41), where he asserts that a mode of production is "constituted by a structure which combines . . . the type of object (raw material) on which it labours, the theoretical means of production available (its theory, its method and its technique . . .) and the historical relations (both theoretical, ideological and social) in which it produces."

By its broadest interpretation a mode of production schema is associated with three major sets of processes: (1) the economic base, (2) the juridico-political organization, and (3) the ideological organization. (I will later focus on a narrower interpretation appropriate for the present analysis.) Each of these three components requires some brief explanation. The economic base is comprised of (a) the productive forces, including all the material conditions for production--natural resources, labor and capital, [2] and (b) the social relations of production, as the set of relations which directly involve control over production and distribution. [3] The economic base is often referred to as "infrastructure" in Marxist literature (e.g., Althusser, 1968) in contrast with the juridico-political (or jural-political) and ideological levels of organization which are

---

[2] The term "natural resources" is more accurate for both traditional and advanced technological context, I suggest, than is the less inclusive term "land." It should also be noted that the use of "capital" in this work is primarily in its liberal or bourgeois sense rather than in its Marxist sense.

[3] Social relations of production, then, includes but is not limited to the "relations established among the producers in the course of their work" (Terray, 1972: 98). It also includes the relations among the decision-makers themselves and between them and the producers.

jointly termed "superstructure." Because the uses of the terms "infrastructure" and "superstructure" and the implications they carry are highly debated and often confused among writers, I have intentionally avoided using them here.

Productive forces and the social relations of production do not exist as two clearly separable levels of a mode of production, but are reciprocally (dialectically) related through time. There may of course exist a differential between the forces of production and the social relations of production in terms of their relative importance in the economic base or the social formation as a whole, and this differential may be expected to shift over time and with changing conditions. Among the Dasanetch branches of production,[4] for instance, it is the social relations of production which are directly responsible for which branches are undertaken and in what way and which may sometimes constitute a serious block to the social formation as a whole adapting to deepening pressures. On the other hand, decisions resulting from the social relations of production are subject to real constraints (direct and indirect) imposed by the productive forces such that the latter may sometimes exert a controlling influence. An example of this is provided by the present Dasanetch situation wherein many production unit heads wish to diversify their productive activities (from stock raising alone to include horticulture), but this action is inhibited by the shortage of suitable land for cultivation, and so forth.

By juridico- (or jural-) political organization I refer to the elements and processes of the system which specify the way in which a society organizes itself into patterns of authority and decision-making at the level of structure above the production unit. The connection between jural-political organization and the economic base of a society is apparent when one considers, for instance, the social division of labor which involves a "hierarchy between direct producers and organizers of production, [and] this hierarchy will require a political and/or ideological sanction . . ." (Terray, 1972: 102). This set of relations within the Dasanetch social formation involves a broad range of social connections inside and between patrilines. Ideological organization is here considered to entail a society's whole set of beliefs and values and their typical expression. In a traditional context such as the Dasanetch's ideological organization includes principles of solidarity along age set or lineage lines (in this respect,

---

[4]A branch of production may now be defined as a combination of forces of production and its immediately associated aspects of the social relations of production which form a typical subsistence activity (e.g., stock raising, hunting, gathering).

its interrelatedness with jural-political relations is obvious), cultural definitions of wealth or value, attitudes toward peace and violence on intra-tribal and
inter-tribal levels, and myth and ritual as they both reflect and generate patterns of social relations. The interrelatedness of the economic base with both
the jural-political and the ideological sets of relations within a traditional social formation is rather well expressed by Terray (1972: 150):

> When pre-capitalist modes of production are dominant . . . juridico-politi-
> cal and ideological phases are involved in the very economic base of the
> mode of production: this involvement invalidates the delineation within the
> socio-economic formation of distinct sectors corresponding to each of the
> phases. The three phases [economic base, ideological phase, juridico-po-
> litical phase] are inseparably involved in the mode of production and have a
> common area of realization . . .

Major components of the mode of production concept frequently do not correspond to conventionally defined social organizational parameters. One clear
example of this may be seen in the realm of kinship relations in traditional societies. Social relations of production necessarily involve kinship relations in
that the latter are critical to an understanding of patterns of land tenure, rights
to products resulting from economic activity, obligations and rights in labor
power control, and other obligations to receive and give (see Godelier, 1972).
Kinship relations are also central to the structure and function of the juridico-
political organization and the ideological character of traditional societies.
Thus kinship can be mapped neither to a particular unit within the S/E system
as defined here nor to a specific component of the mode of production or social
formation. I should point out here that there are certainly other societal features not explicitly taken into account by the mode of production framework or
the system model as developed in this monograph, and these include language,
sexuality and some socialization processes.

Although there is general agreement that a mode(s) of production includes
both the forces of production and the social relations of production (together as
the economic base), there is a lack of consistency in the literature regarding
how much of the remaining social organization or processes are to be included.
A more restricted definition of mode of production may be more useful as a conceptual tool for examining the Dasanetch context--one which includes coherent
sets of relations within the forces and social relations of production only, although these are considered in close and reciprocal relation with jural-political
and ideological processes. The primary advantage of this narrower definition
for the purposes of the Dasanetch study is that while there may be two or three
modes of production defined for the economic base (see below), there exists

only a single set of jural-political and ideological relations at the societal level, although some features within the latter sets of relations may be clearly associated with an individual mode. I shall refer to the jural-political and ideological relations in combination as the <u>associated societal complex.</u> [5]

Environmental processes, like societal relations within the above schema, are associated with the economic base in two ways: (a) as part of the economic base in the form of natural resources (i. e., within the forces of production), and (b) as outside but interacting with the economic base (e.g., those geomorphic and biotic processes in the strata e_2 and e_3 not considered part of the forces of production). The latter category, I suggest, may be termed the <u>associated environmental complex.</u>

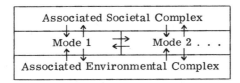

Fig. 6-2. --Modes of Production in Their Environmental and Social Context. Arrows indicate relations of influence.

It is worthwhile reiterating that the inclusion of those relations comprising the associated societal and environmental complexes in this system model which focuses on the modes of production is essential because--among other reasons-- they are critically involved in the <u>reproduction</u> of modes of production. That is, the economic base cannot reproduce itself, but its reproduction depends upon the social formation or society as a whole and the environment as a whole.

If the concept of mode of production is to be a useful tool for understanding traditional societal/environmental change, it is necessary to develop a means of identifying distinct modes on the basis of recognizably coherent sets of processes within the forces of production and social relations of production. I will suggest some criteria for distinguishing modes later in this chapter. It is of some importance here, however, to briefly deal with the theoretical issue of whether there exists a minimal number of modes of production which must exist for any given society. I submit that there is no logical reason why a soci-

---

[5]Associated societal complex, as defined here, is roughly equivalent to the Marxist term "superstructure."

ety must, as some literature suggests (for example, Althusser in Althusser and Balibar, 1970; Terray, 1972), involve at least two modes of production. The utility of social formation as a concept or an historical analysis of that formation does not necessarily depend on the existence of two or more modes, as many Marxists have been prone to accept. To the contrary, analysis of a social formation and its changes may be carried out on alternative structural levels, including the dynamics of components within one mode of production as well as on the level of intersection of modes. This will perhaps become clearer in the discussion below and in the last chapter.

Mode of production and system concepts in combination. --Fig. 6-3 shows the mode of production components in the context of the S/E system, with the associated environmental complex subdivided into its geomorphic and biotic organizations.

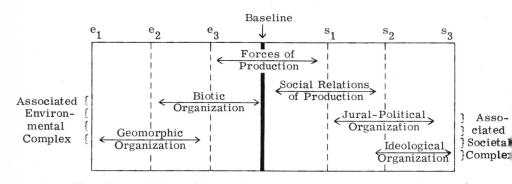

Fig. 6-3. --A Mode of Production Conceptual Overlay on the Societal/Environmental System.

The concept of mode of production now basically defined, it is useful to elaborate how the concept may be usefully combined with the S/E system framework.

Since the forces of production include both societal (labor, capital) and environmental (natural resource) components, as a single category they do not correspond to a specific subsystem as the system is defined. The respective environmental and social aspects of the productive forces may be conceptualized as separate with regard to the human control over the social aspects (e. g., the optional forms of utilization of labor power and the optional pursuit of a range of production branches) as contrasted with the relatively limited human control over most environmental processes. On the other hand, there is an essential unity among these environmental and social forces of production in their combined role in directly comprising the material basis for the production process. Thus, whereas the contrastive character of social and environmental processes is emphasized by the S/E system model, the concept of mode of production facilitates viewing them as a whole. Similarly, the mode concept as developed here emphasizes the parallelism between environmental and societal processes (as environmental and societal associated complexes) with reference to the mode(s) of production (Fig. 6-2), and in this way contributes to breaking down the functional dichotomy so widely conceptualized by system analysts.

Another utility of the mode of production concept when superimposed on the S/E system relates to its different set of categories which are defined according to their relation to overall productive and reproductive processes. The contrasting groupings of relations[6] within the mode concept (e.g., between forces of production and social relations of production) contribute to the understanding or identification of incongruities within the system and the forces leading to change and resistance to change. This I shall attempt to demonstrate in later discussion. In fact, it is perhaps the lack of correspondence of categories between the system and mode concepts which enriches the possibilities for understanding of this immensely complex set of societal and environmental relations.

Identifying distinct modes of production. --An explicit definition of the number and character of modes of production within traditional societies has rarely been attempted in the literature. Instead, a rhetorical and vague usage of the mode of production concept has predominated, justly raising the issue of whether the concept is employed because of its Marxist origin or because of its real value as a tool for analysis.[7] The precise number and identity of modes for a particular society may be determined by sorting the various branches of production according to their distinct properties of the productive forces and social relations of production. Below are a set of possible criteria for this sorting process and a few comments on those criteria which are proposed by Terray (1972).

---

[6]For example, between the forces of production and the social relations of production, and between the economic base and the jural-political organization.

[7]Meillassoux's and Terray's attempts to deal with the concept are quite exceptional in this regard.

Typically, two or more modes of production may interact with each other in at least two primary ways. First, they interact through their mutual connection to the same associated societal (and environmental) complex (see Fig. 6-2). Second, they may interact through direct overlap of their own components. This latter type of interaction may include overlap in the form of the same producers, the same environmental resources (land, etc.), the same production organizers or overlapping criteria for appropriation of the product or utilization of the forces of production. Much of the literature regarding modes of production assumes a clear disjunction between different modes of production and that the utility of the mode concept is bound up with this distinctness. Such a disjunction is not an accurate reflection of reality for the Dasanetch context, nor for many traditional contexts. But far from being a negative statement about the usefulness of the concept of mode of production, I submit that the existence of overlap in processes between modes affords a more dynamic interpretation of production processes over time, thereby increasing the value of the concept as a whole.

Terray (1972), in his effort to develop the notion of mode of production (drawing heavily from Meillassoux's analysis of the Guoro), offers two major criteria for determining the number and character of modes of production: the instruments of labor and the forms of cooperation. Although a helpful departure for considering the Dasanetch material, I have found it more fruitful to consider a broader set of criteria, one which in particular avoids the danger of a technological (cf. Leslie White, 1959) or economic determinism. Without offering a full critique of Terray's schema here, [8] a couple of basic points may suggest why I have arrived at the scope of criteria given below. First, although his assertion of the significance of cooperation and its different forms within traditional economies is important, the definition of cooperation he offers[9] is not sufficiently broad. For example, complex cooperation, as ". . . the use of a collective work implement" (Terray, 1972: 115) is, I suggest, a reification of human relations and in fact may be quite inconsistent with those relations. This is true, to cite only one instance, when the form of human relations (e.g., relations among decision makers for the production process)

---

[8]I intend to offer a fuller critique in a forthcoming paper treating more directly the concept of mode of production, and the present critique cannot do justice to the broad set of issues involved.

[9]Terray's classification of the forms of cooperation is: complex cooperation; simple cooperation; and individual activities (1972: 115).

changes over time, while the implements used in production--even the ownership and use of them--may remain the same. [10] Thus the collective or non-col-
lective nature of the work implement(s) is only one of a number of aspects of
cooperation which is characteristic of a branch of production, and a consideration of this aspect alone distorts the many patterns of human cooperation involved. Second, a more complex set of parameters than that suggested by Terray offers increased opportunity for meaningful distinctions to be drawn between modes and for more subtle but important shifts in productive and reproductive processes to be recognized.

The criteria I am suggesting are helpful in analyzing the Dasanetch
productive system (and those of traditional societies more generally) by virtue
of distinguishing modes of production are as follows.

1. Production Unit Composition. The composition of the production unit
    associated with the given branch of production (e.g., household, ex-
    tended household, age set mates, non-kin females from geographi-
    cally proximal households).

2. Labor Organization: Simple vs. Complex. Simple is defined here as
    that form of productive labor where the results of productive activity
    are a direct function of the laborers as separate individuals, i.e.,
    the product resulting is additive or summed from individuals' labor.
    Complex, on the other hand, is specified as that form of productive
    labor where there is specialization of labor tasks such that the re-
    sults of productive labor represent collective labor greater than the
    sum of its contributors as individuals.

3. Production Unit Organization: Age and Sex. The specific organiza-
    tion of direct producers (laborers) within the production unit along
    the lines of age and sex.

4. Control over Labor Power. The correspondence, or lack thereof,
    between the direct laborer in the production branch being considered,
    and the ultimate controller of that individual's labor power.

5. Ownership and/or Control of Land and Capital. Ownership and/or
    control (in many instances the latter is a better index of social rela-
    tions than is ownership) of land and capital in the production process
    may be private, semi-communal or communal. Any of these may
    require more specification.

6. Criteria Used in Shaping Forces of Production. The relative empha-
    ses among various social obligations, maximization of economic
    wealth, environmental conditions, etc., in forming decisions as to
    the specific uses of the forces of production.

7. Agents and Patterns of Product Allocation (Appropriation). The pos-
    sible range of persons appropriating the product includes the labor-
    ers themselves, the controllers of labor power (where different), own-
    ers or controllers of capital involved, and so forth. Pattern of prod-

---

[10] In Marxist literature this is formulated as a contradiction between the
forces of production and the social relations of production.

uct allocation refers to wealth concentration vs. redistribution, use
for consumption vs. exchange, etc.

Although other criteria could be included or substituted[11] in this set, I believe these to be useful as a means of establishing the number and basic character of modes for a society. When the existing branches of production (with
their associated forces and social relations of production characteristics) do
not cluster readily into recognizable modes, at least two alternatives exist in
the analysis. First, the parameters might be hierarchized (e.g., Labor Organization: Simple vs. Complex might be emphasized relative to Production Unit
Organization: Age and Sex). Second, the production system may be treated as
one complex mode, with subsequent analysis of internal structural and functional variation. This contrasts with the position taken by Terray, Althusser and
others.

The seven criteria offered here deal directly with the economic base,
but to varying degrees they are bound up with relations outside the base. Extremely diverse environmental resources and forms of capital associated with
two different branches of production may be grouped within the same mode of
production (see below). This does not imply, however, that a meaningful analysis need not take into account the environmental aspects of the forces of production. The present study of societal/environmental relations stands in strong
contrast to such an interpretation.

It now remains to apply the concept of mode of production to the Dasanetch system specifically. When the above seven criteria are considered
for the forces and relations associated with the Dasanetch branches of production (stock raising, horticulture, fishing, hunting, gathering), two modes seem
clearly distinguishable. These may be identified as:

Mode I - stock raising and horticulture

Mode II - fishing, hunting and gathering.

On the basis of the description of these socioeconomic activities presented in
earlier chapters of this monograph, the two modes are easily separated by six
of the seven criteria. Points of overlap between the two modes do occur
with regard to land and capital ownership and control (as fundamentally adult
male ownership and/or control). Numerous minor overlaps, of course, also
occur.

---

[11]For example, the environmental resources utilized, or the degree of con-
vertibility of the products of labor among different branches of production might
also be considered as an indicator of the relative closeness of those branches.

A brief digression to consider a couple of these criteria as they might be characterized for the Dasanetch context may help suggest possible refinements for their use more generally. For criterion 2, Dasanetch labor organization associated with both stock raising and horticulture--both components of Mode I--may be classed as complex (see above definition) since both involve significant division of labor in such a way that the whole labor effort is greater than the sum of the individual laborers.[12] By contrast, fishing, hunting and gathering--all components of Mode II--generally can be classified as simple in labor organization. with products able to be produced by the action of isolated individuals. These three branches of production are often not performed by individuals, but with certain notable exceptions such as the hunting of crocodile, topi and gazelle by adult males who operate with a definite organization and strategy, the labor of combined individuals is essentially additive. Groups of women who visit a food gathering area together and who sometimes process the gathered plant parts together, as well as groups of males fishing together, usually act in simple cooperation.

Criterion 3 (production unit organization along age and sex lines) does not immediately provide for a clear separation of the branches of production into modes. But a closer view reveals this separation more likely. The predominant sex associated with each branch of Mode I (males for stock raising and females for horticulture) receives subsidiary labor power from the opposite sex (either seasonally as in the case of horticulture, or more ongoing support as in the case of stock raising). These two branches of production are inverses of one another in this respect, and thus may be seen as complementary in their inclusion within one mode of production. The alternative mode of production, i.e., Mode II (fishing, hunting and gathering) contrasts strongly with this in that its labor is well-differentiated along sexual lines, with subsidiary or additional labor supplied by younger members of the same sex.[13]

---

[12]In stock raising. for example, the resultant products of milk, hides, new stock and so forth require a differentiation of labor among adult bachelor males, very young to adolescent boys, and women and girls. Horticulture likewise necessarily involves a complex rhythm and organization of differentiated labor, from the phase of cutting, burning and preparation of the plot, through planting and harvesting.

[13]It is important to note that all the discussion of "production unit" presented in this and previous chapters refers to that production associated with stock raising and horticulture. This unit, it will be recalled, is formed primarily by the household (adult male, his wife or wives and his unmarried children), even though there are frequently labor power, capital and product sharing ar-

Variation and changing relations among modes. --Dominance of one mode of production over another is a complex problem, the understanding of which is valuable in analyzing change in a social formation and environment. Unfortunately, it is neither clearly defined nor discussed to any satisfactory degree in the literature. Nevertheless, since the issue is part of the major concern of this monograph, namely system change and resistance to change, some attempt to clarify it is needed. Three dimensions within which one mode may be considered dominant over another (though these are not intended to be exhaustive) are:

(1) Ideological. A dominant mode may be judged by the analyst to be more congruent with, or structurally bound up with, the prevailing ideological organization of the society.

(2) Volume of Production. A dominant mode of production may be seen to account for substantially more of the overall material or service production than does the other mode(s).

(3) Social Relations. A dominant mode may be judged structurally more central to the maintenance or reproduction of the prevailing social relations such as political structure, marriage relations, etc.

In any particular societal context there may be no clear dominance of a single mode along the three dimensions noted above. This situation is especially likely to occur when a whole social formation or its system of production more narrowly defined is undergoing a period of large-scale or intensive change. [14]

In the case of the Dasanetch system there is a clear dominance of Mode I (stock raising and horticulture) over Mode II (fishing, hunting and gathering) within all three dimensions. The strong dominance of stock raising in particular within the ideological dimension is reflected in the Dasanetch's cultural definition of wealth, the strong stock emphasis in myth and ritual, the system of naming, attitudes toward other tribes and among tribal segments, [15] and the strong biases against hunting and fishing as a means of subsistence. The vol-

---

rangements among production unit heads. These inter-household sharing relations occur primarily within patrilineages, and among age mates, bond friends and affines. Because stock raising and horticulture together comprise the vast majority of production within Dasanetch society, the term production unit (unless otherwise stated) refers to its form in Mode I.

[14] Consider, for instance, the second dimension of volume of production. If, over time, the subdominant mode increases in importance to become dominant itself. logically there is a point at which the two modes are equal in importance, and this situation may not be trivial in duration. The same principle applies to the other two suggested dimensions。

[15] The reader may recall from Chapter 4 that the Inkabela tribal segment is the dominant one, serving as a sort of "template" for social structure and social relations. Consequently it is significant that this segment has a strong bovine ideology whereas some of the segments of lesser strength have less resistance to diversification (i. e., the Eleli, Rieli and Naritch segments).

ume of production accounted for by the different modes has undergone radical change in recent years, but mode I relations are still clearly primary on the societal level. The third dimension suggested above, that of social relations, is also changing rapidly, but for the tribe as a whole these changes are so far mostly the result of an increasing reliance on horticulture as opposed to stock raising and therefore represent a shift within Mode I. While neither mode can be traced to its own set of characteristics within the associated societal complex, the two modes do have different degrees of congruency with it. Dasanetch social relations have evolved concurrently with stock raising as the central productive activity so that thus branch of production (and thus Mode I) is intimately related to the structure and function of social processes ranging among ideology, kinship, socioeconomic exchange, etc. New emphases in social relations such as change of land and labor relations, are primarily bound up with horticultural activities and are defined around Mode II only for a small though increasing proportion of the tribe. [16]

Differences in dominance over space, time and organizational level are even more in evidence for the Dasanetch when branches or production within a mode are examined. A nearly reverse emphasis exists, for instance, between stock raising and horticulture within the Naritch segment of the east bank of the Omo River as compared with most Inkabela of the west bank. This difference is even more accentuated between the Rieli and the Randel. The Rieli are primarily dependent on horticulture and Mode II branches of production, whereas the Randel are almost entirely dependent on stock raising and are extremely reluctant to diversify to horticulture. Certainly, there has been a marked shift in emphasis from stock raising to horticulture for the tribe as a whole as well as for most individual tribal segments, and this "downgrading" in terms of the Dasanetch system of values is congruent with the larger shift in emphasis from Mode I to Mode II. The Dasanetch increasing reliance on Mode II in recent years does raise the pertinent question: does the subordinate mode exist harmoniously within the framework of the dominant one and the associated societal and environmental complexes, from which it may in fact be considered to have generated. or are there significant tensions arising within the system? We shall return to this question later.

Before proceeding to a detailed analysis of specific change within the Da-

---

[16] Mode II is already dominant among some elements of society (i. e., among portions of the Rieli and Eleli tribal segments in particular) and is presently increasing rapidly in importance for a very large number of households.

sanetch S/E system and a possible means of redressing that change which is destructive, a brief exposition of the processes of feedback as a system process is necessary.

Forces of System Change and Resistance to Change:
Positive and Negative Feedback

A given change or "deviation" occurring anyplace within a system may or may not be immediately linked to another process within that system. Of those which are linked to another process in a way which is perceptible, the relationship may be one whereby the deviation is counteracted (NEGATIVE FEEDBACK) or where the deviation is reinforced or amplified (POSITIVE FEEDBACK). These types of system processes are shown in briefest form below.

TABLE 6-1

A CLASSIFICATION OF SYSTEM PROCESSES

Dominant Relation of Processes	System Effect
Antagonistic	NEGATIVE FEEDBACK Deviation counteraction[17] Subtraction
Independent	Additive
Reinforcing	POSITIVE FEEDBACK Deviation amplification Multiplication

Some assessment of the particular state of a set of societal/environmental relations and its possible future significance can be made through understanding the interaction of these processes within the system. Since such an assessment is a major goal of the present study, some brief clarification of the nature of positive and negative feedback processes in the Dasanetch societal/environmental relations is useful.

Negative feedback processes are those involving self-regulation of a system whereby a deviation within that system is counteracted with the result that the system tends to be regulated to a particular state. Negative feedback processes, when dominant within a system, tend to render that system "stable,"

---

[17]Deviation counteraction, or negative feedback, processes are also termed "error activated" processes (see Hoffman, 1971).

i. e., relatively invariant for a particular state and with regard to specific disturbances.[18] Such a stable state may be highly dynamic rather than static, however. But negative feedback processes are not always characterized by a tendency to contribute to system stability, as for example when the feedback over-
compensates or overshoots in countering the change in question or when the
feedback is distorted (Boyd, n. d.).

Positive feedback processes, or deviation-amplifying processes, occur
when "the output of a system or process is ultimately fed back as an input to the
same system or process so that the process feeds on itself, resulting in a vi-
cious circle" (Boyd, n. d.). Positive feedback processes may characterize a
system when: (1) a system's negative feedback processes break down such that
the positive feedback takes over, or (2) a new variation takes hold as deviation
selectively amplified by natural events (Hoffman 1971). This type of feedback
tends to contribute to system change, or self-feeding variance from a particular state with regard to specific disturbances. But as with negative feedback, a
generalization about the relation of this type of process to system stability or
change is not always accurate. Deviation-amplifying processes may, for instance, have system stabilizing or change resistance effects, even in the short
run, as when a system is reproduced on a higher level at the expense of stability of lower level components (e. g., maintenance of Dasanetch production units
through continual and simultaneous in- and out-migration of individuals [see
Chapter 5]). Any system strongly dominated by positive feedback processes producing change will likely become stabilized, given sufficient time, if through no
other means than the evolution of new system characteristics or system breakdown, after which the processes of change and change resistance continue. To
quote Wilden in his book System and Structure, ". . . all runaway systems
(such as a forest fire or a supernova) are inexorably controlled, in the long run,
by negative feedback at a second level. Second order negative feedback always
takes the form of the emergence of a metasystem (the elaboration of new structures, morphogenesis) or the destruction of the [eco]system involved" (1972:
209). Maruyama (1963) describes the survival of any living system as dependent on two basic processes: (1) morphostasis, whereby a system maintains
constancy in the presence of deviation, through negative feedback,[19] and (2)

---

[18]As Boyd (n. d.) points out, equilibria states of a system may be stable or
unstable, i. e., a given equilibrium state may be stable under some deviations,
yet unstable under others.

[19]Counteracting forces, however, may also take the form of opposing positive feedback forces.

morphogenesis, whereby a system changes its basic structure in response to deviation-amplifying or positive feedback forces.[20] Breakdown of the system may occur when positive feedback processes exist without adequate structural response by the system.[21] Since a particular positive feedback process may be merely part of an oscillation within a homeostatic system where the same homeostatic conditions subsequently are reestablished, or it may contribute to a new system state, some time framework needs to be supplied to distinguish between the two. It is important to remember that system change does not depend upon the assurance of positive feedback processes, although they may be significant in its generation or its intensification.

In identifying a process as either positive or negative feedback, it is critical to be explicit about which components the feedback loop is being considered with respect to. Following are a couple of illustrations of each type from the Dasanetch S/E system:

Negative feedback processes:
(1) The decentralized and age seniority-oriented jural-political system functions as a negative feedback force with regard to disputes and social unrest resulting from depleted tribal wealth.

(2) Productive diversification functions as a negative feedback force with regard to the immediate hunger which accompanies depletion of domestic herds.

Positive feedback processes:
(1) Deterioration of the plant communities of the plains functions as a positive feedback force with regard to the depletion of domestic herds.

(2) Productive diversification functions as a positive feedback force with regard to the weakening of the Dasanetch ideology favoring domestic stock accumulation.[22]

The fact that example (2) of both the positive and negative feedback forces given above involves the same process underscores the necessity of specifying the other term of the feedback relationship. Even during the same period of time,

---

[20] Morphogenesis may actually involve an elaboration or a simplification of the system's structure.

[21] This corresponds to the "runaway" system as described by Bateson (1972).

[22] An apparent paradox is involved here: the changing environmental and economic conditions necessitate significant diversification, which in turn calls for a weakening of the cattle ideology--itself an integral and vital part of the highly stable set of Dasanetch social relations (see Chapter 4); but the complete destruction of this ideology would threaten the strong and flexible set of social relations which are important if long range adaptive change is to occur. This problem will be dealt with in detail in the concluding chapter.

a feedback process may have both deviation amplifying and deviation counteracting effects, depending on which level of system organization one is viewing and also the state of the system at a particular time.

It remains to make clear the distinction between stability of a system and what is desirable or "good, " and conversely, between instability and what is undesirable or "bad. " This is particularly important considering the frequent bias in many system analyses dealing with the environment which at least implicitly associates stability or equilibrium with a desired state of relations. As just one example of this distinction, a set of societal/environmental relations which has existed as a traditionally desirable and homeostatic system may, in a greatly changed environmental or political-economic context of a larger dimension, be considered to be in a "better" or more desirable state if it is unstable, i. e., with the capacity for change. In the same way, the maintenance of stability of a traditional set of societal/environmental relations under these circumstances could be considered "bad" from the standpoint of that society's survival. Of course, in attributing such qualities to stable and unstable sets of relations, it is of the first importance to be clear about the specific objectives or goals involved. I will deal with this issue in detail in the next chapter.

CHAPTER 7

RECENT SYSTEM CHANGE

AND THE BUILDING

OF A SOLUTION

Introduction

The preceding chapters have described much of the general character of
both the Dasanetch society and their lands in the lower Omo basin. Although
there have been many references and some detailed description made of societal and environmental changes which have occurred in recent decades, the
present chapter treats the more major of these changes explicitly. Following
the discussion of specific changes resulting from two selected inputs to the S/E
system, I will offer some generalizations about the existing system of S/E relations and then turn to the matter of possible solutions to the existing economic
and environmental deterioration in particular.

Change within the societal/environmental system has occurred as a result
of deviations originating both internal and external to the system, but externally
induced change has had far greater significance in producing the present state
of the S/E relations. Consequently, the inputs selected for detailed discussion
in the sections to follow are of this type. Some of those inputs which have actually occurred are listed below; these vary greatly in the magnitude of their
effects on the system.

Source of Change	Point of Entry into System
1. Governmental restriction of western and southern Dasanetch territory.	1. Subsystem S; Stratum s_2; Unit$_{19}$: Tribal Population and Territory.
2. Regional geomorphic change causing Lake Rudolf retreat.	2. Subsystem E; Stratum e_2; Unit$_5$: Lake Rudolf.
3. Influx of disease organisms from surrounding regions.	3. Subsystem E; any unit of e_1; Subsystem S; Stratum s_1; Unit$_{11}$: Domestic Stock, or Stratum s_2; Unit$_{19}$: Tribal Population and Territory.

254

4.	Taxation by Ethiopian government.	4.	Subsystem S; Stratum s_2; $Unit_{16}$: <u>Tribal Capital: Amount and Distribution</u>.
5.	Raiding by neighboring tribes.	5.	Subsystem S; Stratum s_2; $Unit_{11}$: <u>Domestic Stock</u> and/or $Unit_{16}$.
6,	Introduction of new domesticated plants (e. g., by missionary).	6.	Subsystem S; Stratum s_1; $Unit_{13}$: <u>Horticulture</u>.
7.	Regional tectonic change producing stratigraphic uplift or other change.	7.	Subsystem E; Stratum e_3; $Unit_1$; <u>Local Depositional and Tectonic Patterns</u>.
8.	Periodic grain contributions by the Ethiopian government.	8.	Subsystem S; Stratum s_1; $Unit_{13}$: <u>Horticulture</u>.

I have selected the first two inputs listed above to analyze in some detail, as each of them has had a pervasive and profound effect on the whole system of Dasanetch societal/environmental relations.

Two Major Change Inputs to the Dasanetch S/E System: Territorial Restriction and Lake Level Change

Some brief comment regarding the form of the discussion to follow is necessary. Although I attempt to trace changes precipitated by two inputs to the S/E system in a step-wise fashion, to a degree, it may be seen from the system models which compositely show the societal and environmental changes (e. g., Fig. 7-5) that deviation occurs non-linearly throughout the system. It is possible to logically trace the movement of change among particular units of the system which are of interest or importance, however, and this is attempted in some detail. Further, although the system relationships described may be analyzed using simulation techniques, I have chosen to present the basic system changes in more general form in the present work.

Case I: Territorial restriction of the Dasanetch. The exclusion of the Dasanetch from much of their traditional tribal territory was apparently an action taken following an agreement between the Kenyan and Ethiopian governments (see Chapter 1). This description does not deal exhaustively with the system of changes following this input, but instead treats the various aspects selectively on the basis of the objectives of this study.

The Ilemi plains of Sudan[1] largely constitute the portion of the Dasa-

---

[1]There has been a recent boundary negotiation whereby Kenya has acquired possession (in addition to the political jurisdiction, which they have had since the 1940's) of part of the Ilemi region.

netch's traditional territory which is now prohibited from their use for settlement and for herding. This exclusion was first carried out in the mid-1930's.
The Ilemi-associated lands are now regularly patrolled by armed Kenyan police
whose major control measure is seizure of any stock found there. On occasion,
Dasanetch have reportedly been shot and killed by the Kenya police.[2] There
have been periods since the initial restriction when the Dasanetch (and their
neighbors, the Turkana and the Inyangatom) were allowed temporary grazing
rights in part of the Ilemi lands. These have included a period just before the
1957 war between the Dasanetch and the Turkana (Os Buma),[3] and for shorter
periods in some recent years of severe drought (e.g., 1966, 1970 and 1972).
As described in the section in Chapter 5 on seasonal movements, there are few
places within the prohibited zone which the Dasanetch attempt to use with any
frequency, even though the tribe's economic situation is critically deteriorated
and most west bank Dasanetch informants consistently maintain that the best
grazing lands of the region are within the prohibited area. This is a matter,
understandably, of deep resentment on the part of the Dasanetch who consider
the British, Kenyan and Ethiopian authorities to have consistently denied them
access to their traditional lands which are essential to their survival.

A rough estimate of the drastic change in the territory of the west bank
Dasanetch may be made on the basis of older informants' descriptions of traditional seasonal movements and settlement, and on police and other authorities'
reports:

traditional territory = 6,590 sq. kilometers (km^2)
present territory = 1,375 km^2

Other factors (see below) have even further effectively reduced the available
lands for the Dasanetch, and the significance of this territorial size for the
west bank population of ca. 9,400 will be discussed below.

The following is an attempt to trace the immediate impact and the proliferation of change throughout the S/E system. These changes may be followed

[2]Some Kenya police officers maintained that Dasanetch, Inyangatom and
Turkana individuals are only shot when they are in the prohibited zone and are
believed to be armed, or when they in fact open fire first. Others made no
such distinction. During the course of my field work I heard of at least five to
eight Dasanetch individuals killed by Kenya police between Kibish and Lomogol,
though a precise number is virtually impossible to obtain due to conflicting reports from both the police and the Dasanetch. Similar conflicts occasionally
occur between the Kenya police and the Inyangatom (the northern neighbors of
the Dasanetch), near Kibish (see Fig. 1-2).

[3]This was reported to me by a former Kenyan police officer in charge of
the northwest Kenya district, Mr. Whitehouse.

step-wise in Figs. 7-1 and 7-2 for the societal subsystem (see also Fig. 7-5). The point of entry into the system is into the s_2 stratum, specifically into the unit entitled Tribal <u>Population and Territory</u>, U_{19}. From the discussion of the system in Chapter 6, one may predict that the change will diffuse from this unit toward the units which are connected with it (see Fig. 6-1), and/or toward the units of adjacent strata, including the units of s_1, the latter being adjacent to the system baseline. In tracing the movement of change from the point of entry into the units of s_1, there is one unit of s_1 which is immediately and profoundly affected, that entitled <u>Seasonal Movements and Settlement</u>, U_{12} (see figure below). The immediate effect on the processes of U_{12} is a severe restriction of the options for seasonal movements and settlement, with the best grazing lands being denied to the Dasanetch (Fig. 7-1). This restriction of seasonal movements is associated with an increase in the density or concentration of herds. The movement of change proliferates within the subsystem from this point, and one of its impacts is on the s_1 unit entitled <u>Domestic Stock</u>, U_{11}, since the concentration of stock significantly increases the communicability of existing diseases with a resulting increase in stock disease and death, leading to a decline in the number of cattle. As deterioration of grazing potential (carrying capacity) of lands occurs, reduction in milk yields and an increasing suitability of small stock (sheep and goats) relative to cattle to existing environmental conditions also occur.

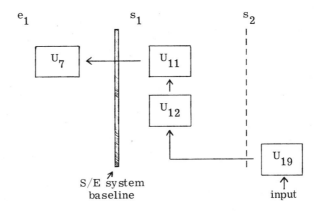

Among the pathways of change movement from U_{11} is that across the baseline to the e_1 unit, <u>Plains Environments</u> (U_7). Grazing pressure from the increased concentrations of stock (a constituent of U_{11}) causes overgrazing of the available pasturage in the plains (U_7); this in turn leads to a deterioration of the

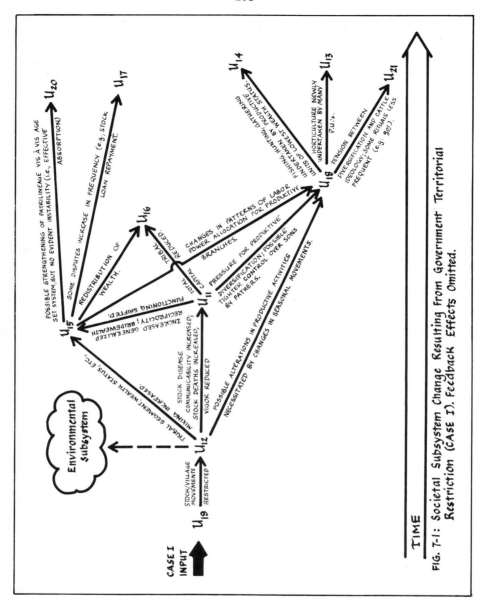

FIG. 7-1: Societal Subsystem Change Resulting From Government Territorial Restriction (CASE I). Feedback Effects Omitted.

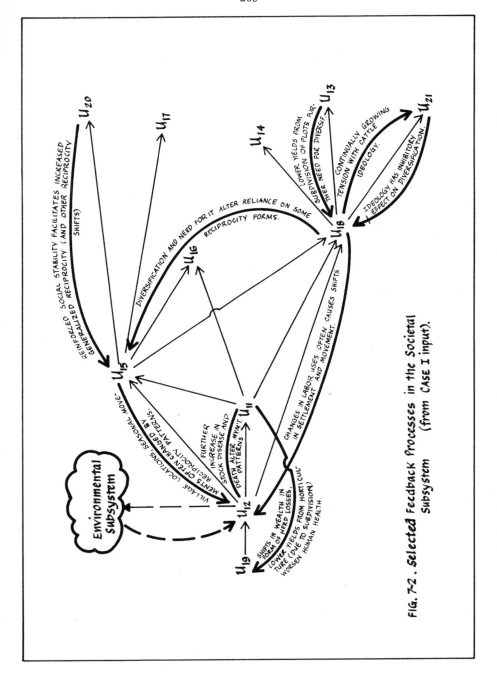

FIG. 7-2. Selected Feedback Processes in the Societal Subsystem (from CASE I input).

plant communities, as detailed in Chapter 2. The number of cattle concentrated by the territorial restriction is sufficiently in excess of what the land involved can support to activate a feedback leading to further deterioration of the plains (this assertion is substantiated below). What develops is a positive feedback loop between these two units (U_7 and U_{11}): the more overgrazing occurs as a result of large domestic herd concentrations, the greater the deterioration of the plains corresponds to a reduced grazing potential of these lands, so that an even greater overstocking of animals occurs (with a corresponding reduction of stock vigor and susceptibility to disease, etc.). The overall effect of this progressive feedback loop on the plains is to reduce the quality as well as the amount of pasturage available within the s_1 unit <u>Domestic Stock</u> (U_{11}). It also profoundly and adversely affects the constituents Herd Composition and Herd Size (see Fig. 6-1): the number of stock is reduced due to disease and death as a result of decreased vigor and resistance to disease, and a strong tendency develops for the proportion of small stock to increase relative to cattle. Thus the composition of herds is changed markedly. This increase of small stock (especially sheep with their ability to graze nearly to the ground surface) in turn accelerates the deterioration of pasturage, thereby further aggravating the positive feedback effects.

The two-directional flow of change between <u>Seasonal Movements and Settlement</u> (U_{12}) and <u>Domestic Stock</u> (U_{11}) is now apparent. To continue this selected trajectory of change, the increased concentration of animals due to seasonal movement constraints (U_{12}) results in a higher communicability of disease (U_{11}). In the other direction, herd size changes, the shift in emphasis from cattle to small stock and the presence of stock disease (all components of U_{11}) alter seasonal movements of both stock and settlement. Although a traditional Dasanetch response to a high incidence of herd disease has been to expand the territory grazed, the government restriction from their traditional lands precludes this stabilizing mechanism. Meanwhile, the domestic stock become an even greater burden on the lands to which they are confined, and the resultant progressive deterioration of the plains vegetation results in decisions by production unit heads and herders which further concentrate stock in the locales with relatively better conditions. These two-directional flows of change, then, form a positive feedback loop.

Finally, $Unit_{12}$ (<u>Seasonal Movements and Settlement</u>) and U_7 (<u>Plains Environments</u>) are also involved in a positive feedback loop. As the patterns of stock movement change and stock are concentrated, the character of the plains is altered, e.g., reduced total plant cover, reduced ratio of palatable to unpalatable plant species, and bush invasion. Again, the reduced carrying capacity and altered patterns of different range conditions are responsible for feedback effects to seasonal movement patterns. Thus a positive feedback loop exists which involves the three units U_7, U_{11} and U_{12};[4] this larger loop is comprised of the three smaller loops described above.

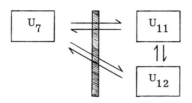

The most critical points of strees which have developed within the S/E system as a result of this loop are clearly (a) the severe overgrazing and range deterioration, and (b) the reduction of stock vigor and numbers for many production units,[5] with resultant starvation facing the Dasanetch. The establishment of the entire positive feedback loop asserted above depends critically on the fact that overgrazing occurs with respect to the grazing land available; that is, that the number of stock present is greater than the number of stock supportable (the carrying capacity) by the grazing lands available. This assertion will be supported below.

Before treating the possible redress mechanisms to these changes, and the blocks to the actual occurrence or effectiveness of such mechanisms some other pathways of system deviation need at least brief mention. These could all be elaborated considerably, but are necessarily only dealt with in a limited fashion here.

Figs. 7-1, 7-2 and 7-5 trace the movement of change through the societal subsystem, i.e., the subsystem of input for Case I. The pathway of change from U_{11} to U_{18} is in the form of pressure on (traditional) production unit heads to diversify productive activities. Elements of the Dasanetch ideological

---

[4]This feedback loop will hereafter be noted as $U_{7-11-12}$.

[5]Under conditions of slight overgrazing, the reduction in stock numbers could lead to a new equilibrium state with both a reduced load-bearing capacity for the range lands and a reduced number of stock. However, under the severely overgrazed conditions which obtain for the Dasanetch, this leads to a positive feedback.

system (U_{21}) are in turn affected through the changes and pressures in U_{18}: namely, significant incongruity[6] exists between the strong ideological emphasis on cattle (and stock generally) and the diversification of productive activity with a lessened reliance on stock raising. Economic survival, for many production units, necessitates the overturning of or at least disregard for the ideological emphasis on stock to the degree that productive diversification can be rationalized by the decision makers. Another impact on U_{21} is that the passing of some rituals (e.g., gol, the bridewealth completion ceremony) which require stock slaughter is made difficult by diminished herds.[7] It should be pointed out that although the Dasanetch ideological emphasis on cattle is presently far out of balance with the land's existing low potential for a stock-based economy, this ideology very likely developed under conditions where such an emphasis was fundamentally in balance with the environment. In fact, it is quite likely that such an ideology was in relative balance with existing conditions up until the recent territorial restriction.

Another major pathway of change moving from U_{11}, U_{12} and U_{16}, is that of the processes represented in U_{15} (Patterns of Exchange and Social Mixing). This has taken several forms. First, a strong utilization of generalized reciprocity (see Chapter 5) exists whereby wealth redistribution has accompanied the reduction in total tribal stock wealth. As discussed below, this wealth redistribution in the face of environmental stress and decreasing tribal capital has had the effects of averting some short-term strife but possibly inhibiting longer term adjustment. Second, some balanced reciprocity patterns have been altered; for example, the bridewealth system has been modified with regard to both the number of stock paid and the number of years used for payment. Third, some types of negative reciprocity have reportedly increased in frequency, such as stock loans which remain unpaid and are consequently more apt to result in disputes, or other stock debts not met. Fourth, mixing of tribal segments has increased as a result of changed settlement and stock movement patterns, and this has undoubtedly had an impact on the social relations associated with bar-

---

[6]Incongruity occurs under the following condition: when two units of a system are directly connected in a way which necessitates the value of each to remain within a certain range in order for the other's processes to be maintained without disruption, incongruency occurs when the value of one of the units does not fall within the designated range.

[7]My field data indicate a marked decrease in the percentage of males who have completed bridewealth payments and the gol ceremony over a period of over four decades.

tering, marriage, etc. Changes in reciprocity and patterns of social mixing in turn make change inputs to <u>Juridico-Political Processes</u> (U_{17}), in the form of pressure for settlement of disputes around acts of negative reciprocity, and possible disturbance of balance between the social organizational principles (U_{20}) of age set (<u>hari</u>) and clan (<u>tur</u>).

Although they form the backbone of change movement within the societal subsystem, these major pathways of change must be viewed non-linearly and with their complement of feedback processes (see Fig. 7-2) in order to fully envision the impact of change on this subsystem. Fig. 7-1 shows U_{15} (<u>Patterns of Exchange and Social Mixing</u>) and U_{18} (<u>Production Unit Organization and Labor</u>) to be pivotal units in the initial diffusion of change so that one may predict these two units to be centrally involved in the set of feedback processes also. Thus, for example, Fig. 7-2 shows the relative success of productive activities alternative to herding to have direct feedback effects on the process of labor power allocation (U_{18}) itself.

Figs. 7-3 and 7-4 treat diffusion of change within the environmental subsystem in a manner parallel to the other subsystem. Since the Case I input of territorial restriction is to the societal subsystem, the environmental subsystem receives its input of change from societal processes; this input is to four different units within the e_1 stratum. Little diffusion of change occurs beyond these four units, but that which does occur is of great importance, such as the feedbacks involving those units concerned with the soil and its dynamics (U_3 and U_4), <u>Edaphic Character</u> and <u>Local Topography and Drainage Features</u>, respectively. There are two secondary positive feedback loops within this subsystem: between <u>Plains Environments</u> (U_7) and <u>Edaphic Character</u> (U_3), and between <u>Local Topography and Drainage Features</u> (U_4) and <u>Edaphic Character</u> (U_3). These may be considered secondary in that their perpetuation depends on continued input, in the form of overgrazing, for the social subsystem. On the basis of the plains ecological studies described in Chapter 2, it may well be that ecological deterioration in large portions of the plains has now progressed to the point where these lands will not recover within the foreseeable future, even with an easing of grazing pressure.

The spread of (Case I) change from the point of input is viewed compositely for the S/E system in Fig. 7-5. Among the positive feedback loops which develop (and are loci for change), there is a strong asymmetry among them in terms of their behavior. Specifically, all of the positive feedback loops in the system are broken if the loop $U_{7-11-12}$ is itself broken. Consequently, this

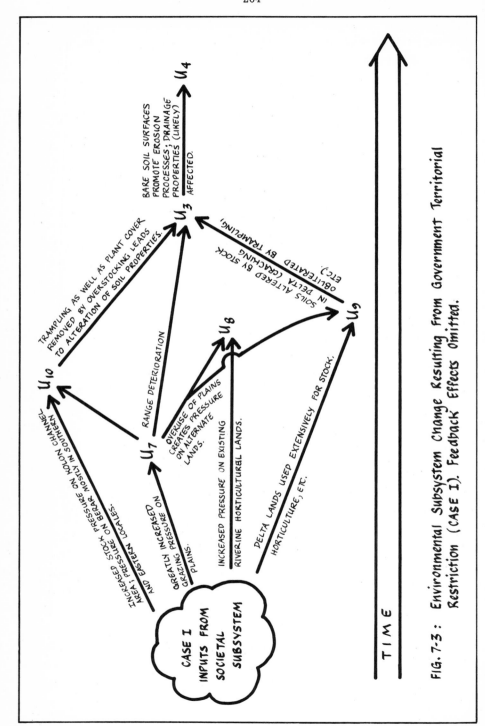

FIG. 7-3 : Environmental Subsystem Change Resulting From Government Territorial Restriction (CASE I). Feedback Effects Omitted.

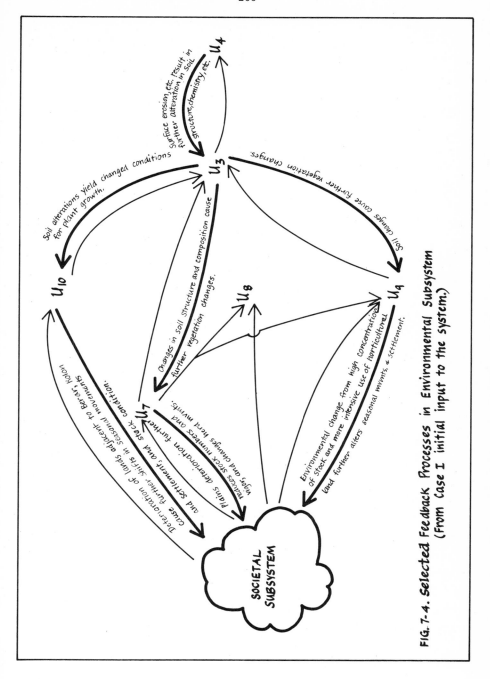

FIG. 7-4. Selected Feedback Processes in Environmental Subsystem
(from Case I initial input to the system.)

loop will be referred to here as the <u>primary</u> positive feedback loop.

The primary positive feedback loop ($U_{7-11-12}$) occurs across the S/E interface (system baseline) whereas those of U_{7-3} and U_{3-4} are embedded within the environmental subsystem. There are no such positive feedback loops embedded within the societal subsystem, and the question may arise as to why, considering the strong proliferation of change there. One possible explanation may rest with the possibility of new alternatives as responses to stress which may be created within the societal subsystem. That is, the very infrastructure or components of units (or even some units themselves) may be altered, dropped or created within this subsystem compared to the environmental subsystem, precisely because of the non-mechanistic or conscious nature of many of its workings. One example may serve to illustrate this potential. Deepening and widening societal tensions with serious social disruption might result if the bride-wealth system (a component of U_{15}), as a major locus of defining social interaction patterns and indeed stability, becomes unable to function in its traditional form. This, I suggest, has been a possibility ever since the Dasanetch cattle herds began declining markedly, placing a real strain on the system of stock transfers. Instead, the institution of bridewealth was modified along the lines of longer terms of payment, reduced spectrum of relations receiving payment, and fewer total number of stock paid. Had this alteration of the major institution of bridewealth not occurred, it is likely that there would have already been serious disruption of the reciprocity system in general and the marriage patterns in particular (other components of U_{15}), juridico-political processes (U_{17}) with resulting severe social strife, and relations among members of individual patrilineages (U_{18} and U_{20}), to name only a few.

In sum, the input of territorial restriction to the system has resulted in a self-perpetuating (or runaway) deterioration within the system, especially along the lines of: (1) environmental breakdown in the plains in the form of reduction of total plant cover, invasion of bush and unpalatable plants, and disruption of natural faunal assemblages, soil erosion, and (2) economic breakdown within the major production activity, stock raising, through reduction of stock vigor, increase in disease and death, and reduced milk yields. These have generated strong pressure on production units to diversify their production activities to horticulture, fishing, gathering and hunting.

The positive feedback loop $U_{7-11-12}$ depends crucially on the relationship between the number of cattle present and the number of cattle that the land will support, specifically on the assumption that the territorial restriction has

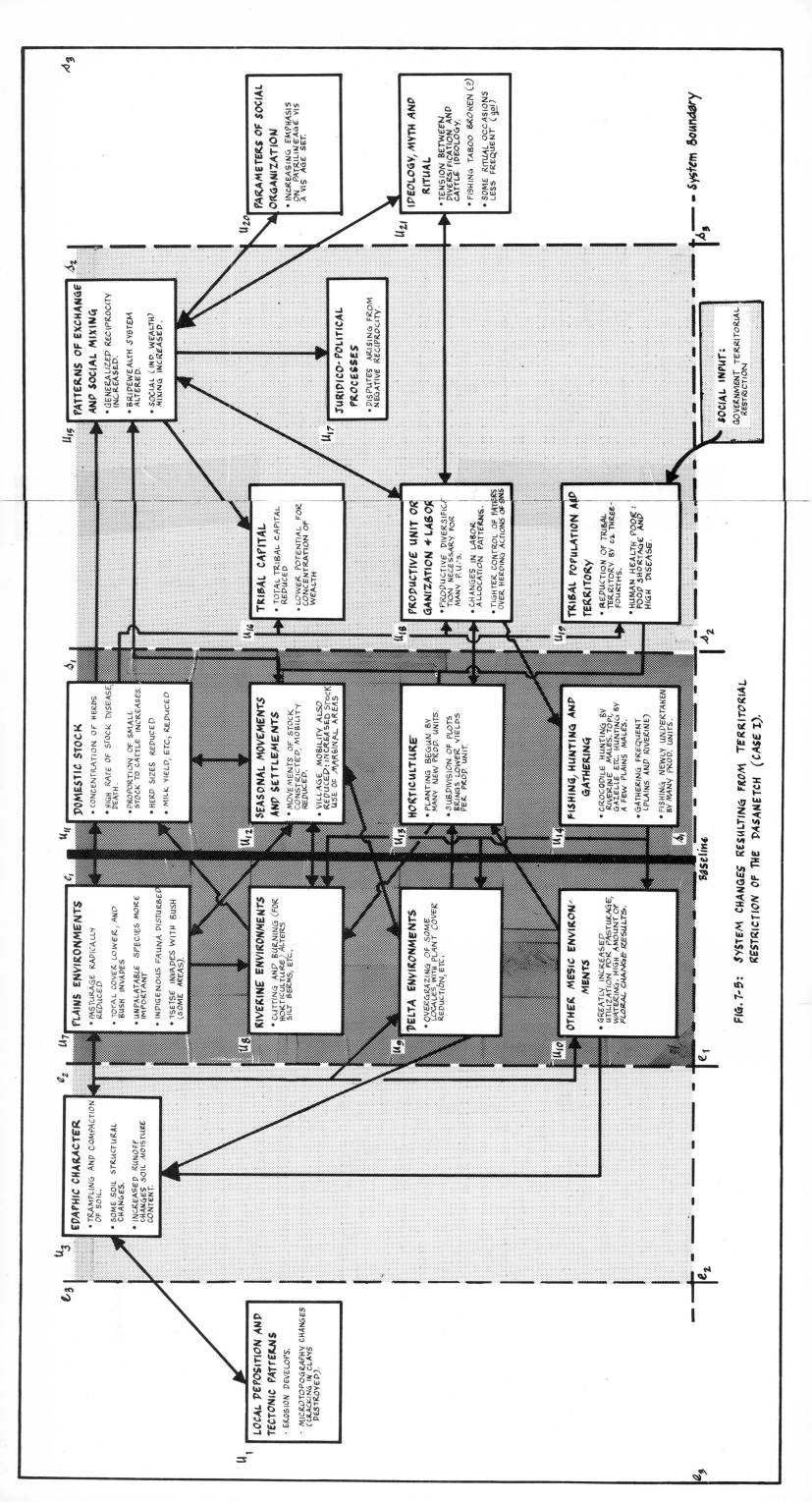

FIG. 7-5: SYSTEM CHANGES RESULTING FROM TERRITORIAL RESTRICTION OF THE DASANETCH (CASE I).

caused significant overstocking. The most direct method of establishing the existence of overstocking would be to cite annual stock censuses for the period of decades involved (i. e., since the 1930's), but unfortunately no such information exists. Consequently, the following discussion establishes, in the absence of this data, the outcomes of the possible states of the system. Subsequently, I will argue which state of the system is most probable. It should be recalled that this study deals primarily with the Dasanetch and their lands on the west bank of the Omo River, and this applies also to the following section.[8]

The two possible states of the system are, simply stated, that the primary positive feedback loop, $U_{7-11-12}$, is actually functioning (such that Dasanetch herds are being depleted), or that no such positive feedback is operative (the herds are not being depleted). These two possible states may be traced to relationships which hold among the following three variables:

(a) x: the number of stock required for subsistence for the Dasanetch.

(b) y: the number of stock that the land will support[9] (i. e., the stock-carrying capacity).

(c) z: the number of stock actually present.

First, as stated earlier, the number of stock actually present (z) is unknown, but both the number of stock required (x) and the number of stock supportable (y) can be computed with information available. In order to make these computations, the following facts are necessary:

size of west bank Dasanetch lands at present: 1, 375 square kilometers (km^2)

size of west bank Dasanetch population: 9, 440[10]

Using ecological categories set out in the Atlas of Kenya (1969), the land of the Dasanetch may be rated between categories V and VI.[11] In his utilization of

---

[8]This is justified since the west bank social units (except for the narrow riverine zone), seasonal movements and political economic processes are essentially distinct from those of the east bank.

[9]The assumption is made here that the Dasanetch derive 100 per cent subsistence from herding. This issue will be treated further in the discussion of diversification, below.

[10]This population figure is based upon an assumed average of four persons per hut, although the figure may be more accurately placed at five persons per hut.

[11]These ecological zone designations are based on moisture-vegetation correlation. In the case of the Dasanetch lands, the correlation is not maintained since its moisture index indicates a more favorable vegetation situation than actually exists (see Chapter 2) due to the severe overgrazing.

this classification system for analyzing pastoral lands and economies, Pratt (1968) states that for land intermediate between these two categories, each person requires 4.25 units of stock for subsistence.[12] Thus:

number of stock required for
Dasanetch subsistence   = number of people x number of stock required per person

$$x = 9,440 \times 4.25 = 36,120$$

On the basis of Pratt's data, the amount of Dasanetch land required to support a single unit of stock is 27 hectares per unit of stock.

number of stock supportable = amount of land / amount of land per stock

$$y = \frac{137500}{27} \text{ ha (hectares)}$$

$$y = 5,093$$

Combining the results of these computations it may be concluded that the number of stock required for subsistence by the Dasanetch is much greater than the number of stock that the land will support (i.e., $x > y$). The outcomes of the various states of the system can best be explicated by characterizing these states with respect to the two variables, the number of stock supportable (y) and the number of stock present (z), and then interpreting them. The possible states of the system are as follows:

state 1: the stock present are greater than the stock supportable ($z > y$).

state 2: the stock present are equal to the stock supportable ($z = y$).

state 3: the stock present are less than the stock supportable ($z < y$).

Considering state 1, if the system is in this state then it is in a positive feedback (among units$_{7-11-12}$) of the nature described above. Because no accurate estimate exists for the number of stock actually present, the relationship between x and z cannot be deduced; however, I will briefly state the three possibilities. If the number of stock required is less than the number present ($x < z$), then on the basis of the above conclusion that the number of stock required for subsistence is greater than the number the land will support, we may conclude that the number present is greater than the number supportable. Since this is a runaway condition and is highly unstable, eventually the number of stock required will be greater than the number of stock present, given no external inputs. The second possibility—where the number of stock present and the num-

---

[12]I am convinced that this ratio is lower than that required for the Dasanetch, primarily for the reasons of low milk yield resulting from poor stock health (see Chapter 5) as well as poor human health conditions. One stock unit is equivalent to one mature head of cattle.

ber of stock required are equal (x = z)—asserts that the Dasanetch have access
to an adequate number of stock. Since we are considering state 1, this condition means that over time, the number of stock present will be reduced and the
situation will reduce to the number required being greater than the number present (x > z). Finally, under the condition where the number of stock required is
greater than the number present (x > z), given state 1, the system is both in a
runaway condition and the Dasanetch do not have an adequate number of stock
for their subsistence (x > z > y). In other words, under the assumption that
stock raising provides the Dasanetch's entire subsistence, they are in starvation conditions. Notice that while the possibility of the number of stock required being greater than the number present (x > z) can initially be distin-
guished from the previous ones, both of the other alternatives (x = z and x < z)
will reduce to the first over time. This is true since the conclusion was drawn
above that the number of stock required is greater than the number of stock supportable (x > y) and because, in such a runaway system, the number of stock
present (z) is continuously being reduced, so that whether or not originally the
number of stock present exceeds the number of stock required, the number of
stock present will, over time, fall below the number required. This exhausts
the possibilities under state 1.

State 2 and state 3 may be collapsed for the purposes of discussion. Under the condition that the number of stock present is less than the number supportable, there is no positive feedback loop immediately apparent. However,
given the conclusion that the number of stock required is much greater than the
number supportable (x > y), it is possible to conclude that the number required
is greater than the number present. In other words, we may conclude that under the assumption that the Dasanetch derive their total subsistence from stock
raising, they already are in a state of starvation.

In summary, then, either the system is in a runaway condition (driven by
the positive feedback $U_{7-11-12}$) or the number of stock present is less than the
number required by the Dasanetch for their subsistence, or both: in any case
they are in starvation conditions. My strong conviction is that at present the
system is in a runaway condition where the number of stock required is greater
than the number present, and the number present is greater than the number
the land can support, with the Dasanetch facing starvation. The following additional lines of evidence have led me to this conclusion.

   (a) Stock diseases are of epidemic proportions, with the most serious
      ones including bovine pleuropneumonia, rinderpest, anthrax and black-

quarter.[13]

(b) I have collected a large number of stock histories of production unit heads, and these nearly uniformly indicate stock deaths (through disease) of sufficient proportion to result in serious herd depletion.

(c) When the large-scale ecological deterioration of Dasanetch rangelands (see Chapter 2) is considered together with the lack of alternative grazing areas available for the Dasanetch's stock, continued overgrazing and loss of stock may be inferred.

(d) The bridewealth system of the Dasanetch has undergone changes over the past fifty years which indicate a reduced average stock wealth.

A brief elaboration of the last of these lines of evidence is relevant here. Data from about 200 informants concerning bridewealth histories, including the records of some complete sub-age sets (modo) of males living in the plains,[14] were collected. These data were sorted into a number of groups according to the time of each informant's first marriage. Two of these groups are summarized here: (a) those males marrying their first wife (min gudoha) near the Turkana/Dasanetch war of about 1928 (os kalas), combined with those first marrying near the war between the British and Italians in the area (os italia) in the late 1930's; (b) those males marrying their first wife around the Dasanetch/ Turkana war of 1957 (os buma). The occurrence of bridewealth payment completion within the first ten years of marriage was computed for these two groups:

	First marriage in period of late 1920's to late 1930's:	First marriage in period near 1957:
Bridewealth payment completion within ten years:	79%	17%

I suggest that these data are a relatively accurate indicator of the average social wealth for their respective periods. (Other dimensions, such as the total amount promised and shifts in small stock vs. cattle payment, etc., have also changed, and these will be described elsewhere.)

Two possible interpretations of the above figures are: (1) the ratio of average wealth for the two periods is explained by strong redistributive mechanisms operative in the Dasanetch system (described in Chapter 5); (2) the ratio of average wealth for the two periods is explained by herd depletion, i.e., as evidence for the positive feedback $U_{7-11-12}$. If the ratio is to be explained by

---

[13] Per personal communication with Dr. Getachew Bekele, the Ethiopian government veterinarian working among the Dasanetch for a short time in 1972.

[14] Riverine (non-stock-raising) persons were excluded from the sample.

redistributive mechanisms, the Dasanetch population must have increased sufficiently to match this redistribution of stock.[15] Since the redistribution ratio is
approximately 4:1, the population would have to have grown by 400 per cent in
about 40 years. In order to achieve this increase in population, the Dasanetch
would have to have one of the highest population growth rates recorded, well
over 3 per cent. This is highly improbable, particularly in view of the extremely poor health conditions in general throughout the tribe.

I conclude, then: first, that the number of cattle required for Dasanetch
subsistence is greater than the number of stock actually present; second, that
the latter is in turn greater than the number of stock supportable by the land;
and third, that the Dasanetch face starvation.

Case II: Lake Rudolf southward retreat in the lower Omo basin. --This
change input is first examined in isolation from the effects of Case I, after
which the two will be considered in combination. To examine the impact of
Case II separately from the effects of the territorial restriction described
above is only hypothetically possible, since by the time the major effects of the
lake withdrawal began to be felt, the repercussions of the tribe's restriction to
less than one-quarter of their traditional territory were already being felt.
There was very likely a time lag of several decades before the consequences of
the lake movement became major ones.

The cause of the lake retreat is still uncertain, though Butzer (1971) offers evidence that it resulted from a reduction in rainfall in the Ethiopian highlands, which in turn lessened the Omo River flow into the lake.[16] The level of
Lake Rudolf has changed greatly within the past hundred years or so, and these
changes have had a great impact both on the physical environment and on the
lives of the Dasanetch. The lake has fluctuated repeatedly in a range of 20 meters, between 15 meters above and 5 meters below the present level, according
to Butzer (1971). His calculations suggest that there was a 30- to 40-year period of rising of the lake level prior to 1898, and a 60-year period of lowering of
the level since that time, and none of the periods of lake rise have caused significant changes in the meandering or gradient of the river. The lake level drop
since the late 1890's occurred rapidly, exposing much of the flats adjacent to

---

[15]Assuming no basic structural changes in normative redistributive patterns occurred.

[16]The Omo River, it may be recalled, is the main river feeding Lake Rudolf.

the river and part of Berar (Sanderson's Gulf) by 1908. This lake level drop, Butzer asserts, exposed about 280 square kilometers of new land in the immediate delta, about the same expanse in Berar, and about 560 square kilometers of land emerged altogether in ten years.

There was a recent lake advance during the early 1960's, involving a rise of about 5 meters and submerging more than 300 square kilometers (Butzer, 1971). This recent northward migration of the lake, with its submergence of delta lands, has adversely affected many Dasanetch who have, over the past decades, used the lowermost delta for settlement, horticulture and herding. The following discussion deals primarily with the repercussions of the lake withdrawal. The most recent lake level rise, while of significance for an understanding of the state of the Dasanetch situation, may nevertheless be considered of secondary importance.

The proliferation of change within the S/E system is shown (without feedback effects) in Fig. 7-6; a representation of these changes in the context of Case I will be presented in the next section. Initially, Lake Rudolf (U_5) was dramatically affected by the loss of input to the lake, whereby the northern terminus of the lake was moved about 30 kilometers southward, a remarkable scale of geomorphic change for such a short period of time. From this unit of introduction, the change proliferates within the E subsystem.

One pathway of change which may be traced, for example, to U_4 (Local Topography and Drainage Features), since the water content and drainage properties of large tracts of newly exposed lands in the modern delta are greatly affected. Much land which was previously submerged by the lake apparently remained moist or poorly drained due to its proximity to the new lake terminus, but much of the delta mudflats (now with huge cracking patterns described by Butzer, 1971) underwent a drying out. Insofar as drainage has been greatly altered in the lands once covered by or adjacent to the lake, it is logical to predict that other soil properties such as soil nutrients and structural features related to moisture content (U_3), etc., would also be altered, though no data has been collected on these variations. Soil character alterations in combination with drainage and micro-topographic changes (U_4), are accompanied by shifts in vegetation patterns within the delta, minimally in the form of large tracts of semi-aquatic and aquatic vegetation in the lowermost delta region (U_9) being replaced by a mosaic of more xerophytic vegetation communities (see Chapter 3).

A second major pathway of change from the point of input (U_5) to the rest

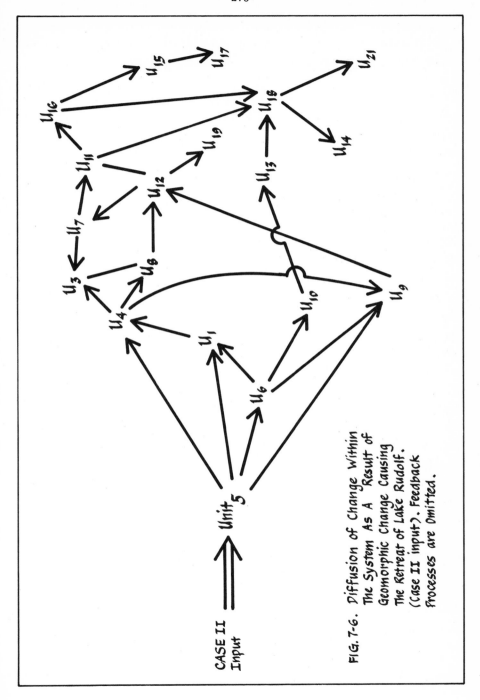

FIG. 7-6. *Diffusion of Change Within The System As A Result of Geomorphic Change Causing The Retreat of Lake Rudolf. (Case II input). Feedback Processes are Omitted.*

of the E subsystem is that occurring through the impact of the lake withdrawal
on the Omo River (U_6). With the southward shift in the terminus of the river,
or a drop in its base level, the river has been subject to minor changes during
the past 70 to 80 years (Butzer, 1971). Changes in downcutting, depositional
patterns (e.g., along silt berms), flooding of natural levees and other features
have significance for other aspects of the system. Descriptions of ecological conditions in the early decades of this century by older Dasanetch informants consistently include reports of a large shift toward more xerophytic vegetation in areas of the riverine transition zone and the adjacent flats (U_8). e.g.,
from relatively lush grassland and shrub grassland to tree/shrub steppe with
significant bare area. These reports support the thesis of a decrease in soil
moisture and improved drainage, likely due to water table shifts associated
with the lake withdrawal. It may be recalled from Chapter 3 that significant
decrease in soil moisture content in both the riverine transition zone and the
adjacent flats zone is suggested by the presence of large, dead riverine shrubs
in what presently are much more xerophytic vegetation zones. The Dasanetch
also describe their abandonment of large tracts of horticultural (and grazing)
lands. made necessary by the reduction of lateral inundation and flooding from
the Omo River and the reduced water content in Kolon channel (Fig. 1-2). Thus,
with changed moisture content and drainage properties (U_3, U_4) came changed
conditions for plant life near the river (U_8). The southward progression of riverine forest and woodland along the natural levee is one major shift in plant life,
and this is described in detail in Chapter 3. Tsetse fly (U_8) has also migrated
southward along with the riverine forest and woodland, and it is now abundant to
a latitude slightly south of Rati (Fig. 1-2). The significance of this disease car-
rier's influx for the Dasanetch will be discussed below.

The mesic, or relatively wet, environments (U_{10}) associated with Kolon
channel and Berar (Sanderson's Gulf) have also undergone substantial change
subsequent to the lake drop. A large expanse of exposed mudflats in the southern portion of Berar has resulted, with resultant colonization by large stands of
salt-tolerant grasses. According to Dasanetch descriptions, Kolon channel
(U_{10}) did receive water inflow or strong seepage from the Omo River at a point
along the river in the northern section of Dasanetch territory during the early
decades of this century. When this flow or seepage ceased, [17] the nearby vege-

---

[17] As Chapter 3 points out, there do remain several small localities along
Kolon which have year-round standing water, presumably from seepage from
the plains to the west. The southern extreme of Kolon receives water from the

tation correspondingly became more xerophytic, lowering its grazing potential and precipitating radical changes in stock movement patterns. Thus, Kolon was lost as a resource for heavy grazing by domestic stock just at a time when it would have been relied upon more heavily by the Dasanetch because of the reduced grazing potential along the Omo River.[18]

Geomorphic change which resulted in the lake withdrawal, then, has caused change nearly throughout the environmental subsystem. It is now possible to briefly trace the change movement into the societal subsystem.

A striking contrast exists between the societal impacts of environmental changes occurring in the modern delta and those resulting from changes occurring farther north along the Omo River (U_8), particularly from Rati northward. Generally speaking, the exposure of modern delta lands (e.g., Nairobi, Erdete) once submerged resulted in expanded possibilities for horticulture (U_{13}), domestic stock herding and settlement (U_{12}). Although the west bank Dasanetch near the lake, predominantly of the Inkabela and Oro tribal segments (see Chapter 4), did gain substantial new resources from the newly exposed lands, the long-term significance of this gain was partially offset by the recent lake rise. Even though the location of a given production unit's horticultural land within the modern delta lands exposed as a result of the lake retreat often shifted due to fluctuating moisture and other conditions, this area was the source of much grain which was essential to the survival of many Dasanetch. Many production units also became dependent on the lower delta's pasturage to support their stock, especially cattle. The availability of pasturage in the delta has in fact been critically important to the survival of domestic stock for many years during drought periods, but this dependence has been augmented by the intense overgrazing of the west bank lands in recent years.

The magnitude of lake advance in the 1960's has certainly been small relative to the lake retreat near the turn of the century, but this recent rise has nevertheless had significant effects which may be briefly summarized. First, flooding and heavy inundation has destroyed much of the horticultural lands previously gained. Second, a large amount of grazing land (and settlement area)

Omo River when the latter is flooding and water is backed up from the Omo River junction with Lake Rudolf.

[18]Further, some Dasanetch report that along with the large number of shrubs and trees which have developed along Kolon channel in recent decades, tsetse has also become abundant there (north of the Rati latitude) during rainy periods, with the result that many stock are excluded at those times.

has been lost, and this has produced a concentration of stock in the remaining parts of the delta and on the west bank. Third, pressure on owners of utilizable horticultural lands to subdivide their lands has increased. Finally, the spread of malaria-carrying mosquitoes into the newly submerged and adjacent lands has added pressure for evacuation of delta inhabitants to the west bank.

Large-scale economic consequences of the southward lakeshore movement have also occurred from Rati northward. According to elderly informants from the Eleli tribal segment, settlement in the riverine zone on the west bank north of Rati was relatively dense in the early decades of this century, i.e., the period immediately following the lake retreat. Many villages, mostly Eleli, were situated within the transition zone and the adjacent flats, especially at Nyibuni (Fig. 5-12). Grazing of stock was common throughout the more open grasslands adjacent to the river, and many who lived here also engaged in horticulture. At that time the riverine zone was an economically mixed area, with an emphasis on production branches alternative to stock raising on the part of productive units of low wealth status. There have been several major dimensions of social effects of the environmental changes already described for Dasanetch in this section of the riverine zone. The movement of the trypanosome-carrying tsetse fly (U_8) southward along the levees and laterally across the adjacent flats and into contiguous dense bush within the plains caused large numbers of stock deaths (U_{11}), forcing large-scale evacuation to the drier plains. This invasion by tsetse radically altered the seasonal movement patterns (U_{12}) of those Dasanetch settled in or utilizing the riverine zone north of Rati, and these people had no recourse but to move their stock from the relatively lush grazing lands near the river. The changed settlement patterns and seasonal movements were in turn responsible for increased social mixing (U_{15}) among tribal segments (en) and also across differences in wealth status. Those households with few or no stock who had inhabited the riverine zone, for the most part, did not move to the plains, but instead were obliged to remain near the river where they could engage in horticulture when possible as well as fishing, hunting and gathering. Some who lived in the plains but who lost many stock migrated into the riverine zone and undertook these same alternative productive activities. Nearly all Eleli informants reported large losses of stock when tsetse migrated into Dasanetch lands, and the total stock capital for the Eleli segment as a whole was greatly reduced (U_{16}). Confronted with the pressure to move to the plains, those Eleli evacuating with their stock did not have many options for new settlement. The lands to the south of Kalam (nodes 1, 2, 3 and to some degree, 4;

see Chapter 5) and in the modern delta were traditionally Inkabela lands (with other segments mixed among them) and almost devoid of Eleli, so that that region did not offer a real possibility for in-migration. The plains to the north of Kalam were already intensively utilized by the Randel segment, although with some Eleli also present. It was therefore into the latter area, and especially the lands just north of Kalam, that most of these Eleli from the riverine zone migrated. Some Eleli did move to the east bank of the Omo River, primarily to Dielirieli and Turangole (Fig. 5-12), where they were able to establish because of socioeconomic ties with age mates, affines or patrilineal relations. East bank lands north of Rati, however, did not provide opportunity for settlement or utilization by stock because of tsetse infestation and also danger of the much feared Hamar tribespeople who sporadically came to the Omo River from the highlands to the east.

A large number of Eleli informants reported a marked change in their patriline's patterns of productive activities during the 1930's, involving various combinations of economic diversification (U_{18}), subdivision of their horticultural lands and begging of land or planting rights from relatives and friends. The Eleli have been of lower economic status and thus more diversified in productive activities than most of the Inkabela and Oro for many years; this is certainly true of them relative to the strongly pastoral Randel and Koro segments. For many Eleli patrilines, therefore, the loss of stock wealth resulted more in a shift in emphasis of subsistence activities rather than in a whole new set of activities. Others, however, were forced to attempt subsistence through fishing, hunting (especially of crocodile) and gathering (U_{14}) for the first time. It is important to note that the Eleli segment shares the strong cattle ideology of the dominant Inkabela segment, so that considerable structural tension is created as productive diversification progresses.

Presently, the Dasanetch settled in the riverine area north of Rati are almost entirely Eleli, with a few Oro and Rieli. These households are almost invariably very poor, as are a large percentage of those settled in the modern delta. The plains-dwelling Dasanetch who move to this northern segment of the Omo River do so only under dire economic pressure through loss of their domestic stock. There are many other plains Dasanetch, however, who come to the riverine zone on a seasonal basis for horticulture as a supplement to stock raising or for supplemental gathering of food, etc. Virtually the whole riverine zone from Rati to the northern border of Dasanetch lands (including riverine forest/woodland, transition zone and adjacent flats) is now infested with tsetse,

with the evacuated lands totaling at least 105 km^2. A potentially tragic footnote
to the description of the existing situation of these people is the possible impend-
ing diffusion of the tsetse-carried trypanosome causing human sleeping sickness, now reported in the riverine zone north along the Omo River. The period
of time remaining before its possible migration into Dasanetch lands is not
known.

In summary, significant changes have occurred throughout much of the
Dasanetch S/E system as a result of the lake withdrawal, i.e., the Case II input, and these changes have involved serious large-scale environmental shifts
and breakdown of economic strength in particular. The Case II change input to
the system was to the environmental subsystem, subsequently profoundly affecting the societal subsystem (see Fig. 7-6), with strong feedback processes occurring from the societal subsystem to the environmental subsystem. Considered alone, however, the impact of the lake withdrawal, even with the resultant
invasion of tsetse, would have had less impact on the Dasanetch had it not been
for the territorial restriction described earlier. Much land previously utilizable for stock was lost with the invasion of tsetse, for instance, but theoretically there would have existed the possibility of utilizing plains lands elsewhere.
Stated in another way, the domestic stock losses caused by tsetse (and from
other disease-carrying organisms associated with the changes following the
lake withdrawal) could quite possibly have been redressed by the natural growth
of herds in relatively adequate pastures elsewhere. If this rebuilding of herds
through expansion to good grazing lands to the west had occurred, only the loss
of horticultural lands north of Rati and its related effects would have stood as
disruptions of socio-economic relations. This offsetting of stock losses through
expansion into the western plains (e.g., the traditional Dasanetch lands in the
Ilemi region of Sudan) was not possible, however, so that it is now necessary to
consider the situation precipitated by the lake withdrawal in the context of the
governmental territorial restriction of the Dasanetch.

Combined effects of territorial restriction and lake withdrawal. --Settle-
ments and stock previously located in the riverine area, as described above,
evacuated to the plains at least several decades after the major lake withdrawal
began. Overlapping in time with this westward movement to the plains, large
numbers of Dasanetch moved eastward into the area from the newly restricted
western plains. The increased stock pressure on rangelands north of Kalam in
particular which resulted from these two geographical movements, contributed

greatly to that land's severe ecological deterioration.[19] Descriptions of earlier times by Randel elders who had utilized the region between Kalam and the
Nakwa village area (see Fig. 5-12) previous to the influx of humans and stock
from the east and the west clearly indicate that radical ecological changes followed: changes consistently reported to involve drastic reduction of grass (and
total) cover and increase in unpalatable shrubs (both disturbance indicators described in Chapter 2).

The magnitude of the resultant economic (stock-raising) hardship may be
appreciated by a brief examination of the following figures:

$1 \ / \ 1.2$ = number of stock required / number of stock supportable in
for Dasanetch subsistence   traditional tribal territory

$7 \ / \ 1$ = number of stock required / number of stock supportable in
Dasanetch lands after restriction
from western plains

$8 \ / \ 1$ = stock required / stock supportable after restriction
from western lands and evacuation
of riverine lands

The last ratio, $8/1$, most clearly suggests the severity of the Dasanetch situation with regard to overstocking of their lands (under the assumption that they
subsist from stock raising).

In system terms, the environmentally instigated exclusion of Dasanetch
from the riverine lands accelerated the primary positive feedback loop $U_{7-11-12}$
which was detailed in the Case I discussion. Consequently, the other system
effects generated by this primary positive feedback loop also are augmented by
the input of lake withdrawal in Case II (as is indicated in the summary diagram
of Fig. 7-7). Some of the production-related effects of the Case I and II inputs
which are convergent are: (a) crowding of the Dasanetch and their stock out of
the western plains (Case I), and crowding of them and their stock out of the riverine zone (Case II); (b) subdivision of horticultural plots, with reduced crop
yields and subsequent pressure for more land and/or undertaking of other alternative productive activities (Case I), and loss of a large amount of riverine horticultural land with pressure for more land and/or other alternative productive
activities (Case II); (c) decreased stock-carrying capacity of the presently
grazed plains due to overgrazing, etc. (Case I), and decreased stock-carrying
capacity of the riverine zone due to woodland and bush development and tsetse
invasion (Case II). The combined effect of these two major inputs has been to

---

[19]The convergence of the ecological effects of deterioration of the range
from overgrazing and the strong erosion associated with stratigraphic uplift is
pointed out in Chapter 2.

destroy much of the plains vegetation and the Dasanetch herds, leading to economic disaster for huge numbers of Dasanetch.

The argument presented in Case I involved an assumption that the Dasanetch attempt to subsist solely by stock raising. The overstocking ratio (number of stock units required / number of stock units supportable) derived, however, indicates that it is not possible for stock raising to serve as the sole source of their subsistence. Therefore, it is imperative that the vast majority of Dasanetch production units undertake to diversify their productive activities. The following discussion deals with the feasibility of diversification, given present social and environmental conditions.

Productive Diversification: A Solution Internal to the System?

The generation of the primary feedback loop ($U_{7-11-12}$) has led to the serious consequences of large-scale range deterioration, domestic stock losses, small stock increase over cattle and reduction of available food for the Dasanetch. A potential counteraction or negative feedback to this environmental and economic breakdown exists internal to the S/E system, namely productive diversification to horticulture, fishing, hunting and gathering. On the basis of the stock and carrying capacity figures cited earlier, it is possible to conclude that fully 87 per cent of Dasanetch subsistence must be derived from production activities alternative to stock raising, given present conditions. Consequently, some assessment of the potential for diversification under the existing environmental and social conditions is of importance. Some general considerations for changing this potential through external human input to the Dasanetch S/E system are discussed later.

The Dasanetch have been somewhat diversified in production for many decades or even longer. It may be recalled from Chapter 5 that the four alternative production branches are unevenly practiced by the Dasanetch, however, with the households of lowest economic status subsisting entirely from activities other than stock raising and the wealthiest ones relying almost entirely on their stock. Assuming a willingness to diversify on the part of the Dasanetch production unit head, there still exist environmental constraints which inhibit the occurrence and effectiveness of horticulture in particular. These include the irregularity of rainfall and river flooding, the drying out of traditional planting areas along the Omo River levees, Kolon channel and the western edge of Berar (Sanderson's Gulf), and the recent submergence of large

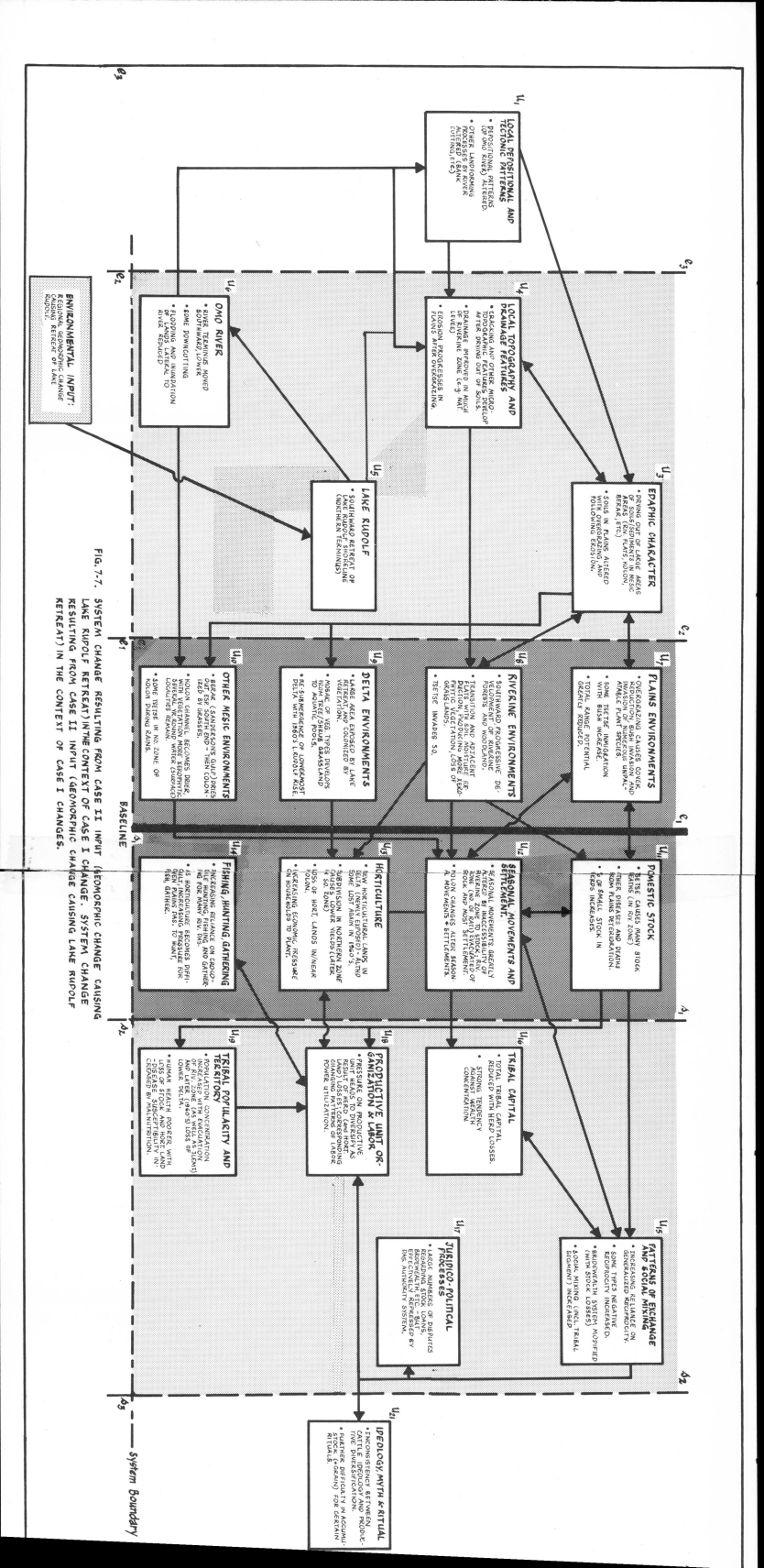

FIG. 7.7. SYSTEM CHANGE RESULTING FROM CASE II INPUT (GEOMORPHIC CHANGE CAUSING LAKE RUDOLF RETREAT) IN THE CONTEXT OF CASE I CHANGE. SYSTEM CHANGE RESULTING FROM CASE II INPUT (GEOMORPHIC CHANGE CAUSING LAKE RUDOLF RETREAT) IN THE CONTEXT OF CASE I CHANGES.

areas of the modern delta. All of these constraints have been described in earlier chapters. Among the societal constraints on diversification, three are of
primary significance: (1) the ideological emphasis on stock and stock raising;
(2) Dasanetch reciprocity patterns; and (3) the level of technology available to
the Dasanetch. The major operative features of these societal constraints are
summarized below.

Among the relatively undesirable (from the Dasanetch cultural standpoint)
alternatives to stock raising, horticulture is the least resisted by the Dasanetch.
Even rather wealthy patrilines have temporarily engaged in horticulture from
time to time, such as after severe stock losses from epidemics or raids by
neighboring hostile tribes.[20] Hunting and especially fishing, as described earlier in this book, have strong cultural stigmas attached to them and are avoided
whenever possible; gathering is done in varying intensity but generally increasing in importance with reduced wealth status.

The fact that horticulture is considerably more palatable to the majority
of Dasanetch than are the other alternative production branches is not only related to the tribe's long-term practice of associating horticulture with the rebuilding of herds, but also to the parallelism of many socio-economic features
associated with both stock raising and horticulture, with horticulture less dis-
ruptive of the normative patterns of social relations.[21] Dominance of the Inkabela tribal segment over the other Dasanetch segments, however, serves to
maintain the bias toward stock raising in the tribe as a whole, since the Inkabela segment is characterized by a strong ideological emphasis on stock. Thus
the comparatively greater subsistence emphasis on horticulture (and the other
alternatives) by culturally subdominant segments such as Eleli and Rieli does
not immediately result in a corresponding weakening of the ideology within
those segments which dictates maximization of stock. Instead, a strong lag
exists between the actual undertaking of alternative productive branches on the
one hand and an ideological shift away from an emphasis on stock on the other
hand.[22] Overall, the strong and pervasive ideology based on stock greatly

---

[20]Traditionally, herd losses have been redressed in several ways: (a) natural reproduction of stock, (b) raiding of neighboring hostile tribes, and (c) horticulture, followed by bartering of the grain for stock.

[21]It may be recalled that these two production branches are paired under
one mode of production, mode I (see Chapter 6).

[22]The Randel and Koro segments are ideologically and in practice even less
tolerant of production alternatives than the Inkabela, and for this reason face
even more severe immediate disaster than do some other segments.

slows the development of a willingness on the part of Dasanetch household heads to diversify their productive activities beyond the barest minimum deemed necessary for survival.

A second way in which the ideological emphasis on stock inhibits the potential of diversification for counteracting the primary positive feedback loop of the system concerns the transformation of available grain into small stock. Although some production units do retain a certain amount of the grain harvested, most who subsist by a combination of stock raising and horticulture utilize much of it for such exchange. This "upward" transformation of wealth, from grain to small stock (and to cattle when possible) is carried out by most production unit heads, even when their particular units are well below subsistence level. The decision to effect this transformation of material goods through exchange certainly coincides with the dictates of the dominant ideology and is supported by at least one frequently expressed line of economic reasoning: stock have an additional positive value when compared with grain in that they provide food (milk) on a sustained basis in the case of a female adult. Nevertheless, it must be pointed out that the conversion of grain to small stock not only serves to reduce the food value gained from the grain, but further augments the already critically serious deterioration of the rangelands, thus reinforcing the primary positive feedback loop. [23]

The Dasanetch's strong wealth redistributive patterns in the form of generalized reciprocity (see Chapter 5) result in a superficial alleviation of hunger for many. But considered in a larger temporal perspective, such redistribution results in a lag in the perceived severity of economic deterioration on the part of many production unit heads. This in turn produces a lag in the productive diversification undertaken, which by definition inhibits the breakage of the primary positive feedback loop and thus perpetuates environmental/economic breakdown. This strong redistributive system of exchange, on the other hand, has also been described as an important factor of the high level of stability in Dasanetch social relations.

I have earlier described the level of Dasanetch material technology as extremely limited, i.e., in the sense of implements present or known to them on any broad scale. This is an important reason for the low effectiveness of those alternative production activities undertaken by the Dasanetch. They lack such essentials, for instance, as strong rope or cord, fishing nets, metal for

---

[23]This is true since the additional small stock obtained through exchange are frequently from surrounding tribes.

fishhooks, blades for digging, etc. Related to this poverty of material technology, and augmented by the absence of a suitable organizational technology, is the existing low feasibility of the Dasanetch making simple environmental modifications which would greatly enhance the horticultural potential of their lands (see below).

All of these forces operate in combination to reduce both the incidence of productive diversification by the Dasanetch and the success of such diversification as is attempted. Diversification certainly does represent a temporary alleviation of hunger for many Dasanetch, and relative to other pastoral people the tribe has shown a remarkable ability to accept the need for such a shift in their productive efforts. But although there has been and is a certain degree of diversification which appears to counter the primary positive feedback loop, a serious question exists as to whether--in the absence of accompanying measures--the diversification lessens or in fact augments the problem. This has serious implications for the measures suggested by some persons and institutions external to Dasanetch society, as I will briefly elaborate below. At any rate, it is clear that the degree of productive diversification which is likely within the existing Dasanetch social and environmental framework is inadequate for solving the large-scale breakdown already in progress within the system of societal/environmental relations.

Finally, insofar as diversification tends to weaken the ideological emphasis on stock, unlimited adoption of production alternatives could result in major disruption of the whole set of social relations which are intimately tied to that ideology and which are critical ingredients in the high level of social stability. Since it is this very social stability which may be of tremendous value in effecting a long-range solution to the situation as described in these pages, this should be a matter of real concern for any who plan significant inputs to the Dasanetch political economy. I will deal with this difficult issue following the next section.

System Change and the Mode of Production Concept

Both major inputs of change described above may now be viewed in the context of the concept of mode of production. These remarks are by no means intended to be exhaustive of the possible generalizations regarding S/E system change and the mode of production concept. Rather, they are intended to stimulate further thought on the matter and to elucidate some aspects of the Dasanetch situation specifically.

Fig. 7-8 indicates the diffusion of change (excluding feedback processes) among the components as defined earlier.

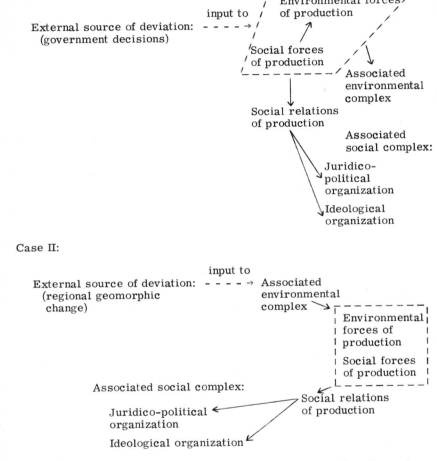

Fig. 7-8.--Flow of System Change and the Mode of Production Concept

These two flow patterns are similar in terms of the patterns of articulation among the components associated with a model

When the complete set of S/E system effects are taken into account, it becomes possible to assess the overall degree of incongruity (as defined earlier in this chapter, see footnote 6) among components of the two Dasanetch modes of production. The primary positive feedback loop $U_{7-11-12}$ is embedded in one component set of processes of a mode, i.e., all three member units of this loop, are within the forces of production. While the rangelands (U_7), domestic herds (U_{11}) and seasonal movement patterns (U_{12}) progressively change as parts of the positive feedback cycle, corresponding adjustment in the social relations of production (in the form of productive diversification)--itself not part of the positive feedback loop--does not obtain, and a growing incongruity between the forces and the social relations of production results. Similar to the classical Marxist formulation of the contradiction between the forces of production and the social relations of production within advanced capitalist society, incongruency within the Dasanetch S/E system along these lines involves a potential development of the forces of production (e.g., fishing and hunting) which remains an unrealized potential partly due to the character of the social relations of production. In fact, the character of Dasanetch social relations of production (and one step removed, the ideological organization), through the process of inhibiting the occurrence and effectiveness of productive diversification, reinforces the breakdown of the forces of production. [24]

It is possible to predict, on the basis of the criteria for identifying modes which were suggested earlier, the nature of some specific changes which will occur within the S/E system with regard to identified modes of production. Diversification for most Dasanetch production units, for example, may be predicted to occur within the same mode (e.g., from stock raising alone to stock raising and horticulture in combination--both branches being of mode I) whenever possible, as opposed to involving a different mode (e.g., from stock raising alone to a combination of stock raising and fishing--branches of mode I and mode II, respectively). This is suggested by my field data and is likely related to the fact that engagement in an alternative branch of production which is within the same mode entails relatively less discrepancy in specific forces of production and social relations of production involved, and thus has a higher chance of success for the production unit in question. Diversification from

---

[24] A significant aspect of the ideological bias against productive diversification concerns the major source of unutilized labor power among the Dasanetch, i.e., adult males. Theoretically, diversification could be facilitated either by these males participating directly in herding (thus freeing the energies of younger males for the less prestigious production alternative to stock raising), or by the adult males themselves undertaking substantial production along the lines of fishing, etc. These are not realistic possibilities within the present context, for the ideological reasons already discussed. In this way the unutilized male labor, as a component of the social relations of production, constitutes a serious block to development of the productive forces which is necessary for Dasanetch survival.

stock raising to production including horticulture (both in mode I) instead of fishing, etc., is of course, more consistent with the ideological emphasis on domestic stock. There are certainly notable exceptions to this generalization, as when the resources needed for the more closely related branches are not available (e.g., stock or horticultural land) or when prevailing ideological tenets lead to a different decision (e.g., from fishing and gathering in mode II, diversification to horticulture in mode I instead of hunting in mode II).

Summary: Existing State of Dasanetch Lands and Socioeconomics

The analysis of the last chapters has led to a number of conclusions about the Dasanetch people and their lands. Those conclusions relevant to the existing state of affairs are briefly summarized here, with the objective of emphasizing both the severity of the situation which has developed and the necessity of considering a number of aspects of the matter integrally in framing any solution.

Among both environmental and societal processes, there is an acceleration of change occurring to such a marked degree that it appears that no acceptable solution to the problems already described can be achieved within the system as it now stands. This is primarily true because of change inputs from forces external to the system which have generated a progressive environmental and economic deterioration. A strong and growing pressure for productive diversification has developed in recent decades. Insofar as the Dasanetch have responded to this pressure in the form of actually undertaking subsistence activities alternative to stock raising, there have been varying degrees of disruption of traditional socio-economic patterns. In spite of this (and in some ways because of it), the Dasanetch have shown a willingness to accept the imperative for diversification, with almost no external aid, and this distinguishes them from many pastoral peoples of East Africa. There are strong forces which inhibit the process of diversification, however, and these may even augment the progressive environmental and economic deterioration I have described.

It is important to bear in mind that concomitant with massive economic and environmental deterioration within the S/E system is a high degree of flexibility and balance within the matrix of Dasanetch social relations. This apparent societal stability in the face of such intense economic disruption results from (1) strong wealth redistributive pressures (see Chapter 5) which insure that a lowering of the total tribal wealth is accompanied by a continuing lateral distribution of that wealth which remains (e.g., stock, horticultural land); (2) a

highly flexible juridico-political system (see Chapter 4) whereby disputes and
other social tensions are effectively handled so that major social disruptions do
not really occur; (3) an intricately and effectively balanced set of social organizational principles whereby the functioning of clans (and patrilineages within
them), age sets and moieties are mutually reinforcing, and what antagonistic
relationships exist between them are largely counterbalanced. The important
generalization about the situation of the Dasanetch and their lands is that while
the essential character of Dasanetch society is protected from serious immediate disruption, the condition of both the economic sector and the environmental
sector is one of continual deterioration of critical proportions. It is likely that
the social processes which are here identified as stabilizing forces, however,
will themselves undergo deterioration and possible breakdown, given sufficient
time.

Barring any significant external input which serves to alleviate the conditions now facing the Dasanetch, they will continue to be subjected to worsening
environmental and economic conditions and will possibly undergo large-scale
cultural disintegration over the long run. One cannot spend any extended time
with the Dasanetch people and observe the nearly uniform indifference with
which their situation is regarded by the powerful political and economic forces
which are in large part the source of their desperate condition and which continue to deeply influence their lives by holding the only possible key to their survival, without comprehending at least part of their resignation as well as their
deep frustration. Only an external input which begins to address the interrelated matters of the condition of their land, their domestic stock, the need for
diversification and the existing set of social institutions can provide an answer
to the conditions described in the preceding pages.

An Approach to Partial and Full Solutions
to Dasanetch S/E System Instability

Notwithstanding the importance of the ecological approach, the commonest
failure in development planning is the scant regard that is given to the human
factor. Wherever there exists a human population, it is certain that there
will exist also a complex of ethnic, biological, and social influences, which
unless they are understood and accommodated by the development plan, will
introduce such an unpredictable element that one can not place confidence in
the projected outcome. (D. J. Pratt [1968: 5])

There have been few attempts by Ethiopian or foreign institutions to alleviate the hunger and destruction in the lower Omo valley, and those which have
been made have either been ineffective or of a one-dimensional nature such that

they have not seriously addressed the existing problems or they have in fact
aggravated them. Although there have been a few attempts by the government
to innoculate and treat the Dasanetch's domestic stock, this has been only by
individuals present for a very short while so that Dasanetch suspicions of them
as foreigners were not able to be overcome. There is virtually no aid to the
Dasanetch for improving their limited and primitive farming and fishing implements, nor for developing more lands for horticulture (see Chapters 5 and 7).
On some occasions in the past few years some grain has been given to (and
quickly absorbed by) the Dasanetch by the Ethiopian government. But medicine is essentially not available to the Dasanetch to any significant degree,
and diseases including trichoma, tuberculosis, malaria and others are ram-
pant. There is an American missionary family, the J. R. Swarts, who live
near Kalam. They and their helpers sell some medicine to the Dasanetch, and
they have also introduced some new crops and methods of planting in small
scale along the Omo River near the mission. It is critical that all these and
future forms of aid be evaluated carefully in terms of their impact on the whole
system. For this reason I have chosen to conclude this monograph with a discussion of possible solutions based on the preceding analysis.

Before discussing aspects of possible solutions, I wish to suggest several
dimensions essential to include in any solution to the Dasanetch S/E system
instability. First, any discussion of partial or full solutions should specify
what properties constitute an "acceptable" solution or system outcome. Second,
possible solutions may be considered to be basically internal or external in
character, depending upon whether they mobilize resources only from within
the system as it is presently constituted or whether they depend on resources
from outside the system. Third, possible solutions should be evaluated from
the standpoint of whether they are basically absorptive in nature, i.e., whether
they absorb or reduce some of the undesired change within the system but at
best provide only a temporary or stopgap solution to the social and environmental problems (e.g., in the Dasanetch case, fail to counteract the primary positive feedback loop, $U_{7-11-12}$), or whether they contribute to a long-range solution. Some brief comment regarding these three dimensions may serve as a
useful introduction to evaluating some specific possible actions.

Not all possible solutions to the serious destruction within the Dasanetch
S/E system are equally desirable or acceptable. For example, allowing the primary positive feedback process as identified to continue unchecked resulting in
mass starvation and disease with consequent drastic reduction of the population,

wholesale environmental destruction in the plains which is irreversible for the foreseeable future, and breakdown of the highly stable traditional Dasanetch set of social relations is, by the values explicitly stated below, not an "acceptable" solution. On the other hand, a radically changed production system, but one which preserves the basic social and cultural integrity and minimizes destruction of the natural resource base would, by the same set of values. be acceptable. In order to deal with such alternative outcomes, it is necessary to state the parameters along which possible future Dasanetch S/E systems may be sorted according to degree of desirability or acceptability, since these assumptions strongly condition the discussion of solutions below.

A "desirable" future condition of the Dasanetch S/E system I will define as one wholly in keeping with the Dasanetch's own value system relative to their established modes of production and accompanying environmental and societal organization, while not creating regional disruption along such lines as transmitting and being a reservoir of serious communicable diseases, furthering natural resource destruction, engaging in serious inter-tribal warfare, etc. On the basis of the present study alone, this state of affairs, however desirable, is wholly unrealistic at present, due to externally induced changes already instituted in the Dasanetch S/E system of relations. Consequently, although such a desirable state is useful as a reference point, it is necessary to turn to the notion of "acceptability."

I will define an "acceptable" solution[25] as one which produces a set of productive relations deemed necessary from the standpoint of Dasanetch economic survival and unavoidable regional pressures, while at the same time maximizing congruity with their traditional system--except insofar as the Dasanetch themselves develop different goals for a system which are possible within the larger political-economic context. The proposed solution outlined below attempts to provide for the maximum amount possible of self determination by the Dasanetch over their own future.

As for the second and third necessary considerations in forming a solution which were suggested above, if the conclusions drawn from the discussion of the Case I and II change inputs are correct, any adequate solution to existing S/E system breakdown must have the property of breaking the positive feedback loop $U_{7-11-12}$. Since the counteracting forces internal to the S/E system have

---

[25]This "acceptable" state, as characterized here, does not represent the thoughts of the majority of Dasanetch at present, but does, I believe, correspond to an increasing sentiment among them as they now face the clear issue of survival.

been judged to be at best absorptive, it is necessary to focus attention on the possible externally derived solutions. The major externally induced measures which might be suggested as possible solutions to existing environmental/economic destruction within the S/E system include: (1) domestic herd reduction and size control, (2) domestic stock inoculation, (3) construction of boreholes for water, (4) increase in Dasanetch tribal territory by government agreement, (5) Dasanetch human population control, and (6) assistance in developing alternative production branches. Considered alone, each of the measures listed either fails to break the primary positive loop $U_{7-11-12}$, or breaks the loop at least temporarily but with effects unacceptable in terms of destruction of the environment, the herds and/or the Dasanetch themselves. I offer several examples to support this assertion.

Consider the first action: domestic herd reduction and size control. If this measure alone were to be adopted, what effects would occur? Herd control would necessarily include the reduction of the present herds to a point where the stock present equal the number of stock supportable by the land. For the present area of the west bank Dasanetch, the number of stock supportable was computed to be slightly less than 5,000 stock units. This number of stock is adequate to support slightly under 1,200 people, whereas the west bank Dasanetch number approximately 9,500. Thus herd control without suitable accompanying measures constitutes a "solution" which fails to provide for over 80 percent of the population.

The second proposal, calling for domestic stock inoculations, may easily be shown to be inadequate as a solution. Although the results of this measure would include an initial decline in the rate of stock deaths and therefore a possible increase in food supply, the altering of the relationship between the number of stock supportable and the number of stock present would only intensify the degree of overstocking in the longer run. Thus, without substantial additional measures of a complementary nature, the net result would be an acceleration of the primary positive feedback loop in the system of S/E relations. A similar line of thought disqualifies the third measure, water borehole construction, as also contributing to the problem if undertaken without accompanying actions.

The fourth proposal, increase in Dasanetch tribal territory by government agreement, is also clearly inadequate. Assuming full subsistence from stock raising, the 9,440 west bank Dasanetch would require 10,832 square kilometers of land suited to grazing (based on the information presented in the discussion of Case I earlier in this chapter). Note that the tribal lands prior to

the initial territorial restriction in the 1930's included some 6, 590 square kilometers. It is possible that these 6, 590 km^2 of land at one time were adequate
for the Dasanetch population, but this amount falls far short of the amount
needed for the existing population (even allowing for a certain amount of reliance on production other than stock raising). In sum, a large-scale territorial
addition to the present Dasanetch lands is inadequate and unfeasible. First, it
is highly unlikely that such an amount of territory as would be needed could be
negotiated, especially considering the fact that other tribes in the region (e.g.,
the Inyangatom) also have dire need of more territory. Further, a major immediate effect of greatly increased tribal lands would be a rapid increase in domestic stock herd size. Given an increased wealth status and the option of selecting from among the possible branches of production a production unit head will
almost invariably select stock raising, for reasons already elaborated. Thus
the accumulation of stock will, over time, create precisely the same situation
the elimination of which was the objective of the territorial increase, but on a
larger geographic scale.

I turn now to presenting an idealized solution which more fully addresses
the Dasanetch situation. After briefly evaluating the possibility of effecting
such an idealized solution, I will proceed to a proposal which combines feasibility with the necessary spectrum of action identified here.

The first component of an idealized solution involves the breaking of the
primary positive feedback loop and consists of direct inputs to two of the three
system units involved in that loop:

1st Component:

Description	Intended Outcome	Input to Unit
Water boreholes	Water more generally available: stock dis-tribution improved	U_7
Stock inoculations	Increased stock vigor and reduction of deaths	U_{11}
Expansion of tribal territory	More grazing land available; pressure on rangelands reduced	U_{19}

Result: Breakage of primary positive feedback loop, $U_{7-11-12}$.
But although the expansion of tribal grazing lands could have the initial effect of
breaking the runaway condition, this breakage can be successful in the longer
run only if the amount of land provided creates a situation where the number of
stock supportable is equal to or greater than the number of stock required for
Dasanetch subsistence. One may easily predict that the central cultural posi-

tion of stock in Dasanetch ideology will lead to herd buildup until once again the stock present will exceed the stock supportable. This would be augmented by the inoculation of herds which will lead to a decrease in stock death and disease. [26] The intention of creating boreholes is to make water more generally available during the drought months, thus reducing herd concentrations around the few traditional water holes. But the effectiveness of boreholes assumes both a territory adequate to support the number of stock present and some schema which prevents the otherwise predictable overgrazing of lands proximal to the boreholes.

The general answer to these difficulties is contained in the measures taken under the second component of the proposed solution, Herd Control.

2nd Component:

Description	Intended Outcome	Input to Unit
Control over size of herds	Maintenance of herds below overstocking level	U_{11}
Control over the movement of herds	Protection of grazing lands	U_{12}
Control over composition of herds	Protection of grazing lands	U_{11}

Result: Prevention of reoccurrence of primary positive feedback loop $U_{7-11-12}$.

The purpose of specifying a schedule of herd movement, then, is to prevent the common situation in pastoral lands of East Africa: the destruction of grazing lands proximal with boreholes which were supposedly established to alleviate the deterioration of herds and rangelands. Similarly, control over the composition of herds is designed to prevent the destruction of grazing land. As described in an earlier section of this book, the increasing proportion of small stock (especially sheep) in Dasanetch herds has seriously accelerated ecological breakdown in the plains. The optimal ratio between cattle and small stock will vary as a function of the type of rangelands involved, the availability of water, the desired rate of reproduction, and other factors. The most advantageous balance of stock types must be estimated for the range conditions present in Dasanetch lands specifically.

---

[26]There have been some attempts by external agencies (e.g., Ethiopian government, foreign missions) to inoculate both Inyangatom and Dasanetch cattle. These have understandably met with deep suspicion by many stock owners, and at any rate represent expenditure of resources which inevitably only worsen the situation when they are unaccompanied by other necessary measures.

But if the Dasanetch's herd sizes are fixed at a level necessary to prevent rangeland destruction, either the population must be stabilized or the size of the herds must continuously be adjusted upwards to compensate for the increasing population. The latter alternative is not acceptable as it would lead to a situation where once again the overstocking condition would occur. A third component, then, must be added to the idealized solution.

3rd Component:

Description	Intended Outcome	Input to Unit
Human population control and medical care instituted	Population balanced with natural resource base; acceptable level of health maintained	U_{19}

Result: Prevention of starvation conditions and natural resource base depletion, and creation of desirable human health conditions.

Finally, the fourth component of the idealized solution:

4th Component:

Description	Intended Outcome	Input to Unit
Productive diversification to horticulture, fishing, hunting, gathering	Minimal subsistence provided for Dasanetch population	U_{18}

In addition to providing subsistence for the precentage of the population in excess of that taken care of by stock raising, diversification of productive activity would achieve a certain independence from domestic stock raising and the attendant risks of destruction of the tribe's food source by periodic stock epidemics. The following table suggests some possible external inputs associated with the alternative production branches which address the sources of resistance to those branches within the S/E system.

Productive Branch	System Internal Resistances	Possible External Input
Horticulture	Limited total amount of land with even periodic suitable conditions; stock ideology	Simple irrigation (e.g., open ditches) on natural levee backslopes to expand horticultural lands;[27] simple tools for digging and cutting

[27]At present, the Swart family at the Kalam mission are experimenting on a small scale with windmills as a means of delivering water from the Omo River to the levee backslopes.

Fishing	Lack of material (and organizational) technology; stock ideology	Simple fishing implements (e.g., nets, rope, hooks)
Hunting	Lack of technology; decreasing game population due to deteriorating environment; stock ideology	Simple material items for hunting; basic wildlife range management program
Gathering	Low yield and high variability due to semi-arid environment; deteriorating environmental conditions; stock ideology	Conditional on type of environmental management (if any)

Each of the system characteristics listed above which have historically precluded the development of effective alternatives to herding is addressed by an external input with the exception of the one category which crosscuts all of the productive alternatives: stock ideology. A major concern rests with the fact that the strong stock ideology so permeates the social organization of the tribe that any solution which fails to provide for at least some stock raising will fail to be acceptable to the Dasanetch and will very likely be unsuccessful over any significant period of time. Therefore, a balanced and long-term solution should include at least some raising of stock as one constituent of Dasanetch productive activity, along with the promotion of the alternative subsistence activities of horticulture, fishing, hunting and gathering.

It would be highly distorting of the preceding analysis to present this idealized solution as one capable of resolving the Dasanetch dilemma without attempting to determine the probability of its implementation within the larger political-economic context, particularly at the regional and national levels. Stated in their most general form, three important constraints on applying the idealized solution which operate at these larger levels are: (1) limited financial resources, (2) limited number of trained personnel, and (3) priority of development potentially contributing more to the national economy. There are also a number of other difficulties with implementing the idealized solution, and these concern the Dasanetch's particular geographical position and historical relations (e.g., between the Dasanetch and contiguous tribes), relations among the national governments involved, and other circumstances peculiar to the context of the larger system. Several of these may be concretely stated:

1. The expansion of Dasanetch tribal territory to its former boundaries is made difficult by the fact that these lands also have been traditionally occupied by the Turkana and the Inyangatom tribes. For this reason it is unlikely that the Dasanetch's claim to these lands could be recognized by other national governments (for example, Kenya) who have responsibility for the other tribes involved. To honor fully all three of the tribes' claims to these lands would destroy their range value through overgrazing.

2. It is questionable whether or not the government(s) involved would be willing, if able, to commit sufficient resources to adequately control herd sizes, herd composition and herd movements within the context of the present Dasanetch lands. Further, pervasive external controls over the Dasanetch people and their lands without their participation would not be welcomed by them, and indeed would likely meet with ultimate failure if attempted by outside forces. Thus the whole matter of what constitutes a legitimate and effective controlling agency must be confronted.

3. The components of the idealized plan described above must, in order to actually effect a solution, be made operative nearly simultaneously. Considering the difficulties in instituting some of them, this is highly unlikely. Consequently, the result could be similar to that described earlier for the instances in which the component solutions are applied separately. Specifically, depending on the order in which the above component solutions are applied, they may actually intensify rather than alleviate stress within the S/E system.

The idealized solution described above, therefore, is not a practicable one given the existing conditions. It is, however, still useful in that it identifies a set of parameters which any workable solution must take into account. I wish to suggest an outline of a workable plan which is a significant step in the direction of a full solution to the Dasanetch dilemma. These measures do not constitute an immediate or full solution; nor are they intended as the only possible combination of actions, but rather as one schema which offers a real possibility of success and which moves the whole system much closer to an acceptable state. I present it here only in brief form, sufficient only to communicate its essential features.[28] All four aspects of the proposal are intended to be implemented together.

I: Allocation of some portion of the Dasanetch's original territory, though less than the full area claimed.

II: Institution of a plan for domestic stock herd control which focuses on the limitation of the number of stock which utilize the newly allocated lands (and to some extent, the movements of those stock), but with little control over the lands now occupied.[29]

---

[28] Medical and population control measures are omitted here; these would presumably be the next necessary phase of an effort toward a full solution.

[29] Perhaps some portions of what is presently Dasanetch territory, i.e.,

III: Undertaking of aid to the Dasanetch for productive diversification, specifically in the form of horticulture and fishing in a way which will bring the Dasanetch up to subsistence level (that is, alternative production minimally needs to supply the difference between the required subsistence level and the portion provided by stock raising).

IV: Utilization of Dasanetch social organizational principles in carrying out the economic and environmentally oriented changes, in order to increase the effectiveness of any external inputs through maximizing Dasanetch cooperation and success in coping with and having significant input to the measures taken.

V: Maximization of Dasanetch roles in decision-making, both through traditional and newly formed administrative means.

It is possible, for instance, to envision a scenario of development and assistance along the above four dimensions which includes some of the following details.

The Dasanetch secure an increase in territory which includes a limited amount of their traditional lands; this occurs through successful negotiations between the Ethiopian and Kenyan governments. With the participation of representatives of the Dasanetch tribe (selected by the tribe), the Ethiopian government (or other outside agency) involved draws up a plan to equitably partition the newly awarded lands (and possibly some of the existing territory of the Dasanetch) into sections.[30] These sections are allocated for domestic stock use (not necessarily for residence) to specified social units (e.g., patrilineally defined units) within the tribe.[31] After a survey to approximate the stock-carrying capacity of the sectioned land, the government, in consultation with tribal representatives,[32]

---

those which are relatively ecologically intact (e.g., lands just east and southeast of Koras Mountain) could also be brought into the herd control schema.

[30]Some of the Dasanetch lands at present are so degraded, ecologically speaking, that it is not clear that they should be included in the sectioning play; such a decision might be made primarily on the basis of available human organizational resources. In the case where much of their destroyed lands are not included, there is perhaps no reason why controls need be exercised there, at least during the first phases. Sections are drawn in a fashion which incorporates ecological information gathered on the newly opened territory.

[31]I suggest grazing and stock control units based on the patrilines because the lineage structure is traditionally most closely related to stock ownership, inheritance and herding control. Consequently, the degree of social adjustment required by the new economic arrangement is minimized.

[32]Again, it is critical to rely on the traditional political structure of the Dasanetch for tribal representatives, not political offices imposed on the tribe by the external government as has happened in the past (see description of government chiefs in Chapter 4).

fixes the maximum number of stock allowed in each section. In both the partitioning of the land and the specification of the maximum number of stock allowed in the section, variation in range conditions for different localities and seasons is taken into account. Enforcement of the stock limitations for the sections is by the local government or development authorities, whereby stock in excess of the limit specified for the section are confiscated by the authorities after a series of agreed-upon measures to be taken by the tribal social unit concerned have failed. Matters such as disputes arising from the legal confiscation of excess stock by the authorities, the proportioning of stock among production units included in one grazing section, and conflicts regarding claims for access to a particular section by Dasanetch individuals are handled by the already established system of authority relations within the tribe. This situation results in a sustained though limited milk and meat yield for the Dasanetch, as well as provides a minimal number of stock which are critical to the maintenance of social relations. The food yield from the stock is not sufficient to meet full subsistence requirements for the tribe, however, so that the social units involved (and those with no stock) turn to alternative productive activities (or intensify their present involvement in them), particularly horticulture at the outset.

The government or other agency renders material aid to support the development of new lands for horticulture. Using the simple irrigation technique of open ditches from the river channel to selected natural levee backslope localities, the latter receive water during the flood stage of the Omo River. The backslope localities selected for horticulture are contiguous whenever possible, in order to facilitate more efficient control. A coordinator from the government or agency who is responsible for the initial phases of the project meets and confers with traditional production unit heads (or natural authority figures of a larger patrilineally based unit) regarding the allocation of the labor power they control (e.g., wives, daughters and sons). Normative patterns of Dasanetch labor allocation are thus employed. Labor power is allocated to the horticultural project by voluntary agreement from the various production units; the coordinator has the responsibility for the supervision of this labor power and also the techniques employed. The coordinator also enters into negotiation with the Dasanetch production unit heads regarding the allocation of the horticultural product. In return for donating labor power at their disposal, the production unit heads are guaranteed a minimum return by the project director(s) (this serves to prime the process until the project is functioning to produce a sufficient amount of product when the guarantee will be a proportion of the crop involved proportional to the labor power committed). Further, agreements are reached between the production unit heads and the coordinator concerning the system of allocation of the product. The crop yields are stored in a central place with respect to the area they are harvested in, and this storage system holds the bulk of the product, dispensing it to the appropriate production unit at the prearranged rate. This last measure, i.e., a rationed release of grain rather than the release of the full allotment at once, helps to discourage the recipients of the product from attempting to transform their grain into stock. Distribution of the allocated grain among kin, age mates, etc., is of course under the control of the production unit head (or appropriate wife) involved, i.e., in a fashion congruent with Dasanetch tradition.

Although no detail is suggested here, implements for fishing (as well as some organization) form an additional important element in diversification of production for the Dasanetch. At least for the immediate future, however, fishing will be less acceptable to the Dasanetch than horticulture, and hence should likely be of secondary (though increasing) emphasis.

There are several underlying characteristics of the secnario which merit some further comment. A commitment is made and executed by the outside agency to involve the maximum number of Dasanetch in the decision making which concerns, for example, the identity of the social unit which is awarded the section rights and responsibilities and the rate of dispensation of the crop yields. This commitment will finally take the form of a Dasanetch "shadow" structure whereby each member of the outside agency participating in the project trains a Dasanetch in the execution of his or her duties. The limitations imposed on the new land section guarantees the protection of the rangelands as a natural resource. The fact that any stock in excess of the number specified for a section will be confiscated discourages the Dasanetch from attempting to accumulate additional stock, or alternatively, such attempts to accumulate stock will be naturally offset by the fact that these excess stock will be subject to the severely overgrazed conditions of the lands already deteriorated which are not under the control scheme. Simultaneously, the recognition of this upper limit to herd size encourages the tribal units to diversify. Under this scenario the redistributive pressures on the wealthier stock-holding patrilineages to distribute their stock--an important aspect of Dasanetch social stability--may continue, since the number of stock that they are allowed will be limited. Insuring that a significant portion of their subsistence can be derived from their herding activity allows the whole system of social relations based on stock to continue functioning, thus maintaining social cohesion. The overall effect of this scenario would be to weaken the stock ideology to the extent that diversification and herd control are progressively accepted. Both the commitment to encourage participation by the Dasanetch and the sensitivity to the structural principles of their traditional social organization when allocating herding sections promote cooperation and a drive toward self-sufficiency on the part of the Dasanetch. The weakening of the Dasanetch stock ideology will likely, in the long run, lead to basic level social structural changes since, as has been stressed repeatedly in this analysis, the society's system of social relations are deeply rooted in this ideology. Even though basic level change will ensue, however, its gradual nature will allow it to be adaptive and to develop largely from the internal evolutionary potential of Dasanetch society.

I suggest that the solution outlined above achieves the following goals:

(a) It breaks the primary positive feedback loop (of environmental and herd deterioration) by creating a balance between the load-bearing capacity of the rangelands and the number of stock allowed on that land.

(b) It maintains the herding activity to the extent that it allows the continuation of the normative patterns of social relations based on stock (though with the numbers of stock for social transactions reduced).

(c) It introduces conditions which both encourage and support the establishment of alternative economic activity.

(d) It gradually undermines the cattle ideology, without threatening the associated patterns of social relations--thus allowing adaptive change which is gradual but large scale.

(e) It preserves the balanced flexibility of the social units (patriline, age set, and moiety) and allows the Dasanetch significant control in the choice of the unit appropriate for the economic activity involved.

(f) It insures that the herd control and the horticultural project will have the maximum chance of succeeding by employing outside agents, and by making provision for the return of that control to the Dasanetch as part of its program--thus trading off an initial lack of autonomy for the Dasanetch against the successful establishment of programs which include the autonomy and self-sufficiency of the tribe as stated objectives.

(g) It involves relatively little in the way of either personnel and material aid, while promoting the self-sufficiency of one of the member tribes of the nation.

In addition to the measures described in the scenario, less immediate but no less important projects must subsequently be introduced, such as: population control, stock inoculations, educational and material aid regarding methods and implements for fishing and hunting (the last of these could very likely be instituted from the outset).

The integrated solution proposed here is severe with respect to disrupting some of the most central traditions of Dasanetch society in the long run. This, I conclude, is unavoidable in any plan which adequately responds to the plight in which the Dasanetch now exist; a purely pastoral way of life is no longer possible in this region. The key to successfully transforming from a pastoral political economy to one highly mixed in productive activities (but weighted against pastoralism) is a gradual and multilevel shift to the alternative production organization--one respecting the Dasanetch traditional social organization and system of social relations. In addition to maintaining the high level of social coherence which obtains for this particular society and providing for a long-range adaptation of the society to its changed conditions, this type of solution, I suggest, represents the minimum long-range expenditure of resources which will render the tribe self-sufficient and simultaneously avoid destruction of their natural resource base.

I have had two major objectives in this study—namely, the analysis of a specific set of societal/environmental interactions in a manner which makes clear the origin and nature of existing conditions as well as provide a basis for the formulation of a solution, and the development of a conceptual framework which is broadly applicable to the study of societal/environmental relations in other contexts. The success of the second of these objectives may be evaluated by the reader, and I myself will offer a critique of this approach elsewhere. As to the first of these objectives, my association with the Dasanetch has contributed immeasurably to transforming my previously intuitive grasp of the relations between societies and their natural surroundings into a more systematic and explicit means of understanding. It is my profound hope that this study may contribute to lessening the pain and destruction which these proud people face each day of their lives.

APPENDIX A

PLANT SPECIES COLLECTED IN THE

LOWER OMO RIVER BASIN

PTERIDOPHYTA

POLYPODIACEAE
Actiniopteris radiata (Swartz) Link

ANGIOSPERMAE: DICOTYLEDONES

ACANTHACEAE
  Barleria acanthoides Vahl
  B. eranthemoides C. B. Cl.
  Blepharis linariifolius Pers.
  B. persica (Burm. f.) Kuntze
  Crossandra nilotica Oliv.
  Ecbolium anisacanthus (Schweinf.)
    C. B. Cl.
  E. revolutum (L.) C. B. Cl.
  Hypoestes verticillaris (L. f.)
    Roem. & Schult.
  Justicia anselliana (Nees) T.
    Anders.
  J. caerulea Forsk.
  J. flava (Vahl) Vahl
  J. odora (Forsk.) Lam.
  J. striata (Klotzsch.) Bullock
  J. sp. (=Carr 255)
  Peristrophe bicalyculata (Retz.)
    Nees
  Ruellia patula Jacq.

AIZOACEAE
  Corbichonia decumbens (Forsk.)
    Exell
  Trianthema triquetra Willd.
  Zaleya pentandra (L.) Jeffrey

AGAVACEAE
  Sansevieria ehrenbergii Bak.

AMARANTHACEAE
  Achyranthes aspera L.
  Aerva persica (Burm. f.) Merr.

Celosia argentea L.
C. populifolia Moq.
C. schweinfurthiana Schinz
Cyathula orthacantha (Hochst.)
  Schinz
Dasysphaera prostrata (Gilg) Cavaco
Digeria muricata (L.) Mart.
Psilotrichum elliottii Bak.
P. ghaphalobryum (Hochst.) Schinz
Pupalia lappacea (L.) Juss.
P. lappacea (L.) Juss. var. orbicu-
  lata Schinz
Sericocomopsis pallida (S. Moore)
  Schinz

ANACARDIACEAE
  Heeria reticulata (Bak. f.) Engl.
  Lannea floccosa Jacl.
  Rhus natalensis Bernh. ex Krauss

ANNONACEAE
  Uvaria leptocladon Oliv. ?var. nov. ?
    (=Carr 543)

APOCYNACEAE
  Adenium obesum (Forsk.) Roem. &
    Schult.
  Saba florida (Benth.) Bullock

ASCLEPIADACEAE
  Calotropis procera (L.) Ait
  Caralluma russelliana (Brongn.)
    Cuf.
  C. somaliea N. E. Br.

301

Curroria volubilis (Schlecht.)
Bullock
Leptadenia hastata (Pers.) Decne
Pergularia daemia (Forsk.) Chiov.
Sarcostemma viminale (L.) R. Br.
Tacazzea apiculata Oliv. S. lat.

BALANITACEAE
Balanites aegyptiaca (L.) Del.
B. orbicularis Sprague
B. sp. (=Carr 859)

BORAGINACEAE
Cordia crenata Del.
C. sinensis Lam. (C. gharaf)
Heliotropium indicum L.
H. ovalifolium Forsk.
H. somalense Vatke
H. steudneri Vatke
H. supinum
Trichodesma zeylanicum (L.) R. Br.

BURSERACEAE
Boswellia hildebrandtii Engl.
Commiphora africana (A. Rich.)
Engl.
C. boiviniana Engl.
C. madaga scariensis Jacq.
C. sp. (=Carr 227)

CAPPARACEAE
Boscia angustifolia A. Rich. var.
angustifolia vel sp. aff.
B. coriacea Pax
Cadaba farinosa Forsk. ssp.
farinosa
C. gillettii R. A. Grah
C. glandulosa Forsk.
C. rotundifolia Forsk.
Capparis fascicularis DC. var.
elaeagnoides (Gilg) De Wolf
C. fascicularis DC. var.
fascicularis
C. tomentosa Lam.
Cleome brachycarpa DC.
C. parvipetala R. A. Grah.
Crateva adansonii DC.
Maerua crassifolia Forsk.
M. oblongifolia (Forsk.) A. Rich.
M. subcordata (Gilg) De Wolf

CELASTRACEAE
Hippocratea africana (Willd.) Loes.
Maytenus senegalensis (Lam.) Exell

CERATOPHYLLACEAE
Ceratophyllum demersum L.

CHENOPODIACEAE
Suaeda monoica J. F. Gmel.

COMBRETACEAE
Combretum aculeatum Vent.
Terminalia brevipes Pampan.

COMPOSITAE
Delamerea procumbens S. Moore
Helichrysum glumaceum DC.
Kleinia kleinioides (Sch. Bip.)
M. R. F. Taylor
K. longiflora Oliv. & Hiern
Pluchea dioscoridis DC.
P. ovalis (Pers.) DC.
Sphaeranthus ukambensis Vatke &
O. Hoffm.
Vernonia cinerascens Sch. Bip.
V. sp. (=Carr 333)

CONVOLVULACEAE
Hildebrandtia obcordata S. Moore
Ipomoea aquatica Forsk.
I. sinensis (Desv.) Choisy ssp.
blepharosepala (A. Rich.) Meeuse
I. sp. (=Carr 728)
Seddera hirsuta Hall. f. var. hirsuta

CUCURBITACEAE
Coccinia grandis (L.) Voigt
C. sp. (=Carr 618)
Cucumis dipsaceus Spach
C. figarei Naud.
Kedrostis gijef (Gmel.) Jeffr.
K. foetidissima (Jacq.) Cogn.
Luffa ?echinata Roxb.
Momordica rostrata A. Zimm.

DICHAPETALACEAE
Tapura fischeri Engl.

EBENACEAE
Diospyros scabra (Chiov.) Cuf.
D. sp. (=Carr 578)

ELATINACEAE
Bergia suffruticosa (Del.) Fenzl

EUPHORBIACEAE
Acalypha fruticosa Forsk.
A. indica L.
Euphorbia grandicornis Goebel

303

E. heterochroma Pax
E. hypericifolia L.
E. tirucalli L.
E. triaculeata Forsk.
Jatropha fissispina Pax
Phyllanthus amarus Schumach. &
Thonn.
P. maderaspatensis L.
P. reticulatus Poir.
P. sp. (=Carr 411)
Ricinus communis L.
Securinega virosa (Willd.) Pax &
K. Hoffm.
Tragia hildebrandtii Muell. Arg.

GENTIANACEAE
Enicostema hyssopifolium (Willd.)
Verdoorn

LABIATAE
Basilicum polystachyon (L.)
Moench.
Hyptis pectinata (L.) Poit.
Leonotis nepetifolia (L.) Ait. f.
Leucas ?glabrata R. Br.
L. nubica Benth.
Ocimum americanum L.
O. Hadiense Forsk.
O. Kilimandscharicum Guerke
Orthosiphon somalensis Vatke
Plectranthus sp. (=Carr 739)

LEGUMINOSAE: CAESALPINIOIDEAE
Cassia didymobotrya Fres.
C. italica (Mill.) F. W. Andr. ssp.
micrantha Brenan
C. nigricans Vahl
C. occidentalis L.
Delonix elata (L.) Gamble
Tamarindus indica L.

LEGUMINOSAE: MIMOSOIDEAE
Acacia brevispica Harms
A. drepanolobium Sjoestedt
A. horrida (L.) Willd. ssp.
benadirensis (Chiov.) Hillcoat &
Brenan
A. mellifera (Vahl) Benth. ssp.
mellifera
A. nubica Benth.
A. paolii Chiov.
A. reficiens Wawra spp. misera
(Vatke) Brenan
A. senegal (L.) Willd.
A. seyal Del.

A. sieberana DC.
A. tortilis (Forsk.) Hayne ssp. spi-
rocarpa (Hochst. ex A. Rich.)
Brenan
Dichrostachys cinerea (L.) Wight &
Arn.
Mimosa pigra L.

LEGUMINOSAE: PAPILIONOIDEAE
Canavalia cathartica Thou.
C. virosa (Roxb.) Wight & Arn.
Crotalaria polysperma Kotschy
C. pycnostachya Benth.
Indigofera arrecta A. Rich.
I. ciferrii Chiov.
I. coerulea Rosb. var. occidentalis
Gill. & Ali
I. hochstetteri Bak.
I. oblongifolia Forsk.
I. schimperi Jaub. & Spach.
I. spicata Forsk.
I. spinosa Forsk.
I. tinctoria L.
I. volkensii Taub.
Ormocarpum trichocarpum (Taub.)
Engl.
Rhynchosia minima (L.) DC. var.
prostrata (Harv.) Meikle
R. pulverulenta Stocks
Sesbania sesban (L.) Merr. var.
nubica Chiov.
S. sericea (Willd.) Link
S. somalensis Gillett
Tephrosia purpurea (L.) Pers. var.
pubescens Bak.
T. uniflora Pers.
T. uniflora Pers. ssp. uniflora
Vigna luteola (Jacq.) Benth.
V. radiata (L.) Wilczek. var. sublo-
bata (Roxb.) Verdc.
V. unguiculata (L.) Walp. ssp. cylin-
drica (L.) Van Eselt

LORANTHACEAE
Loranthus sp. (=Carr 880)
Plicosepalus sagittifolius (Sprague)
Danser
Tapinanthus aurantiacus (Engl.) Dan-
ser

MALVACEAE
Abelmoschus esculentus (L.) Medic.
Abutilon figarianum Webb
A. fruticosum Guill. & Perr.
A. graveolens W. & A.

A. hirtum (Lam.) Sweet
A. pannosum (Forsk.f.) Schlecht.
Hibiscus micranthus L.f.
H. sp. (=Carr 857)
Pavonia patens (Andr.) Chiov.
P. zeylanica (L.) Cav.
Senra incana Cav.
Sida rhombifolia L.

MELIACEAE
Trichilia roka (Forsk.) Chiov.

MENISPERMACEAE
Cissampelos mucronata A. Rich.
Cocculus hirsutus (L.) Diels

MORACEAE
Ficus sycomorus L.

NYCTAGINACEAE
Boerhavia erecta L.
Commicarpus plumbagineus (Cav.)
Standl.
C. stellatus (Wight) Berhaut

NYMPHAECEAE
Nymphaea lotus L.

OLACACEAE
Ximenia americana L.
X. caffra Sond.

OLEACEAE
Jasminum abyssinicum DC.

ONAGRACEAE
Ludwigia leptocarpa (Nutt.) Hara
L. stolonifera (Guill. & Perr.)
Raven

PASSIFLORACEAE
Adenia venenata Forsk.

PEDALIACEAE
Sesamothamnus busseanus Engl.
Sesamum latifolium Gillett

PISTACEAE
Pistiai stratiotes L.

POLYGALACEAE
Polygala erioptera DC.

POLYGONACEAE
Polygonum senegalense Meisn.
forma albotomentosa R.A. Grah.

PORTULACACEAE
Portulaca foliosa Ker. Gawl.
P. oleracea L.
P. quadrifida L.
Talinum portulacifolium (Forsk.)
Schweinf.

RHAMNACEAE
Ziziphus mauritiana Lam.
Z. mucronata Willd.
Z. pubescens Oliv.

RUBIACEAE
Kohautia caespitosa Schnizl.
Tarenna graveolens (S. Moore)
Brem.

RUTACEAE
Fagara chalybea (Engl.) Engl.

SALVADORACEAE
Dobera glabra (Forsk.) Poir.
Salvadora persica L. var. persica

SAPINDACEAE
Allophylus macrobotrys Gilg
Aphania senegalensis (Juss.) Radlk.
Cardiospermum helicacabum L. var.
halicacabum
Haplocoelum foliolosum (Hiern) Bul-
lock
Lepisanthes senegalensis (Poir.)
Leeuh.
Melanodiscus oblongus Taub.

SCROPHULARIACEAE
Stemodia ?serrata Benth.
Striga hermonthica (Del.) Benth.

SIMAROUBACEAE
Harrisonia abyssinica Oliv.

SOLANACEAE
Lycium sp. (=Carr 225)
Nicotiana tabacum L.
Solanum hastifolium Dunal
S. incanum L.
S. sp. aff. longestamineum Dammer
S. nigrum L.
S. sepicula Dunal
Withania somnifera (L.) Dunal

STERCULIACEAE
Melochia corchorifolia L.
Sterculia sp. (=Carr 340)

TILIACEAE
Corchorus olitorius L.
C. trilocularis L.
Grewia bicolor Juss.
G. fallax K. Sch.
G. tenax (Forsk.) Fiori
G. villosa Willd.

ULMACEAE
Celtis integrifolia Lam.

VAHLIACEAE
Vahlia goddingii E. A. Bruce

VERBENACEAE
Phyla nodiflora (L.) Greene
Premna resinosa Schauer

Priva adhaerens (Forsk.) Chiov.
Svensonia Laeta (Fanzl. ex Walp.)
Moldenke

VITACEAE
Cayratia ibuensis (Hook. f.) Suesseng.
Cissus cactiformis Gilg
C. quadrangularis L.
C. rotundifolia (Forsk.) Vahl
Cyphostemma sp.

ZYGOPHYLLACEAE
Tribulus cistoides L.
T. terrestris L.
Zygophyllum simplex L.

ANGIOSPERMAE: MONOCOTYLEDONES

AGAVACEAE
Sansevieria ehrenbergii Bak.

ARACEAE
Pistia stratiotes L.

COMMELINACEAE
Commelina benghalensis L.
C. forskaolaei Vahl

CYPERACEAE
Cyperus alopecuroides Rottb.
C. articulatus L.
C. laevigatus L.
C. longus L.
C. maritimus L.
C. rotundus L.
C. teneriffae Poir.
Scirpus maritimus L.

GRAMINEAE
Aristida adscensionis L.
A. keniensis Henr.
A. mutabilis Trin. & Rupr.
Cenchrus ciliaris L.
C. setigerus Vahl
Chloris roxburghiana Schult.
C. virgata Sw.
Chrysopogon aucheri (Boiss.) Stapf
var. aucheri
Cymbopogon schoenanthus (L.)
Spreng. ver. proximus
Cynodon castylon (L.) Pers.
Dactyloctenium giganteum Fischer &
Schweickt.

D. sp. nov.
Digitaria macroblephara (Hack.)
Stapf
Dinebra retroflexa (Vahl) Panzer
Echinochloa haploclada (Stapf) Stapf
Enneapogon brachystachyus (Jaub. &
Spach) Stapf
E. cenchroides (Roem. & Schult.)
C. E. Hubb.
Enteropogon macrostachyus (A. Rich.)
Benth.
Eragrostis cilianensis (All.) Lutati
E. namaquensis Nees var. diplachnoides (Steud.) Clayton
E. namaquensis Schrad. var. diplachnoides (Steud.) Clayton
Eriochloa nubica (Steud.) Thell.
Heteropogon contortus (L.) Roem. &
Schult.
Lintonia nutans Stapf
Loudetia phragmitoides (Peter) C. E.
Hubb.
Panicum coloratum L.
P. maximum Jacq.
P. meyeranum Nees
P. poaeoides Stapf
Perotis patens Gand. var. parvispicula Robyns
Phragmites australis (Cav.) Steud.
P. ?karka (Retz.) Steud.
Schoenefeldia transiens (Pilg.) Chiov.
Sehima nervosum (Willd.) Stapf
Setaria acromelaena (Hochst.) Dur.
& Schinz

Sorghum verticilliflorum (Steud.) Stapf

S. virgatum (Hack.) Stapf

Sporobolus consimilis Fres.

S. fimbriatus Nees var. latifolius

S. helvolus (Trin.) Dur. & Schinz

S. marginatus A. Rich.

S. pellucidus Hochst.

S. pyramidalis Beauv.

S. spicatus (Vahl) Kunth

Stipagrostis hirtigluma (Trin. & Rupr.) De Winter

Tetrapogon cenchriformis (A. Rich.) Clayton

T. tenellus (Roxb.) Chiov.

Tragus berteronianus Schult.

Urochloa setigera (Retz.) Stapf

Vossia cuspidata (Roxb.) Griff.

LILIACEAE

Urginea indica (Roxb.) Kunth

Asparagus sp.

PALMAE

Hyphaene ?thebaica (L.) Mart.

TYPHACEAE

Typha sp.

APPENDIX B

METHODOLOGY: ECOLOGICAL STUDIES

Two major types of transecting methods were used for studying plains vegetation. First, line-belt transects were done in a stratified random manner at
three sites within each of the three zones established for the disturbance gradient investigation. Each transect was 90 meters in length and 10 meters in
width (5 meters on either side of the transect tape). Line intercept was recorded along the tape for all woody species, and herbaceous plants were recorded as grasses or forbs. All woody species and their heights were recorded
throughout the belt area. The following were recorded for 5 m^2 samples at 0,
30, 60 and 90 m values along the tape: soil character, % total plant cover, %
ground cover (less than 1 m), % woody cover, grass height, and herbaceous species present along with Braun-Blanquet values. Also noted for the transect
area were general type of land use, presence or absence of termite mounds
(and any associated vegetation), and patchiness in vegetation pattern.

Second, circular plots (radius = 15 meters) were used more generally
throughout the plains of the lower basin, as well as within the transition zone
and adjacent flats of the riverine zone. These were selected in a stratified random manner. All species were rated on the cover-abundance scale as used by
the Zürich-Montpellier school of phytosociology, and on the sociability scale.
Geomorphic and edaphic character were noted, and some soil samples were
taken. Total vegetation cover, woody vs. herbaceous cover, presence and character of termite mounds, and land use were also recorded.

Successional changes leading to the advanced state of riverine forest were
investigated along the south to north gradient on inside bends of the Omo River.
At each riverine site, general collection and description were done, and belt
profile transects were made for physiognomic characteristics. These transects were made perpendicular to the river bank, 100 meters long by 14 meters
wide (7 meters on either side of the transect tape). Line intercept was recorded for all plants taller than 1 meter. Within each 30-meter segment,
Braun-Blanquet sociability and cover estimates were recorded for all species,
as were total cover, cover of plants greater than 7 meters, and ground cover

(less than 1 meter in height). Woody individuals at least 2 meters high were tabulated by species, height, basal diameter and number of stems, parallel position on the tape, and crown width along the tape. Point-center quarter transects were utilized for a more precise description of floristic and structural changes. These transects were modified slightly from Cottam and Curtis (1956). L-shaped transects were constructed with one axis roughly parallel to the river and the other axis perpendicular to it, in order to compensate for any vegetation pattern paralleling the river. Sixty points, separated by 20-meter intervals, were included in each transect. Within each quarter the nearest tree or shrub taller than 2 meters was recorded by species name, basal diameter, number of stems, height and distance from the point. Ground cover was noted along with any interesting phenomena such as species patchiness, dead woody plants, litter thickness and composition, fauna and human activities.

SELECTED DASANETCH ORAL TRADITION

Early history of Inkabela (Sheer) and Oro[1]

NEUPE

Long ago, the "Shir" were all "Neupe." The Neupe split into two groups disagreeing on where to go for grass for the cattle. One group of Neupe went "Upland" to the other side of Amodet; the other group of Neupe (Shiri) went to the lower land, Turkikwell. When they entered Turkikwell, they fought with the Koro. Ĩgudan (the old name for Oro) then stayed with Neupe. After Turkikwell they moved to Kalolikongoli, on the south side of Lodwar. Both Neupe and Ĩgu-dan all came to this place (after moving many times in between). But there was no grass, so they looked for grass and saw rain in the distance. One young man went out alone, found some footprints of people, and followed them until he found some cow dung. So he followed the dung until he found a large trail used by cattle to go to Lake Rudolf for water. He followed this path until he found an abandoned village site; he thought this village was of Koro. He returned to his village that evening telling the men there what all he had seen, that he hadn't seen the actual people, and that he didn't know where they went or what tribe they are. He had seen grass, so they could move. The Neupe (and Ĩgudan) ar-rived there and saw the rain far off. So the old man sent four or five young men to look at this land to see if there were rain and grass there so they could move. There they saw some cattle of Koro, who had brought their cattle from the other side when the rains came. When they saw them some thought they were Koro and some didn't know. Some said that they should go close and see the owners of the cattle. But others said if the Koro would chase us then some of us are not as fast: "If we go there the Koro will kill us, " they said.

They waited there awhile, then returned to their village to talk with the Koro, who told them that there was grass and water there and that they didn't

---

[1]The name for Sheer in oral tradition regarding this period was Nyeupe; that for Oro was Ĩgudan.

know who the people were. When they got there, they met the Koro at the water place where they talked. Neupe (and Īgudan) said they had heard the noises of cattle and had come to see. And the Neupe told the Koro where their village was and that they wanted to move on this "side" (other side from Koro). The Koro said yes and they agreed to be on different sides of the water hole. Vigana went back to the Koro village to talk together. Then two Koro men went back to the Neupe village where they finished by saying "Peace." Neupe said they wanted to move so Koro said there was grass on "their" side and to come there tomorrow. So the next day, Neupe moved nearby. Then the Koro (Neupe-Īgudan) left the village with the young ayi and cattle and sent the rest of the stock to the water. Then they went to the Koro village. One Koro man came to talk with them when they arrived, saying "Go and sit in our shady place there." The Neupe-Īgudan said to each other, "Ah, now they are showing us a shady place, another is bringing us an ayi to eat, we are the guests of the Koro." They then went to see the shady place, but there were thorns everywhere and it was a bad place. The sage thorns had dried up and fallen off and no man had swept it off. So they said, "Now, where will we sit?" Another said, "This is bad." And they sat on their "kara," and said, "Hold your spears ready for trouble." They thought the Koro cattle came into the village and the Koro bled them and milked them and brought both blood and milk to the Neupe-Īgudan, both wooden vessels were full. They (Koro) mixed the two full vessels together very fast spilling much of them on the ground. As the Neupe watched, they said, "This is trouble!" The Koro gave them the milk and blood to drink. They drank it. The Neupe then said, "We haven't seen our cattle and this afternoon we will go and check them. If they come back to our village we will come back here." The Koro said good. But the Koro said, "Just one more thing. If there will be trouble between us, our blood will spill like this we have spilled today." The Neupe said, "Yes, that's right." Then the Neupe-Īgudan went back to their villages to talk. They said to the old people, "Today we have seen trouble." They both recounted the story with the Koro (enemy tribe). They told them of the bad shade place, of the welcome with blood and milk which the Koro spilled, of drinking the milk with blood and telling the Koro they would leave to look after their cattle, and of the last comment by the Koro about blood-spilling if a war were to begin between the Neupe and Koro. The old men said to the younger, "You have been fooled! Remember this: this is trouble! Watch the Koro carefully. If the Koro did these things, they want to kill us so watch them!" When the Neupe young men had returned from the Koro village, there was a big meeting and everyone came together (both the Īgudan and Neupe). They talked a long time until one old man said, "Tomorrow we will build a huge village together." The old man said to bring one eute (dati) which he broke up into many pieces and gave one to each man. Each man then placed blood and milk on the side of the village toward the Koro. Each man with two spears and bow and arrows hid in a hole inside the outer one. In the morning, the Koro came to start trouble and they fought until the Neupe chased them away, and the Neupe killed more Koro than the reverse. The Neupe stayed here five more days and there was no trouble; they took the dead bodies as far away as possible because they would smell badly. After five days they moved to this side [north] of Lodwar. They stayed there a long time without seeing anyone, then they went southwest. When they got there the young men went on ahead (this side) and saw the Turkana (who were looking for grass) as they were. They were friendly and the Neupe say, "We will move here tomorrow." So the Turkana said they would also move there and they would be friends.

Remarks on early Eleli history

Informant: Bilili

Long ago, on the other (south) side of Lodwar, the Sheer told the Koro to kill the Eleli. Why? Because the Sheer were jealous of the Eleli. So, the Koro came to kill the Eleli, therefore some of the Eleli came to this side of Lodwar, then to Labur. The Sheer and the Koro stayed there (in Ger, on the other side of Ladwar) a few years. Later, one day the Koro called the Sheer to their village, gave the Sheer men a place to sit and brought them two full wooden vessels--one of blood and one of milk--and told them to mix them. The Sheer wouldn't and admitted their defeat. The Koro men then said, "You told us to chase the Eleli away--we did it and they were many. Now, we who chased the Eleli away want to kill you, the Sheer." The Sheer were surprised. Both the Sheer and the Īgudan (Oro) were chased out by the Koro. The Oro went around to Ilyaret, into Nikīi and settled in Lōgoro. The Sheer entered the present Les Dasanetch country by themselves and stayed below Labur for a long time; the Eleli arrived first, though. A few Koro came to Labur and killed some Sheer there, then came on into Les Dasanetch country, where the Eleli lived.

Origin of Galbur clan (Inkabela segment)

Informant: Ekorisep

Once upon a time there were two men. They lived in Lake Rudolf, and had long hair, dark skin, and only one foot each. One was named Galbur. Near the lake was a village. Young boys from this village used to herd the village cattle every day to Lake Rudolf. When they came back to their village with the cattle, however, the cattle would give no milk. The women of the village became angry and accused the young boys of drinking the milk. This happened every day. One day the father of one of the boys, Shardetch, [1] told the boys to stay home in the village, and let him (the father) herd the cattle. He took the cattle to Lake Rudolf and went to sleep in a shady place. When he returned home, the women again cried, "There is no milk." So he said he would herd them alone again the next day. The next day he again took the cattle to Lake Rudolf, but this time he hid in the trees to watch. He saw two men come out of Lake Rudolf and pass among his cattle, milking them. Then Shardetch saw them go back into Lake Rudolf. He was afraid and stayed hidden. That evening he returned to the village and his wife cried again. He told her to be quiet and then told her the story of the two men, saying, "These are not the men of the land, they are from the water." The next morning Shardetch did not go back to Lake Rudolf. Instead he went to the village of a diviner. He told the man his story, and said, "I am afraid of them, they are from the water. Now what should I do?" The diviner answered: "Catch one of the men by his arm. Then he will first change into a snake, then into an elephant, then into a rhinoceros, then into a water buffalo, then into a hippopotamus, then a lion, then a leopard, then into a scorpion, then into a spider--then he will turn back into a man if you, Shardetch, would keep holding him." So the man went back to Lake Rudolf and caught one of the men by the arm (the other one escaped back into Lake Rudolf). After the lake-man changed to all the animals, Shardetch stood with nothing in his hand--then the man reappeared in his hand, this time with a normal head and still with long hair. He then took the water-man back to his village. He brought a goat and slaughtered it, he took out the blood and stomach contents, and spread them on the water-man's body, then put the goat skin across his shoulders and down his back. He then put the water-man inside his hut and he was quiet. During the night the other water-man came and walked around and around the village, calling in a high voice, "Galbur! Galbur!" (water-man)--

---

[1]Informant indicated Shardetch to be a member of the Sheer.

again and again, until the next morning, when he went back into Lake Rudolf. (Galbur was the name of the captured man.) He, the other man from Lake Rudolf, continued to call for Galbur for four days. On the fifth day, Galbur asked for food and water. He asked Shardetch, "Tell me one thing: if I am your first child of your first wife, tell me. If I am younger say so." Shardetch said, "You will be my first child." Galbur said thank you and stayed. Shardetch then gave Galbur one heifer, saying, "This is your cow." Galbur then said, "If this is my cow I want to use my cattle brand and my mark on the ears." Shardetch agreed and brought him a knife and a branding iron. Galbur then cut the cow's ears (split in two) and gave her her brand. Galbur then called Shardetch "my father." (Galbur has used the brand from Lake Rudolf ever since.)

BIBLIOGRAPHY

ALTHUSSER, L., and BALIBAR, E. (1970) Reading capital. London, New Left Books, 340 pp.

ANDERSON, G. D., and TALBOT, L. M. (1965) Soil factors affecting the distribution of the grassland types and their utilization by wild animals on the Serengeti Plains, Tanganyika. Journal of Ecology, v. 53:33-56.

AUSTIN, H. H. (1899) Journeys to the north of Uganda. II. Lake Rudolf. Geographical Journal, v. 56:347-70.

_____. (1902) A journey from Omdurman to Mombasa via Lake Rudolf. Geographical Journal, v. 19:669-90.

BARAN, P. (1957) The political economy of growth. New York, Monthly Review Press, 308pp.

BATCHELDER, R. B., and HIRT, H. F. (1966) Fire in tropical forests and grasslands. U.S. Army, Natick Laboratory Technical Report 67-41-ES. Natick (Mass.), U.S. Army Materiel Command, 380pp.

BATESON, G. (1972) Steps to an ecology of mind. San Francisco, Chandler, 545pp.

BELL, R. (1971) A grazing ecosystem in the Serengeti. Scientific American, v. 225:14, 86-93.

BOHANNAN, P., and DALTON, G. (1962) Markets in Africa. Garden City, Anchor, 762pp.

BOYD, D. (n.d.) An introduction to systems and system analysis. Manuscript, in preparation.

BROOKE, J. W. (1905) A journal west and north of Lake Rudolf. Geographical Journal, v. 25:525-31.

BUNTING, B. T. (1965) The geography of soil. Chicago, Aldine, 213pp.

BUTZER, K. W. (1970) Contemporary depositional environments of the Omo Delta. Nature, v. 226(5244):425-30.

_____. (1971) Recent history of an Ethiopian delta. The University of Chicago Department of Geography Research Paper No. 136, 183pp.

BYRAM, G. M. (1948) Vegetation temperature and fire damage in the southern pines. Fire Control Notes, v. 9:34-36.

316

CARR, C. J. (1976a) Ecological studies along the Omo River, Ethiopia. Journal of Biogeography, in press.

_____. (1976b) Plant ecological variation and pattern in the lower Omo Basin. In Y. COPPENS, F. C. HOWELL, L. L. ISAAC, and R. E. F. LEAKEY (eds.), Earliest man and environments in the Lake Rudolf Basin. University of Chicago, in press.

CAVENDISH, H. S. H. (1898) Through Somaliland and around and south of Lake Rudolf. Geographical Journal, v. 11:372-96.

CERULLI, E. (1942) Il Linguaggio dei tirma populazione dela zona de la lago Rudolfo. Oriente Moderno, v. 22:26-35.

_____. (1956) Peoples of Southwest Ethiopia and its borderlands. Ethnographic Survey of Africa, Northeast Africa Part III. London, International African Institute, 148pp.

DAUBENMIRE, R. (1968) Ecology of fire in grasslands. Advances in Ecological Research, v. 5:209-66.

DE VOS, A. (1969) Ecological conditions affecting the production of wild herbivorous mammals on grassland environments. Unpublished manuscript.

DUPREY, G., and REY, P. (1973) Reflections on the pertinence of a theory of the history of exchange. Economy and Society, v. 2:131-63.

DYSON-HUDSON, N. (1966) Karimojong politics. Oxford, Clarendon, 280pp.

EATON, J. (1963) Political economy. New York, International, 254pp.

EDWARDS, D. C., and BOGDAN, A. V. (1951) Important grassland plants of Kenya. Nairobi, I. Pitman, 124pp.

EVANS-PRITCHARD, E. E. (1960) The Nuer. Oxford, Clarendon, 271pp.

FERGUSON, C. A. (1975) Language in Ethiopia. London, Oxford University, in press.

FIRTH, R. (1951) Elements of social organization. London, Watts, 257pp.

_____. (1965) Primitive Polynesian economy. London, Routledge and Kegan Paul, 385pp.

GILLETT, J. B. (1955) The relation between the highland floras of Ethiopia and British East Africa. Webbia, v. 9:459-66.

GLASCOW, J. P., and DUFFY, B. J. (1961) Traps in field studies of Glossia pallides. Austen Bull. Ent. Research, v. 52:795-814.

GODELIER, M. (1972) Rationality and irrationality in economics. London, New Left Books, 326pp.

GOOD, R. (1964) The geography of flowering plants. London, Longmans, 518pp.

GOODLAND, R. J. A. (1965) On termitaria in a savanna ecosystem. Canadian Journal of Zoology, v. 43:641-50.

GULLIVER, P. (1951) A preliminary survey of the Turkana. Communications from the School of African Studies, University of Capetown, New Series No. 26, 25pp.

_____. (1955) The family herds. London, Routledge and Kegan Paul, 271pp.

GULLIVER, P., and GULLIVER, P. H. (1953) The central Nilo-Hamites. Ethnographic Survey of Africa, Part VII. London, International African Institute, 106pp.

HEADY, H. (1960) Range management in East Africa. Kenya Department of Agriculture and East African Agriculture and Forestry Research Organization cooperating with the United States Educational Commission in the United Kingdom. Nairobi, Government Printer, 125pp.

HEDBERG, O. (1962) Mountain plants from southern Ethiopia collected by Dr. John Eriksson. Arkiv för Botanik, v. 4:421-35.

HEILBRONNER, R. (1972) Understanding macroeconomics. Englewood Cliffs, Prentice-Hall, 242pp.

HERSKOVITZ, M. J. (1926) The cattle complex in East Africa. American Anthropologist, v. 28:230-72, 361-80, 494-528, 633-64.

_____. (1952) Some problems of land tenure in contemporary Africa. Land Economics, v. 28:37-45.

HESSE, P. R. (1955) A chemical and physical study of the soils of termite mounds in East Africa. Journal of Ecology, v. 43:449-61.

HOFFMAN, L. (1971) Deviation-amplifying processes in natural groups. In HALEY, J. (ed.), Changing families. New York: Grune and Stratton, 353pp.

HOHNEL, L. von. (1894) Discovery of Lake Rudolf and Stefanie. London, Longmans, Green, v. 2, 397pp.; trans. by Nancy Bell (Frank Cass Press Reprint, 1968).

JACOBS, A. H. (1968) Masai marriage and bridewealth. (Paper presented at Society and Law Workshop, 28-30 March). Nairobi, University College (mimeograph), 16pp.

KEAY, R. W. J. (1959) Vegetation map of Africa south of the Tropic of Cancer. UNESCO. London, Oxford University Press, 23pp.

KENYA. (1969) Atlas of Kenya. Ecological potential. Nairobi, Government Printer, 103pp.

LEONTIEFF, N. de. (1900) Explorations des provinces équatoriales d'Abissinie. La Géographie, v. 2:105-18.

MacGILLIVARY, D. (1967) East African livestock survey. 2 vols. UNDP, Rome, Food and Agricultural Organization, 494pp.

318

MANDEL, E. (1969) Marxist economic theory. New York, Monthly Review, 797 pp.

MARX, K. (1967) Capital, Vol. 1. New York, International Publishers, 807 pp.

MAUD, P. (1904) Exploration in the southern borderland of Abyssinia. Geographical Journal, v. 23:552-79.

MEILLASSOUX, C. (1964) Anthropologie économique des Guoro de Côte d'Ivoire. Paris, Mouton, 383pp.

NALDER, L. F. (ed.). (1937) A tribal survey of Mongolla Province. London, International Institute of African Languages and Cultures, 42pp.

NAVEH, Z. (1966) The need for integrated range research in East Africa. Tropical Agriculture Trin. v. 43(2):91-98.

OLLMAN, B. (1971) Alienation: Marx's conception of man in capitalist society. London, Cambridge University Press, 325pp.

PAULI, E. (1950) Die splitter-stamme nordlica des Rudolfsees. Annali Laternai, v. 14:61-191.

PHILLIPS, J. (1936) Fire in vegetation: a bad master, a good servant and a national problem. Jour. S. Arr. Bot. 2:35-45.

_____. (1965) Fire as a master and servant: its influence in the bioclimate regions of the trans-Sahara Africa. Tall Timbers Fire Ecology Conference, v. 5:7-109.

PICHI-SERMOLLI, R. (1957) Una carta geobotanica dell'Africa orientale. Webbia, v. 13(1):15-132.

POLANYI, K. (1957) Trade and market in the early empires. Glencoe (Illinois), Free Press, 382pp.

PRATT, D. J. (1968) Rangeland development in Kenya. Annals of Arid Zone, v. 7(2):177-208.

PRATT, D. J., GREENWAY, P. J., and GWYNNE, M. D. (1966) A classification of East African rangeland, with an appendix on terminology. Journal of Applied Ecology, v. 3:369-82.

RATTRAY, J. M. (1960) The grass cover of Africa. FAO Agricultural Series No. 49. Rome, FAO, 62pp.

RICCI, M. (1943) Usanze funerati degli Arbore, degli Amarr e degli Gheleba nel sud Etiopico. Rassegna di Studi Etipici, v. 3:214-22.

RINEY, T. (1964) The economic use of wildlife in terms of its productivity and its development as an agricultural activity. First FAO African Meeting on Animal Production and Health, Addis Ababa. Rome, FAO, 35pp.

SAHLINS, J. (1972) Stone age economics. Chicago, Aldine-Atherton, 348pp.

SALISBURY, R. F. (1962) From stone to steel. Melbourne, University of Melbourne, 232pp.

SCHNEIDER, H. K. (1957) The subsistence role of cattle among the Pakot and in East Africa. American Anthropologist, v. 59:278-300.

SMITH, A. D. (1896) Expedition through Somaliland to Lake Rudolf. Geographical Journal, v. 8:221-39.

_____. (1897) Through unknown African countries. London, Arnold, 471pp.

_____. (1900) An expedition between Lake Rudolf and the Nile. Geographical Journal, v. 16:600-639.

SMITH, G. D., et al. (1960) Soil classification, a comprehensive system (7th Approximation). Washington, U.S. Department of Agriculture, 265pp.

STIGAND, C. H. (1910) To Abyssinia through an unknown land. Philadelphia, Lippincott, 352pp.

TERRAY, E. (1972) Marxism and "primitive" societies. New York, Monthly Review, 186pp.

TURNER, T. S. (1973) Nature and society among the Northern Kayapo. Unpublished manuscript.

VANNUTELLI, L. (1899) L'Omo: viaggio di esplorazione nell'Africa orientale. Milan, U. Hoepli, 650pp.

WALSH, J., and DODSON, R. G. (1969) Geology of Northern Turkana. Mines and Geological Department of Kenya, Report 82. Nairobi, Government Printer, 42pp.

WEAVER, J. E., and CLEMENTS, F. E. (1938) Plant ecology. New York, McGraw-Hill, 601pp.

WEISS, P. (1971) Hierarchically organized systems in theory and practice. New York, Hafner Publishing, 263pp.

WEST, O. (1965) Fire in vegetation and its use in pasture management with special reference to tropical and subtropical Africa. Commonwealth Agricultural Bureaux. Bucks (England), Farnham Royal (mimeographed), 53pp.

WHITE, L. A. (1959) The evolution of culture. New York, McGraw-Hill Press, 378pp.

WHYTE, L. L., et al. (eds.). (1969) Hierarchical structures. New York, American Elsevier, 322pp.

WILDEN, A. (1972) System and structure. London, Tavistock, 540pp.

THE UNIVERSITY OF CHICAGO
DEPARTMENT OF GEOGRAPHY
RESEARCH PAPERS (Lithographed, 6×9 Inches)

(Available from Department of Geography, The University of Chicago, 5828 S. University Ave., Chicago, Illinois 60637. Price: $6.00 each; by series subscription, $5.00 each.)

106. SAARINEN, THOMAS F. *Perception of the Drought Hazard on the Great Plains* 1966. 183 pp.
107. SOLZMAN, DAVID M. *Waterway Industrial Sites: A Chicago Case Study* 1967. 138 pp.
108. KASPERSON, ROGER E. *The Dodecanese: Diversity and Unity in Island Politics* 1967. 184 pp.
109. LOWENTHAL, DAVID, et al. *Environmental Perception and Behavior.* 1967. 88 pp.
110. REED, WALLACE E. *Areal Interaction in India: Commodity Flows of the Bengal-Bihar Industrial Area* 1967. 210 pp.
112. BOURNE, LARRY S. *Private Redevelopment of the Central City: Spatial Processes of Structural Change in the City of Toronto* 1967. 199 pp.
113. BRUSH, JOHN E., and GAUTHIER, HOWARD L., JR. *Service Centers and Consumer Trips: Studies on the Philadelphia Metropolitan Fringe* 1968. 182 pp.
114. CLARKSON, JAMES D. *The Cultural Ecology of a Chinese Village: Cameron Highlands, Malaysia* 1968. 174 pp.
115. BURTON, IAN; KATES, ROBERT W.; and SNEAD, RODMAN E. *The Human Ecology of Coastal Flood Hazard in Megalopolis* 1968. 196 pp.
117. WONG, SHUE TUCK. *Perception of Choice and Factors Affecting Industrial Water Supply Decisions in Northeastern Illinois* 1968. 96 pp.
118. JOHNSON, DOUGLAS L. *The Nature of Nomadism* 1969. 200 pp.
119. DIENES, LESLIE. *Locational Factors and Locational Developments in the Soviet Chemical Industry* 1969. 285 pp.
120. MIHELIC, DUSAN. *The Political Element in the Port Geography of Trieste* 1969. 104 pp.
121. BAUMANN, DUANE. *The Recreational Use of Domestic Water Supply Reservoirs: Perception and Choice* 1969. 125 pp.
122. LIND, AULIS O. *Coastal Landforms of Cat Island, Bahamas: A Study of Holocene Accretionary Topography and Sea-Level Change* 1969. 156 pp.
123. WHITNEY, JOSEPH. *China: Area, Administration and Nation Building* 1970. 198 pp.
124. EARICKSON, ROBERT. *The Spatial Behavior of Hospital Patients: A Behavioral Approach to Spatial Interaction in Metropolitan Chicago* 1970. 198 pp.
125. DAY, JOHN C. *Managing the Lower Rio Grande: An Experience in International River Development* 1970. 277 pp.
126. MAC IVER, IAN. *Urban Water Supply Alternatives: Perception and Choice in the Grand Basin, Ontario* 1970. 178 pp.
127. GOHEEN, PETER G. *Victorian Toronto, 1850 to 1900: Pattern and Process of Growth* 1970. 278 pp.
128. GOOD, CHARLES M. *Rural Markets and Trade in East Africa* 1970. 252 pp.
129. MEYER, DAVID R. *Spatial Variation of Black Urban Households* 1970. 127 pp.
130. GLADFELTER, BRUCE. *Meseta and Campiña Landforms in Central Spain: A Geomorphology of the Alto Henares Basin* 1971. 204 pp.
131. NEILS, ELAINE M. *Reservation to City: Indian Urbanization and Federal Relocation* 1971. 200 pp.
132. MOLINE, NORMAN T. *Mobility and the Small Town, 1900–1930* 1971. 169 pp.
133. SCHWIND, PAUL J. *Migration and Regional Development in the United States, 1950–1960* 1971. 170 pp.
134. PYLE, GERALD F. *Heart Disease, Cancer and Stroke in Chicago: A Geographical Analysis with Facilities Plans for 1980* 1971. 292 pp.
135. JOHNSON, JAMES F. *Renovated Waste Water: An Alternative Source of Municipal Water Supply in the U.S.* 1971. 155 pp.
136. BUTZER, KARL W. *Recent History of an Ethiopian Delta: The Omo River and the Level of Lake Rudolf* 1971. 184 pp.
137. HARRIS, CHAUNCY D. *Annotated World List of Selected Current Geographical Serials in English, French, and German* 3rd edition 1971. 77 pp.
138. HARRIS, CHAUNCY D., and FELLMANN, JEROME D. *International List of Geographical Serials* 2nd edition 1971. 267 pp.
139. MC MANIS, DOUGLAS R. *European Impressions of the New England Coast, 1497–1620* 1972. 147 pp.
140. COHEN, YEHOSHUA S. *Diffusion of an Innovation in an Urban System: The Spread of Planned Regional Shopping Centers in the United States, 1949–1968* 1972. 136 pp.

141. MITCHELL, NORA. *The Indian Hill-Station: Kodaikanal* 1972. 199 pp.

142. PLATT, RUTHERFORD H. *The Open Space Decision Process: Spatial Allocation of Costs and Benefits* 1972. 189 pp.

143. GOLANT, STEPHEN M. *The Residential Location and Spatial Behavior of the Elderly: A Canadian Example* 1972. 226 pp.

144. PANNELL, CLIFTON W. *T'ai-chung, T'ai-wan: Structure and Function* 1973. 200 pp.

145. LANKFORD, PHILIP M. *Regional Incomes in the United States, 1929–1967: Level, Distribution, Stability, and Growth* 1972. 137 pp.

146. FREEMAN, DONALD B. *International Trade, Migration, and Capital Flows: A Quantitative Analysis of Spatial Economic Interaction* 1973. 202 pp.

147. MYERS, SARAH K. *Language Shift Among Migrants to Lima, Peru* 1973. 204 pp.

148. JOHNSON, DOUGLAS L. *Jabal al-Akhdar, Cyrenaica: An Historical Geography of Settlement and Livelihood* 1973. 240 pp.

149. YEUNG, YUE-MAN. *National Development Policy and Urban Transformation in Singapore: A Study of Public Housing and the Marketing System* 1973. 204 pp.

150. HALL, FRED L. *Location Criteria for High Schools: Student Transportation and Racial Integration* 1973. 156 pp.

151. ROSENBERG, TERRY J. *Residence, Employment, and Mobility of Puerto Ricans in New York City* 1974. 230 pp.

152. MIKESELL, MARVIN W., editor. *Geographers Abroad: Essays on the Problems and Prospects of Research in Foreign Areas* 1973. 296 pp.

153. OSBORN, JAMES. *Area, Development Policy, and the Middle City in Malaysia* 1974. 273 pp.

154. WACHT, WALTER F. *The Domestic Air Transportation Network of the United States* 1974. 98 pp.

155. BERRY, BRIAN J. L., et al. *Land Use, Urban Form and Environmental Quality* 1974. 464 pp.

156. MITCHELL, JAMES K. *Community Response to Coastal Erosion: Individual and Collective Adjustments to Hazard on the Atlantic Shore* 1974. 209 pp.

157. COOK, GILLIAN P. *Spatial Dynamics of Business Growth in the Witwatersrand* 1975. 143 pp.

158. STARR, JOHN T., JR. *The Evolution of Unit Train Operations in the United States: 1960–1969—A Decade of Experience* 1976. 247 pp.

159. PYLE, GERALD F. *The Spatial Dynamics of Crime* 1974. 220 pp.

160. MEYER, JUDITH W. *Diffusion of an American Montessori Education* 1975. 109 pp.

161. SCHMID, JAMES A. *Urban Vegetation: A Review and Chicago Case Study* 1975. 280 pp.

162. LAMB, RICHARD. *Metropolitan Impacts on Rural America* 1975. 210 pp.

163. FEDOR, THOMAS. *Patterns of Urban Growth in the Russian Empire during the Nineteenth Century* 1975. 275 pp.

164. HARRIS, CHAUNCY D. *Guide to Geographical Bibliographies and Reference Works in Russian or on the Soviet Union* 1975. 496 pp.

165. JONES, DONALD W. *Migration and Urban Unemployment in Dualistic Economic Development* 1975. 186 pp.

166. BEDNARZ, ROBERT S. *The Effect of Air Pollution on Property Value in Chicago* 1975. 118 pp.

167. HANNEMANN, MANFRED. *The Diffusion of the Reformation in Southwestern Germany, 1518-1534* 1975. 248 pp.

168. SUBLETT, MICHAEL D. *Farmers on the Road. Interfarm Migration and the Farming of Noncontiguous Lands in Three Midwestern Townships, 1939-1969* 1975. 228 pp.

169. STETZER, DONALD FOSTER. *Special Districts in Cook County: Toward a Geography of Local Government* 1975. 189 pp.

170. EARLE, CARVILLE V. *The Evolution of a Tidewater Settlement System: All Hallow's Parish, Maryland, 1650–1783* 1975. 249 pp.

171. SPODEK, HOWARD. *Urban-Rural Integration in Regional Development: A Case Study of Saurashtra, India—1800–1960* 1976. 156 pp.

172. COHEN, YEHOSHUA S. and BERRY, BRIAN J. L. *Spatial Components of Manufacturing Change* 1975 272 pp.

173. HAYES, CHARLES R. *The Dispersed City: The Case of Piedmont, North Carolina* 1976. 169 pp.

174. CARGO, DOUGLAS B. *Solid Wastes: Factors Influencing Generation Rates* 1977.

175. GILLARD, QUENTIN. *Incomes and Accessibility. Metropolitan Labor Force Participation, Commuting, and Income Differentials in the United States, 1960-1970* 1977. 140 pp.

176. MORGAN, DAVID J. *Patterns of Population Distribution: A Residential Preference Model and Its Dynamic* 1977.

177. STOKES, HOUSTON H.; JONES, DONALD W. and NEUBURGER, HUGH M. *Unemployment and Adjustment in the Labor Market: A Comparison between the Regional and National Responses* 1975. 135 pp.

178. PICCAGLI, GIORGIO ANTONIO. *Racial Transition in Chicago Public Schools. An Examination of the Tipping Point Hypothesis, 1963–1971* 1977.

179. HARRIS, CHAUNCY D. *Bibliography of Geography. Part I. Introduction to General Aids* 1976. 288 pp.

180. CARR, CLAUDIA J. *Pastoralism in Crisis. The Dasanetch and their Ethiopian Lands.* 1977. 339 pp.

181. GOODWIN, GARY C. *Cherokees in Transition: A Study of Changing Culture and Environment Prior to 1775.* 1977.

182. KNIGHT, DAVID B. *A Capital for Canada: Conflict and Compromise in the Nineteenth Century.* 1977. 359 pp.

our
Environment

Dams and Levees

Kevin Hile

KIDHAVEN PRESS

An imprint of Thomson Gale, a part of The Thomson Corporation

THOMSON

★

GALE ™

Detroit • New York • San Francisco • New Haven, Conn. • Waterville, Maine • London

For more information, contact
KidHaven Press
27500 Drake Rd.
Farmington Hills, MI 48331-3535
Or you can visit our Internet site at http://www.gale.com

LIBRARY OF CONGRESS CATALOGING-IN-PUBLICATION DATA

Hile, Kevin.
   Dams and levees / by Kevin Hile.
     p. cm. — (Our environment)
   Includes bibliographical references and index.
   ISBN-13: 978-0-7377-3559-8 (hardcover)
   1. Dams. 2. Levees. I. Title.
   TC540.H45 2007
   333.91'214—dc22

                                    2007015980

ISBN-10: 0-7377-3559-7
Printed in the United States of America

contents

chapter one

Changing Water's Course

Rivers are very important to the survival of plants, animals, and people. They are a source of fresh water to drink. They help move fresh soil and minerals around so that plants can grow better. They act like liquid highways for fish and other animals to travel in from one place to another. People use them to transport goods from port to port, too. Rivers also erode mountains and hills. Over millions of years, they change our planet's landscape. They can turn rocky mountains into fertile hills, and they can even create canyons, such as the Grand Canyon in Arizona. This process of water wearing away the land is called erosion.

Rivers flow downhill with the force of gravity. They follow the landscape from high mountains

Lakes are often created by a dam.

or hills down to lakes or oceans. Sometimes, though, this natural flow can be stopped or slowed by a dam or a levee. A dam is anything that blocks water from flowing down a river. It can result in the formation of a lake, creating new habitats while flooding others.

Levees are barriers that run along the side of a river or along an ocean coastline. They prevent water from overflowing shorelines. Levees serve an important function by making floods less severe or preventing them entirely. When there is too much flooding, natural habitat for plants and animals can be washed away. Floods, too, affect people who live near rivers or oceans.

How Rivers Work

Rivers are more complex than they might seem. They get their water not only from rain, but also from melting ice or snow, from beneath the ground, or from the surrounding soil. Smaller rivers —streams, creeks, or rivulets—flow into each other to form larger rivers. Of all the water on Earth—330 million cubic miles (1,375.5 million cu km) of it—less than 0.01 percent of it is contained in rivers.

An area of land that is supplied with water from a single system of linked rivers and streams is called a watershed. The plants and animals living in a watershed can depend on each other for survival, and their health depends on rivers and streams.

Plants around the rivers help filter out animal waste or chemicals that make the water less healthy to drink. The river, in turn, provides water for plants, and some animals eat those plants.

When rivers eventually flow into lakes, seas, or oceans, they carry with them soils, minerals, nutrients from decaying plants and animals, and even oxygen. Rivers can therefore supply oceans with food and oxygen needed to help fish and other creatures thrive. In many instances, rivers do not pour directly into the sea. Instead, they often spread out into deltas, fertile wetlands surrounded by a fan of little rivers that feed into the ocean.

Rivers often spread out into deltas. The Mississippi River Delta is shown here.

Deltas are great habitats for birds, fish, mammals, and reptiles. All of the natural land through which rivers flow can be changed dramatically by dams and levees. Sometimes this is for the better, but sometimes for the worse.

Natural Dams and Levees

Dams and levees have existed in nature since the first rivers formed billions of years ago. Sometimes they form when silt, rocks, branches, or leaves clog up a river. Other times wild animals build them on purpose. Beavers are famous for building dams. A beaver is a large rodent that lives in the

A beaver stands on top of its dam.

water and will cut down trees and shrubs with its strong teeth and make a dam. Beavers build dams to give them easier access to food and to protect themselves from predators such as wolves or coyotes that do not hunt well in the ponds that form behind dams.

When a beaver builds a dam, it can have a good result on the environment. Beaver dams can create wetlands for other animals to live in, for example. They also reduce excessive erosion and help retain important soil nutrients for plants. Beaver dams, just like human dams, can also interrupt fish migrations or cause floods, however.

Levees can form naturally, as well. Usually this is from fine soil—called silt—building up over time near riverbanks. When the silt and other dirt and rocks carried by the river get high enough, they form a levee. The levee is like a high embankment, which keeps more water in the river and prevents or lessens flooding.

Long ago, human beings observed the advantages of natural dams and levees. They decided to build their own dams and levees for the benefit of people.

Early Man-Made Dams and Levees

Early people probably built dams out of mud and logs before recorded history. The first dams for which historians have a record, however, date back to ancient Egypt. Almost 5,000 years ago, a dam called the Sadd el-Kafara was constructed by the Egyptians along the Nile River to provide fresh water to the ancient city of Memphis. It was nearly 350 feet (107m) wide and was made of loose stones and gravel covered in limestone. Because it was so crudely built, the dam eroded away after only a few years. The ancient Egyptians therefore decided dams were not practical to construct, and they abandoned such projects.

The next civilization to seriously pursue dam building was in Mesopotamia. Around the year 2000 B.C. the people there constructed an earth dam across the Tigris River just north of the city of Baghdad. Much later the Roman Empire, which was famous for its architectural achievements, also constructed dams. During the height of their civilization, the Romans made great advances in dam building. Around the year A.D. 100 they started using mortar and blocks of concrete to build much stronger dams.

The dams these ancient people built were of a type called **gravity dams** or **embankment dams**. If they are made primarily of dirt, they are described as **earthen dams**. These are dams that hold back water simply because they are so wide, thick, and heavy that water cannot get by them. Later, in 13th-century Europe, architects invented the **arch dam**. Arch dams use a curved shape to make the dam more stable. Because of this, the

A gravity dam in Japan. Gravity dams were first built in ancient times.

arch dam does not have to have walls as thick as those in a gravity dam.

Thirteenth-century Spaniards were particularly famous for their skill at building dams. Don Pedro Bernardo Villarreal de Berriz was the first European to write an important book on how dams should be built. Don Pedro's designs would help inspire the later advancement of the **buttress dam**, which uses supports, called buttresses, that rest against the wall of the dam to add strength to it.

Levees, also known as **dikes**, have also been in use since ancient times. Dating back about 3,000 years, the Egyptians and the Sumerians used levees to control river flooding just as is done today. But levees are not always constructed just along riverbanks. They can also be used to keep ocean coastlines from flooding. One of the most famous levee systems existing today is along the coast of the Netherlands in Europe. Much of the Netherlands is very close to, or even below, sea level. The Dutch people there had to build levees to keep their land from becoming permanently submerged under water.

From Colonial Times to Today

The Spanish eventually brought their dam-building knowledge to America as they settled areas such as Florida and California in the 17th and 18th centuries. By this time the British were also colonizing the eastern coast of North America. Many historians believe that the first dam built in North America was completed in 1634 in South Berwick, Maine. Early North American dams were usually fairly small and intended to help generate power for grist and saw mills.

The first really ambitious construction projects to control rivers in North America were levees. In the 18th century, French settlers in what is now Louisiana began building levees to control the Mississippi River's floods around New Orleans.

Hoover Dam is considered a modern-day marvel. Lake Mead, one of the world's largest man-made lakes, was created by Hoover Dam.

Levee construction along the Mississippi really took off in 1928, after the U.S. government became involved in constructing levees to stop repeated floods. Today over 27,000 square miles (69,930 sq. km) of land along the Mississippi River is protected by more than 1,500 miles (2,414 km) of levees.

The Mississippi levee system is considered an amazing architectural achievement. Another modern-day marvel is the Hoover Dam. Straddling the Colorado River between Nevada and Arizona, the Hoover Dam was completed in 1935. A combination gravity-arch dam, it stands 700 feet (213m) tall and creates one of the world's largest man-made lakes: Lake Mead. It also is used to generate electricity.

Hoover Dam was one of the first megadams ever constructed. From the 20th century to the present day, there has been a trend to build larger and larger dams. With growing human populations needing water and electrical power, there is considerable pressure on governments to build these megastructures.

chapter two

Why Build Dams and Levees?

People build dams and levees either to use water as a resource or to protect themselves from the damage that too much water can do. Dams are very useful tools, which is why there are about 79,000 dams in the United States. Of these dams, about 5,500 are considered to be "large" dams. The oldest use of dams was for people who wished to have more water to drink. They could also use the water to grow food. By blocking a river with a dam and creating a lake, the amount of water available for people increases greatly. Farmers often build their own dams, usually creating embankment dams because they are fairly cheap and easy to construct.

Two kayakers enjoy Lake Powell. The lake was created by the Glen Canyon Dam in Arizona.

In a prosperous society such as America's, dams are often used to create lakes for recreation. In 2004 it was estimated that 23,185 dams existed in the United States so that people could boat, swim, water ski, and fish. But there are more practical uses for dams, too.

Mining and Shipping

Dams are commonly built to keep water away from people. Sometimes this is done so people can have a dry place to live. Other times it is so they have a dry place to work. For example, miners use dams to prevent areas they are mining from being flooded. Valuable metals, rocks, or gems can be found in lakes, rivers, or in valleys that are flooded. In order to get at these minerals more easily, mining companies will build dams to divert water away from their digging project. Dams can also be built to contain mine waste.

When miners dig out the raw ores they are looking for in the ground—especially metal ores—they send the ore to a hydrometallurgical plant. Here the ore is ground up and treated with chemicals to remove the desired metal. The leftover fine dirt and chemicals used in the milling process cannot simply be dumped in a river or lake. Many of the chemicals are poisonous to people and animals. The muddy mixtures of fine dirt and chemicals are called tailings. They are dumped into a **reservoir** contained by a **tailings dam**. Tailings dams keep pollution from mines from escaping into the environment. If these dams fail, a major ecological disaster can occur.

Helping Ships and People

Dams are also useful to make it easier for ships to travel down rivers. Some rivers, during the summer, can dry up or become too shallow to navigate. This is true of some rivers in the United States that are very important for shipping, such as the Ohio, Allegheny, and Monongahela rivers. Often, dams are used together with **locks**. A lock is a section of a canal or river with solid gates on

Dams and locks are often used together to make it easier for boats to travel from one place to another.

either end. The water level between the gates can be raised or lowered so that a boat can travel from one level of the river or canal to another.

A more familiar use of dams and levees is to stop flooding. They are necessary because so many people like to live and work near rivers, lakes, and oceans. Living in a home that is on land near water level can be dangerous, though. It can also be hazardous to live downstream along a river that has a potential for flash floods.

A flash flood is a sudden flood that usually occurs after a heavy rain. Communities that live below mountains where there is a lot of rain are especially vulnerable. To protect such cities and towns, dams are built that can contain sudden increases in water. The water can then be released slowly over time so that there is no flooding.

Dams are often built to protect towns and cities from flooding.

Sometimes it takes several dams to do this and not just one. For example, near Webster, New Hampshire, five dams have been erected to stop floods in the Merrimack River basin.

Power Generation

Besides controlling the water in rivers and lakes, and near oceans, another important use of dams is to create electricity. More than 20 percent of the electrical energy used by people on our planet comes from **hydroelectric dams**. Such dams have been used since 1878, when the first hydroelectric dam was built in Northumberland, England. Hydro-electricity is energy that is produced from falling water. Water rushes through a kind of tunnel in the dam called a **penstock**. The penstock leads to a **turbine**. The turbine, which looks like a giant boat propeller, is turned by the water. The turning turbines are hooked up to generators, which then create electricity. The room where the generators are maintained is called the dam's **powerhouse**.

Building a hydroelectric dam is a difficult and expensive project. Engineers have to first divert water away from the natural course of the river so that the dam can be erected on a dry riverbed. To do this, **cofferdams** are built. Cofferdams are temporary dams that change a river's course so that it flows down a channel or tunnel. These channels or tunnels also have to be built beforehand to prepare for the main dam's construction.

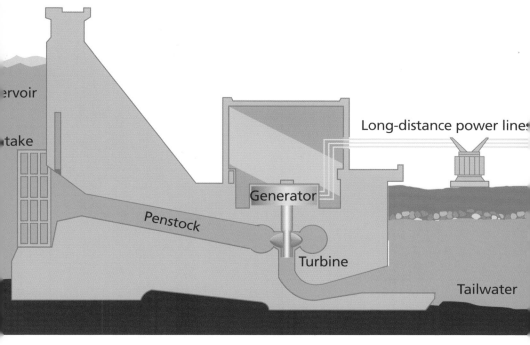

How a hydroelectric dam works.

Once the dam is completed, water is allowed to return to the original riverbed. A reservoir is then created as water builds up behind the dam. Precautions are taken so that the dam operates properly. For example, because debris—silt, rocks, branches, and such—flows down a river, screens are used to filter out this material. If it were not filtered out, the debris could clog the turbines and cause them to fail. Fish screens are also put in place to keep fish from being sucked into the turbines.

Finally, **spillways** are built to control water overflow. Spillways are like the channels or tunnels used during the building of a dam. Instead of

The Grand Coulee Dam in Washington State is a functioning hydroelectric dam.

diverting water all of the time, though, spillways are used to let excess water go around the dam in times when there is too much water in the reservoir. If there were no spillways, then the excess water could flow over the dam and cause a great deal of structural damage.

In a world where much of the energy used creates pollution, dams are seen by many people as a clean and renewable energy source. Burning coal or oil pollutes the air, and generating nuclear power creates dangerous nuclear waste. A hydroelectric dam, however, uses only water and creates no harmful waste.

chapter three

Dangers to Wildlife and People

Despite the many advantages dams and levees have for collecting drinking water, aiding river transportation, and creating electricity, there are downsides as well. Whenever people do something that changes the planet's natural environment, there are consequences. Many environmental groups, scientists, and private citizens are concerned about the way dams and levees can harm both wildlife and human communities.

Habitat and Property Destruction

The most obvious problem caused by a dam is that it floods land that was once dry. Any plants and

The spillway of the Itaipú Dam, the world's biggest dam.

land-dwelling animals that once lived there will either drown or be forced to live somewhere else. According to scientific surveys, dams are responsible for affecting about half of the species that are currently considered endangered. Ideally, engineers would study the landscape near a dam to determine what the resulting flooding will do and weigh that against the benefits of building the dam. Environmentalists fear, however, that wildlife impact is only a minor concern to businesses and governments that wish to build dams.

The world's biggest dam, the Itaipú Dam on the Paraná River between Brazil and Paraguay in South America, was built to generate power. It is 643 feet (196m) high and more than 4 miles (6.4km) long. It generates 12,600 megawatts of power, enough to provide electricity for 10 to 12 million households. It has also created a reservoir that is 125 miles (201km) long. The reservoir and surrounding area has destroyed or damaged about 270 square miles (700 sq. km) of forest. Also, in one survey conducted from 1977 to 1978, over 27,000 animals were killed that year when they were caught in the dam.

The Impact of Dams

Dams not only flood areas that are upstream, they also impact what is downstream. They are known to increase erosion of riverbanks. Screens and filters in a dam prevent silt, sand, and rocks from flowing down a river. These materials no longer collect on the river's edge, so instead more soil and rocks are worn away from the downriver banks and from river bottoms.

The result of this erosion is that rich soils that are good for plants are washed away. Surrounding wetlands that are great places for animals to live can dry up. This can happen along the river or in the estuary area, where a river meets the ocean.

Not only is there a loss of habitat for animals as a result, but humans are affected, too. Farmers who need rich soils find that plants do not grow as well.

Both dams and levees alter the natural, seasonal floods that occur near rivers. These naturally occurring floods deposit fresh soil near rivers that help plants thrive. Dams and levees, however, stop flooding, and so the river area lands are not replenished by new soil.

A Chinese villager carries an armoire. He and his family have to relocate because of the construction of the Three Gorges Dam.

New reservoirs can also displace people from their homes. There have been many cases where a dam created a new reservoir, and people who had homes there had to move. The Chinese government has completed the huge Three Gorges Dam on the Yangtze River. The dam is 1.45 miles (2.3km) long, 607 feet (185m) high, and will generate 18.2 million kilowatts of power when it begins operating in 2009. Its reservoir is 360 miles (493km) long and will submerge 13 cities and over 1,500 towns and villages. About 1.2 million people will be displaced. Also, there are still many archeological and paleontological sites along the Three Gorges area where the dam is built. Remains of dinosaur fossils still undiscovered, as well as ancient Chinese civilizations, could be lost forever due to the dam's reservoir.

Effects on Fish

Dams have a big impact on fish. First, they deprive fish of habitat. Many fish live in and around rock beds on river bottoms. When dams prevent rocks from going downstream, there are fewer rocks for fish to use as habitat. River estuaries that are destroyed by dams are also prime habitat for fish. About 80 percent of the fish that people catch each year for food depend on estuaries for survival. Without them, people will have less to eat as well.

Second, dams change water temperature. Turbines and generators can heat the water. On the

This fish ladder, located on the Rhine River, is the largest in Europe.

other hand, water stored upriver in the reservoir can be cooler than normal. Many fish that live in rivers have adapted to survive under certain temperature conditions. When these temperatures change, they can suffer from stress and are more likely to become sick.

The third problem is that dams prevent fish from migrating. Many fish depend on migration for survival. One of the best-known migratory fish is the salmon. There are many types of salmon in the world, and most either migrate between oceans and rivers, or sometimes just up and down rivers. They do this to travel to places called spawning grounds, where the fish lay their eggs. Salmon are known for returning to the same spawning grounds every year. If they cannot reach them, they will die and the eggs will not hatch to produce young salmon. Some dams, though, are equipped with **fish ladders** (also called **fish passes**), that allow fish to swim around dams. This is not always the case, however.

When Disaster Strikes

Some effects of dams and levees on the environment are gradual, taking years before they are noticed. When dams and levees are destroyed or damaged by disasters—such as hurricanes or earthquakes—the devastation can be quick.

Structures can break because of human error. This was the case with England's Sheffield Dam on the River Loxley. It had just been completed when, on March 11, 1864, the dam broke and caused the Great Inundation that killed 270 people. Investigators later determined that the dam broke because it was not built correctly. A more recent example of a dam failure came in 1976,

The Teton Dam burst on June 5, 1976. Its failure caused the deaths of fourteen people and millions of dollars worth of damage.

when the Teton Dam near Idaho Falls, Idaho, failed. This gravity dam had just been finished in 1975, but it could not hold up against spring rainfall. Its collapse killed fourteen people and caused almost $200 million in damage.

Because dams are anchored to the earth, they can be damaged by earthquakes and landslides. The destruction of the St. Francis Dam near Los Angeles resulted in the second worst disaster in California history (the 1906 San Francisco fire was the worst). Built on the San Francisquito fault line, the dam was not only located on unstable ground but was also built of substandard materials. When it failed on March 12, 1928, the flood cost 600 people their lives.

Typhoons or hurricanes cause considerable damage to dams and levees. In 1975 Typhoon Nina destroyed the Banqiao Reservoir Dam in China and resulted in the deaths of over 170,000 people. In the Netherlands, where much of the land is protected from flooding by dikes, there was a huge flood in 1953 known as the North Sea Flood. It caused 1,836 deaths. Afterward, the Dutch government created the Delta Plan. From 1958 until 2002, a massive effort was made to build up the dikes along the coast and rivers. Over 8,000 miles (12,874km) of levees were completed in the project.

A helicopter drops sandbags to try and repair one of the levees that failed when Hurricane Katrina hit New Orleans in 2005.

Hurricane Katrina

The worst disaster in recent history occurred in New Orleans, which was hit by Hurricane Katrina in late August 2005. The levees along Lake Pontchartrain, built to protect the city from floods in just such a case, failed. Many of them were earthen levees and were not strong enough to resist the hurricane's force. Most of the city flooded, and residents were evacuated. Not only were homes and businesses destroyed, but pollution was a huge problem afterward. Sewers backed up, and the "Industrial Canal" area, where there were many chemical plants, was heavily damaged. Sewage and toxic chemicals seeped into the floodwaters. There were many stories of dogs and other animals drinking from the floodwaters and dying within hours. Today, the now-dry soils of New Orleans are heavily contaminated. On dry days, when dust blows through the air, it is feared that just breathing could make people sick, especially children and the elderly.

Without dams and levees in place in all of these cases, the damage to the environment and to people's homes and lives would have been much less severe. The question is whether people can do anything to fix or avoid these problems.

chapter four

The Future of Dams and Levees

As technology advances and people become more aware of how important a clean environment is, will they find alternatives to dams and levees? People will always need energy sources and clean water, but many groups concerned with the environment feel there are better ways to get them.

Wiser Alternatives

Although dams help people collect freshwater and to generate electricity, there are other ways to do these things. One very good way to have more fresh drinking water available is to recycle used water. Water that goes down drains can be reused for purposes other than drinking, such as for watering yards or flushing toilets. Recycled water such as this is called gray water. Using more gray water makes more freshwater available.

Conserving water can make dams less necessary. Clean water can also be obtained from the oceans through desalination, or removing the salt from it. A **desalination plant** is a kind of factory that takes saltwater from the ocean and removes the salt to create clean water for crops and drinking. Another

A worker at the Tampa Bay Seawater Desalination Plant explains how the rows of filters behind him help remove salt from seawater.

way to get clean water is to collect rain. Rain that falls on roofs can be collected and saved in big storage units called cisterns. Finally, everybody could use more showerheads, appliances, and toilets that are designed to use less water.

Relying Less on Dams

Energy alternatives are also available that could make hydroelectric dams less essential. Although there are some disadvantages to solar and wind power, technology is improving to make these sources of energy more efficient and less expensive. There is also a new technology on the horizon called fuel cells. Fuel cells are like batteries. Instead of using poisonous acids like traditional batteries do, fuel cells use hydrogen and oxygen. When these two elements combine, they produce energy and water. The energy is used to power machines, and the leftover water does not damage the environment. Other alternative sources of energy are also being researched. One is biomass, which is plant and agricultural waste that can be burned for fuel.

To reduce flooding—another reason dams, and especially levees, are built—there are natural alternatives. Many floods are the result of human interference in nature. By draining out the water and filling in wetlands with dirt so that they can be turned into suburbs and farms, people have destroyed wetlands that control floods naturally.

Wind turbine generators are an alternative energy source that could decrease the need for hydroelectric dams.

Rivers that once curved and meandered with the landscape have been forced to flow through straightened paths. Rivers are straightened so that ships can navigate them more easily, and to prevent seasonal flooding. Crooked rivers, however, run more slowly, which allows more plants to grow along the shores. While seasonal flooding does happen with natural, curving rivers, dangerous flash floods are much less likely to occur when rivers are not artificially straightened.

Still another way to control flooding is to dig **bypass channels**. These channels are like canals that give water a second path to flow down when there is too much water in the river. Bypass channels have a positive side effect, too: They provide additional habitat for wildlife.

When it comes to people being affected by flooding, there is one very obvious solution: Move away from rivers and oceans. Unfortunately, people are attracted to life along shorelines. Also, ocean and river ports are places where there are a lot of jobs and businesses that attract people. However, with planning, people could build homes on ground high enough not to be flooded. There are also ways to construct houses so that they are less likely to be damaged by floods.

Repairing the Damage

There is a growing movement in the United States to tear down dams and levees. Numerous environmental groups are involved, but so are individual citizens, such as fishermen who see the benefits to migrating fish. These people have started to convince the U.S. government that fish and environmental concerns sometimes outweigh the need for electricity. The first large dam in America to be removed with the help of the government because of environmental concerns was the Edwards Dam on the Kennebec River in Maine. It was destroyed in 1999 to help endangered fish such as the shortnose sturgeon.

Studying Dams and Levees

Meanwhile, in the Pacific Northwest dams are also being removed to help salmon migrate. Salmon are already in trouble because of overfishing. Commercial fishing companies have recognized the need to help salmon breed to guarantee there will still be salmon in the future. Despite growing support for removing dams, though, many scientists believe that not all dams should be destroyed. There are many types of dams and they affect the environment in different ways. These scientists want more studies to be done to determine which dams are causing the worst problems. Only those dams, then, would be torn down.

Research has shown that, when it comes to levees, placing them farther from riverbanks helps reduce flooding. When levees are not close to riverbanks, the amount of floodplain increases.

This gives water more places to go so that it does not flow over the levees and into cities and towns. This strategy, like bypass channels, also creates new wildlife habitat.

Future Trends

Today there are two sides to the debate about controlling the world's waters. Because the world's population is increasing greatly, some see the need for more dams and levees to serve people's needs. Others feel that the environmental costs will exceed the benefits. There is great pressure in countries such as China and India, for instance, to build more dams to generate electricity and store

The Three Gorges Dam in China was built to generate electricity and store water.

water for the billions of people who live there. This is why China has built the huge Three Gorges Dam. It is why the trend in many countries is to build more large dams.

More recently, global warming has become a new reason to build dams. In drier areas, many people get their water from melting snow in nearby mountains. As the planet warms, however, these mountains may lose their snow permanently to melting. Because of this, California's governor, Arnold Schwarzenegger, announced in January 2007 that many more dams should be built to capture water from the mountains and store it.

Change Is Needed

There is a great deal of resistance to changing the current levee system in the United States, too. Because so many cities, towns, and farms have come to depend on them for flood control, it would cost millions of dollars to change the location of levees or to move populations away from floodplains.

In the end, the environmental and property damage caused by the current system of dams and levees is likely to cost more than if we take steps to return rivers and oceans to their natural states. When people first started building dams and levees, they did not understand the consequences to wildlife, plants, and people. Now we do understand.

Glossary

arch dam: A dam that uses a curved shape to shift water pressure toward the sides.

buttress dam: A dam that is strengthened with vertical supports.

bypass channels: Long channels or ditches dug near a river to give excess water a place to go without flooding surrounding land.

cofferdams: Temporary dams used to divert water away from a riverbed while a permanent dam is being built.

desalination plant: A water treatment plant that takes saltwater from the ocean and converts it to freshwater.

dikes: Levees used to keep floodwaters from populated areas.

earthen dams: Simple gravity dams or levees constructed primarily of dirt and rocks.

embankment dams: *See* gravity dams.

fish ladders (or fish passes): A series of low, water-filled steps built next to a dam that allows migrating fish to swim up- or down-stream.

gravity dams: Straight dams that are built thick, heavy, and strong enough to block water. Also called embankment dams.

hydroelectric dams: Dams used to generate electricity by making use of the energy from falling water.

locks: Gated canals where water can be raised or lowered to allow ships to pass between bodies of water of varying elevations.

penstock: A tunnel in a hydroelectric dam that funnels water toward a turbine.

powerhouse: A large room in a hydroelectric dam that contains the turbines and generators.

reservoir: A lake or pond created by a dam.

spillways: Channels or tunnels used to divert excess water around a dam to prevent water from flowing over the top of a dam.

tailings dam: A dam used in mining operations to contain waste soils and chemicals.

turbine: A propeller-like device used in hydroelectric dams to transfer energy from running water to a generator.

For Further Exploration

Books

Lesley A. Dutemple, *The Hoover Dam*. Minneapolis, MN: Lerner, 2003. A thorough history of the construction of the Hoover Dam. Includes discussion of its operations in modern times.

Lynn M. Stone, *How Are They Built? Dams.* Vero Beach, FL: Rourke, 2002. An introduction to the history of dams. Explains different types of dams and their environmental impact, and describes some of the world's major dams.

Web Sites

Energy Kid's Page (www.eia.doe.gov/kids/index.html). A site from the U.S. Energy Information Administration with a great deal of information about energy, plus activities, games, and a glossary. Includes an excellent explanation of hydropower.

Energy Resources (http://home.clara.net/darvill/altenerg/index.htm). This Web site, created by British science teacher Andy Darvill, provides easy-to-understand explanations of all sorts of alternative energy sources, including hydropower, solar, wind, geothermal, biomass, tidal, and others.

Environmental Literacy Council (www.enviro literacy.org/article.php/539.html). The ELC has great articles on all sorts of environmental concerns. This particular page is all about floods, including the impact of dams and levees.

Science News for Kids (www.sciencenews forkids.org/articles/20050921/Feature1.asp). This general science facts page for young Web surfers is packed full of information, including this particular page that has an article on Hurricane Katrina and how it damaged New Orleans's levees.

SimScience (http://simscience.org). A site created by the National Science Foundation that includes, among other simulations, computer animations explaining how dams crack.

TVAKids (www.tvakids.com). The kid's page of the Tennessee Valley Authority. The site explains what the power company is doing to lessen the impact their dams have on fish. It also has pages about electrical safety and power generation that is environmentally friendly.

Index

Picture credits

About the Author

Kevin Hile is a freelance writer and editor based in Michigan. A graduate of Adrian College, where he met his wife, Janet, he has been a reference book editor for almost twenty years. Hile is a former Detroit Zoo volunteer who is currently a docent and Web site manager for the Potter Park Zoo in Lansing. Deeply concerned about the environment, animals, and wildlife conservation, he is also the author of *Animal Rights* (Chelsea House, 2004) and *Little Zoo by the Red Cedar* (MSU Press, 2007). Hile is a regular contributor to Thomson Gale's Contemporary Authors series. This is his first book for KidHaven Press.